The
Pathless
Way

The surface of the earth is soft and impressible by the feet of men; and so with the paths which the mind travels. How worn and dusty, then, must be the highways of the world, how deep the ruts of tradition and conformity!

WALDEN

The Pathless Way

John Muir and American Wilderness

MICHAEL P. COHEN

THE UNIVERSITY OF WISCONSIN PRESS

Published 1984

The University of Wisconsin Press
114 North Murray Street
Madison, Wisconsin 53715

The University of Wisconsin Press, Ltd.
1 Gower Street
London WC1E 6HA, England

First printing

Printed in the United States of America

For LC CIP information see the colophon

ISBN 0-299-09720-X

for Jesse,
and the mountains in his life

Contents

x *Contents*

Acknowledgments

The perspective of this book is the result of dialogue, and the voice, though my own, cannot be separated from those of others. First of all I am indebted to Norman Clyde and Carl Sharsmith, my first teachers in the mountains. Most of my ideas about wilderness matured while I wandered the mountains with Gary Colliver and Dennis Hennek; much of the thinking here may be theirs. While I was a student, James McMichael taught me much of animated nature, itinerary, and the flow of water, Jay Martin paid close attention to the sources of my ideas and the way I expressed them, and Pete Clecak reminded me of social and economic realities. George Sessions and Bill Devall influenced the final writing of this book, constantly testing its ideas against their ecological consciences. Sam Allen, my editor, provided a fine sense of craft and countless hours of labor. Valerie Cohen contributed to my sense of landscape, and much more.

I received encouragement from Donald Wesling and Robert Engberg. Steve Hickman and Connie Metherell generously provided a good environment for writing. Shirley Sargent shared materials and ideas with me. Michael Ross was always willing to walk with me and contribute his perspective.

I would not have gotten far without Mary Vocelka at the Yosemite Research Library, Loraine Warren at the Southern Utah State College Library, or Ronald Limbaugh at the Stuart Library of the University of the Pacific; Mr. Limbaugh has been a constant friend for Muir scholars, where a friend has been essential. The staffs of the Huntington Library and the Bancroft Library at the University of California were more than helpful. Much of the work on this book was supported by a research fellowship from the National Endowment for the Humanities.

A slightly shortened version of chapter 5, "Stormy Sermons," appeared in *The Pacific Historian*, volume 25, Number 2 (Summer 1981), pages 21–37. I thank them for the right to reprint this material.

Introduction

This book is not a biography of John Muir. Although it has a firm
foundation in biographical fact, it is not meant to retell the life. Instead I chose to occupy myself with what I call Muir's spiritual journey. I was interested in his thinking while in the mountains, and
his struggle to articulate his views to people who were not in the
mountains. I wanted to know what kinds of philosophical questions
he asked, and what kinds of answers he received while he wandered
in the Sierra. I wanted to investigate the conscious decisions he made
and how he embodied them in his writing. I was particularly interested in Muir's ethics. What was a right relation between Man and
Nature, and how could that relationship be transacted? Why, for
instance, had he become an advocate of National Parks? I wanted
to know what his life meant, but I found that to be an impossible,
if not arrogant, question. So I began to ask what his books suggested about his life, or mine.

Just as Muir felt no desire to separate himself from the mountains he loved, or to treat them as objects, so I have felt for many
years now. Further, I knew that when I began to question Muir's
decisions, I was also exploring my own thoughts about the mountains, and about parks. I do not wish to deny a simple fact. This
book about Muir is also a book about my own thinking; and not
only my own thinking, but the thinking of a whole community, of
my generation. Muir has always had a special place in our hearts,
and we have often thought of him while we sat around campfires,
walked through the woods, or climbed the walls of Yosemite. Much
of this book is about the questions my friends began to ask when
they learned that I had written a dissertation about Muir while at
school. The overriding issue they raised was not only about Muir,
but about me: why was I going to school in the city if I was inter-

ested in Muir and mountains? Throughout this book, that theme surfaces again and again, because I put that question to Muir himself. Why did he spend so much time writing about the mountains when he could have remained in them?

Muir was a writer in the end, and so am I when I write this book. He chose to devote his life to telling people about the wonders of the mountains, and I hope some of the wonders come through here. His life, as far as I have been interested in it, is to be found in his writings. And I have chosen to take him seriously by putting my questions directly to his texts. No doubt Muir has also become a powerful figure in the American consciousness, and as a result in my own consciousness. But I am only interested in the mythical Muir insofar as he tried to create this figure. My own transactions seek neither to destroy nor recreate his mythical stature. I think America needs to imagine him as a monumental figure, but for myself, I wanted to know how the myth came into being, and what it meant. We need the myth and also the text.

Many of my friends insisted on asking hypothetical and even fantastic questions about Muir. What would Muir think, one wanted to know, if he came to Yosemite in 1957? What group of climbers would he find most congenial? That is an interesting question. Was Muir a Taoist, a Zen Buddhist, a pantheist? asked one friend. He deserved an answer, not a dismissal. Another friend wanted to know what would have happened if Muir had become friends with Ishi. That was a profound question, but I was not sure I could answer it. Then there were the paradoxes of Muir's life. How could he hate bookmaking so much in the 1870s and yet become a writer? How was it possible for the young man who hated tourists to become the genial narrator of *Our National Parks* who encouraged all kinds of tourism? How was it possible for Muir to advocate so much road and trail construction after the turn of the century?

So I began to ask those kinds of questions. Did Muir really develop an ecological perspective? Did he become truly enlightened while wandering in the Sierra? What happened to his enlightenment when he tried to bring it down from the mountains? Did the Sierra Club really represent his true attitudes? Was he successful in the politics of conservation? The most serious issue was raised by Pete Clecak, a member of my doctoral committee, who wondered whether

Muir's life might represent a shallow victory or a rich, complex American tragedy.

I finally realized that I could only deal with these issues — particularly the last one — by attempting to write a book which judged the late Muir in the context of his younger self. I would try to ask the important questions which revealed the significance of particular facets of Muir's life. I would follow his conscious decisions about the important themes in his life. And yet I saw, as I began to write, that I would not be able to answer all of my friends' or my own questions. Indeed, I found that I sometimes merely articulated the complexity of the questions, as Muir saw them and as I see them today. That is perhaps as it should be. Many of the issues Muir explored are eternal and have no final answers. Perhaps what he had to teach was that a man might never solve all the problems he began to uncover when he asked, What is the right relationship between Man and Nature, Civilization and Wilderness? But without wondering, without thinking deeply about these questions, a man could not become himself. And in this sense I realized that Muir's life, like my own experience in the Sierra, could be best appreciated as an unending meditation on the meaning of life. No book could ever exhaust that meditation, just as no book will ever exhaust the mystery and wonder of the mountains.

A Note to the Reader

In the pages that follow, the Valley always refers to the Yosemite Valley, as it does in Muir's writing; the Club is always the Sierra Club; and the Commission, the National Forestry Commission formed by the National Academy of Sciences in 1896.

Walk, Thousand Mile Walk, and First Summer refer to those events in Muir's life as distinguished from the published accounts of them indicated by *Walk, Thousand Mile Walk,* and *First Summer.*

The
Pathless
Way

1

|\|\|\|\|\|

The Machine and the Flower

"I wish I knew where I was going," he wrote to his close friend, Jeanne Carr. "Doomed to be 'carried of the spirit into the wilderness,' I suppose." John Muir was twenty-nine years old in the early fall of 1867 when he left Indianapolis on the journey which was to bring him to California. This was no vacation. He was departing from old friends, and from an old life, on his way toward he knew not what. He would learn by going where he had to go, and as he departed, he was not certain that he would ever return.[1]

Something strange had happened to the eldest brother in the Muir family. After he had left the farm seven years earlier, in September of 1860, his brother David had written to him, "The folks think it funny that you never date your letters nor write your name at the end." As if he had become a voice with neither name nor time. And now, in September of 1867, he wrote to his youngest brother, Daniel. "In case anything should befall me," he began, as he settled his material affairs in careful and detailed completeness. To Daniel he must have sounded melancholy and deeply disturbed. So when the letter concluded, "I hope you will not infer from all this that I am going into great danger," the family might have had good reason to be troubled by brother John's state of mind.[2]

A journal from this excursion has been published, but one is struck by important differences between the hand-written notebook and *A Thousand Mile Walk to the Gulf*, edited by William Freder-

3

ick Badè. Although the notebook Badè used is probably not the original, since Muir recopied most of his original journals and since the introduction is clearly written in the language he learned in Yosemite, nevertheless, one is surprised by the contents of this handwritten document. For one thing, it was written in the past tense, unlike most of Muir's journals, suggesting that he was constantly looking forward. The days were not organized by the calendar, but were simply numbered consecutively; the numbers ran into the fifties, and then ceased altogether around the time Muir became ill toward the end of October. These structural features suggest that Muir was entering a new life, not to be measured by the old standards of calendars or watches, but lived one day at a time, and then left behind. A third feature is the style of his drawings. They are undoubtedly original and are pasted into the notebook. Many include, carefully and prominently, portraits of Muir himself as a part of the scene; indeed this is probably the most self-conscious of all Muir's journals. Below the first sketch, which depicted Muir outside Louisville, Kentucky, as he planned his journey, he wrote, "The world was all before them where to choose." Did these words mean that Muir thought of himself in terms of Milton's unhappy couple, exiled from the Garden? Certainly he carried the great Puritan epic, *Paradise Lost*, in his backpack, along with his plant press, his Bible, and a copy of Burns's poems. But what Garden had he left, and what Wilderness did he seek? One might even ask, was he Adam, or Eve, or both?[3]

If he was setting out to be an American Adam, on a model articulated by Thoreau, then he seemed not yet aware that like Thoreau he was, as one critic says, cleansing the "conventional or traditional man; in order precisely to bring into being the natural man." Yet he was conscious of making another fresh and new start, perhaps not of his own choosing. That had become a pattern of his life during the sixties: leaving the farm, leaving the university, leaving the United States for Canada, then leaving the woods of Canada for work in the city of Indianapolis, and finally nearly leaving his eyesight behind in a machine shop. Now he was leaving civilization behind altogether. He felt, almost immediately, the precariousness and loneliness of his situation, and it took him more than a month on the road before he could begin to make some sense of his attitudes as he wrote in his journal. He slowly began to realize that he was approaching a new and boundless perspective, which I like to compare to the one Thoreau began to develop in his last years, after *Walden.* Muir began consciously and categorically to deny, point by point, many nineteenth-century assumptions about God, Man, and Nature.[4]

He was not only leaving civilization and community for the wilderness. He was also discarding the values he had learned in a farming community, in an academic community, and in the industrial city. He was attempting to reestablish a new set of values congruent with the laws of the Universe. This is the significance of the inscription "John Muir, Earth-planet, Universe" that is written inside the cover of this and a succeeding journal which pertained to Muir's first winter in California. He had left the Garden for the Wilderness, and knew that his family and Christian friends would think of him as an outlaw. He wrote to Jeanne Carr that he wished he could be more moderate in his desires, but could not.

It is hard at first to see what Garden he thought he was leaving as he began his self-enforced exile. From a century away, his life in the 1860s hardly seems idyllic. Yet so much had opened up for him during those years. After the authoritarian dominance of his father at home, the University of Wisconsin must have seemed almost edenic. He found himself surrounded with people who were not only *doing* things, but also treated him with respect. Even in Muir's worst times, the new world that opened to him in Madison must have been wonderful in its intellectual richness and social possibilities. When he traveled on to Canada, and later to Indianapolis, he discovered that he could find a place for himself as a valuable working member of a community. It was this society which he saw as a Garden.

Why had he left? That was a more complex question. Not simply because he injured his eye in an industrial accident, not because he was tired of the new group of friends he had established; no, it was because he knew that he had gotten somehow onto the wrong path in life, and had run into a dead end. He needed to make a new beginning.

MACHINES

> *Things are in the saddle*
> *And ride mankind.*
>
> Emerson, Ode Inscribed
> to W. E. Channing

Muir's inventive genius — if that is what it was — allowed him to escape from the farm. But the ticket out of a confining rural life had led into a terrible trap. When he exhibited his devices at the State Fair in Madison, he had no idea how far he could travel on them. They were, after all, only devices whittled from wood and designed to measure time and temperature. But what did they say about him? Even if they were taken as works of genius by a public which worshipped technology, his family continued to remind him in letters from home that he must keep humble. Such pressure must have only made him wonder more about the mental gifts he possessed.

When he established himself as a student at the university, he continued to impress his friends and acquaintances with inventions which had harnessed the theme of time in Ben Franklin fashion. A rotating study desk organized hours of study for a student, who appeared to one friend "as if chained, working like a beaver against the clock and desk"; a loafer's chair discouraged sloth with a sharp gunshot sound; an "early rising machine" threw John out of bed each morning, and seemed to say, "Early to bed, early to rise . . ." — all of these machines were designed to reduce a man to an efficient mechanism, to make him a machine. Behind them was a need to hoard time which Muir had developed during his days of heavy labor on the farm. Making the most of time could be measured in terms of *efficiency*. And the theme of efficiency followed in Muir's work as he learned to turn out brooms at a prodigious rate for the Trout Brothers in Canada, and later developed automated manufacturing systems for Osgood Smith and Company in Indianapolis. Time was, of course, Money. What had begun as a diversion, as an entertainment, as an expression of Muir's need to think and do something exceptional, became as the years went by a means toward what? He wasn't sure.[5]

He hoped that his work with practical machinery was "done for the real good of mankind in general," hoped that it was a kind of true philanthropy to make brooms, rakes, or wheels more efficiently and cheaply. He wrote to his brother Daniel in 1863, "To what end do we receive life and health from God if not to do good and to be good." Did he think that making machines was a way of doing his duty to God? Perhaps he did. He was a conventional, shy, moralistic young man when he arrived in Madison. He wanted to help the people of a seemingly utopian community which had accepted him. But something in this clockwork mentality refused to run smoothly.[6]

What did a machine mean? As an image of God's world, a machine might suggest that the world, the Creation itself, was a clockwork mechanism. And of course the first thing to remember was that machines made perfect sense. If they were properly designed they never made a mistake and nearly never wore out, thus surpassing their creators, and suggesting the possibility that men could, with the aid of their technology, follow their dreams to perfection. Muir inscribed "All flesh is grass" on one clock he had fabricated. His father had liked that; it suggested that John was not becoming too worldly as he pursued his hobby. Yet his father also suspected that his son's interests in science, philosophy, and technology were driving him away from God. Machines were more than a hobby.[7]

The reply that Muir later remembered giving to his father's accusations rang with Ben Franklin's philosophy. If men needed to read the Bible, as his father argued, then the person who made spectacles was serving Man and God. His father replied, as he remembered, that there would "always be plenty of worldly people to make spectacles." The answer that Ben, the inventor of bifocals, had given was "that the most acceptable service we render to Him is doing good to His other children." Young John on the farm, nocturnal maker of machines, agreed.[8]

Perhaps modern humanism is based on the assumption young John had accepted. A trust in the goodness of machines goes still deeper and becomes a religion, a faith in Man, and insists that human problems are soluble by people, through technological or social means. If this is modern humanism, then Muir was becoming a humanist, as he argued with his father and made his machines. He wasn't just making things, he was making himself into a maker of things, and integrating himself into the machinery he helped create — the machinery of technology, and the machinery of society. And he was using a God-given gift to help other people.[9]

Indeed, he scarcely thought that he had any personal choice in the matter. He wrote to his brother from Indianapolis, "I have about made up my mind that it is impossible for me to escape from mechanics, I begin to see and *feel* that I really have some talent for invention, and I just think that I will turn all my attention that way at once." Yet his feelings were mixed about the course his life was taking. Perhaps he was ridden by his mechanical abilities. If he had no choice in his fate, he also knew that he was sacrificing other desires which he had nourished through his youth. And writing to his brother several months later, he described in detail a grisly industrial accident which had mangled a sawyer. Life in a machine shop or sawmill was grim and sometimes horrifying. The industrial accident was a common fact of life, and he had to fear the same fate for himself. He didn't wish to waste his life in a machine shop, nor did he wish to lose it to a machine. He was clearly confused about the direction his life had taken when he wrote to Jeanne Carr, "I should like to invent useful machinery, but it comes, 'You do not wish to spend your lifetime among machines and you will die ere you can do anything else.'"[10]

Before the industrial accident which nearly blinded him in 1867, Muir had already suspected that his interest in machines was an obsession which would lead to disaster, be it a slow wasting away of his life, or a quick maiming. It was one thing to argue the value of spectacles, and another to blind oneself in a machine shop. He knew there was another path for him. "How intensely I desire to be a Humboldt!" he had written once. Since 1862 he had been increasingly fascinated with botany, and he was encouraged in this pursuit most of all by Jeanne Carr. During the years between 1862 and 1867 he had realized that he couldn't do everything. If he spent all his time thinking, then he scarcely had any time for seeing. When working on new machinery, he wrote, "my mind seems to so bury itself in the work that I am fit for but little else." In 1867 he must have realized, as a shock, that he had been blinding himself all along. The trouble with botany, though, was that it seemed to be quite irrelevant to the realm of human society. If he chose to become a Humboldt, wandering in the fields and forgetting everything else, who would approve of him? Consequently he would feel a tremendous need to justify himself. In Jeanne Carr he had at least one person who, he hoped, could understand his need to wander in God's fields.[11]

THE MACHINE AND THE FLOWER

When John Muir went to Madison he was fortunate in becoming an intimate friend of Ezra and Jeanne Carr. This couple became Muir's second family, and when they moved to Oakland shortly after he took up residence in Yosemite, the relationship continued to deepen and grow.

Although Muir credited Dr. Carr with laying before him the "great book of Nature," it was Jeanne Carr who taught him something of the spirit in which the book might be read. Indeed he may have felt that the relationship with the Carrs paralleled his relationship with his parents. He remembered in later years that his mother had encouraged him to emulate Humboldt and become a world traveler, against his father's wishes. So too, he expressed his hope to become a Humboldt to Jeanne Carr, not to her husband. But the Carrs, unlike the Muirs, were of one mind about most things.[12]

They were active Grangers, especially after they came to California. They believed in the agrarian future for the West. They believed in practical education, and in particular encouraged professional training for women. Though Ezra Carr spoke and acted on this educational policy in Wisconsin, and eventually became Superintendent of Education for California, some of his professional colleagues believed that Mrs. Carr was the guiding power of the family. But he was the *public* figure.[13]

Though Dr. Carr taught Muir chemistry, he was most committed to education in agriculture and forestry — to hard scientific facts as the foundation for an equitable society. When he came to California, as a professor of agriculture, Dr. Carr became a public figure by trying to influence the future course of the new University of California. He wanted it to be an agricultural school, wanted it to give farmers the professional status they needed, wanted it to be an agent of change. He openly supported and acknowledged the help of Henry George during his battle with the administration of the university, and certainly stood by George in calling for an equitable division of California's agricultural land. He believed in a new agrarian society based on wise use and foresight. In a speech about forestry that he gave in 1873, he quoted the gospel of George Perkins Marsh, insisting that *"Social man* repays to the earth all that he takes from her bosom. . . ." For Carr, men had to deal fairly with Nature if they hoped to profit from their use of her.[14] This was the gospel he inherited from George Perkins Marsh.

Jeanne Carr, equally interested in the importance of a new agrarian community, argued in one speech to a Grangers group that the meaning of Christianity was being carried forward by groups like the Grangers who acted upon the creed "Love thy neighbor, help thy neighbor." Like her husband, she was a Christian and a humanist, but she was not so tied to practical affairs as he was, and she was more literary minded. In fact, she knew Ralph Waldo Emerson. She was more likely to be congenial to Muir's purely spiritual interest in botany.[15]

Further, Muir may have seen in the Carrs an admirable model of nineteenth-century social relations between men and women. Men were expected to be practical and scientific; they used their reason and followed their duty. Women were allowed to dwell closer to Nature, perhaps because they did not have to manipulate her for society's benefit, or perhaps because they were themselves viewed as part of her. They learned to love, not harvest, the flowers. Perhaps this was not the way life needed to be, but there it was, two opposing postures toward Nature: the educator who followed a scientific and practical path toward a more profitable mode of agriculture, and his lovely wife who always called him "Dr. Carr," and for herself cared only to botanize because the study offered personal pleasure and spiritual wholeness. The professor, not surprisingly, tended to look upon Nature as a mechanical system which could be utilized, while his wife was pleased by the infinite diversity and beauty of the Creation.

Perhaps I make this dichotomy too severe. Yet these two perspectives are real, not only as the opposite poles of the Carr family, or the socially determined attitudes of men and women, but as two voices which have eternally spoken in human minds. In the last few centuries we have heard more of the male voice, the Doctor's voice, which says that there is very little point in speaking to the world when there is work to be done. The male voice shuts itself off from life itself: "He says that woman speaks with nature. . . . But for him this dialogue is over. He says he is not part of this world, that he was set on this world as a stranger. He sets himself apart from woman and nature." This is a passage from a modern feminist, but it is not so far from the warning which Jeanne Carr insisted on giving to John Muir, when he was buried in his work on machines: "You do not know how we hold you in our memories as one apart from all the other students, in your power of insight into Nature, and the simplicity of your love for her. I think you would love her if she did not turn *mill wheels* or grind anybodies *grist.*" The path of mystical vision. To follow it he would have to be sensitive to what civilization would call the woman in him. When Jeanne Carr suggested that she and Muir engage in an exchange of thoughts through letters, he eagerly accepted.[16]

For her, John Muir had the "eye within the eye," but she knew that he needed to be reminded constantly, or he would lose his vision. She also knew that Muir could follow a path that she would have chosen had she not been born a woman. She once hoped to emulate David Douglas, the "Patron Saint of Tree Worshippers," who botanized through the forests of western America. Muir, another Scot, could perhaps become the living inheritor of that tradition, as she could not. When Muir set out on his walk through the South looking for "the greatest extent of virgin forest," her hopes went with him.[17]

In her notes for an article she wrote about Muir when they were both older, Jeanne Carr compared him to the Patron Saint of Ecology, Saint Francis of Assisi. She also described her one wonderful Sierran outing with Muir and his friends in terms of Saint Francis. "We carried no tent that 'our brother the sun' and 'our sisters the moon and the stars' might be always with us." "We were willing to lose ourselves," she said. In fact she was at least partially responsible for creating this kind of courage in Muir himself. When she wrote to him while he was in Yosemite, she reminded him that he was close to the "great mother," and she once commented that one had to capitalize "Valley" for the same reason that one capitalized "Jesus." She had, in other words, a most powerful and liberating effect on Muir and loosed him, as he only slowly realized himself, from the bonds of patriarchal thinking, from seeing Nature only as commodity. She gave him the support he needed if he was to take a solitary path and a loving attitude toward Nature.[18]

His own conversion to this way of thinking is vividly dramatized by an early Yosemite journal. Muir had recycled a notebook in which he had earlier transcribed notes from reading or listening to lectures on "Principles of Physics or Natural Philosophy Designed for etc ditto"; he used the uninked backs of the pages for penciled notes in Tenaya Canyon. The inked notes were standard academic fare, but in his penciled notes he thought about "the chemistry of mountains," taking what the nineteenth century would have called a wild and mystical view of Nature, inappropriate for scientists. "Im breathing the granite again. The mtns. are getting back into my blood," he wrote. This was a perspective like that of a modern feminist: "We know ourselves to be made from this earth. We know this earth is made from our bodies. For we see ourselves. And we are nature. We are nature seeking nature. We are nature with a concept of nature." Perhaps Jeanne Carr had been trying to tell him the same thing after his accident when she wrote, "He gave you the eye within the eye, to see in all objects the realized ideas of His mind." He would have to use not just his eye, but all his senses, to absorb the spirit of the mountains.[19]

One might also recall that Jeanne Carr was a member of the committee which awarded Muir the prize for his inventions at the Wisconsin State Fair. As she continued to interest herself in his progress when he came to the university, one day she visited his room with her young sons. One particular device caught her attention there:

But to me the most captivating piece of mechanism was an apparatus for registering the growth of an ascending plant stem during each of the twenty-four hours. . . .

A fine needle, threaded with the long hair of a fellow studentess, when attached to the plant, made the record faithfully upon a paper disk marked to indicate minute spaces with great exactness, while the rustic clock ticked the minutes and hours away.

What are we to think of the machine, Muir's making it, and Jeanne Carr's praise? Granted that it was a fine and delicate work, but it was part and parcel with that obsession about time and measurement. A vine harnessed to a clock and a pen. In times of dearth, William Blake once commented, take out line and measure. Perhaps she was encouraged because this device at least did not say that all flesh was grass, did not measure death, but instead reminded one of ascending life. But like all the rest of Muir's machines, it reduced the living flow of Natural life to rule and order. She must have suspected that Muir himself was harnessed and confined like the vine growing near the window of his room.[20]

Certainly he came to know something about the difference between wild and cultivated plants some years later, and knew too that the pattern of his own life bore a striking resemblance to their lives. In a passage of his journal, which he later blotted out, he said,

Some plants take on themselves the forms & habits of society & civilization quite readily, but generally speaking soon return to primitive simplicity of life in all things & I too like a weed of civilization feel a constant tendency to return to primitive wildness.

Well perhaps I may become a proper plant and repent of my outlawry to society, but if so I must, like a revived methodist learn to love what I hate & to hate what I most intensely & devoutly love.

It is hard not to believe that Jeanne Carr helped him to realize this truth about himself. Even as he had left Indianapolis a month before this self-discovery, following his immoderate desires toward the "wildest, leafiest, least trodden way," he had asked Jeanne Carr, "Is not your experience the same as this?"[21]

If he had fallen away from society and his social duties, she had provided the apple, or even taught him to eat it. Knowledge for its own sake, or for his own sake, heart-ravishing knowledge, was what he sought in the wilderness. In his journal, he pondered this sin, if sin it was. The copy of *Paradise Lost* he carried told him about Eve and the Garden, and he recognized the wrong done to Nature and to Eve by Milton's patriarchal thinking. "We are taught that this thing called death is an Evemade accident — a deplorable punishment for the oldest sin — the enemy — the 'archenemy' of life . . ." Like Adam, Muir scrupled not to eat, but did. Unlike Adam, he would not be sorry. The oldest sin, against the God of the Old Testament, against the God which society had invented to enforce its rules: this was the desire for knowledge, the desire to eat from the trees and worship them. If it was woman's sin, so be it. He suspected that this doctrine which men had invented came from a fear of women, of Nature, and finally of death. An acceptance of Nature on her own terms involved the acceptance of Man's rightful place in Nature.[22]

THE BLACKSMITH AND THE BOTANIST

Early in his Walk through the South, Muir began to notice "Nature's grandeur in . . . abrupt contrast with paltry artificial gardens." At Mammoth Caves he was disappointed with the "parlor taste" of "fashionable hotel grounds" when compared to the divine beauty of Nature. The gardens included "many a beautiful plant cultivated to deformity, and arranged in strict geometrical beds, the whole pretty affair a laborious failure." So much for Man's work. The gardens were like plowed fields, which was not surprising. When Muir conversed with a typical man who lived in the region, he found him to be "one of the useful, practical men — too wise to waste precious time with weeds, caves, fossils, or anything else he could not eat." Men who thought in these terms failed to distinguish between Nature and culture, he realized.[23]

What was happening to the Muir who had been so proud of the straight furrows he had plowed in his father's fields, who knew the secret was a sharp, well-designed and forged plowshare? He was alienating himself from society, its aesthetic taste and its values. Still, he continued to carry within himself a vestigial faith in Man's works. He could not ignore the technology of gristmills and machines in Kentucky and Tennessee. He could not help criticizing southern society for being far behind the age of "speculation and invention so characteristic of the North." He thought the South was a "primitive country" as he listened to the talk of Providence he heard from a Tennessean:

"I believe in Providence," said he. "Our fathers came into these valleys, got the richest of them, and skimmed off the cream of the soil. The worn-out ground won't yield no roastin' ears now. But the Lord foresaw this state of affairs, and prepared something else for us. And what is it? Why, he meant us to bust open these copper mines and gold mines, so that we may have money to buy the corn we cannot raise." A most profound observation.

Providence was what they had instead of Progress, Muir guessed. But he must have wondered which doctrine was worse, the one northern man dreamed, or the one southern man believed. Muir was not yet ready to understand that the northern sort of energy and industry was more damaging to Nature in the long run than the lazy indifference of the southerners he talked to. In any case, the South would enter the industrial age, and he was beginning to suspect the kinship at the root of both doctrines, the implicit trust in Man's dominion over Nature. North and South, on the farm and at the foundry, men believed that God gave them the earth; after they cut down trees and exhausted the soil, it was time to rip open her bowels and heat up the forge.[24]

How could he justify his seemingly impractical wanderings to people he met along the way, people who believed that men must work, people who often did him personal kindness? A blacksmith, for instance, welcomed Muir to share his bread, because the young man offered to pay. In his journal Muir simply dismissed the man's "musty orthodox arguments," but in a later note to himself he wrote that the story would have to be told in full. And later he reconstructed their discussion.[25]

"Hammer in hand, bare-breasted, sweaty, begrimed, and covered with shaggy black hair," this blacksmith of Tennessee could not understand how any "strong-minded man" could be wandering around aimlessly, just because he loved plants and wanted to "get acquainted with as many of them as possible." When Muir attempted to repeat this man's arguments, he was also recreating a dialogue within himself. A threatening figure had asked, was Muir a man? The blacksmith was a materialist, and in his reconstructed dialogue Muir had him arguing like a character invented by Hawthorne: "These are hard times, and real work is required of every man that is able. Picking up blossoms doesn't seem to be a man's work at all in any kind of times." Muir responded, or so he reported, with the example of Solomon the wise botanist, and with the words of Christ. "Consider the lillies and how they grow," said Christ. Jeanne Carr was fond of this aphorism. And so Muir claimed mighty scriptural authority for his own occupation. This argument might have satisfied a country blacksmith, as Muir claimed it did, but the nagging suspicion remained that he was not doing a real man's work. The pursuit of wisdom for its own sake, even by a Solomon or Christ, was suspect in post-Civil War America, North or South.[26]

Was Muir willing to follow his own way, unsupported by human company or approval? He found that it was not entirely possible. He was lonely, even though he received occasional letters from his brother Daniel and Jeanne Carr. He needed to justify himself even if he rejected the doctrines of the people he lived among. He would have to be solitary indeed. The most serious problem in this regard came when he rejected the doctrines of Providence and Progress. He could still try to justify his own way in Christian terms, because he knew that certain men like the blacksmith or even his father could only listen to ethical arguments about the book of Nature when they were given in the language of the Bible. But he also knew that he was struggling bitterly with the language as well as the morals presented in the Bible.

The blacksmith's argument would haunt Muir. Men in this world got their bread by doing "real" work, not by loving flowers. A man would have few friends to feed him if he never did anything of material significance. If Muir refused to see Nature as commodity, and thus refused to take the male role by working, he also knew that he couldn't go without bread. Later in his journal he wrote, "A serious matter is this bread which perishes, and, could it be dispensed with, I doubt if civilization would ever see me again." That was a big if. Hunger was a fact of life in the wilderness, as it was in civilization. And a botanist had to eat just as a blacksmith did. What would happen if he didn't eat? That was a lesson which waited for him at Bonaventure.[27]

BONAVENTURE

Death is the mother of beauty, mystical,
Within whose burning bosom we devise
Our Earthly mothers waiting, sleeplessly.
                    Wallace Stevens, "Sunday Morning"

"I gazed awe-stricken as one new-arrived from another world," he said, as he looked at the moss-draped live oaks of Bonaventure Graveyard. In the narrative of his stay there, which he rewrote at least three times, Muir revealed the most significant turning point in his journey through the South. At Bonaventure he learned to accept his own death.[28]

After reaching Savannah, he hoped to find letters and money waiting for him. He found no word. And so the journal entry for that day ends with one word, "*Alone.*" He visited Bonaventure the next day, and after his money again failed to arrive, he finally decided to camp there because he was afraid of the loitering Negroes who were so noticeable around town. He assumed that they would be too superstitious to visit the graveyard after dark. And so, for that matter, would he be unlikely to happen upon any whites. Men were afraid of graveyards because they were afraid of death. And they were afraid of death because they were superstitious. Just as they believed the story of Eve in the Garden, so that story formed the center of a doctrine which disabled the thinking of the "civilized swarm of christians so called." Thus Muir came to see himself as making journeys, every day as he walked from his camp to town, from the world of the dead to the world of the living. He came to prefer the world of the dead, which he perceived as "one of the Lord's most favored abodes of life and light."[29]

In Bonaventure life was at work everywhere, remedying the work of men, corroding iron and marble, leveling the hills of earth over the dead, replanting, and "obliterating all memory of the confusion of man." Meanwhile, Muir's fast drew out toward physical weakness. And so when he thought about death, he was surely thinking about his own. As he meditated and wrote in his journal he began to accept, in fact to insist, on the "beautiful blendings and communions of death and life, their joyous inseparable unity." Thus he learned to shuck off what he thought of as a Christian doctrine that death was to be feared. In a civilized world, he realized, "the most notable & incredible thing that a wild fanatic can say is, 'I fear not to die.'" Yet without question, he realized that one could only accept the interpenetration of life and death in Nature if one also accepted one's own death.[30]

But something else was operating on him. In a letter to his brother Daniel, written two years later, he tried to account for the effect of fasting on his consciousness. Daniel was at that time studying medicine, so John put the issue to him as a medical problem, yet he also described his experience in visionary terms: "the forest trees seemed to be running round in a circle chase and all the streams by the roadside seemed to be running uphill." He was experiencing a new and strange reality, where Nature flowed in patterns which transcended scientific laws of regulated time and space. He was seeing strangely. He was leaving the world of machines and entering a mystical perspective, though scarcely yet aware of it.[31]

He was radically transformed by his five-day stay at Bonaventure, but he was not joyous. On the contrary, even later, after he had received letters and money, even after he had celebrated with a "jubilee of bread," he found himself melancholy. On October 15, when he reached Florida, he was out of sympathy with Nature: ". . . not a mark of friendly recognition, not a breath, not a spirit whisper of sympathy came from anything about me, and of course I was lonely." And so he tried to account for his morbid, melancholy state of mind. Perhaps it was a result of his "starving unfriended condition" the week before at Bonaventure. He was unreasonably apprehensive about alligators, and a noise behind him, made by a tall white crane, "handsome as a minister from spirit land," made him fancy his own demise in the jaws of death.[32]

He responded to this unhealthy state of mind with as much discipline as he could, talking to himself in his journal about courage and cowardice, accepting the truism that "no man knows himself,— or rather no man knows his future self, if he did he would be a prophet, & far more . . ." And finally he went to Nature for solace, despite his fear of her. He tried to listen to the palm tree, just as he had listened to the live oaks of Bonaventure. This was his course in discipline, and it allowed him to finally accept what he had announced in Bonaventure, but in more concrete terms. A man might be repelled by alligators, snakes, and other members of God's family. He might fear his death in the jaws of Nature's wild creatures. Yet these antipathies, he argued, were the morbid productions of "the proprieties of civilization." Here is the best example of the difference between the original and the published versions of *Thousand Mile Walk*: Muir later revised this phrase to read "ignorance and weakness," thus deemphasizing the degree of his own rebellion during this journey. And in his notebook he drew a picture of a smiling alligator watching a happy brother devour a man. He hoped that he had reformed his attitude, once he had seen the alligators "at home."[33]

One might argue that Muir was simply following the ascetic discipline revealed in his account of conquering the fear of water in *Story of my Boyhood and Youth*. There, he was ashamed to discover that he could panic and nearly drown. His cure for this weakness was to throw himself back into the water, over and over again, shouting to himself, "Take that!" But the kind of discipline he was learning in Georgia and Florida was notably different because he was appealing to a higher power than self, and attempting to accommodate himself to a still unknown world-view which was deeper, larger, and more powerful than one based on self-interest. And in that, there is all the difference. He wasn't conquering himself, but allowing something long dormant in his soul to grow. He was beginning to think of human life, his own included, from an eternal perspective. He was beginning to see his limits as a man. He was learning the humility necessary to any true vision of Nature.[34]

LORD MAN

The world, we are told, was made especially for man — a presumption not supported by all the facts.

Thousand Mile Walk to the Gulf (p. 354)

A man might starve in the wilderness. If he did, the blacksmith might have argued, he had only himself to blame. But there was other evidence that men were not the crown of creation. At first Muir was horrified to realize that Nature herself had no need to welcome Man into her own arms. Her alligators were not his friends, and her briars did not allow him to pass unscathed. Her murky pools often held murky dangers for Man, who was apparently not her chosen favorite. The swamps of Florida, for instance, held worse fates than starvation. His encounters with all sorts of dangerous species, from the

Spanish bayonet to the microbes which caused malarial fevers and typhoid, led Muir to believe that the natural inhabitants of the earth did not necessarily comfort a pilgrim seeking the warm breast of Nature. And so he learned in concrete detail what he had suspected before, that the world was not necessarily made for men.

"Why," he began to ask himself, "should man value himself as more than a small part of the one great unit of creation?" Indeed *he* had ample evidence that *he* was not suited to the tropics, but knew that this was not to be blamed on Nature. Just as a man might invent a doctrine which blamed Eve for death, so too, "when man betakes himself to sickly parts of the tropics and perishes, he cannot see that he was never intended for such deadly climates." A man might blame the "first mother," or consider his difficulty "a providential chastisement for some self-invented form of sin." Only his monumental egocentrism, his anthropocentrism, made him believe that his own death at the hands of the elements was important. In fact, Man was simply not a necessary member of the biological community in such places. He passed away there because he never belonged in the first place. Muir was beginning to acquire a biocentric outlook.[35]

When he did begin to suspect that civilized Man had a totally misconceived notion of his own exalted position in Nature, Muir ran up against his education. I have mentioned that Ezra Carr drew heavily on the theories of George Perkins Marsh. Marsh's *Man and Nature*, in turn, has been taken by no less an authority than Lewis Mumford as the "fountainhead of the conservation movement."[36]

Certainly Muir would draw upon many of the details of Marsh's monumental book when he came to argue for the preservation of the forests in the seventies and the nineties, but he saw during his Walk that his philosophy was founded on quite different assumptions about Man's place in Nature. Man was the center of Marsh's theory of conservation, and was central to the original title of his book, *Man the Disturber of Nature's Harmonies.* Marsh had argued well enough to convince a skeptical Sir Charles Lyell that Man had been a dominant force in the landscape, that Man was one of the most important ecological forces on earth. Marsh did not doubt Man's

supreme power over Nature, and only wished to discourage its mis-
use. He tried to convince civilized men that their energies ought to
be directed by foresight, rather than by ignorance, war, tyranny,
and misrule, as had been the case in past history. Ezra Carr followed
Marsh in pointing out that Man changed Nature, produced "mutations" which were "unforeseen through natural consequences of acts
performed for narrower and more immediate ends."[37]

Yet neither Marsh nor Ezra Carr had questioned Man's ultimate
supremacy. Marsh's biographer explains that "there was nothing sacred about Nature; man must rebel against her demands, subjugate
her, and create his own order in her world." This clearly contradicted
the perspective that Muir had gathered at Bonaventure. Imagine how
Muir might have responded in 1867 to this seminal passage from
Man and Nature:

The fact that, of all organic beings, man alone is to be regarded as essentially a destructive power, and that he wields energies to resist which,
nature – that nature whom all material life and all inorganic substance
obey – is wholly impotent, tends to prove that, though living in physical
nature, he is not of her, that he is of more exalted parentage, and belongs
to a higher order of existences than those born of her womb and so sub-
missive to her dictates.

Muir would have immediately recognized the central paradox in
Marsh's torturous argument. How could Man's destructiveness be
a sign of his "exalted parentage"? Further, Marsh's argument was really
only another version of God's Providence toward His spiritual creation, Man. Though it was more enlightened than the version of Providence Muir had heard in Tennessee, though Marsh insisted that the
earth had been given to Man "for usufruct alone, not for consumption, still less for profligate waste," still this doctrine insisted that
the world was given to Man.[38]

Muir labeled this prideful conception of Man's place in the universe with the epithet "Lord Man." And if Muir had been familiar
with Marsh's essay "The Study of Nature," which was printed in
the *Christian Examiner* in the year he entered the university at Madison, he would have learned that the life of a man was "a perpetual
struggle with external Nature," fought for economic comfort. In an

argument which seemed almost a response to Thoreau's *Walden*, Marsh argued that Man rose not by his ability to do without, but "in proportion to the magnitude of the physical inconveniences and wants he successfully combats and finally vanquishes." It was in this sense that Man became the "rightful lord" of Nature by rebelling against her forces and commands.[39]

Muir would have found himself, too, described in Marsh's essay: "When he sinks to be her minister, to make those laws the rule of his life, to mold his action to her bidding, he descends from the sphere of true humanity, abdicates the sceptre and the purple with which the God of nature has invested him, and becomes a grovelling sensualist or a debased idolator. Whenever he fails to make himself her master, he can but be her slave." Clearly Muir had become a "debased idolator" when he had chosen to learn from Nature rather than subdue her. And so the flow of his ecological thought was far more radical than that of Marsh, or than that he had heard from Ezra Carr. Later, when he would ally himself to the conservationist heirs of Marsh's thought, he would do so not because he agreed philosophically, but because he needed political help. In 1867, the flow of American ecological thought divided, and Muir took the deeper, more dangerous way.[40]

How could Man take dominion over Nature when he was, really, Nature's jack-of-all-trades, master of none? It was absurd. The alligator ruled the swamps because he was made in and for the environment which was his home. Yet Muir knew that there was a "numerous class of men" who had a "precise dogmatic insight of the intentions of the Creator," and regarded Him in anthropomorphic terms, as a "civilized, law-abiding gentleman." For these men, the Creator simply provided His sheep, whales, cereals, cotton, iron, etc. But Muir had learned that all the world was not given to Man. He knew that Man could not walk on water, and asked, "Why does water drown its lord?" He believed that men were made from the same material as all other creatures, "from the dust of the earth, from the common elementary fund." He could no longer believe the "closet researches of clergy," and refused to see Nature through the eye of Christian dogma. After this rebellion, he could "joyfully return to the immortal truth and immortal beauty of Nature."[41]

AN ETHICAL DILEMMA: BEARS, COYOTES, MEN, AND SHEEP

Well, I have precious little sympathy for the myriad bat eyed proprieties of civilized man, and if a war of races should occur between the wild beasts and Lord Man I would be tempted to side with the bears.

Draft version, *Thousand Mile Walk to the Gulf*

With these words Muir concluded the section of his journal which recorded his experiences in Florida's swamps and forests.[42] Later, when he revised this passage, he decided that men were only "selfish," not "blind," and that it would be more appropriate for him to "sympathize" rather than to "side" with the bears. And yet he saw, when he went to California, that even sympathy was not a practical possibility; either one sided with Man, or one sided with the predators which Man fought as enemies.

At issue was Man's choice to take dominion. Who had a right to hunt in the fields of the Lord? And what if a man was pasturing his sheep in those fields? While Muir worked as a shepherd for Smokey Jack and Patrick Delaney, he found himself having to defend their flocks from bears and coyotes. He must have hoped, as so many have through human history, that pastoral life would allow him to escape the hypocrisies of society, but instead he found that he was drawn into conflicting loyalties. While he read Shakespeare and tended his flocks, he discovered that there was no possibility of reconciling Nature's laws and Man's: "I used to imagine that our Sabbath days were recognized by Nature, and that . . . there was a more or less clearly defined correspondence between the laws of Nature and our own." But he was learning that such was simply not the case, and it was particularly clear in the battle between men and other predators. For instance, coyotes (which he called wolves) were "the greatest of all enemies of the California sheep-raiser"; to Muir, they seemed beautiful, loved by God. In fact, he particularly admired their style of hunting. But as a shepherd he was responsible for defending the sheep from predators. When he began to herd Smokey Jack's sheep, at Twenty Hill Hollow, his own sympathies were clear: "The sheep of my flock are unhappy creatures, dirty and wretched, miserably misshapen and misbegotten and I am hardly sorry to see them eaten by those superior beings, the wolves." But given the nature of his duties, several weeks later Muir could only say that he wished he had not seen a coyote approaching the flock. His journal does not indicate that he shot the coyote, but certainly that would have been his responsibility as a sheep man's employee.[43]

The issue returned that same summer when he was tending Patrick Delaney's sheep near North Dome on the headwaters of Yosemite Creek. This time the predator was a bear, the first one that Muir had ever seen at home. The Sierran canyons, Muir knew, were the homes of bears, where they reigned as kings until Man happened along. And though he wrote in his journal that he would like to know his "hairy brothers" better, he also returned to camp for a rifle to shoot this one. "Fearing he might attack the flock I reluctantly went," he penciled into his journal, although the final draft indicates he would only have shot the bear "if necessary." Fortunately, Muir never had to shoot that bear, or any other. But he knew that he might have to if he continued his work as a shepherd.[44]

Two years later, on finding a dead Yosemite bear, he could only write an elegy:

Bears are made of the same dust as we, and breathe the same winds and drink of the same waters. A bear's days are warmed by the same sun, his dwellings are overdomed by the same blue sky, and his life turns and ebbs with heart-pulsings like ours . . . His life not long, not short, knows no beginnings, no ending. To him life unstinted, unplanned, is above the accidents of time, and his years, markless and boundless, equal Eternity.

Muir could try to be like Saint Francis in his acceptance of brotherhood with the beasts, and he could try to live a life like the bears, which was measured by eternal time. Yet he knew what a heresy this was to Christians, who killed bears with no pangs of conscience, who claimed that bears had no souls. It was not possible to be a Saint Francis while defending a flock of domestic sheep from a wild environment. And so Muir gave up his hopes for being a shepherd, if he ever seriously had any.[45]

In a larger sense though, all of men's works were created at the expense of Nature, so Muir found himself in an uncomfortable dilemma. It was only a partial solution to his problem that he could sympathize with the wild beasts. He knew that siding with them was virtually impossible if a man were to get his bread in a civilized way. There was always bread to be considered. He would never solve this problem in a satisfactory manner.

THE FLIGHT FROM ORTHODOXY

The greater part of what my neighbors call good I believe in my soul to be bad, and if I repent of any thing, it is very likely to be my good behavior.

Thoreau, Walden

Muir had begun the bold and arduous task of reexamining values he had absorbed during his first thirty years of life. It was not a project he was likely to complete very quickly. Because the world was not divided into neat dualities, it was difficult for him to establish a coherent set of beliefs that would replace those he had learned in civilization. As he rebelled against the doctrines enforced upon him in his youth, he rejected at first almost everything he had learned which might be called cultured or civilized. Sometimes his excitement might have led him toward a more radical position than he realized. But he was following a life of principle, not wise policy, as he walked through the South and came to California. It did not trouble him yet that his values would be a social liability for the rest of his life.

He thought that he would begin to solve his philosophical dilemma by simply escaping from civilization, and going solitary into the woods. And he attempted to establish a set of implicit resolutions. As I see them, he would:

- Leave civilization and society, and enter the self-consistent realm of Nature

- Forget the workings of machines and start considering the way plants, flowers, beasts — and his own soul — grew

- Reject the false and abstract doctrines of Christianity and learn his philosophy directly from Nature

- Liberate himself from the social expectations of manliness, and accept himself as an equal though humble member of Nature's community

— Leave Man's arbitary time, and enter Nature's eternal realm

— Cease to believe that Man was the Lord of Creation, or was providentially given dominion, and accept the limitations of human aspirations

— Cease to see Nature as commodity, and accept her true responsibility to herself

— Cease to believe that philanthropy was the highest good. He would pledge his allegiance to Nature.

Though they were not entirely new aspirations, in 1867 he decided it was time to test them. What made his later life so remarkable was that he realized how fruitless his past had been and how meaningless it would be to keep up with the times. He tried to step out of history. He realized that the education he sought wasn't available at any university, on any farm, or in any machine shop. He had to seek reality outside any social realm. It was not easy to retire from society, though Muir himself would later suggest that he easily shed the doctrines and lessons which had been taught to him through his youth. "I never tried to abandon creeds or code of civilization; they went away of their own accord, melting and evaporating noiselessly without any effort and without leaving any consciousness of loss." This wasn't true. The process was far more conscious, and far more trying than he wished to admit at the time or in later years. For that reason it is important, if one wishes to grasp a true picture of those crucial years, to be skeptical of his late written narratives. It is more important to suspect the versions of his journals edited by William Frederick Badè. And even the more accurate edition by Linnie Marsh Wolfe sometimes omits Muir's most radical statements. In the past, few of Muir's editors or biographers have wanted to consider just how rebellious and radical he was in the late 1860s.[46]

As he battled for his own spiritual integrity, it must have seemed to him that he was "between two worlds, one dead, the other powerless to be born." Between two worlds. One can see this dilemma in a number of ways. It was a personal and spiritual crisis for Muir to leave behind his father's farm and his father's values as well. But discarding his father's version of the Bible was a longer process. And he finally learned that he would have to reject a belief in "a clearly defined correspondence between the laws of Nature and our own." As he began to realize the full implications of this decision, he was living in California, working as a shepherd, and apparently reading Shakespeare. The very Shakespeare he read was likely to provide heavy doses of Christian humanism, and contained the implicit doctrine that the laws of Nature were intimately connected to the laws of human history, as a sort of mirror. But even in Florida Muir could see that a God "who believes in the literature and language of England" is "purely a manufactured article." He would have to live by that discovery. Just as he realized that "in the free unplanted fields there is no rectilinear sectioning of times and seasons," so he had to accept the fact that in the "invisible, measureless currents" of Nature, no doctrinal signpost from his past would do him any good.[47]

In this sense, Muir's tense and excited state of mind during this period reflects not just a personal crisis, but a crisis in world-view of the kind experienced particularly by scientists and philosophers during historical epochs when, suddenly, nobody is sure exactly what the world is like. Though Muir saw his dilemma as a personal one, he was participating in a broader crisis of values which plagued many of his clear-thinking contemporaries. His choices represented radical responses to the deterioration of the Christian faith, and to a seemingly chaotic situation in an academic world during the years which preceded and followed the publication of Darwin's *Origin of Species*. Muir would begin to think in Darwinian terms in California during the seventies, but from early in the sixties he realized that at the root of all his confusion was the false doctrine that Man was the Lord of Creation. When he left civilization behind, he thought he was on a true path toward the heart of Nature.[48]

2

The Glacial Eye

GOING LIGHT

For many of my generation, Muir's rebirth in Yosemite a century ago was a model of the kind of life worth living. But we found, strangely, that when we discussed his example with our parents and teachers they saw his life during that period as an evasion of responsibility. Muir too felt keenly a pressure to return to society and settle down. He talked about it in his letters and in his journal. After he had left his mechanical inventions and had determined to devote the rest of his life to studying the inventions of God, he wrote to Jeanne Carr in February of 1869 that a friend had sent him a "large sheetful of terrible blue-steel orthodoxy" calling him from "clouds and flowers to the practical walks of politics and philanthropy." Muir knew he was not ready to settle down, and when he commented, "Mrs. Carr, thought I, never lectured thus," he was reminding himself and Jeanne Carr of something which went deeper than words.[1]

Not only did she second his views, agreeing that guiding tourists in Yosemite was a distasteful job, but she also began to import society to him. Emerson, William Keith the artist, Asa Gray the Harvard botanist, and many others sought Muir out in the Valley because Jeanne Carr sent them to him. She and her friends also sent books to Muir; in fact, she sent the books she had been reading. Thus he continued his academic education as he read Lyell's *Principles of Geology*, Tyndall's *Hours of Exercise in the Alps*, Ruskin's

28

book *Of Mountain Beauty*, and undoubtedly many other works pertaining directly to the studies he was pursuing. Jeanne Carr had embarked on a study of evolution when she came to California, and probably Muir began to read Darwin and his commentators seriously at this time. But most important, she reminded him that he was not simply escaping from nineteenth-century realities, but was engaged in an attempt to find a place where a man of integrity and sensibility truly belonged.

"I have no fixed practical aim, but am living in constant communion with Nature & follow my instincts & am most intensely happy," he wrote to his brother Daniel in 1871. But probably Muir was rarely so confident of the direction his own life had taken. He justified himself in his journal, arguing that the rest of the family had all settled down, and there was perhaps room for one of the eight to carry on an experiment in life. All the rest were "exemplary, stable, anti-revolutionary," so he could be spared for something else.[2]

It is impossible for me not to draw certain parallels. Thoreau had written, during the Mexican War, that the State itself exerted tremendous force on the individual. "You must live within yourself, and depend upon yourself, always tucked up and ready for a start, and not have many affairs," he said. He knew what it meant to *go light* by leaving the baggage of civilization behind. He felt the burden that my generation has felt, far more impersonal and institutionalized than the forces which worked on Muir. Going light requires that the wanderer turn away from the affairs of state.[3]

I remember the meeting of a poetry association on a campus of the University of California in 1969. The group enthusiastically discussed Gary Snyder's *Myths and Texts*, admiring Snyder's use of John Muir's vision on Mount Ritter. But the group's advisor, a Shakespeare scholar, interrupted our reverie and argued that Eliot's *Waste Land* was the last great poem of the twentieth century. There was nothing left but the heavy baggage of civilization, he said. "These fragments I have shored against my ruins." We were young, and many of us would be drafted out of graduate school into Viet Nam. None of us could hope to be a Prince Hal, but we were not ready to take drugs and die. I had gotten a deferment and enrolled in classes before sneaking off guiltily to the mountains. I did not know enough to respond to the professor with lines from Eliot's *Four Quartets:*

> *We shall not cease from exploration*
> *And the end of all our exploring*
> *Will be to arrive where we started*
> *And know the place for the first time.*

And I didn't know Snyder's poem, "For the Children," which reminded of a new discipline that reached beyond wasteland:

> *stay together*
> *learn the flowers*
> *go light*

This would be our answer to the twentieth century. And it had been Muir's answer too. Going light requires that the wanderer forget the nightmare of modern history.[4]

When John Muir arrived in Yosemite Valley he had no reason to believe that he would become the voice of Yosemite, nor did he suspect that he would win a national audience when he began to articulate the theory of the glacial evolution of Yosemite's landscape. All he knew was that he felt blessed, wholly free, reborn. That was enough encouragement to counterbalance all of the social pressures to come back and settle down. Even if his pursuits were neither practical nor rational, they seemed to suit him. When we arrived at Yosemite, however, we had Muir's example of the right way to live in the mountains.

At issue here is a way of life which has transcended Muir's time, and has come to be an archetypal experience. Muir's way of going light in the mountains is likely to remain a long time in the American imagination. When we explore the way in which Muir's wanderings began to take direction in Yosemite, the principles which led to his style of travel in the mountains, what do we find essential?

One is tempted to construct an imaginary dialogue:

"John, when did you stop carrying that plant press, and why?"

"When I discovered I could learn more by studying the plant where it was."

This would be factually wrong, since Muir continued to collect plant specimens and send them to botanists and friends, particularly to Asa Gray, director of Harvard's herbarium. Nevertheless it is true to the spirit of Muir's changing consciousness. He realized that he was gathering impressions which would grow cosmic in scope, that he couldn't take a waterfall, a storm, or even a flower with him when he found it in the wilds. He could store impressions in his memory, but it was better to see that Nature as discipline required giving up any other home but the wilderness. Collecting is an anthropocentric activity. A man gathers around himself all of his experience, a list of the birds he has seen or a list of the mountains he has climbed, a collection of color transparencies. Even in the late nineteenth century scientists were making a very slow transition from categorizing, collecting, and building systems to a Darwinian view that such collections were only evidence, *abstracted,* and thus deceiving, of the flux of Nature. The problem, as Muir discovered at Smokey Jack's sheep camp, was that a man could rarely see the flux in Nature, could not see geological change, or biological change. It was a process beyond his everyday scope. But collecting, gathering specimens, and then taking them home to be classified and indexed discouraged seeing these living organisms among their neighbors. Wood's *Botany* gave a false notion about botany. It did not describe the world as man experienced it, or even *as it was experiencing itself.* Museums were graveyards of Nature.

Muir finally realized a dynamic theory, but was never able to put it completely into practice. It would have led him to a more radical view of the wilderness experience, and a greater distrust of man and his books.

The implications are obvious now, however. "Take only photographs and leave only footprints" — as the Sierra Club used to advise — is not a guide to experience of the wilderness, because it misses the point of the experience itself. One shouldn't leave even footprints, for they will become a beaten track, and the photographs are worthless anyway. These days all the traveler's experiences are designed to insulate him from the truth he confronts. He takes snapshots or buys postcards. Even the most urban commentator recognizes the disappointment with Nature which results from putting it on a time schedule, setting up bleachers, and viewing it through a camera. This is not the way things ought to be. From my childhood I remember the venerable Park Naturalist Carl Sharsmith speaking to us as we sat around the campfire in Tuolumne, where they never progressed to putting up a slide projector and screen. Carl described the tourist who attempted to *take* a picture of huge Mount Dana;

and what was the end product?—a little rectangular piece of cardboard with a small rubble heap depicted on its surface. Going light requires that a man cease to use any method of perception which mediates between himself and Nature.[5]

My imaginary interview resolves a problem I have always had. Why, I have always wondered, am I so irritated by the fellow who comes along on a walk in the mountains with his bird book or flower book or camera, who wants to make sure he *knows* what he is seeing by finding it in the book he carries or in a viewfinder? It is precisely because he is following someone else's interpretation, even forming his own perceptions not by what he enters, but by what he brings. He doesn't even try to see Nature in her own terms.

So: the deep meaning of going light reveals the state of mind a mountaineer develops in the wilderness. What, we ask, must he leave behind? Muir may have gone into the Sierra alone, but did he seek solitude? Not entirely. Emerson argued that "to go into solitude, a man needs to retire as much from his chamber as from society. I am not solitary whilst I read and write, though nobody is with me." Perhaps, then, one can only go relatively light, and relatively solitary, into the mountains.[6]

ITINERARY

John! Were you an itinerant, or did you truly have an itinerary? Muir's answer was a paradoxical "yes" to both questions. When he had left on the journey described in *Thousand Mile Walk to the Gulf*, he had carefully consulted maps and had planned his route, which led for most of the journey from city to city. His journal indicates that every time he attempted to go cross-country he ran into unanticipated, sometimes overwhelming problems. So he frequently stuck to main traveled roads. But in California his route became more radically an escape from cities and civilized routes of travel. Further, where his itinerary in the Walk led downstream to the thick rich life of the tropics, in California he ascended toward austere alpine environments. Either way he would be following the flow of Nature, but in California he became conscious of his direction. Following Nature's ways required, first of all, that he give up all artificial paths.

So it is not surprising to discover Muir announcing at the very beginning that he would disdain modern methods of travel.

In 1872 he described the journey he had made four years earlier, when he first came to Yosemite. He contrasted his own method of travel to that of the typical tourist, whose journey by stage and steam resulted in "memories made up of a motley jam of cascades and deserts and mountain domes." The big gun of a railroad "belched" tourists against the "targets of the golden State." What was the point, he wondered, when time, space, and travelers were annihilated by the process? The newest ways were not the best ways, and so Muir and a companion walked across California, by any road they chanced to find. Because they had plenty of time, they proposed to drift leisurely mountainward. In that way they could make the most of their time and place.[7]

Muir portrayed himself as a botanist who drifted until lost in a kind of heaven-on-earth filled with "plant clouds" and carpeted with a "firmament of flowers." There in the Central Valley was a lake of "solar gold," whose source was the Sierra. The botanist stopped at one point, dipped into this lake, and came up with a strict accounting of California's wealth per square yard. The yield was staggering — 165,912 open flowers, a million mosses, all sorted into nine or ten natural orders, sixteen species. Such was the wealth of Nature in California, and Muir could, on occasion, tally it as well as an accountant. But it would be ten years before he could clarify what this wealth was good for. In 1868, he was only passing through.

Perhaps one might think of him mining the plant gold of the Central Valley, as Thoreau had plumbed his Walden Pond. But the walls of Muir's Valley awaited him. Thoreau waited until winter to measure the depth of his pond, but Muir continued his walk that April and met the winter of the Sierra. Thoreau could never find the source of Walden, but Muir rambled into the mountains, followed the tenuous path which led from the rich land of the Central Valley to its source in the Sierra. Muir sought beyond the transcendental tradition; he was going into the flow.

He continued to speak in a tentative tone of voice as he recorded his thoughts in his journals. He may have been collecting specimens and sensations, he may have been drifting on a random path, yet he knew that one day his observations would cohere. So too, when writing his geological observations for publication in 1871 and again in 1873, he began to describe the Sierra as a kind of book. Its glacial history was "blotted and storm-beaten," with chapters "stained and corroded," but still readable. And so too, when he concluded an essay about a "raid" to the Tuolumne country, he described the grand rocks as "books never yet opened" to which he would go in the future, "a library, where all kinds of rock-structure and rock-formation will be explained, and where I shall yet discover a thousand waterfalls."[8]

His mountain rambles were filled with the lessons of rocks and the songs of waterfalls: serious study and pure pleasure. He was not willing to sacrifice either. In fact, he had been content since his first summer to reconcile himself with the possibility that he might never be able to read the grand page of the Sierra's history. Nature, he knew, was deep and difficult, and a man's powers shallow. "Yet why should one bewail one's poor feeble ignorance. The beauty is visible and that we can enjoy, though the grand mechanical causes may lie beyond our ken." At this point in his intercourse with mountains it was sufficient to know that the Sierra had meaning, even if he could not read it. At this point he could delight in his experience. This seemed to require very little discipline, at least not by a definition of the term a contemporary might accept. So he reminded himself, even in 1872, that he would "rather stand in what all the world would call an idle manner," because "so-called sentimental, transcendental dreaming seems the only sensible and substantial business that one can engage in." He was not ready to narrow his attention to bookmaking.[9]

He was not ready to narrow his attention at all. Just as he refused to settle down, so he refused to accept any confined vocation because his own aims were so diverse. When he wrote his early narratives for the *New York Tribune* and the *Overland Monthly*, he had difficulty integrating his sensations and perceptions about botany and geology. In Muir's narrative account of the first ascent of Cathedral Peak one commentator observed his "equal interest in the abundance of flowers and the structure of the peak." Of course. How could he separate the pleasures of granite from the pleasures of white heather? The rock and the flower were interfused.[10]

All of this mingling of the senses was a good deal more disciplined than it might have seemed. Muir was not on vacation in the Sierra; he was, rather, learning to inhabit the mountains. This activity was his life. He was neither botanist nor geologist, but a whole man in a whole Nature, yearning. No wonder he was not single-minded. No wonder he didn't wish to narrow his attention to the pointed aims which a technical education might have given him. Everything was interesting to him. He scarcely was aware of the serious split in consciousness which seemed to be man's fate, the split between knowledge (the grand mechanical causes) and spirit (the beauty). Muir wanted them both, and never thought that they could be separate.

What would have happened if Muir had taken an excursion with Clarence King, the tough-minded product of Yale's Sheffield Scientific School and a member of the Whitney Survey? Though Jeanne Carr once hoped to introduce the two to each other, they would never walk through the Sierra together, or agree about its origin. But their differences went deeper than geological theory. I imagine them together: King would be suspicious of Muir for many reasons, and would play the role of geologist working. Muir would be interested in everything around, would stop every so often to examine a flower and to marvel at the view, to grin slyly while running his hand over a particularly fine sheet of glacially polished rock. King would stand by, tense-jawed, growing impatient, waiting to proceed with their serious geological investigations. Muir might well laugh when short-legged and stocky Clarence had trouble walking through the talus. But King would try to get in the last word. For him, anyone like Muir who had not narrowed his attention was an amateur. King hoped that "the ambitious amateur himself may divert his evident enthusiastic love of nature into a channel, if there is one, in which his attainments would save him from hopeless floundering." Well, King was more charitable than Whitney, who simply dismissed Muir as a sheepherder.[11]

Muir in turn contrasted his own leisurely method of study with the businesslike methods used by the men of the Whitney Survey when they went to the mountains. "I had remained winter and summer for two years," he said. "I did not go to them for a Saturday, or a Sunday, or a stingy week, but with unmeasured time, and independent of companions or scientific associations." He took his

studies seriously, but had a difficult time putting a name to his occupation. Later, when he called himself a "self-styled poetico-trampo-
geologist-bot. and ornith-natural, etc.!!!" he was looking back with
humor on a serious personal problem of the early seventies. His independence might have begun as a matter of necessity, but later,
when he could have become involved in either academic or dollar
geology, he refused both, thus never establishing himself as a professional scientist, naturalist, or interpreter.[12]

We are still faced with problems in defining this occupation,
or even finding a space for it in our busy lives. Muir was not ready
to be an interpreter precisely because he was still satisfactorily engaged as a student. Though he did work as a guide, and as a sawyer
for the hotelkeeper, James M. Hutchings, he spent most of his time
unemployed, as far as the world could understand. He saw a need
to continue his commerce with Nature, not with men. In return, his
neighbors in Yosemite saw him as an unpleasant and perhaps troublesome vagabond, certainly a capable young man, but unwilling
to work. So perhaps we still see him, though with increasing sympathy. He cultivated this image in his early narratives, letters, and
journals, and suggested that he had attained a perfect idleness and
a careless life. "I only went out for a walk, and finally concluded
to stay out till sundown, for going out, I found, was really going
in." But he was not so careless, and his rambling, wandering style
of life was, beneath the surface, strenuous, exacting, and disciplined.
Only he had departed from mechanical science and abstract philosophical musings. If he was going to avoid the errors of the others
who tried to grab the seamless whole of Nature by one handle, he
was also going to keep an open mind, and an open life.[13]

Although it may not have been very surprising to Muir, to a modern reader it might seem strange that a budding botanist suddenly
began to interest himself intensely in geology. The growth of interest
was so gradual that he might scarcely have been aware of the way
it inhabited his brain. On the other hand, there is the surprising
passage from his journal, written in Little Yosemite at Washburn
Lake, on the night of October 7, 1871: "I spring to my feet crying:
'Heavens and earth! Rock is not light, not heavy, not transparent,
not opaque, but every pore gushes, glows like a thought with im-

mortal life!'" This passage illustrates as well as anything what had happened to him. Certainly, if he were following the Humboldt tradition, all natural sciences were only methods used to approach the grand and whole cosmos. But Muir had also been following a path which led him into a more and more simplified ecological system. He had, in other words, simplified his life by simplifying his environment, to the point where he was awakened by the stark primitive contrasts which surrounded him. The Sierra itself demanded to be considered in its full and divine light, which was geological. George Shaller argues that "mountains and deserts, with their spare life at the limit of existence, make one restless and disconsolate; one becomes an explorer in an intellectual realm as well as in a physical one." But Muir had transcended the restlessness Shaller speaks of. In the realm of cloud and rock, Muir awakened to the Sierra as an organic whole. So he was led into the wilderness within and without, and he would not cease until he had plumbed the depth of the Sierra's natural history, as well as his own.[14]

MOUNTAIN JOY

He had never seen a landscape like the Sierra before that day when he peered over a ridge and saw Bridalveil Fall. He was not prepared for the sublimity of the rocks and waters of Yosemite. When he looked down at Bridalveil from a distance, he thought he was observing a "dainty little fall," certainly not higher than sixty or seventy feet. When he actually began to appreciate the magnitude of Yosemite, he was overpowered by its grandeur. "Oh, no, not for me," he later remembered thinking. This is what sublimity has always meant. Sublime Nature forces a man to reevaluate not just what he sees, but what he is and what he is capable of understanding.[15]

I doubt that any new visitor to Yosemite can adjust himself quickly enough to the reality he finds. Either he dismisses the features with a quick glance, or else he is overcome. In many ways the shock may be more extreme for the modern traveler who comes bursting out of the tunnel at fifty miles an hour, glides past Bridalveil before he even smells the ferns and mosses, and finds himself under the immense face of El Capitan. But Muir was not a man to let first impressions determine his attitude toward a landscape. As Yosemite grew in him, the first lesson he had to learn was the necessity of adjusting his own senses so that he might be able to read a landscape which was written in such massive characters.

Yosemite required a sensibility which could only be cultivated in Yosemite. Because he was so small, and the mountain so large, Muir began to discipline his own mind and body. And as he grew wiser in the ways of mountains, he began to extend his explorations out of the Valley. Each excursion became a discipline in itself, and as he received more than he had hoped, he began to reevaluate the expectations his education had given him, to reeducate himself in Yosemite.

He started with the basic texts. He read Humboldt. He read Lyell's geology, those books of Tyndall's which presented the physicist's view of the mountains, and probably Agassiz's glacial studies. He read Darwin, and probably Asa Gray's commentaries on evolution. He began to read or reread Emerson seriously, especially after he met the man in Yosemite. He suffered through Ruskin's aesthetics of mountains. His interest in geology, natural history, evolution, and aesthetics became a major theme in his letters. But now, more than in the past, his education was being directed. He tested his reading every day as he wandered in the mountains, discarding ideas which did not harmonize with the reality he lived in. This was a more mature and more studious Muir than the traveler in *A Thousand Mile Walk to the Gulf*, who had no base camp, and who did not know where he was going. On the Walk he had carried Burns's poems, Milton's *Paradise Lost*, Wood's *Botany*, and the New Testament. Now his library grew, and it could hardly keep up with his own growing consciousness.[16]

As a resident of the mountains, he soon equipped himself with the necessary means to interpret his experience to himself. Yet his reading of Emerson might have reminded him that books were for the scholar's idle times. "When he can read God directly, the hour is too precious to be wasted in other men's transcripts of their readings." Books were not the tools which would allow him to cross that thin invisible line between the finite and the infinite, the temporal and the eternal. So Muir's method of study came to be characterized by the austerity of the human resources he allowed himself.

He would finally have to listen to Nature, not to men's theories of natural history, aesthetics, or philosophy. Once he was truly a part of the wilderness, he recognized the limits of ideas as tools for revelation. Thus one might define going light.[17]

The most obvious problem was the separation between so-called "objective" and "subjective" experience. Despite his desire to uncover a modern scientific theory of mountain building in Yosemite, he could never forget the intense mountain joy he felt. He could never give up this ecstasy for any simply material explanation of the Sierra's geology. So he found himself caught between the progressive views of scientists like Darwin, Tyndall, and Gray, and the more personal and traditional attitude of someone like Ruskin. He knew he was unlike the scientists he read. In the summer of 1872 he wrote to Jeanne Carr that he had "a great longing for Gray, whom I feel to be a great, progressive, unlimited man like Darwin and Huxley and Tyndall." But after Gray's visit he commented to her, "He is a most cordial lover of purity and truth, but the angular factiness of his pursuits has kept him at too cold a distance from the spirit world." So too, when he read Tyndall that fall, Muir was dissatisfied with the physicist's analysis of "intense mountain enjoyments." Tyndall tried to account for himself by considering his own genetic heritage, or his own evolution. Muir, on the other hand, decided that mountain joy was a primary property of man. "I think that one of the *properties* of that compound which we call man is that when exposed to the rays of mountain beauty it glows with *joy.*" Mechanistic science could not account for ecstasy.[18]

 On the other hand, when Muir read Ruskin he discovered that "Mountain Glory" and "Mountain Gloom" were little more than a restatement of old Christian dualities between heaven and hell. Indeed, Ruskin offered an example of peasant mountaineers, degraded because "familiarized with certain conditions of ugliness and disorder produced by the violence of the elements around them." Ruskin believed that all the universe presented itself to Man "under a stern aspect of warning" with "good and evil set on the right hand and the left." Muir knew there was no sin in the mountains, and no "dead unorganized matter." So Ruskin's idea of "foulness" seemed absurd, and Muir could confidently predict, "were he [Ruskin] to dwell awhile among the powers of these mountains, he would forget all dictionary differences between the clean and the unclean and he would lose all memory and meaning of the diabolical, sin-begotten word *foulness*." Muir had come to realize that Ruskin's "aesthetic distance" and the scientist's "objectivity" had this in common: neither perspective allowed the human to become a part of his environment. Both perspectives were limited and flawed.[19]

Fortunately Muir could find more congenial company in Yosemite on occasion. With Joseph Le Conte he sat one night above Tenaya Lake, embosomed in the mountains. Le Conte wrote, "The deep stillness of the night; the silvery light and deep shadows of the mountains; the reflection on the water, broken into thousands of glittering points by the ruffled surface; the gentle lapping of the wavelets upon the rocky shore – all these seemed exquisitely harmonized with one another and the grand harmony made answering music in our hearts." Mind you, these are the words of a confirmed evolutionist, a professor at the University of California. Like Muir, he suspected that the life of a scientist was more than science.[20]

So Muir could not make the kind of dogmatic judgment that Clarence King expressed. For King, Tyndall represented the "liberating power of modern culture which unfetters us from the more than iron bands of self-made myths." King was sure that he had replaced the archaic model of Ruskin's thought with the modern "objectivity" of Tyndall. If he gave up the Ruskin who attempted to invest the mountains with consciousness, King did so against his feelings, and because Ruskin "helps us to know himself, not the Alps." But Muir knew that no desire to separate oneself from the world could be successful. In the mountains, on the mountains, a part of the mountains; a man had to listen to the music he heard.

There are no harsh, hard dividing lines in nature. Glaciers blend with the snow and the snow blends with the thin invisible breath of the sky. So there are no stiff, frigid, stony partition walls betwixt us and heaven. There are blendings as immeasurable and untraceable as the edges of melting clouds. Eye hath not seen, nor ear heard, etc., is applicable here, for earth is partly heaven, and heaven earth.

If there were no dividing lines in Nature, then why in the world should a man try to fragment himself? This was the lesson of Tuolumne Divide, where Muir realized that a glacier had flowed *uphill* and over a ridge into Tenaya Canyon. This was a lesson about life. The tops of the mountains flowed into the bottom of heaven, the finite merged with the infinite. The message of an old Zen saying was clear: "When you get to the top of the mountain, keep on climbing."[21]

When he had accepted himself – all of himself – in the mountains, he had found a kind of practical immortality in "vast, calm, measureless mountain days." Even when he wrote in his journal in August, "this good and tough mountain-climbing flesh is not my final home, and I'll creep out of it and fly free and grow," he knew that he had already tasted immortality. But he continued to struggle with a duality between body and soul, a doctrine which he found difficult to transcend. He knew this much: when he wandered in the mountains, he found no walls that he could not cross on his own two feet. And so he began to wonder whether his finite body could be a means for reaching the infinite. His body, which experienced pleasure, had contact with Nature, was a part of Nature. But his soul was a part of the Spirit of Creation. He had been taught that the world was composed of matter and spirit. Did they have to be separate? He would have to study himself more carefully before he could answer that question. For now he would follow the paths of the glaciers.

METHOD OF STUDY

This was my "method of study": I drifted about from rock to rock, from stream to stream, from grove to grove. Where night found me, there I camped. When I discovered a new plant, I sat down beside it for a minute or a day, to make its acquaintance and hear what it had to tell. When I came to moraines, or ice-scratches upon the rocks, I traced them back, learning what I could of the glacier that made them. I asked the bowlders I met, whence they came and whither they were going. I followed to their fountains the traces of the various soils upon which forests and meadows are planted; and when I discovered a mountain or rock of marked form and structure, I climbed about it, comparing it with its neighbors.[22]

He could never call this kind of occupation work, in fact it seemed more like pure pleasure. Even in an essay entitled "Exploration of the Great Tuolumne Cañon" he refused to distinguish among the activities normally denoted by the words "explore," "study," "wander," "follow," and "drift." He continued to wonder, as he wrote in his journal, whether his "methodless rovings" and "lawless wanderings" would advance him along the path of "grave science."[23]

But there had always been a central assumption behind his personal style of mountain travel and mountain study. His life was predicated on the Emersonian dictum, "We must trust the perfection of the creation so far as to believe that whatever curiosity the order of things has awakened in our minds, the order of things can satisfy." This had been the rationale for all of nineteenth-century science. But even Emerson had divided his investigation of Nature into the kinds of truths which separate disciplines yielded, while Muir wished to integrate all disciplines into his study. One might ask how much the order of things might satisfy one man, in one place, at one time. Muir wanted it all, and as his studies began to take direction from the ice scratches and boulders, as he began to trace back the soils and waters to their fountains, he believed that he had found the Way. Still, he knew that the order of things was deep, and that man was shallow, that the order of things was eternal, and that man was mortal. He recognized that a perfect creation could answer our questions, but was under no obligation to do so. Certainly he hoped that he could take a step toward perfect health by using all of his senses and faculties. That in itself was satisfying.[24]

Muir had also inherited a disciplined approach to the creation from Louis Agassiz, who had introduced the method of close inspection and comparison to American schools. Agassiz told the student to look closely and long at natural objects. But when it came to glacial studies, Muir was in a quandary. Agassiz's glacial studies, *Études sur les Glaciers*, was the definitive text. Agassiz had lived *on* them, and had studied their mechanics, and determined what glaciers were. As he kept his attention on these geological agents, he had asked what were their origins, how did they move, how were they influenced by external agents, and how did they change their environment? Muir needed to know these things, but he could not observe them in the Sierra. He felt a need to witness a landscape in the midst of a glacial age, and already hoped to go to Alaska for that purpose. But in 1873 Muir had to accept Agassiz's findings, and could only look at rocks the glaciers had carved. He started not on the glaciers, but in the Sierran canyons. The glacier as a geological agent provided a possible answer to his primary scientific concern: "In particular the great Valley has always kept a place in my mind. How did the Lord make it? What tools did He use? How did he apply them and when?" But Muir's insistence on the glacial origin of Yosemite only took him one step toward deeper questions.[25]

Since he could not study the glaciers as they created the Sierra, he had to apply another man's theory. He had to create a mental experiment by imagining what glaciers would have done in the Sierra. So he began to see the landscape as a glacier might. He followed his imagination back into the wilderness, testing the glaciers of his mind against the canyons, cliffs, and domes, hoping that mind and matter would become one. He was no longer traversing the landscape in a random way, but blending into it, following its own laws. By September of 1873, his studies had become a good deal more focused, and he had begun to investigate the importance of rock structure: "No scientific book in the world can tell me how this Yosemite granite is put together or how it has been taken down. Patient observation and constant brooding above the rocks, lying upon them for years as the ice did, is the way to arrive at the truths which are graven so lavishly upon them." He had entered so completely the secret life of glaciers that he described his observations as if he were a patient, brooding river of ice. He planned to demonstrate his sympathy to the landscape by wearing "tough grey clothes, the color of granite," and then he would "reproduce the ancient ice-rivers and . . . dwell with them."[26]

Given this kind of mystical commingling of himself with the history of the Sierra, it was only natural that he would also begin to describe himself as climbing down rocks like a glacier: "I then began to creep down the smooth incline, depending mostly upon my hands, wetting them with my tongue, and striking them flatly upon the rock to make them stick by atmospheric pressure." He was learning about glaciers by imitating them, and his study became increasingly a physical activity. As he climbed through the steep and seemingly inaccessible canyons, he began to call upon not simply his imagination, but his physical discipline. As he journeyed back and forth through natural history, following the glacial footprints, he was directed through time and space.[27]

BODY AND SOUL

Muir was deeply troubled by the doubleness of his life in the mountains, and it is instructive to explore his dilemma. On the one hand, he had learned to value his physical sensations, especially after he had nearly been blinded. On the other hand, he often wondered whether he wouldn't have preferred to be all mind, all spirit, and consequently bodiless. He found the method of scientific study introduced by Agassiz congenial because it was based on close inspection of the objects in Nature. But Muir felt, along with Agassiz, that a scientist's duty went beyond "angular factiness." "Philosophers have yet to learn that a physical fact is as sacred as a moral principle. Our own nature demands from us this double allegiance," Agassiz had said. Muir believed this maxim, and believed further that his senses and soul were sacred but independent when his body and mind wandered in the wilderness. And so he sometimes wondered if he were not two separate beings, as Agassiz suggested, on two separate errands. I think of a contemporary parallel — George Shaller and Peter Matthiessen walking together in the Himalaya, one on a spiritual quest and the other faithfully following his science. Muir felt the need to write both journals, and hoped they would cohere.[28]

His early attempts were clumsy. "Explorations in the Great Tuolumne Cañon" was a perfect example of his problem. The essay was divided into two halves, the first one devoted to geographical observations, and the second half to observations of self. He wanted to report a unity of the two enterprises, but found he had to split his vision in order to explain it. Further, he ended up portraying himself in dualistic terms; the body acquired daytime knowledge, while the mind and memory became active at night. He knew that physical exercise, climbing the canyon walls, was an important part of his method of study, and he knew that his austere method of mountain travel had something to do with the remarkable sense of health he attained. After a climb of 5,000 vertical feet, when he ate his "craggy bowlder of bread" and drank his cup of tea, he could argue that

no healthy man who delivers himself into the hands of Nature can possibly doubt the doubleness of his life. . . . Soul and body receive separate nourishment and separate exercise, and speedily reach a stage of development wherein each is easily known apart from the other. Living artificially in towns, we are sickly, and never come to know ourselves. Our torpid souls are hopelessly entangled with our torpid bodies, and not only is there a confused mingling of our own souls with our own bodies, but we hardly possess a separate existence from our neighbors.

Sometime after he published this essay, Muir blotted out this whole passage and attempted to deemphasize the "capacity that our flesh has for knowledge," but he was deeply troubled, because sometimes he thought his body had been so completely and so mindlessly in control that he trusted it against his own advice.[29]

His body acted intuitively, and seemed not to require that he scrutinize the rock, or exercise his will at all. The line between body and rock seemed to disappear, along with the separation of "objective" and "subjective" experience. His wild body was quite simply a part of the wilderness which he had learned to trust. But the wild body was a very special and highly attuned organism, not to be mistaken for the tame one. Wild legs could accomplish more in the dark than civilized legs in the day, even when "piloted by the mind that owns them." This fine-tuning was the result of discipline; and it was only possible for the adjusted, experienced traveler who had left his fears behind. This is by no means the typical backpacker's experience, as one can learn on any summer day by watching the long lines of overladen and grim-faced hikers trudging down the trail from Tuolumne Meadows toward the lower canyons of the Tuolumne River.

But "soul life," he knew, gave an intimation of the eternal: after the whole body had opened up as an eye during the day, the soul awoke and crossed that boundary into "realms that eye hath not seen. . . . Brooding over some vast mountain landscape, or among the spiritual countenances of mountain flowers, our bodies disappear, our mortal coils come off without any shuffling, and we blend into the rest of Nature, utterly blind to the boundaries that measure human quantities into separate individuals." So the two lives were necessarily linked, and the only way to become "part and parcel of Nature" was to attain such a fine edge of physical fitness that one didn't even notice it. Muir said that he was in such good health that he "knew nothing about it."[30]

The palpable separation of soul life from limb life was not easily come by. Once arrived at, there was a loss of any feeling of separateness. The mind knew the body, because one was part of the other, but each followed its own way. This experience is described by Delores LaChappelle when she talks about skiing powder snow. There is some point at which a good skier ceases to consciously steer the skis; in fact, conscious control actually impedes his motion through the snow. The skis follow the body, and the will follows the body downhill through the turns. LaChappelle recognizes that this state of consciousness depends on complete trust in Nature. Such an experience, if one can call it that, requires full commitment, no turning back. Climbers in Yosemite have noticed that it's always at the beginning of the second day that inexperienced or exhausted climbers retreat from routes on the faces of El Capitan.[31]

What, then, could Muir make of Tyndall's statement that "imagination . . . must be strictly checked by reason and by observation"? This seemed the reverse of Muir's own experience, and confused the issue. If it was anything, imagination was soul life and was based on observation, though more subtle. It reminded the observer of all the things he did not see, and did not hear. It wasn't simply a "mental picture," and certainly wasn't "unreal." No, imagination reminded Muir of the "sweet music of the tiniest insect wings," and the sounds of avalanches in the past; it saw "crystals of the rock in rapid sympathetic motion," and heard "the sound of stars in circulation." It reminded him that "the whole world is in motion to the center." It extended the physical senses until they approached the infinite.[32]

There was nothing soft-headed or sentimental about this. Muir did not think of himself as airy or effusive during this period of his life. He wrote to one friend, in 1872, "You'll find me rough as the rocks and about the same color — granite."[33]

TRAVELING THE GLACIAL PATHWAY

As Muir sought a way to tell people about his method of study, he gave up trying to explain the dialectical relationship between soul life and limb life. It was implicit in his activity and could be dramatized through narrative essays. When Jeanne Carr sent a letter from him on to *Overland*, where it was published as "A Geologist's Winter Walk," Muir's progress as a professional writer turned a corner. The essay tells a good deal about the man who needed to get into shape and who was capable of thinking seriously about the purely athletic side of his explorations. He dramatized the way soul life was built upon sturdy limb life as the way of the soul became the path of the glacier.[34]

He began to follow the pathway of the Tenaya Glacier, climbing out of the Valley from Mirror Lake toward Tenaya Lake. Tenaya Canyon is still trailless through most of its length, and even today the Park Service tries to discourage casual hikers from traversing it. Yet a competent rockclimber may make the journey during the season of low water in several hours. And if it is a difficult canyon, it is also a rewarding one. The sculpture of the inner gorge and surrounding domes is particularly dramatic and very steep. As with any fine mountain ramble, the beauty of the landscape is inseparable from its technical difficulties.

So near and yet so far from the crowded Valley, it is another world. I have scrambled on its walls, bathed in its waterfalls, climbed on its cliffs, walked through forest to its abrupt edges, and even once floated shamelessly through its depths in a helicopter. But it has always been most real when I walked it alone. How many times have I gone there on a crowded summer afternoon, crossing Snow Creek, passing under the great northwest face of Half Dome, and finding myself alone in the world of rock and water? May such places always be feared by those who do not belong in them, and may such deep shadows and smooth granite walls continue to lure those who are ready for the more austere lessons of the wilderness. Hidden in those massive planes of polished rock are gardens filled with singing ouzels. Though one might be the only human traveling in the depths, one is never alone.

Muir followed this path because it was the most direct route from the Valley to the winter of the backcountry. It was February, and it must have been what we call a drought year. Muir's desire to follow this glacial pathway indicated his own changing perspective. Where he had earlier wished to brood upon the rocks and wear grey, now he wished to move, and in so doing he was running toward his final transformation, thinking and seeing like a glacier.

He did not take his excursion lightly, since he had been in the city, and was aware that a winter storm might isolate him in the backcountry. Tenaya Canyon is a world of avalanche; Cloud's Rest, runneled with avalanche courses, is a reminder of rushing snow. But as he said, he was "seduced by the voice of Tissiac," Half Dome, the guardian of the canyon; "never did her soul reveal itself more than now." This was also a hint to the scientist in him, for he was interested in proving that Tissiac was not half a dome at all, but a whole and glacially carved monument, whose front had been chiseled by the Tenaya Glacier. Unfortunately, he was carrying a heavier burden than usual. He was a scientific expedition, not a man. He had been weakened by city life, and hoped that "a fast and a storm and a difficult cañon were just the medicine." But he also confessed, "I was anxious to carry my barometer and clinometer through it, to obtain altitudes and sections." He was not going light, for his city legs would have to carry civilized devices and a mechanistic attitude into the wilds. This arithmetical work was not the sort of thing Muir ever enjoyed, but it was the kind of evidence that the scientific world demanded.

Almost immediately he slipped on the polished apron of Mount Watkins and fell. And with the fall went all of his tools, except those which were a part of his more intimate self. This was a shock that he needed. He "felt degraded and worthless," and addressed his feet with disdain. He blamed his clumsiness on his intercourse with "stupid town stairs and dead pavements." But now that the "town fog had been shaken from both head and feet" he was prepared to enter Nature's realm on her own terms: "I determined to guide my humbled body over the most nerve-trying places I could find; for I was now awake." Once Nature had disencumbered him of superfluous paraphernalia, he could rescue his fallen body and become whole.

As Muir recounted his adventure, his essay became more explicitly about getting into shape, and dramatized Muir's successive movement through states of fitness and states of mind. He was "determined to take earnest exercise the next day," and was free to confront his true self. In his first bivouac he reacquainted himself with the rock. "No plushy boughs did my ill-behaved bones enjoy that night, nor did my bumped head get a spicy cedar plume pillow mixed with flowers. I slept on a naked boulder, and when I awoke all my nervous trembling was gone." On the second day he was prepared to find flowers where others might only find terror, and he even parodied the gothic style of landscape description. Here was beauty, "Ay, even here in this darksome gorge, 'frightened and tormented' with raging torrents and choking avalanches of snow."

His own clumsiness was a result of his lack of fitness, just as a gothic perspective was a result of fear. The canyon itself provided more than enough of "the one big word of love that we call the world," and provided more than Muir had a right to expect, considering the condition in which he approached it. Doing without, disciplining oneself; though it sounds rather puritanical, this regimen was necessary to the only experience Muir found valuable. If he wished to travel this path, he would have to follow Nature's rules and he would have to simplify his aims. There was only room enough for a man in Tenaya, not for an expedition.

The next day he arrived at Tenaya Lake, which was frozen and was transparent in the sunlight, manifesting "myriads of Tyndall's six rayed water flowers, magnificently colored." These ice flowers reminded Muir of the days when the whole canyon had been a *mer de glace*, and reminded him that the glaciation of Yosemite might be imagined not as a catastrophic epoch, but as a uniform flow of compacted snowflakes — snow flowers who slowly carved out the beautiful structures of a mountain mansion.

After conditioning his mind and body by following the path of a glacier, he was able to return two days later for another excursion. He climbed around Half Dome and Cloud's Rest in one day, constantly moving and observing, making the most of his life:

Not one of all the assembled rocks or trees seemed remote. . . . I ran home in the moonlight with firm strides; for the sun-love made me strong. Down through the junipers; down through the firs; now in jet shadows, now in white light; over sandy moraines and bare, clanking rocks; past the huge ghost of South Dome rising weird through the firs; past the glorious fall of Nevada. . . . All of this mountain wealth in one day!

As his narrative accelerated, he began to capture the freedom of movement in his language. He was traveling Nature's glacial highways at her own pace, or even faster, passing waterfalls, transcending day and night, transcending his own human limitations, until he was able to measure the sublime landscape with his whole being.[35]

As he traveled upstream back into time and returned with renewed vision, he used the images of sun and moon to suggest the structure of his activity, the two sides of it. The sun, associated with the body, ruled the time of close observation, but Muir's body absorbed the light and carried him back into the shadowy world of the moon. Day and night merged as he ran through the mountains. As he moved through the flowing landscape, his joyful vision partook of the present, yet contained the depth of history that the canyon represented.

Jeanne Carr had once quoted a passage from Tyndall's *Hours of Exercise in the Alps* in a letter: "Much as I enjoy the work, I do not think I could have filled my days and hours in the alps with clambering alone. The climbing in many cases was a peg on which a thousand other 'exercises' were being hung." But Muir could not justify his own mountaineering in such mechanical terms. It is interesting to consider the possibility that Muir's barometer and clinometer had been gifts from Tyndall, as one writer suggests; if that were so, Muir was consciously dramatizing his departure from Tyndall's method of study. Certainly Muir could not separate his exploration of self from his exploration of the mountains. They were simultaneous and intermingled. His narratives would demonstrate why a man had to inhabit his own body and follow it into the wilderness. "[We] live with our heels as well as head, and most of our pleasure comes in that way," he once wrote.[36]

THE EXPLORER SIMPLIFIES HIS TOOLS

Probably Muir was not responsible for the title "A Geologist's Winter Walk." But it was an apt name for his essay because of its fine sense of understatement, and because it invited comparison with Thoreau's "A Winter Walk," wherein young Henry began to explore his own higher latitudes. Thoreau could imagine that he was a polar explorer as he skated along the frozen river behind Concord. So too

Muir had imagined, as he ran through the canyons of Yosemite, that he dwelled in the glacial age of the Sierra. Though the Transcendental tradition flowed from Emerson to Thoreau and Muir, neither of the younger men were strict followers of Emerson. If the self they began to discover was suggested in Emerson's essays, both men found in practice that they had to entrust themselves to Nature far more than Emerson did. The old sage had argued that Nature was the first influence upon the mind of Man, but for Muir Nature became the alpha and omega of life. And so he parted with his teacher when he realized that he would be more faithful to the primary influences on his life.

Emerson had suggested the significance of the Transcendental experience in "Nature": "In the woods, we return to reason and faith. . . . all mean egotism vanishes. I become a transparent eyeball; I am nothing; I see all; the currents of the Universal Being circulate through me; I am part or parcel of God . . . In the wilderness . . . man beholds somewhat as beautiful as his own nature." But this kind of disembodied experience was suspiciously empty. For instance, Emerson could not decide whether the power to produce this cosmic state of mind resided in Man or in Nature. Even his colleagues in Concord suspected that Emerson's Nature was too etherialized, too abstract, and as a result they further suspected that Emerson saw not Nature at all, but himself.[37]

From the beginning of his stay in California, Muir had discarded the image of the "transparent eyeball" and had begun to speak of the human body as a "sponge steeped in immortality." He was delighted to find that the body contained "such multitudes of palates, or that this mortal flesh, so little valued by philosophers and teachers, was possessed of so vast a capacity for happiness." He could delight in purely animal pleasures, and was sure that these too had their spiritual satisfactions. When Muir read and annotated Emerson's *Essays* in the Sierra, he found himself disagreeing with the Concord sage. Edwin Way Teale has recorded the most striking of Muir's departures:

Emerson observes: "There is in woods and waters a certain enticement and flattery, together with a failure to yield a present satisfaction. This disappointment is felt in every landscape." Muir dissents: "No — always we find more than we expect."

And so Emerson only provided a ladder to Muir's vision. After he had climbed to the top, Muir kicked the ladder away. Then he was far above, and alone.[38]

His faith in himself and in Nature was more absolute than Emerson's could ever be. "Winter blows the fog out of our heads," he wrote while returning one fall to his home in the mountains. "Nature is not a mirror for the moods of the mind." When Muir thought about the natural history of Man, he understood, as Emerson had not, that the human animal had to accept himself as a part of the flow. Man was not above, but was immersed in, his environment.

Now we observe that, in cold mountain altitudes, Spirit is but thinly and plainly clothed. As we descend down their many sides to the valleys, the clothing of all plants and beasts and of the forms of rock becomes more abundant and complicated. When a portion of Spirit clothes itself with a sheet of lichen tissue, colored simply red or yellow, or gray or black, we say that is a low form of life. Yet is it more or less radically Divine than another portion of Spirit that has gathered garments of leaf and fairy flower and adorned them with all the colors of Light, although we say that the latter creature is of a higher form of life? All of these varied forms, high and low, are simply portions of God, radiated from Him as a sun, and made terrestrial by the clothes they wear, and by the modifications of a corresponding kind in the God essence itself. The more extensively terrestrial a being becomes, the higher it ranks among its fellows, and the most terrestrial being is the one that contains all the others, that has, indeed, flowed through all the others and borne away parts of them, building them into itself. Such a being is man, who has flowed down through other forms of being and absorbed and assimilated portions of them into himself, thus becoming a microcosm most richly Divine because most richly terrestrial, just as a river becomes rich by flowing on and on through varied climes and rocks, through many mountains and vales, constantly appropriating portions to itself, rising higher in the scale of rivers as it grows rich in the absorption of the soils and smaller streams.[39]

What an amazing statement this was. Man was a microcosm, in a paradoxical way. He was the highest creature because he absorbed so much of Nature, and he was the lowest because his spirit was so heavily clothed by his descent through history. Muir's meditation suggests that he had begun to absorb and apply a kind of Darwinian thinking to Man. Evolution reminded him of his own membership in a community of all things, the community he might have called Nature. No wonder he wrote to Asa Gray that he had never liked "Darwin's mean ungodly word, 'struggle'!" Man was like a river; he could flow through the creation as Muir had been doing, assimilating those rich nourishing soils through his dynamic immersion in the flux of Nature. He was clothed in the dust of creation. This was what Muir meant by *baptism*. When man immersed himself in the terrestrial, he was in fact immersing himself in the divine.[40]

But this view of man's relationship to the creation did not come to America with Darwin's *Origin*. It was there all along. Humility—"to lie low before God, as in the dust; that I might be nothing but God might be ALL"—this had been the method of study or meditative posture of Jonathan Edwards, the greatest American Calvinist. And humility before Nature was the cornerstone of Muir's own method of study, indeed of his whole life's work. A twentieth-century naturalist like Aldo Leopold might argue that "The two major advances of the past century were the Darwinian theory and the development of geology" because they tore down the wall that Christian thought had erected between man and other forms of life, and because they dramatized man's membership in the community of things, not his lordship over it. But Muir could have inherited that posture toward Nature before he began to study geology or evolution.[41]

Muir in Yosemite was like Edwards precisely because he rejected notions of time and efficiency, rejected the anthropocentric attitudes of the Enlightenment, which might be typified by the philosophy of Ben Franklin. For Edwards, as for Muir, the world was not given to men. For Edwards, "there is some impropriety in saying that a disposition in God to communicate himself *to the creature,* moved him to create the world." A man could only suppose "a disposition in God, as an original property of his nature, to an emination of his own infinite fulness, was what excited him to create the world; and so that the emination itself was aimed at as a last end in creation." There was an old message whispering to Muir out of his earliest religious training: "Suspect thyself much, Man." Thus was Muir's Transcendental faith tempered. He could never think of man as a God, even as a god in ruins, as Emerson argued. He would have to pay serious attention to his own method of study, and would have to suspect that as a man he could always be wrong. If he were to trust himself at all, it would be a result of his mystical, not scientific, insights. Those, he would insist, were the result of Nature's voice, not his own.[42]

What has all this to do with Muir's role as an explorer? Historians of the American West have labeled the period between 1860 and 1900 as the era of the great surveys, devoted to "more intensive scientific reconnaisances and inventories" which would lead to "sober second thoughts as to the proper nature, purpose, and future direction of western settlement." This was the period when Americans began to question their motives and their Manifest Destiny to "conquer" the West. And this was the period when John Muir was learning how to dwell in the mountains. He confronted alone the same wilderness that the giants of western exploration faced with large expeditionary teams. He was in the American West of Powell, King, Hayden, and Whitney; yet he was proceeding by methods totally different from the ones they were using. They brought the city into the wilderness: that was what an expedition had always been. He followed his wild body into the wilderness: that was what his lawless wanderings were. Just as the explorer differed from the discoverer in terms of his mission, so Muir differed from the explorers. Discoveries might be accidental, exploration might be "programmed" by some older center of culture, but Muir's way allowed him to reevaluate his mission constantly.[43]

The questions one asks largely determine the kinds of answers one can hope to receive, and Muir was asking more personal and more basic philosophical questions than the government surveys. Muir was a majority of one and was responsible to his own conscience. He had no direct ties with Sacramento or with Washington. He was not even obligated to follow the doctrine of Emerson. Nature provided his direction, and enforced his integrity. That was how he came to take a place in the American imagination, along with the other explorers of the period. Though his search was more personal at first, it would come to address the same issues —"the proper nature, purpose, and future direction of western settlement." Indeed, none of these issues have been satisfactorily resolved, even as I write, in 1981.

Nor is it a charming coincidence that Muir entered the canyons of the Sierra at about the same time that John Wesley Powell set off in his boat to follow the flow through canyons carved by the Colorado. Muir's Hetch Hetchy, and Powell's Glen Canyon, are gone now, impounded behind dams. Yet both men had attempted to check the tide of unthinking settlement in the West, and both had failed. Now we might look back and see that Muir always knew that the issues were not economic, or scientific, but were philosophical at bottom. What, his friends and family might have asked him, was he doing out in the howling wilderness? People like Powell or Clarence King never had to reach so deeply for their answers. They were part of a larger organization of men and had their duties to perform. Muir would have to appeal to deeper reasons for his quest, and that is what he did.

Why did men go West? Muir recognized his kinship with a new wave of immigrants. Like Galen Clark who was to become the Yosemite Guardian, Muir went to the mountains seeking personal health, and became a student of natural history. He found more than he expected. "Go east, young man, go east!" he wrote in his journal, speaking in his mind to the residents of the cities of California; "earth hath no sorrows that earth cannot heal." Muir, Clark, or John Nelder — who made his home near Giant Forest among the godlike Sequoias — these men were explorers who sought a home in Nature. Their example suggests a new consciousness in the American westward movement, a countercurrent to the advancing tide of civilization.[44]

BIRTH OF THE GLACIAL EYE

As he relived and recreated the geological history of Yosemite, Muir dreamed glaciers. At times he wrote about following their paths, and even sleeping with them, as in a section of one article entitled "Scenes Among the Glaciers' Beds." No wonder he was so enthusiastic when he had a chance to investigate a glacier firsthand. Besides, his method of study insisted that there was no substitute for complete immersion in Nature. The one thing Muir had wholly rejected when he rebelled against his religious training was reasoning from authority. In the final analysis, his findings in Yosemite could only be trustworthy if he could substantiate his imagination not by books on glaciology, but by personal observations.[45]

So Muir made his most decisive single step toward certainty

when he found an active glacier on Red Mountain in October of 1872. He wrote to Jeanne Carr, Asa Gray, Joseph Le Conte – to almost everyone he knew. The article which appeared in the December 1872 issue of *Overland* was substantially that letter. As it appeared in *Overland*, Muir's letter was only a report of work in progress, of "first fruits," and was intended only to substantiate the existence of glaciers in the Sierra. He did not attempt to discuss the personal and geological significance of his findings, but he did use the opportunity to discuss his method of study. As he followed "the footprints of ancient glaciers that once flowed grandly from their ample fountains," he had unexpectedly discovered glacial silt: "Before I had time to reason, I said, Glacier mud, mountain meal!" Like Agassiz, Muir was arguing that scientific observation, cultivated by long practice, became instinctual. After this surprise, Muir became exuberant when he climbed over the terminal moraine and was faced with the prospect of a snowfield, etched with curving lines of dirt and stones. He shouted, "*A living glacier!*" He perceived the green ice in a small crevasse, and was anxious to show by observations how he knew he had found a glacier. These observations confirmed the *form* of the glacier, and should have convinced anyone, Muir thought, but he found that his friends required "proofs of the common, measured, arithmetical kind." So the rest of his narrative, like the rest of his experience with this glacier, was transformed into a survey of moving stakes in an ice field. He dwelled on these dry facts not because he wanted to, but because the exigencies of science seemed to require that he report not his "personal" experience but a mechanical "scientific" experience. Even if scientists refused to accept the whole truth as he had learned it, Muir could at least dramatize his method of study, which he did.[46]

It is clear that he slowly grasped the full meaning of his day on this glacier several years after he first reported it. When he enlarged his essay, which appeared in its new form in *Harper's* as "Living Glaciers of California," Muir had a chance to integrate the spiritual significance of the experience into his narrative. According to John Swett, with whom Muir lived when he came to San Francisco, the essay caused Muir considerable effort and time. The revised essay presented a more complete picture of the Sierran wilderness, and was more carefully worded and structured, but it was also transformed into more than a simple proof of Muir's glacial theory.

When he shifted his moment of enlightenment from his initial view of the glacier to a journey into a crevasse, the essay took on a new symbolic significance. When he contrasted his observations with those of Joseph Le Conte, he established the validity of his method of study.[47]

Though "the Sierra Nevada of California may be regarded as one grand wrinkled sheet of glacial records," Muir focused not on the records, but on the creators of such records. Where did the glaciers live? For the first time the term "wilderness" became prominent in Muir's writing: "The pearly band of summits is the Sierra Alps, composed of a vast wilderness of peaks, variously grouped, and segregated by stupendous cañons and swept with torrents and avalanches. Here are the homes of all the glaciers left alive in the Sierra Nevada." Muir educated himself in this wilderness by immersing himself in it. He described himself first as wandering and then as drawn to the glacial womb. Traveling the "path of the dead glacier," noting the lateral moraines which "bounded the view on either side like artificial embankments," he was directed inexorably into a "grand fountain amphitheater." In this wilderness, this pathless place, he found well-marked glacial highways. This paradox became clearer as he continued to follow the "guidance of a stream," and was urged forward by the "main lateral moraines that stretch so formally from the huge jaws of the amphitheater." He dramatized his own walking as almost passive, simply as a matter of following the topographical invitation which the glacier had left. He did not dwell on his discovery of glacial silt, or even on the form of the glacier itself, but saved his eloquence for a journey down into the womb of the glacier, the *bergshrund.*

A series of rugged zig-zags enabled me to make my way down into the weird ice world of the *Shrund.* Its chambered hollows were hung with a multitude of clustered icicles, amidst which thin subdued light pulsed and shimmered with indescribable loveliness. Water dripped and tinkled overhead, and from far below there came strange solemn murmurs from currents that were feeling their way among veins and fissures on the bottom.

Ice creations of this kind are perfectly enchanting, notwithstanding one feels so entirely out of place in their pure fountain beauty. I was soon uncomfortably cold in my shirt sleeves, and the leaning wall of the *Shrund* seemed really to ingulph me. Yet it was hard to leave the delicious music of the water, and still more intense loveliness of the light.

There is a good deal more than scientific observation operating in this passage, but I will consider first the purely geological significance of Muir's entry into this underworld.[48]

He had made his most dramatic discovery not below the glacier where he found glacial mud, not overlooking it from the terminal moraine, but actually in it, and for good reason. For most laymen, a *shrund* is the surest sign of a live, active glacier, because it is the crevasse which lies close to the head of the amphitheater against the mountain, and it indicates that the ice has been moving down and away from the mountain wall. It is the glacier's point of origin; the winter snows which fill it keep the glacier moving. Even hidden under the snows of winter, the glacier continues its slow sure work of carving out the landscape. Because this is true, Muir had concrete support for his belief in a dynamic Nature, a wilderness that was still being made. Now he had lived what he had only read in Agassiz before.

This kind of close observation became the inevitable starting point when in the revised essay he turned to his differences with Le Conte, who was one of those he ridiculed for making a hash out of glacial theory. Le Conte had actually observed the Lyell Glacier with Muir, but from a distance. Muir recounted the ambiguous report that Le Conte had published, which said that such a glacier was neither true nor typical, but was "in some sense a glacier." Then Muir insisted that imperfect data, acquired from such a distance, was "a sample of rashness sometimes evidenced by scientific observers" who had no previous experience and had made no effort to acquire some when the opportunity presented itself. Le Conte had seen no glacial ice because he hadn't gone into the depths of a glacier. In terms of this controversy, one can understand why Muir wanted to stay in the *bergshrund* longer. Time was needed for complete study; the more time the better.[49]

Entering the glacial womb, Muir was also dramatizing the limits of empirical science. He knew there would always be hidden secrets in Nature, that finally the empirical method could not take him infinitely back into history or the nature of creation. Even in the glacial womb, Muir had not plumbed the depths of geological history. As we will see, the formative influence of the structure of rocks would create an impenetrable barrier to an empirical scientist who wished to explain the mechanical causes of the Sierran landscape.

But there is also a spiritual resonance to Muir's journey into the glacial womb. He was drawn into the world of ice by more than science. If it was a journey to the origin of Yosemite's landscape, it was also a journey into Muir's mind. Indeed, the necessarily brief confrontation between a man and the unclothed reality of wilderness is mentioned in most of Muir's narratives. He always underlined the fact that he needed to return to civilization for bread, and portrayed himself as always in shirtsleeves, whether in a blizzard on Shasta, down in Hetch Hetchy, or in the glacial womb. This was not poor preparation; rather, Muir was attempting to show the limits of any man's experience. Intense unmediated contact with the wilderness was at best temporary. He could not be close to the ice for too long without becoming part of it.

Other post-Emersonian writers wondered about becoming "part and parcel of Nature," particularly Thoreau when he recounted his climb of Ktaadn in *The Maine Woods,* and Melville when he narrated the climb up to the masthead in *Moby Dick.* Thoreau found the summit of Ktaadn hostile because "the tops of mountains are among the unfinished parts of the globe." Nature spoke to him there, but asked him sternly, "Why came you before your time? This ground is not prepared for you. Is it not enough that I smile upon the valleys? . . . Why seek me where I have not called thee, and then complain because you find me but a step mother?" Muir did not share several of Thoreau's assumptions. He neither believed that Nature was making certain parts of the earth for man, nor that she could be hostile. Certainly he found her a cold but very beautiful mother in the glacial womb. He sought her in such a place precisely because she was still at work, and she in turn attracted him maybe even too powerfully, for he needed to resist the urge to stay in her icy depths. Even though he was not on the warm Sierra granite he had learned to traverse barehanded and barefoot, even though his naked fingers were benumbed, and the cold would travel eventually from his extremities to his vital center, he was not ready to give up his faith in Nature.[50]

Melville argued that annihilation was the consequence of becoming part and parcel of Nature. If Muir persisted in following his method of study far enough, with regard only for the spiritual reward, perhaps it would bring him to his final reward. One thinks of Ishmael on the masthead, entertaining that disembodied state of mind that Emerson recommended so heartily:

There is no life in thee, now, except that rocking life imparted by a gently rolling ship; by her, borrowed from the sea; by the sea, from the inscrutable tides of God. But while this sleep, this dream is on ye, move your foot or hand an inch; slip your hold at all; and your identity comes back in horror. . . . And perhaps, at mid-day, in the fairest weather, with one half throttled shriek you drop through that transparent air into the summer sea, no more to rise forever. Heed it well, ye Pantheists!

Melville believed, in other words, that men needed to keep a firm grip on themselves. Men did, alas, inhabit very limited physical bodies, and they were subject to mechanical laws which paid no mind to spiritual states. Worse perhaps was Melville's suggestion that men were also limited spiritual beings. Certainly Ishmael argued that men could go beyond their own spiritual depth. Could a man remain human after he had been immersed in the full power and glory of creation? Or would he, like Melville's Pip when lost at sea, find that his horizon expanded so far, so limitlessly, that he would lose his identity altogether? That is what Muir had to consider when he sought the hard, cold, glacial truth. That was the fascination of the glacial womb.[51]

"Why should man value himself as more than a small part of the one great unit of creation?" Muir had asked during his Thousand Mile Walk. And when he answered, "After human beings have also played their part in Creation's plan, they too may disappear without any general burning or extraordinary commotion whatever," he had established his own view about the possibility of annihilation. He spoke of the death of glaciers in much the same terms he used for men. This might be puzzling until one realizes that for Muir, glaciers, like men, were only a vital part of the Plan.[52]

Aside from calling the *bergshrund* a glacial womb, Muir described the glacier itself as animate. It was not like Melville's transparent sea; it was a living fountain. It had blue veins. In it the light pulsed. Muir lavished his style on glaciers, frequently personifying them. This one was female, was the Mother, but Muir was capable of describing a glacier in male terms as well. He usually caught and removed this kind of sexuality, as in the conclusion to an essay published in 1880, "Ancient Glaciers of the Sierra." In an early draft he had described a brooding glacier, outspread spiritlike over a predestined landscape, and he spoke of "channels furrowed," "basins scooped," and the glaciers which "wither and vanish." The sexuality was clear enough, and did belong in such a vision of genesis. Because the glacier was a creative force with which Muir wished to merge, his identification with the glaciers themselves was a search for an imaginative fusion of self with other agents of Nature. If such a fusion could be an annihilation of self, it could also suggest a rebirth. Muir did not expect God to save him, nor was he unaware of the possibility of death in the wilderness. Apparently he even had dreams in which he saw himself swept away by an avalanche or thrown down a cliff in an earthquake. Even in his dreams he learned to die calmly, as the glaciers had.[53]

When he contemplated the risks he took, he justified himself by remembering that he had been visiting sacred places. Thoreau had said of the mountain tops that "only daring and insolent men, perchance, go there. Simple races, as savages, do not climb mountains — their tops are sacred and mysterious tracts never visited by them." But Thoreau was wrong. Certain men in all times and all cultures have gone to sacred and mysterious places, because that was where one could gain power. Shamans climbed their own kinds of mastheads at the beginning of celestial journeys. And in many rites of sacred initiation men have gone through death and rebirth.[54]

Indeed Muir was reborn as a son of Mother Nature when he returned from the glacial womb. He had acquired a deeper appreciation of his own relationship to the wilderness by living with the agents which shaped it and are still shaping it. He learned to see not as a man but as a glacier might. And he could now answer men like Clarence King, who thought that the Sierra was "the ruins of a bygone geological empire." He had been reborn with a cosmic point of view, which he came to call his "glacial eye."[55]

MUIR'S GLACIAL EYE AND THE MEANING OF WILDERNESS

Indian summer was the season of this baptism in the glacial womb. And Indian summer has always been a special time in the Sierra.

The tourists had gone back to civilization, and Nature was left to her own life. The Sierra seemed to hang suspended in time and space, between life and death. Muir noticed that in the flat light of the season "the sun melts all the roughness from the rockiest landscapes." Indian summer seemed a time of eternal stasis, when the seasons were stilled. In the mind of a god, all natural history was less than a moment.

To the glacial eye born in this still moment, the seasons always recalled the ages. Following the seasons, one followed the path of natural history as it spiraled through creation. In any season one was reminded of all seasons: "When after the melting of the winter snow, we walk the dry channel of a stream that we love, its beds of pebbles, dams of boulders, its pool-basins and pot holes and cascade inclines, suggest all its familiar forms and voices, as if it were present in the full gush of spring." And in the same way the wanderer who walked the glacial pathways could hear the sound of moving ice. The seasons recalled the ages. In the spring, Tuolumne's meadows returned to their previous lives as lakes. And from Fairview Dome one seemed to look down on the end of a long glacial winter each June. But in deep fall, one wandered out onto the blue glacial ice of alpine amphitheaters. The Sierra seemed a sterner place, more of an alien world. One could hear the lonely sound of rocks falling in what Muir called the "cold bloodless solitudes." One journeyed into the deep past. So to Muir, every season had its reminiscent age, and the Sierra contained the zodiac of its own history. Each rock, each landmark, was burnished to its heart with the eternal history of the sun. A man entered his origins there, even his unrecorded glacial history. Muir felt the enchantment of these mountains, and imagined Indians walking through their silent depths for thousands of years, "mountain flowers stuck in their black hair and their wild animal eyes sparkling bright as the lakes." And so he suspected that his glacial eye also absorbed the light of the Sierra.[56]

In these mountain solitudes, in places where he thought men would never settle, he found the answers to questions essential to America's future. He knew what it meant to be reborn in the wilderness. This had never been considered by men who saw only the material uses of the wilderness; because they could not harness the spirit of Nature or run their trains on glacial power, they would never ask where their blessings came from. Was it true that understanding his place in the universe, a man might be made whole? Muir thought so, but he also found this enterprise easier in theory than in practice. It meant finding yourself in a place, by recognizing and following the forces which had created it. Despite the risk of annihilation, Muir had found himself not through his ability to change or take dominion over Nature, but in his ability to follow her laws. As he moved through and took joy from the creation, he became a dynamic force, even as he knew Nature was.

The infinite number of lives, the infinite set of possible awakenings, the myriad possibilities of wilderness, the lace-like fabric of existence. Muir never meant to suggest that there was only one way. He meant only to say that the wilderness offered such an infinite variety of possibilities to men, that it offered so many new lives. Every human, no matter what his disposition, would find his own way, if only he looked for it. A man could wade into the holy stream of the Merced as it flowed through Yosemite, or could baptize himself in the irised spray at the base of a thousand waterfalls, or he could seek the origins of the landscape. Somewhere, if he wandered freely enough, he would enter the flow and begin to take his strength from the fountains. Muir knew that his own way required tracing the flow to its origins, but it was perhaps enough if most people simply immersed themselves in the flow at all. Then they would know how important the fountains were, and would learn to inhabit the earth.

He never ran out of examples. Previously unpublished incidents appeared right up the end of his life — riding an avalanche, rocking in an earthquake, baptizing himself in Yosemite Fall, wandering in the Sequoia groves. He continued to hone the edge of these kinds of simple exercises so that he might show how important they were. "The clearest way into the Universe is through a forest wilderness," he once wrote.[57]

Yet Thoreau had said, "I left the woods for as good a reason as I went there. Perhaps it seemed to me that I had several more lives to live, and could not spare any more time for that one." After two years at Walden he thought he had fallen into predictable paths which had become ruts. Muir too would leave his life in Yosemite, yet he was far less sure that he wished to leave. There was a pivotal point, in September of 1874, when he returned to Yosemite for a short stay, and wrote to Jeanne Carr, "I am hopelessly and forever a mountaineer. . . . Civilization and fever and all the morbidness that has been hooted at me have not dimmed my glacial eye, and I care to live only to entice people to look at Nature's loveliness. My own special self is nothing." Did this mean that he meant "to give himself to the task of interpreting wilderness for others"? Were his years in the Sierra only a preparation for him? Or could he entice people to "look at Nature's loveliness" only as long as he continued to be "hopelessly and forever a mountaineer"? Was the glacial eye to become a tool for social change? Was his old friends' view finally right—would he indeed accept their refining social influences?[58]

It is optimistic to believe that these years were not a temporary retirement like Thoreau's, and were not simply an initiatory period. Perhaps it would be impossible to live the life of the wilderness unless one were committed to it fully. Or one might argue that Muir's later years would be patterned by a kind of periodic cycling through the wilderness. He had to return to the mountains often, whenever he was in danger of being degraded by society. Each time that meant repeating the painful transition of "A Geologist's Winter Walk." It is true that one's re-immersion into the wilderness was as dramatic, radical, and painful an experience as the first baptism, as Muir suggested in many narratives. But the prospect of a future without wilderness was more frightening. One's glacial eye did become dimmed, though there was only one light, and a man had only one life.

3

||||||||||

The Pathless Way
and the Range of Light

If there is such a thing as an awakening, Muir's eyes were opened by the mountains in the early seventies. His journals and letters from Yosemite are filled with references to baptism in light and water. Rock, water, and sunlight were instinct with God. In the morning particularly the trees and mountains were "made one, unseparate, unclothed, open to the Divine Soul, dissolved in the mysterious incomparable Spirit of holy Light!" So it was that he could speak of the Sierra as "Mountains holy as Sinai." He was living in a sacred world, and as he partook of its reality and being he became a part of a world which was not a chaos, but a cosmos. In this way he had come to appreciate a "sense of place," not in any mechanical way, but because he felt himself a part of the spiritual wholeness of the Sierra. He might compare himself to Adam in the Garden, unfallen and alone. Like Thoreau, he recognized his sacred spiritual state as opposite to the profane. He was cleansed by being converted from conventional or traditional man back into natural man. This was what it meant to be awakened. This is what he meant when he wrote to his brother that he had been baptized three times in one day and had "got religion."[1]

The significant awakenings that he wrote about were few: his immersions in the power of Yosemite Fall — at the brink and at Fern Ledge — his ride on an avalanche, his experience of the earthquake, his immersion in the flood storms, and most important, his climbs of Mount Ritter and Cathedral Peak. His mountaineering narratives give the most intense and most complete analysis of the process of enlightenment. All of these moments had certain elements in common, however. They included physical danger, loss of the sense of self, and increased clarity of vision as a result. When describing these timeless moments, Muir frequently used similar language, thus reinforcing the idea that each moment represented one central and powerful human possibility. If there is such a thing as a "wilderness experience," these narratives attempt to say what that might be. It is the most powerful kind of religious conversion, and is not to be seen as anything less than complete rebirth. Awakening, Muir became a religious man.

In the Sierra, he was entering a sacred space. Just as Moses was instructed by the Lord to "put off thy shoes from off thy feet, for the place whereon thou standest *is* holy ground," so too Muir found himself barefoot on the polished rocks near Tenaya Lake. The mountains around Tuolumne Meadows became for him a sacred place, very close to the center of the world or "navel of the earth." There the harsh dividing line between earth and heaven was broken.[2]

On the mountains themselves, he learned to transcend. Not any mountain might do, as we shall see. Certain mountains, like Shasta, Ritter, or Cathedral Peak, had a particular attraction for him. They were isolated temples and seemed to have singular sacred significance, just as Fairweather, Rainier, and Hood would later claim his reverence, whether he climbed them or not. Each mountain was not just significant in itself, but in the relationship it bore to the land surrounding it. Each could possibly be a center of the world. In writing his Sierran experiences, he chose to describe his awakening on Ritter as the archetypal experience.

As a scholar, I would like to be able to use the closest and most immediate responses by Muir to his awakening. But I find in practice that what journal entries he left are less enlightening about the process than are his later narratives, which begin to analyze what he had received. This was also true of his baptism in Yosemite Fall on Fern Ledge. It was only in 1890 that he began to consider fully what had happened to him on that night when he was immersed in the power of water. So too, his climb of Mount Ritter began to take form in his mind, but only took literary form in 1880. It is this narrative, first called "In the Heart of the California Alps," and later "A Near View of the High Sierra," which explores the process of awakening and enlightenment. Thus it remains the seminal text, just as it becomes the central chapter of *The Mountains of California*. Without it, much of what Muir thought in the seventies would lack true and immediate significance to a modern reader.[3]

This is his best narrative and deserves close reading. I believe it is a poem, and its literary structure is comparable to more modern narratives which we have learned to praise, like Hemingway's "Big Two-Hearted River," or Faulkner's "The Bear." Like those narratives, it is about the power of the wilderness and its ability to awaken a heightened consciousness in men.

A NEAR VIEW ON THE NORTH FACE OF MOUNT RITTER

The walk to Ritter was the journey out of self, the wandering toward the center of the world which would later return the mountaineer to his true home in Tuolumne, a new man in a new world, yet the same man in a familiar place. Such is the nature of enlightenment, claim those who believe they know. The journey to Ritter entailed losing one's self and finding it again, the same and yet transformed. The approach to Ritter was a real journey over real mountains, and entailed pain and suffering, but the mountaineer's pain and suffering were only part of a larger spiritual challenge. Muir's narrative was a symbolic structure which embodied that spiritual quest; every incident resonated with meaning.[4]

Muir's way became increasingly difficult as he approached his cosmic mountain. He was well beyond the glacial pathways of the middle Sierra. At one point, while trying to cross a ridge, he was forced to retrace his course, after failing to get up a steep slope of hard snow. He had tried to use the technique that had worked well for him on burnished granite, but after slipping several times, found that the concave snow slope would not yield to the same technique which had always worked on the convex domes around Tuolumne. When he finally set foot on the mountain itself, he made his way "into a wilderness of crumbling spires and battlements, built together in bewildering combinations." The almost repetitive use of "wilderness" and "bewildering" is a clue to Muir's problem. He had learned to travel glacial pathways without thought, but now he was in a truly pathless place, and as he said, his instincts, "usually so positive and true, seemed vitiated in some way," and were leading him astray. Ritter was the sacred mountain, was indeed *ganz andere*, something else.

He was beyond the realm of the familiar, beyond the meadows, beyond the songs of the dun-headed sparrows. He had entered a "massive picture . . . rock, ice, and water close together without a single leaf or sign of life." Further, he "dared not think of descending" since "the dangers below seemed even greater than the cliff in front." Though he knew where he was, he was truly lost and bewildered, largely as a result of his own efforts. What followed was the awakening, and it is worth reading in its entirety:

After gaining a point about half-way to the top, I was suddenly brought to a dead stop, with arms outspread, clinging close to the face of the rock, unable to move hand or foot either up or down. My doom appeared fixed. I *must* fall. There would be a moment of bewilderment, and then a lifeless rumble down the one general precipice to the glacier below.

When this final danger flashed upon me, I became nerve-shaken for the first time since setting foot on the mountains, and my mind seemed to fill with a stifling smoke. But this terrible eclipse lasted only a moment, when life blazed forth again with preternatural clearness. I seemed suddenly to become possessed of a new sense. The other self, bygone experiences, Instinct, or Guardian Angel,— call it what you will,— came forward and assumed control. Then my trembling muscles became firm again, every rift and flaw in the rock was seen as through a microscope, and my limbs moved with a positiveness and precision with which I seemed to have nothing at all to do. Had I been borne aloft upon wings, my deliverance could not have been more complete.[5]

It is no accident that Muir found himself writing this entire section in the passive voice, since he wished to suggest a kind of dual consciousness. The climb happened to him. He could only observe the phenomenon. Here he approached the nearest possible view of the High Sierra, seen as through a microscope, while his body embraced the mountain. He was not certain what force had assumed control.

Perhaps the spirit of science was nearby, since he read the face of the rock as through a microscope. Perhaps in discovering the rifts and flaws of the rock he had read the cleavage of pure rock, untouched by glaciers because it was above them. That was the basis of his theory that in Sierran architecture *"the style always proclaims the nature of the rock."* Or the new sense might have been given by a guardian angel, since he had seemed to receive a sign the night before when "two crimson clouds came streaming across the summit like wings of flame." He had noted in his copy of Emerson, "in your path there is always an angel." Or perhaps, as he suggested in a rewritten variant of this awakening, his body, "finding the ordinary dominion of mind insufficient, pushed it aside." If that was the case, the body itself was a gate to vision, since in that variant he saw "every rift, flaw, niche, and tablet in the cliff." The tablet — new to this variant — suggests that Muir, like Moses, had seen the devouring fire on the top of the mount. In his isolation, "cut off from all affinity," he had received the Law.[6]

Muir was not satisfied with any single answer, and stressed in the phrase "call it what you will" that an explanation was not as important as the actuality. An unknown region in his consciousness had been awakened in this unknown region on Mount Ritter. Do I dare call this satori — "the unfolding of a new world hitherto unperceived in the confusion of the dualistically-trained mind"? I don't see why not. The very difficulty of language Muir wrestled with in explaining his awakening is in harmony with the idea that "satori is the most intimate individual experience and therefore cannot be expressed in words or described in any manner." In any case, the whole structure of Muir's narrative lends credence to his own belief that he had achieved a true awakening. This was no mere athletic event.[7]

There is a particular part of his awakening which I find most significant. It has to do with forgetting one's self and losing all self-interest. It was one thing to receive this blessing while standing in the woods, where Muir once described the peace of forgetting his own existence. It was quite another thing to do so in the midst of intense effort and tension. This process began even while Muir was walking toward Ritter, "limbs moving of themselves, every sense unfolding like the thawing flowers, to take part in the new day harmony." Especially at the beginning of his essay he tried to capture the rhythm of the "watercourse way" of the young Tuolumne River. He was precisely immersed in the flow and drift of Nature:

Down through the midst, the young Tuolumne was seen pouring from its crystal fountains, now resting in glassy pools as if changing back again into ice, now leaping in white cascades as if turning to snow; gliding right and left between granite bosses, then sweeping on through the smooth, meadowy levels of the valley, swaying pensively from side to side with calm, stately gestures past dipping willows and sedges, and around groves of arrowy pine; and throughout its whole eventful course, whether flowing fast or slow, singing loud or low, ever filling the landscape with spiritual animation, and manifesting the grandeur of its sources in every movement and tone.

He found the rhythm of going and pausing inspiring, "leading one far out of himself, yet feeding and building up his individuality."[8]

But on the mountain, when lost, it was not so easy to go with the grain and follow the rhythm of the landscape, as he had while following the glacial pathways. Then he felt the tension which could lead to separation and alienation. Here was a tension which could be transcended, or else abruptly and mechanically terminated. Like Nick Adams fishing on Hemingway's "Big Two-Hearted River," like a student of the art of archery, Muir had to wait until the tension was fulfilled. In his dance on the mountain he had to realize that it was not him, not the mountain, but something beyond them that moved. So it was that he had to accept his death, accept his doom, and view it with no self-interest at all as "a moment of bewilderment, and then a lifeless rumble down the one general precipice." This too was a necessary part of the spiritual journey he had undertaken, and prepared him for an awakening "far out of himself."[9]

Gregory Bateson found this fusion of self and other a key step to ecological thinking, where ontology and epistemology could not be separated. Such a mental state, he argued, was necessary to the ecologist's flexibility, to his *"uncommitted potentiality for change."* Like the bamboo leaf loaded with snow, the mind of the ecologist had to accept the load of information, and wait until his time was ripe and the load fell. The snow would fall from the bamboo leaf, the shot from the archer's bow, and the thought from the ecologist's mind — before it was ever thought. This flexibility required that there was no "myself" different from the rest of the cosmos. Muir had realized this state of mind when he noticed without self-interest that he was like all the rest of the boulders on Mount Ritter, "detached," and "ready to be launched below." The law which let him live was no more an idle chance than the law which might have let him fall. Perhaps we could call this mystical mountaineering; those who know something about this experience insist, along with Suzuki and Snyder, that it is a normal state of mind, that it happens every day. Bateson believed that he had not accomplished such an "other way of thinking," but still suggested that "we should trust no policy decisions which emanate from persons who do not yet have that habit." Such a state of mind, then, is a *powerful source* for human action, and should be recognized as such. For those who accept it, it represents a commerce between the human mind and the Mind of the Universe.[10]

THE LIGHT OF THE MOUNTAIN

After climbing Rainier, Muir said,

One feels far from home so high in the sky, so much so that one is inclined to guess, that apart from the acquisition of knowledge and the exhilaration of climbing, more pleasure is to be found at the foot of mountains than on their frozen tops. Doubly happy, however, is the man to whom lofty mountain tops are within reach, for the lights that shine there illumine all that lies below.[11]

When he emerged from the "terrible shadow" of the North Face of Ritter into the "blessed light," his awakened consciousness expanded into the landscape which surrounded the summit. Sixteen years later he asked himself in his journal why light seemed so much brighter on the top of a mountain after a difficult climb. His answer supports the idea that the awakening on places like the North Face of Ritter infused his being permanently with power.

In climbing where the danger is great, all attention has to be given to the ground step by step, leaving nothing for beauty by the way. But this care, so keenly and narrowly concentrated, is not without advantages. One is

thoroughly aroused. Compared with the alertness of the senses and corresponding precision and power of the muscles on such occasions, one may
be said to sleep all the rest of the year. The mind and body remain awake
for some time after the dangerous ground is passed, so that arriving on
the summit with the grand outlook—all the world spread below—one is
able to see it better, and brings to the feast a far keener vision, and reaps
richer harvests than would have been possible ere the presence of danger
summoned him to life.[12]

So the view from the summit became the harvest, the enlightenment that followed awakening. However, the view from Ritter's summit, or from that of Rainier, could not be understood in aesthetic
or hedonistic terms, because the climber was faced with more than
a pleasing prospect or simple pleasure.

Muir did not feel that a summit was always the best place for appreciating the harmony of a landscape. It was certainly not true on the
top of Half Dome, where views of Yosemite Valley were "far less striking than from any other points, chiefly because of the forshortening
effect produced by looking from so great a height." As we shall see,
the value of summit views was a major issue in Victorian literature
on mountaineering, and for good reason. For now, let me observe
that Ritter was an archetypal mountain for Muir, a "fountain peak"
as he called it, and must be seen as the center of the earth. When
he arrived at the summit of Mount Ritter, he had arrived at the right
place and at the right moment. He had come to the place of origin.[13]

To know what he saw there we must know something about
the special significance of Ritter for Muir, for he thought of it as
a singular peak, not only because of his awakening, but because
it was a holy mountain and had great symbolic significance. Though
he did not attempt to describe the views from the summits of Whitney, Rainier, or indeed any other peak he climbed, his essay on the
climb of Ritter included a thorough and inspired view of the landscape. Why did he know this place would be special, before he had
arrived on its summit?

Mount Ritter became the archetypal mountain first of all because of its geological history. Like Shasta, it was a stark peak and
stood alone. Comparing Shasta to Whitney, for instance, he saw
that "the former is a colossal cone rising in solitary grandeur and

might well be regarded as an object of religious worship; the latter is one of the many peaks of an irregular and fragmentary form." So too, Ritter was the "noblest mountain of the chain" because of its "commanding individuality." Ritter, like Shasta and like the Matterhorn in Europe, was a dark mountain, and nourished a number of glaciers. Though he recorded in his journal that "the glaciers of Ritter number six together," he reported in "Living Glaciers" that it nourished five, and his topographical drawing showed these five glaciers on Ritter as the symmetrical petals of a flower. Nature loved the number five.[14]

The black rock and white glaciers suggest a further significance because of their stark contrast. Shasta, for instance, was a fire-and-ice mountain, and its form represents the primal forces which made the earth. This archaic pattern of imagery is the yin-yang, representing swirling shadow and sun of the cosmic mountain, which Peter Matthiessen has recognized in the landscape of the Himalaya. Ritter, Shasta, and all glacially carved mountains suggested the harmony of contrasting and yet complementary forces. Muir's own ascent of Ritter — his deliberate choice of a route on the North Face — led him through the darkness and into the light. His rebirth was determined by the structure of the mountain, which in turn embodied the glacial history of the Sierra.[15]

Mount Ritter was, as he argued in the *Studies*, "a kind of textbook" which had much to teach. Muir's choice to ascend the North Face was significant in itself, since "every mountaineer and Indian knows that high mountains are more easily ascended on the south than on the north side." The steep north faces were directly above the glacial wombs, which lay in the northern amphitheaters. The climb of Ritter, then, represented a step further in Muir's journey toward the origin of the world. When he climbed onto the rock above Ritter's glacier, he was stepping back into pre-glacial times, onto the oldest rocks of the Sierra — rocks which overlaid the granite of the Yosemite Valley and the domes of Tuolumne. After a near view of Ritter's face, he hoped he would be ready to describe the panorama of Sierran history from the summit.[16]

It was perhaps surprising to Muir that he did not ascend beyond the influence of the glacier when he entered the North Face of Ritter. Even above it, he found the glacier the "most influential agent, constantly eroding backward . . . and enabling gravity to drag down large masses." He himself was almost one of those masses. So his lesson in gravity on the concave North Face was a lesson in geology. The other half of his training had to do with the structure of Ritter's own rock. What made it the "noblest mountain of the chain" was the grain of its living rock. Its "predestined beauty" was a result of its own inner structure. As his precarious position had taught him, the noble face was not a result of upbuilding, but of "universal razing and dismantling" by glaciers and gravity.[17]

COSMIC VISION

As he described the panorama around Ritter, facing south, west, north, and east by turns, he seemed to be describing four separate landscapes. To the south was a "sublime wilderness of mountains . . . peak beyond peak, swelling higher." To the west the landscape spread in flowing undulations of granite, lakes, meadows, and forests toward the hazy Central Valley and the blue mountains of the coast. In the north was the Sierra Crown, the peaks surrounding Tuolumne Meadows. To the east were the Owens and Mono basins. Just as four separate landscapes spread "map-like" from Ritter, so too four separate rivers began their courses from fountains. The headwaters of the San Joaquin, Owens, Tuolumne, and Merced rivers were clustered around his cosmic perch.

From this central mountain, *axis mundi*, the real was unveiled. As Muir's eye roved around the vast expanse, he recognized that he saw not four static views, but a harmonious sequence. The territory was not a map, but a manifestation of flow: "Standing here in the deep, brooding silence all the wilderness seems motionless, as if the work of creation were done. But in the midst of this outer steadfastness we know there is incessant motion and change. . . . Here are the roots of all the life of the valleys, and here more simply than elsewhere is the eternal flux of nature manifested." At the summit of Ritter he had entered cosmic time, at the origin of creation, and only the wheeling of the sun reminded him that he was also a part of the historical present as well as the cosmic eternal. He was standing at the intersection where space and time became one.[18]

I believe it is fair to say that Muir's experience on Ritter is the wilderness experience par excellence. Though it has aesthetic and scientific aspects, it is primarily a religious conversion, followed by a religious vision of a sacred cosmos. His essay on Ritter dramatized what he felt was the primary and archetypal baptism in Nature. Unfortunately, it is never enough to have a vision. One must also justify and explain the significance of that vision, and the structure of Muir's essay on Mount Ritter was designed to do just that. When we approach his essay from an historical point of view, we see it in the context of the Victorian literature of mountaineering. No matter what Muir might have wanted, for the Victorians all human activity fit into neat categories. For the Victorians mountains might have a personal significance, *or* aesthetic significance, *or* scientific significance. Mountaineering could be justified in these terms; but more likely, the justification would be based on one of them as opposed to another. The artist, for instance, would say that his way of seeing mountains was superior to the geologist's. More important, the personal significance had to be justified in socially acceptable terms; climbing a mountain had to be productive, had to make one a better member of society. Muir's belief in the value of mountaineering as a human activity — and my own as well — must be set against the justifications given by Victorians at the inception of the modern sport. At issue is not the climbing of a mountain, but the style the climber adopts.

FOREGROUNDS, MIDDLEGROUNDS, AND BACKGROUNDS IN MOUNTAINEERING

When the Golden Age of Mountaineering in the Alps came to a close in 1865 with Edward Whymper's ascent of the Matterhorn, the Golden Age had only just begun on the American continent. In the summer of 1864, Clarence King and Dick Cotter left their companions of the Whitney Survey with the hope of climbing the highest peak in the Sierra. King dramatized the influence of the British tradition on literature in America: "I rang my hammer upon the topmost rock;

we grasped hands, and I reverently named the grand peak MOUNT TYNDALL." Most of the early mountaineers in the Alps had been scientists, but the literature of Victorian mountaineering which began to appear in the late sixties and early seventies was equally divided between scientific books, such as John Tyndall's *Hours of Exercise in the Alps* or *The Glaciers of the Alps,* and classics written in an aesthetic tradition, such as Edward Whymper's *Scrambles Amongst the Alps* or Leslie Stephen's *The Playgrounds of Europe.* Certainly King's *Mountaineering in the Sierra Nevada* was consciously written in awareness of the issues raised by both traditions, and so too Muir's narratives of mountaineering show his own debt to the literary traditions.[19]

It is well to remember that the culmination of the Golden Age in the Alps was a disaster, at least in the eyes of the British public. Four men were killed in the descent from the Matterhorn, and the reaction in England was dramatic. The *Times* called into question the sense of such activity, and saw climbers as "accepting the equal alternatives of idle boast and a horrible death." The *Times* taunted, "it is magnificent. But is it life? Is it duty? Is it common sense?" And so climbers are still occasionally viewed by civilized commentators as "dilettantes of suicide."[20]

John Ruskin raised a deeper and more lasting issue about the value of the mountaineer's experience. Ruskin's strongest criticism of alpinism came in *Sesames and Lillies,* even before the accident on the Matterhorn. "You dispise nature," he told the mountaineers; "the alps themselves, which your own poets used to love so reverently, you look upon as soaped poles in a bear garden, which you set yourself to climb and slide down again with 'shrieks of delight.'" After the accident on the Matterhorn he revised and enlarged his criticism in the preface to his second edition, explaining that his objection was not to the dangers, but went deeper: "The real ground for reprehension of Alpine climbing is that, with less cause, it excites more vanity than any other athletic skill." He thought that the real beauty of Switzerland was lost "by the country being regarded as half watering place, half gymnasium," and he stated categorically that "the real beauty of the Alps is to be seen and seen only where all may see it, the child, the cripple, and the man of grey hairs." Thus he was linking the idea of aesthetic distance with the reverence of a Biblical point of view. "I will lift up my eyes to the hills" meant that one should lift up only the eyes. One did not climb cathedrals, and "the mountains of the earth are her natural cathedrals." Precisely because of the magnitude of Ruskin's contribution to the aesthetics of mountains in *Modern Painters*, Ruskin had to be answered. Further, Ruskin was himself a member of the Alpine Club.[21]

Tyndall attempted to answer Ruskin from the scientific perspective. Just as Agassiz felt that dangers had to be overcome by complete dedication to science if the mysteries surrounding alpine phenomena were to be solved, so Tyndall claimed that close observation was a necessary tool. The scientist had to learn to live on the glaciers and peaks if he was to understand them. But part of Ruskin's argument was that too much or too close contact with mountains was degrading, as peasants of the Alps seemed to demonstrate. This was the basis for his analysis of "Mountain Gloom." While Muir used his own enlightenment as an answer to Ruskin's theory, Tyndall observed that Bennen, the great alpine guide, was "without a particle of the 'mountaineering gloom,' respecting the prevalence of which among the dwellers of the High Alps Mr. Ruskin discourses poetically, but I am myself rather incredulous." Beyond that was a difference of imagination between Tyndall's sharp scientific eye and Ruskin's desire for the spirit of mystery. "Where Tyndall was 'all concentration,' Ruskin tended to be diffuse," Henry James thought; Tyndall, like Agassiz, advocated close and even microscopic inspection.[22]

King followed this scientific tradition, despite his inclination toward a Romantic view of mountains. He was drawn to the thinking of both Ruskin and Tyndall, and struggled between the scientific and Ruskinian aesthetic views. On the one hand he might say, "No tongue can tell the relief to simply withdraw scientific observation, and let Nature impress you in the dear old way with all her mystery and glory, with those vague indescribable emotions which tremble between wonder and sympathy." But this kind of pleasure was a diversion, and he concluded that "Alpine literature, once lifted above the fatiguing repetition of gymnastics, is almost invariably scientific." Aesthetic views were archaic. Ruskin helped the reader to know Ruskin, not the Alps: "The varying hues which mood and emotion forever pass before his own mental vision mask with their illusive mystery the simple realities of nature, until mountains and their bold natural facts are lost behind the cloudy poetry of the writer." Consequently, on the summit of Mount Tyndall, King saw a dead world with "no sentiment of beauty in the whole scene." The desolate landscape, the ruin of a bygone glacial period, was presented with an "unrelenting clearness," and all he saw was "a fearful sense of wreck and desolation, of a world crushed into fragments." It was, despite King's best literary intentions, a dead world. Even though he desired to avoid any subjective or distorting views, his mechanistic perspective devalued mountains as significant sources of spiritual insight.[23]

Whymper joined King and Tyndall in pointing out the limitations of Ruskin's trust in the distant view. Ruskin, for instance, had said that there was "'no aspect of destruction about the Matterhorn cliffs.'" But Whymper had been on the mountain and knew better. He had heard the "descending masses thunder loudly as guns" as he sat by the side of the Z'Mutt Glacier. On the mountain he had found himself a target for a storm of stones. He knew that the mountains were coming down. Ruskin could believe in the permanent and eternal aspect of the mountains precisely because he had watched them from a great distance. Up close, Whymper watched the stones fall, and reported "a strong smell of sulphur, that told who sent them." Though Tyndall watched the same storm of stones, from nearly the same place, he avoided interpreting their descent personally. To him, they described their proper parabolas and were deflected by the rocky towers. Nevertheless, familiarity with mountains drew the alpinists to an inescapable conclusion that the mountains were falling down, and such close observations led to the further assumption that the rockfall and receding glaciers signaled the slow death of the mountains. Leslie Stephen agreed, and spoke of the situation as true and sad, but still announced that the purpose of his book, *The Playgrounds of Europe,* was "to prove that whilst all good and wise men necessarily love the mountains, those love them best who have wandered longest in their recesses, and have most endangered their own lives and those of their guides in the attempt to open out routes amongst them." Even dying mountains could be a source of spiritual insight.[24]

Stephen justified the activity of mountaineering in aesthetic terms which seemed a diminished version of the spiritual perspective. He argued, "Now the first merit of mountaineering is that it enables one to have what theologians would call an experimental faith in the size of mountains — to substitute a real living belief for a dead intellectual assent." Stephen meant not only that one could measure the magnitude of mountains in terms of muscular exertion, where "every step of the ascent has a beauty of its own," but also, "that which gives its inexpressible charm to mountaineering is the incessant series of exquisite natural scenes which are for the most part enjoyed by the mountaineer alone." Thus began the tradition of making fine distinctions among the scenes in such an incessant series.[25]

Whymper argued that the highest alpine summits "do not usually yield the views that make the strongest and most permanent impressions." For him, impressions from such panoramic views were fleeting and vague, while the most lasting impressions were "those which are seen but for a moment." He preferred the middle distance above all, found neither at the summit nor on some low prominence where the eighteenth-century spectator had trembled in awe. Whymper's own etchings are the best defense of his perspective because they capture the series of natural scenes which the mountaineer encountered along the way to the summit. His defense suggested a right relation between man and mountain: "I think the grandest and most satisfactory standpoints for viewing mountain scenery are those which are sufficiently elevated to give a feeling of depth, as well as height, which are lofty enough to exhibit wide and varied views, but not so high as to sink everything to the level of the spectator." This was the perspective of a man on the mountain, but not of a man who had conquered it. It was a perspective which gave the mountains due respect, even in a modern and materialistic world. Whymper's was a good *secular* answer to Ruskin's criticism. That was as far as it went.[26]

MUIR AND THE ARTISTS

While British Victorian mountaineers were intent on showing the importance of impressions gained along the way to the summit, Muir wished to go beyond their fragmented perspective and assert that the whole ascent was greater than the parts. In the first published version of his narrative he dramatized his search for the right relationship between men and mountains. Even if the reader missed the spiritual message, he would at least know that mountaineering had an aesthetic dimension. The narrative, contrasting his own ascent of Ritter to the activity of two artists whom he brought to Tuolumne Meadows, invited the reader to compare the climber's way with the aesthetic perspective of the artists.[27]

Before the artists arrived on the scene, Muir was already disposed to think of the Sierra as an aesthetic whole; at the same time he recognized that "few portions of the California Alps are, strictly speaking, picturesque." This was because the whole range was "one grand picture, not clearly divisible into smaller ones." He tried to believe that he was the Sierra's "elected artist," framing a picture by throwing up his arms to enclose it. But finally he despaired of such activity and admitted, "I could not help wishing that I were that artist. I had to be content, however, to take it into my soul." Into his soul, indeed. That has always been better than putting it on paper!

So when he returned to Tuolumne Meadows with his two artist friends, he hoped that they would be able to reap this aesthetic treasure. They were very particular artists, however, and were at first disappointed with the scenery, because, as they said, "All this is sublime, but we see nothing as yet at all available for effective pictures." They required foregrounds, middlegrounds, and backgrounds. Finally, when Muir showed them the Sierra Crown, they were satisfied, and "ran here and there, along the river-bends and up the side of the cañon, choosing foregrounds for sketches." Clearly they did not come to gain vision, but to find something which suited their preconceptions about scenery; "Here, at last, was a typical Alpine landscape."

They could spend three days working in Tuolumne, while Muir would spend his three days climbing Ritter, which he called a "grand masterpiece." His own essay offered an alternative way to perceive the Sierra, including "some characteristic pictures, drawn from the wildest places, and strung together on a strip of narrative." He employed the Stephen–Whymper defense. As he moved through the landscape and achieved freedom of eye, his views, taken consecutively along with the experience which informed them, would produce something more than a mechanical combination of foregrounds, middlegrounds, and backgrounds.

If the first day of his excursion was filled with foregrounds—
the "painted meadows, late-blooming gardens, peaks of rare architecture"—then the second day created a "massive picture," pure wilderness, "only the one sublime mountain in sight, the one glacier,
and one lake; the whole vailed with one blue shadow—rock, ice
and water, without a single leaf." He had passed out of the foreground and into the middleground. Later that day, clinging to the
North Face of Ritter, he was lost in the background. So he hoped
his progress through the landscape gave the mountains a significance
beyond that which artists could achieve. When he finally reached
the summit of Ritter he could look around and appreciate the harmony of the scene.

When looking for the first time from an all-embracing standpoint like this,
the inexperienced observer is oppressed by the incomprehensible grandeur
of the peaks, and it is only after they have been studied one by one, long
and lovingly, that their far-reaching harmonies become manifest. Then,
penetrate the wilderness where you may, the main telling features to which
all the topography is subordinate are quickly perceived, and the most un-
governable Alp-clusters stand revealed, regularly fashioned, and grouped
like works of art,—eloquent monuments of the ancient ice-rivers that
brought them into relief.[28]

The lesson was simple enough. Even his friends had admitted
that "art is long, and art is limited, you know." A man could grasp
the true harmony of the mountains only by the process Leslie Stephen had also recommended: "No one can decipher the natural writing on the face of a snowslope or a precipice who has not wandered
among their recesses, and learned by slow experience what is indicated by marks which an ignorant observer would scarcely notice."
Muir was finally suggesting that the artists were ignorant observers,
and when they returned to the Valley together, with the "precious
sketches," he felt that he had gained much more than they had.[29]

THE PRODIGAL SON

Muir wrote to Jeanne Carr in 1872, "I am glad to know, by you and
Emerson and others living and dead, that my unconditional surren-
der to Nature has produced exactly what you have foreseen—that

drifting without human charts through light and dark, calm and storm, I have come to so glorious an ocean." This was very different from the talk of most Victorian mountaineers. Whymper could speak of the "development of manliness, and the evolution, under combat with difficulties, of those noble qualities of human nature — courage, patience, endurance, and fortitude." In similar passages, Clarence King argued that the wilderness was a place where men might develop those noble qualities in a simplified and pure environment, which differed markedly from the cities. To the Victorian, speaking of the wilderness and man's role there was tantamount to visualizing wild Nature as a place where men might exercise their power. As Kevin Starr shrewdly argues, "In Clarence King the mountaineer defied nature, pitting himself against rocks and gorges in a test of courage conceived of as an abstraction and revelled in psychologically."[30]

On the other hand, more modern commentators are likely to see mountaineering as an existential drama, like that of Camus' "Myth of Sisyphus." This perspective has been generally more true among Europeans than among Americans. The twentieth-century British climber George Leigh Mallory spoke to the query "Why do you try to climb Everest?" with an off-hand comment, "Because it is there." He knew the question could not be answered in the terms that had been given. What happened on the mountain was something like a "marriage of ideas about the world with ideas about self." In another place, Mallory attempted an honest answer to the question. He was speaking about Mont Blanc, but the actual summit was unimportant:

Have we vanquished an enemy? None but ourselves. Have we gained success? That word means nothing here. Have we won a kingdom? No . . . and yes. We have achieved the ultimate satisfaction . . . fulfilled a destiny. . . . To struggle and understand — never this last without the other; such is the law. . . . We've only been obeying an old law then? Ah! but it's *the* law.

The mountaineer did not conquer anything but himself; he only learned the law of life.[31]

Americans have rarely understood this view of the challenge of the wilderness. For us, mountaineering has always been a step toward dominion over Nature. Lionel Terray's classic book on mountaineering was translated from the French for British readers in a literal way as *Conquistadors of the Useless* — but was marketed to Americans as *Borders of the Impossible.* In a society where mountaineering could not be accepted by the public as a religious pilgrimage, the only explanations which would make sense were that mountaineering was war, technical victory, or a crucible of character.

While Muir was gone, his artist friends were sure that he had been lost on the mountain, and so he had been, though not in the sense they supposed. When he left the home he had adopted in Tuolumne Meadows he knew that he would sooner or later confront his own ignorance, but he knew also that this had always been the story of the prodigal son. "The sense of peace one finds in Enlightenment is indeed that of a wanderer getting safely home," says one religious commentator. More important, perhaps, was Muir's realization that all the Sierra had become his home. His victory was achieved when he had learned to live according to a law larger than himself, when he had learned to follow a path which he had not made, and for which he had no map. As soon as he had awakened to and recognized the wholeness of the world, he had become whole.[32]

EGO AND GAMES

Sometimes it is difficult to sift the essential from the merely distracting aspects of a human activity. There is no escaping the fact that Muir was quite a competitive mountaineer, especially with regard to Clarence King, who tended to add literary embellishments to narratives of his own ascents. As Kevin Starr argues, "Muir despised King's elaborate self-consciousness, his risk-taking as a form of existential encounter." So Muir frequently deprecated King's exploits — or at least his exaggeration when writing of them — particularly when it came to the difficulty of Mount Tyndall or the inaccessibility of the Grand Canyon of the Tuolumne. Muir's tremendous resolve when he suffered to attain the summit of Mount Whitney in the fall of 1873 can probably be attributed to his competitive drive.[33]

Even late in life he could not avoid measuring his own abilities against those possessed by Galen Clark. Clark was better in chaparral, but Muir excelled in the talus. Galen's pot of oatmeal boiled first, and Muir admired his ability to sleep anywhere. And it is interesting to note that Muir's early employer in Yosemite, James Hutchings, always seemed to accomplish one of Muir's feats right after Muir did; he traversed the canyon of the Tuolumne, and climbed Lyell and Whitney, soon after Muir. Hutchings suspected that when his wife departed from Yosemite in 1873, Muir was responsible.[34]

Did this mean that mountaineering was merely a contest of strength and endurance among men? Certainly there have been stories in Yosemite, for as long as I can remember, about the links among climbing ability, valor, and the sexual prowess of men. Now female rockclimbers collect groups of men who compete for their attentions. The Women's Annapurna Expedition sold T-shirts which said "A Woman's Place is on the Top," suggesting that mountaineering is just sublimated sexual activity. Worse, the myth of mountaineering as conquest may become a social tool which glamorizes the distasteful side of civilization's domination of Nature. Society may idolize the men who climb mountains because they lead the way for the rape of Nature. Is sharing a climb in the mountains like sharing a girl among the fellows, in that it strengthens the notion of group masculinity and power, as Susan Brownmiller argues? When women become great climbers, as they are becoming, are they really struggling against masculine power rather than engaging themselves with the mountains? If that is the case, they learn only the games of an oppressive patriarchal society.[35]

These are not questions which can be dismissed. The relationships among climbing mountains, conquering Nature, and ravishing women are not only obvious, they are to a great extent real. One wonders about the psychological motivation of some alpine climbers. Muir himself joked about short climbers. Why are so many great male alpinists so short—because they try to compensate? We are told by some that climbing is a game, a test of self against arbitrary or perhaps carefully calculated rules. If the spirituality intrinsic in mountaineering is not recognized, mountaineering may become no different than any other competitive game, be it chess or some military activity.[36]

Some climbers have begun to reevaluate their techniques and mo-

tives, and have begun to return to the more austere and less destructive mode of travel Muir advocted. They try to climb "clean" and
"free," by avoiding the pitons which destroy the rock, and by using
their own bodies rather than artificial aids to get them up Yosemite
walls. But that too can become a competitive game. How much protection did you need? someone asks when you return to camp. How
long did it take? Who led the crux pitch? I can remember doing an
early "free ascent" in Yosemite years ago, and returning to the Valley
to discover that others had watched us through a spotting scope to
make sure that we really did the climb as we said we would.

There will always be competition in these kinds of activities,
and there will always be people who engage in them only because
they are competitive. Beyond these superficial vanities, one hopes
there is something which leads to an awareness greater than one's
self. Muir knew the inner awareness, and he wrote his narratives
not in order to congratulate himself on his exploits, not in order
to say exactly what he had accomplished, but to demonstrate what
was essential and enlightening about the activity. A literal-minded
analysis of Muir's narratives is fruitless because they are not about
a literal truth. They are about the eternal quest of the human toward enlightenment. No doubt there is an erotic side to this quest,
but one hopes that it is healthy eroticism. If Muir fictionalized his
exploits, if he was not enlightened, then one can only commend him
because he knew so clearly what the way to enlightenment was like.
He knew that it was more important than personal glory.

I bring up this issue because it dramatizes something which Muir
never expressed explicitly. Recreation is a more complex activity than
it first appears to be. One must discriminate between activities that
lead to enlightenment and those that do not, but must further reflect upon the style, or manner, in which an activity is carried out.
A man can climb the mountains and fail to get their good tidings,
and this happens frequently. We need only read Hunt's *Conquest
of Everest* to realize how completely a mountaineering expedition
can be conceived and carried out as a military campaign against
Nature. Muir's contribution to the literature of mountaineering was
significant not because of his first ascents, but because of the spirit
in which they were made. This has far-reaching implications for
any theory of recreation. It will never be enough to recommend cer-

tain activities. We will always have to consider how the participant engages himself in them.[37]

For a full understanding of what a wilderness experience might be, one must reconsider what a wilderness is. No definition of wilderness that I have read helps much. The Wilderness Act of 1964 says,

A wilderness, in contrast with those areas where man and his own work dominate the landscape, is hereby recognized as an area where the earth and its community of life are untrammeled by man, where man himself is a visitor who does not remain.

I am troubled by the term "untrammeled." At what point have we caught and trapped the wilderness? I would presume that a process of capturing or trapping begins when men try to "open out routes" among the mountains, as Leslie Stephen suggested. A mountaineering route, a trail, or a guidebook seem to be the first tools in a progressive domination of the landscape because these works of men give form to a world which, up to that point, could only have had an internal structure that owed nothing to men. The truly pathless way is a spiritual journey *and* an unmapped landscape. The experience of a wilderness and the wilderness itself are inseparable. Any human tool which mediates between man and mountain separates journey from landscape, and thus alienates Man from Nature. In this primary significance, wilderness is neither an abstract nor a subjective term.[38]

What we have made of the term is another matter. One day I listened to a talk given to a group of agriculture students by a "wilderness expert" from the Bureau of Land Management. He announced that wilderness was a political abstraction about a type of land use; he dated the term from the 1920s, and attributed its use to Aldo Leopold, appropriately enough. He discussed the history of wilderness in America, assuming that history was made up of legislation and bureaucratic machinations, and that it led to the Wilderness Act, Rare I and II, the BLM Organic Act, and FLPMA. What can one say? It isn't the term which is important, but the idea, and the idea goes back a long way, and deep into the spirit of American life. What's more important, when the "wilderness expert" gave witness, he perpetuated the false belief that we *create* wilderness, when in fact we are to be congratulated not so much because we have created wildernesses, but because we have systematically destroyed them. Wilderness is not an invention of man, it is not *whatever* we say it is, and until we accept the full meaning of the pathless way, we will not begin to be able to control our own nature, or understand Nature.[39]

One need not be surprised at the attitude of a man who worked for the Bureau of Land Management. The definitive book on wilderness in America tells us that "while the word is a noun it acts like an adjective. There is no material object that is wilderness." Thus we are ready to think of the word in perfectly subjective terms; wilderness is what men think it is. In a dialectical way, one might argue further that we learn what we think it is in the act of subduing it. However, the author of *Wilderness and the American Mind* goes on to say that the common conception of wilderness is that of a desert, of uncultivated or undeveloped lands, a place where men are absent, a place without paths or roads. A wilderness has been, for the western man, a place where "a person was likely to get into a disordered, confused, or 'wild condition.'" In other words, a place where a man would be bewildered. This definition suggests, at least, that the problem might be that of an ignorant observer rather than a chaotic world. Muir's bewilderment on Mount Ritter was a necessary recognition of ignorance which preceded his discovery that the cosmos was indeed an ordered whole.[40]

Getting lost does not solve one's problems, but it goes a long way toward resolving certain priorities. If the wilderness was a pathless way, then Muir's own drifting was equally a pathless way. There was no paradox in the expression, as he discovered when suddenly on Mount Ritter he was given to see every rift and flaw of the rock. There was no paradox because Muir always knew that "the Sierra, instead of being a huge wrinkle of the earth's crust without any determinate structure, is built up of regularly formed stones like a work of art." Man's experience need be no more disordered than the mountains themselves.[41]

But a man had to be very careful. If the wilderness was on the one hand a pathless place because men had not set up any trail markers, it offered the possibility for following a more transcendent path, set up by the Creator himself. It is no surprise that Muir was never particularly fond of the stairway George Anderson proposed to build up the side of Half Dome. Not only did Muir suspect that such a man-made route was a grave error, but also he was not delighted with the prospect of its completion, when "all may sing excelsior in perfect safety." Then the climbers of Half Dome would not be following the ways of the wilderness, but the ways of other men. The same argument might be made about the John Muir Trail. It is an artificial route, and does not follow the glacial highways Muir was so fond of.[42]

I think of white whales and black mountains. I consider El Capitan as a kind of wilderness, as a kind of Moby Dick, on account of its whiteness, its blankness, and its climbing history. There was always a map on it, if only men were ready to read it. I am not talking about the North American Wall, which is a figment of our aesthetic and cultural imaginations. I am talking about a map which has no human face. I remember that Ahab was appalled at the inhuman face of Moby Dick, and took it upon himself to strike through the mask, with violence. And I think Muir's experience offered an alternative to Ahab's way of reading the face of Nature. One did not have to strike through the mask if one was willing to live on it long enough. Then, in due time, the face of El Capitan would turn translucent.

When Yvon Chouinard and T.M. Herbert went up to El Capitan and named their route the Muir Wall, they were right, because they chose to launch themselves out onto a glorious ocean without human charts. This is the heart of the wilderness experience. If Chouinard and Herbert did not achieve the awakening Muir described, I would be surprised, since they had at least followed the necessary prerequisites. For them the wall must have glowed in the moonlight as if from within, revealing what they knew was beyond. High on the rock, they must have noticed that their ropes grew weightless and lofted in the wind, just as their bodies did. Up there, men became unsubstantial, and the planes of rock more massive. They were neither lost nor found. What might they have answered if someone asked, "Are you all mind, or no mind?"[43]

4

The Way
of Geology

Muir's vision of the Sierra was as fluid as the landscape he had absorbed. The waterfalls of Hetch Hetchy, the glacier
on Red Mountain, the glorious ocean of mountains he had seen from
Ritter: all of these he had absorbed into his soul. His fascination
with the dynamic geological agents tells us much about him. Muir's
Nature was all one, but it constantly expanded and could not be
seen or comprehended in one place. Nature could not be seized, taken
hold of. It eluded any kind of circumscribing. So Muir ran on and
on through the 1870s, further from Yosemite and deeper into the
Sierra, farther from the center of his world, out into the glaciers
of Alaska by the end of the decade. All because he wanted to understand his home in Yosemite, to arrive where he started and know
the place for the first time. That is the nature of spiritual journeys.

Nevertheless, Muir did settle down in Oakland for a while to
write *Studies in the Sierra*. He conceived his book of *Studies* a full
year before his journey into the glacial womb, and he thought of
it as the magnum opus of his Yosemite years; but he continued to
put off the project: he might become distracted from his main work
by writing his thoughts too soon, more than by even "the distasteful
and depressing labor of the mill or guiding." He asked Jeanne Carr
in 1871, "Suppose I should give some of the journals my first thoughts
about this glacier work as I go along, and afterwards gather them
and press them for the Boston wise. Or will it be better to hold my

wheesht and say it all at a breath?" He didn't wish to pick half-formed thoughts, killing them like botanical specimens before they matured and turned to fruit. Even if he could send certain flowers of his experience to the press as decorative essays, he would still devote his energy and enthusiasm to a more substantial and mature project:

Well here it is — the only book I ever have invented. First, I will describe each glacier with its tributaries separately, then describe the rocks and hills and mountains *over* which they have flowed or *past* which they have flowed, endeavoring to prove that all of the various forms which those rocks now have is the necessary result of the ice action in connection with their structure and cleavage. . . . Then, armed with these data, I will come down to Yosemite, where all my ice has come, and prove that each dome and brow and wall, and every grace and spire and brother is the necessary result of the delicately balanced blows of well directed and combined glaciers against the parent rocks which contained them.

The *Studies* became more and less than Muir thought they would be in 1871. He would be true to his own path of thought, and would argue that Yosemite Valley was the end of a grand chapter of glacial history. Yet he finally attempted to show more than a unified, predetermined Sierra as monumental sculpture. He also provided a guide, a way to his own vision. A book which attempted to describe each landmark as a preconceived work of art would have been encyclopedic, and a substitute for the experience of the Sierra itself; he had not wanted to write that kind of book because the Sierra was not simply a collection of monuments: it was flow. But there was a tension in Muir's early conception of the *Studies*. Was he to write a descriptive book, or a guide to vision? Could he do both at the same time?[1]

When we come to the Sierra now, we come to it frequently as if it were a playground. We assume that someone knows how it was created, and that we can go to such an authority if we wish to understand its natural history. But this was not true, we scarcely need to be reminded, for Muir. Even if it were, he would have wanted to make these discoveries for himself. I have seen this self-reliant impulse at work in Norman Clyde, who taught me when he was in his eighties that Nature is only new and original if the observer goes to her each time with a desire to explore once again from the beginning the mystery and wonder.

When we read the standard text by Matthes on Yosemite's geology, we find that he does what Muir did in the *Studies*, taking the reader on an "imaginary" traverse of the range in preparation for seeing the Yosemite as part of the whole Sierra. Further, Matthes's Sierra is imbued with value, as is Muir's, and much of his book's metaphorical structure is indebted to Muir, despite his hesitance to announce his themes in Muir's exuberant, enthusiastic terms. He corrects some of the details of Muir's analysis, yet his perspective is largely the same, suggesting that Muir's very way of seeing has become, if not a part of the tradition of geology as a discipline, then a part of Yosemite and a part of our cultural heritage.[2]

Muir struggled to create the language of Yosemite. As he wrote, he was encouraged by Jeanne Carr to "curtail his poetic exuberance . . . to gain the attention of the scientists." But his choice, when he began to compose, was not between metaphored and unmetaphored prose; rather, he tried to find metaphors which were true to science and to his own vision. As a result he had to ask some basic questions about the cosmos. "Cosmos" is not a word he ever used, just as he only gradually became comfortable with the term "wilderness," yet they became synonymous. He realized that in writing the *Studies* he was describing the creation of the world. The Sierra became a universal mountain range which told the truth about all mountains. He was making his first attempt to describe the nature of Nature, writing a document which would elucidate his world-view.[3]

It is impossible to separate his conceptual problems from his articulation. It is probably not true that he conceived his message thoroughly before he found words, yet it is also clear that writing caused him great agony because his vision was so complete in his mind. "Everything is so inseparably united," he lamented. His vision was too whole to find easy expression in either the language of contemporary science or the language of contemporary literature. There was nothing new about the perspective which Muir wished to communicate, but he was cut off from the tradition of discourse which might have offered him a way of speaking. A perceptive literary critic can find the language Muir sought in the fragments of

Heraclitus, in the Upanishads, the Zend-Avesta, and the Tao Te Ching, where, as one philosopher argues, there is a coalescence among ideas, things, and quality, between the abstract and the concrete. These works, being pre-Cartesian, do not assume the dualism or the division of objective and subjective, knower and known, thinker and thought, matter and spirit. These dualities do belong to our own culture, much as they were inherent in the language Muir had learned. Hence the problem with inherited language: "most of the words of the English language are made of mud, for muddy purposes, while those invented to contain spiritual matter are doubtful and unfixed in capacity and form, as wind-ridden mist-rags." His insistence that matter and spirit were indissolubly united was at the root of this problem, and when Muir took what might be called a vitalist point of view toward Nature, he was not applying it, as Thoreau or early British naturalists had, to plants and animals. He was applying it to the more obdurate aspects of Nature, to the rocks, the glaciers, the weather itself.[4]

He began, while he was writing, to reconsider his idea that the Sierra could be understood as a sculpture. He did not wish to say that it was already completed in its entirety, but he had already committed himself heavily to this view. As a result, the *Studies* itself contains the history of Muir's changing conception of the Creation. Just as there was a tension in the original conception of his book, so there was a tension among the metaphors he chose. He began with the traditional comparison of Nature to a Book, but turned to more organic comparisons to Path, Flow, and Cycle. Finally he began to describe Yosemite as the trunk of a tree which had both roots and branches.

THE LIVING ROCK

He visualized the pre-glacial Sierra as "one vast undulated wave, in which a thousand separate mountains, with their domes and spires, their innumerable cañons and lake basins, lay concealed." If the glaciers were the tools which would "disinter forms already conceived and ripe," as Muir believed, then they "only developed the predestined forms of mountain beauty which were ready and waiting to receive the baptism of light."[5]

Nineteenth-century geophysics could not provide Muir with a history of granites. Beginning as silica-rich sands deposited by rivers, buried in geosynclines at deltas, only to rise again metamorphosed into the lighter batholiths, granite became the heart of new ranges of mountains. With his vision of flow and constant rebirth in Nature, Muir would have welcomed this natural history of rock, just as he would have appreciated the forms of wind captured in the structure of monumental sandstone. But he could not follow the Sierran granite to its origin, so he attributed the evolution of the range to a combination of nature and nurture. He accepted the nature of Sierran granite on faith as an inherent, preordained structure. The nurturing glaciers and later erosive forces were not mysterious at all; they acted as a result of predictable mechanical laws — gravity, chemistry, and meteorology.

Thus he could reveal the evolution of a landscape without discarding his belief that it followed a preordained direction. A teleology was brought in by the back door, so to speak; God had created the strong rocks to stand and the weak to fall away and become soil. He had used His glacial tool, which would follow the grain of the medium and would guarantee this process.

If, "in Sierra architecture, *the style always proclaims the nature of the rock*," it was incumbent upon the geologist to investigate seriously the texture, structure, and nature of granite. After Muir convinced himself that the glaciers were the primary creative forces which had carved the Sierra, the study of rock structure took much of his time and energy. He was convinced that the Sierra was a work of divine art, and came to understand "'He hath *builded* the mountains,' as not merely a figurative but a literal expression." When Muir explored the length, breadth, and heights of the range, he decided that the Sierran granite was all of one piece. This meant that the separate glaciers which followed the first universal ice sheet met and disinterred similar forms all along the axis of the range, cutting canyons that bore a strong familial resemblance. Hetch Hetchy Valley, the canyon of the South Fork of the Kings River, and Yosemite were similar. "Nature is not so poor as to possess only one of anything, nor throughout her varied realms has she ever been known to offer an exceptional creation, whether of mountain or of valley."[6]

But Muir was puzzled by the monumental domes so prevalent in these Yosemities. He wondered if the controlling influence in the landscape was really a ubiquitous set of cleavage planes across the entire range. If that were so, he was troubled to explain the commanding individuality of inspiring landmarks like Half Dome. An early version of the *Studies* reveals his suppressed desire to present a theory of their creation which could not be justified in purely mechanical terms. He wished to see their origin in "seeds so to speak which produce domes," and stated in another early hypothesis that "domes appear to be concretionary in their nature appearing as immense balls partly or wholly buried in undist.[urbed] granite." Here is an implicit linking of theological and scientific vision, which can be traced to his background as a botanist. Wood's *Botany*, which he carried on his botanical excursion to Florida and which probably came to California, makes this link explicit. Under the heading "No Accidents or Caprice in Nature," Wood announced that "the seed of the plant is its redemption. . . . in the grain of the mustard there is literally a *faith*. Plants may teach us lessons in sacred things." Thus Muir spoke of a rock as "conceived and ripe," and described its weathering as "the ripening of one of its cleavage planes, just as the valves of seeds ripen, open, and fall."[7]

He had written in his journal, "While the snow-flowers for Yosemite glaciers were growing in the depths of the sky, the stones for Yosemite temple-walls were growing in the crystalline depths of the mountains." When he described the baptism of a monumental dome into Sierran light, he used Mount Starr King as his example of redemption. Great buds of rock seemed to blossom into the sky:

The beautiful conoid, Starr King, the loftiest and most perfect of the group, was one of the first rocky islets to emerge from the glacial sea into the azure mountain sea, and ere its new-born brightness was marred by storms, must have presented a glorious spectacle, dispersed light like a crystal island over the snowy expanse in which it stood alone. The moraine at the base is planted with a very equal growth of manzanita.

Baptism, birth from one environment to another, the sea of ice replaced by the sea of vegetation — all suggested that Starr King was alive. This suggestion is most obvious in his earliest draft of the *Studies*. Muir loved the domes for their wholeness, and because they suggested that the landscape evolved through an organic process of ripening and growth — this despite the eroding power of glaciers, whose roles were only apparently destructive. The last chapter of the *Studies* concluded, "In all this sublime fulfillment there was no upbuilding, but a universal razing and dismantling, and of this every mountain and valley is the record and monument"; this could only be understood if the reader realized that such an evolutionary process merely separated weak and dying rock from live and growing forms. Basic to this view was Muir's refusal to be stopped by paradox, and the patience to see that the tension and apparent strife were part of a larger harmony. "Opposition brings concord. Out of discord comes fairest harmony," said Heraclitus; "the hidden harmony is better than the obvious."[8]

The living rocks of Yosemite: the scientist had been taught not to invest them with consciousness. But Muir knew that the rocks themselves were alive, and his perspective was likely to be dismissed by the scientific community. Clarence King, for instance, had learned to banish such ideas from his mind. After climbing Mount Whitney he said, "It is hard not to invest these great dominating peaks with consciousness, difficult to realize that, sitting thus for ages in [the] presence of all nature can work, of light-magic and color-beauty, no inner spirit has kindled, nor throb of granite heart once responded, no Buddhistic nirvana-life even had brooded in eternal calm within these sphinx-like breasts of stone." King had been proud of his ability to resist such mythologizing impulses; he sacrificed his soul to gain the objectivity of detachment. He looked at Mount Whitney, saw a hard materialistic reality, and no more. But everything in Muir yearned toward the powerful spirit of the mountains. A year before he climbed Whitney, Muir wrote in his journal, "Glaciers move in tides. So do mountains, so do all things." So when he looked up from the Owens Valley on the day after he climbed Whitney in October of 1873, his perceptions were quite different from the ones King had felt only a month before. He reveled in the rich colors of sky and rock as they shaded magically into each other, orange, blue, crimson, and chocolate.[9]

Muir had not studied the resources of primitive, ancient, or oriental thought which would later allow someone like Gary Snyder to reinvest the mountains with consciousness. Jack Kerouac documented the Snyder perspective in *Dharma Bums:* "'. . . to me a mountain is a Buddha. Think of the patience, hundreds of thousands of years just sittin there being perfectly perfectly silent and like praying for all living creatures in that silence and just waitin for us to stop all our frettin and foolin.'" Snyder has stated that he was influenced by the "Mountains and Rivers Sutra" by Dōgen, wherein the mountains and rivers of the present are the actualization of the word of the ancient Buddhas. In A.D. 1240, Dōgen stated simply, "When we thoroughly study the mountains, this is the mountain training. Such mountains and rivers themselves spontaneously become wise men and sages." The imagery of Muir's journals suggests that this was his personal view. If Dōgen had said "The blue mountains are constantly walking," Muir might have dissented only by correcting his English: "sauntering," Muir might have said; he guessed the mountains were thoughtful and on the move. Yet such views are likely to bring laughter in the West, where we have developed a reductive scientific objectivity. We do not understand Dōgen when he says, "To be 'in the mountains' is a flower opening 'within the world.' Those outside the mountains do not sense this do not know it. Those without eyes to see the mountains do not sense, do not know, do not hear this truth."[10]

The germ of this vision is buried in the *Studies,* although it does not take a more poetic and spiritual form until later, when Muir will say, unashamedly,

No temple made with hands can compare with Yosemite. Every rock in its walls seems to glow with life. Some lean back in majestic repose; others, absolutely sheer or nearly so for thousands of feet, advance beyond their companions in thoughtful attitudes, giving welcome to storms and calms alike, seemingly conscious, yet heedless of everything going on about them. Awful in stern, immovable majesty, how softly these mountain rocks are adorned and how fine and reassuring the company they keep.[11]

If we do not dismiss this as hyperbole, faking, or pathetic fallacy, it is a recognized truth, but not for modern western culture. When Mrs. Carr told Muir to prune the lavishness of his native fancy, or to curtail his poetic exuberance in the *Studies,* she was also telling him to omit the living truth he had seen. Nevertheless, the mountains and domes of the *Studies* were alive, even if he sometimes treated them as objects. Earlier he had driven wooden stakes into living glaciers so scientists would believe that they were alive. Now he found that he would have to describe the fault planes in granite to show its wholeness.

There are undoubtedly many paths to the whole living vision in Nature. I have attempted to describe a part of Muir's path in previous chapters. Richard Shelton is a contemporary poet who has spoken about the sense of the living Sonoran Desert. He says he arrived at the vision of a live and organic landscape through surrealism, at least insofar as his vision appears in his poetry. But below its articulation, before its annunciation in words, the vision comes from living among the rocks and allowing them to speak. We can't be talking to each other; we must be silent if we wish to hear the silent voice of the mountains. What is one to do with a man who insists that the rocks are alive, who insists on saying against all *common* sense that

> *There are families of stones*
> *under the ground.*
> *As the young stones grow*
> *they rise slowly like moons.*
> *When they reach the surface*
> *they are old and holy*
> *and when they break open*
> *they give off a rich odor,*
> *each blooming once in the light*
> *after centuries of waiting.*[12]

You cannot begin to analyze these ideas in western scientific terms, because they do not translate. No attempt to account for such ideas will lead you to appreciate or assent to them. There is really only one thing to do — join the celebration. Running down the talus, singing and shouting, in the spirit of Muir, has always seemed an appropriate celebration. As Kerouac describes it,

I looked up and saw Japhy *running down the mountain* in huge twenty-foot leaps, running, leaping, landing with a great drive of his booted heels, bouncing five feet or so, running, then taking another long crazy yelling yodelaying sail down the sides of the world and in that flash I realized it's *impossible to fall off mountains you fool* . . .

Muir had his own version of this dance on the mountain; it suggests his trust in the mountains, in the living wholeness of the rocks:

If for a moment you are inclined to regard these taluses as mere draggled, chaotic dumps, climb to the top of one of them, and run down without any haggling, puttering hesitation, boldly jumping from boulder to boulder with even speed. You will then find your feet playing a tune, and quickly discover the music and poetry of these magnificent rock piles — a fine lesson; and all Nature's wildness tells the same story . . .

With the vision of living rock comes trust, and also responsibility. I have an anthropological friend who says he knows a Navajo who apologizes to the rocks before he steps into the cab of the bulldozer he operates at a coal mine in northern Arizona. My friend says he cannot personally understand this. Perhaps he has not listened long enough or deeply enough to the wind that blows through the piñon pines, the wind which once blew through the great arches of Navajo sandstone.[13]

When I was a child, I used to follow Carl Sharsmith, the venerable naturalist of Tuolumne Meadows. I remember Carl's anger once when he noticed that someone had casually displaced a group of small erratic boulders which sat in the middle of a particularly fine sheet of glacially polished rock. He knew.

THE GLACIAL PAST

Why should it matter to us that the Sierra is a glacial range? It all depends on us. If we are tourists, the glaciers have created scenery. If we are mountaineers, glaciers have shaped the highest rugged peaks, carving northern amphitheaters and leaving the gentle southern slopes. They have carved the canyons we ascend when we approach the peaks. If we are rockclimbers, the glaciers have disinterred and polished the fine smooth domes of the middle Sierra. If we are shepherds, the glaciers have scooped out huge basins and filled them with the soils which create high meadows. If we are miners, the glaciers have exposed the contact zones at the crest and at the foothills of the Sierra where we shall dig for gold. If we are loggers, the glaciers have left the huge morainal soil beds on the western slope of the Sierra where the beautiful and productive forests now flourish. If we are farmers, the glaciers have supplied the matrix of rich soil in the entire Central Valley, as well as the intricate system of drainage which waters it. All of these blessings are part of the whole story of the creation of the Sierra. At various times Muir considered the Sierra from all these points of view.

But each of these perspectives is finally limited, because all represent a human criterion of use. Muir hoped that his conception of the Sierra as sculpture would turn attention toward its genesis and structure. It was not simply scenery, a playground, or a soil factory. Certainly it was not a collection of sterile monuments. As it created itself, nothing was wasted or a byproduct. No part of the wilderness was accidental.

So much depends on how one imagines the earth's past. For Muir, the glacial history of the Sierra was a peaceful, harmonious era. Just as he found residual glaciers "lingering beneath cool shadows, silently completing the sculpture of the summit peaks," so he imagined the glacial past of the Sierra as "tender snowflowers, noiselessly falling through unnumbered seasons, the offspring of the sun and sea." The glaciers were more than the gouges of the "Master Builder." They were the plows of God, the great soil makers and distributors. They blessed the earth and created the form that a tree of life would one day fill. How could Muir see their reign as anything but harmonious? [14]

When he attempted to imagine the glacial history of the Sierra in peaceful terms, he was trying to avoid a major scientific controversy of the day between what are called the Catastrophists and the Uniformitarians, represented by Louis Agassiz and Sir Charles Lyell. Modern geology accepts a combination of catastrophe and uniformity to explain the creation of the earth, and so did Muir. His own fusion of the two viewpoints reveals the way he attempted to form a coherent theory of natural history. In fact, Muir's method of geological study was created by Lyell, and revised by Agassiz's introduction of the glacier as a major geological agent. One can see the source of geological confusion when one realizes that Lyell's concept of uniformity intertwined methodological and substantive, or cosmic, statements, some of which were accepted by Agassiz and the Catastrophists. There were few geologists who took an absolute stand on these issues.[15]

Lyell's theory of uniformity required first of all that "Natural laws are constant (uniform) in space and time." This was a cornerstone of Muir's philosophy, and he expressed it not only in geological terms, but by appealing to Linnaeus, the botanist: "Linnaeus says Nature never leaps, which means that God never shouts or spouts or speaks incoherently. The rocks and sublime canyons, the waters and winds, and all life structures — animals and ouzels, meadows and groves, and all the silver stars — are words of God, and they flow smooth and ripe from his lips." He saw that this was not a theory about geology alone, but was basic to his conception of natural history as a whole. Lyell had articulated this component of the theory of uniformity as a defense of science against the intrusion of theological dogma. If, for instance, the world was created by miraculous means before men arrived, then men could not listen to the words of God as they came from Nature, but would have to trust the Bible. Lyell had heard too much about the Flood.[16]

In *Principles of Geology*, Lyell wrote the manifesto for the nineteenth-century field geologist, arguing that the geological agents which had made the earth were still at work. He attacked the earlier theory of geology which held that the earth in the present was in a period of repose; he insisted that this dogma was "calculated to foster indolence, and to blunt the keen edge of curiosity." Men who did not believe that the earth continued to change would despond and cease to investigate "those minute but incessant mutations which every part of the earth's surface is undergoing." It was the geologist's job not to "speculate on the possibilities of the past [but to] patiently explore the realities of the present."[17]

Agassiz was Lyell's heir, but his *Études* introduced the glacier, which seemed to be a much more violent and inconstant force than the better-known agents of wind and water. Though glaciation offered an alternative to the deluge which had swept Noah's neighbors away, the introduction of such a massive geological agent seemed to require a revision of uniformity. The American historian Henry Adams wondered whether the glacier was not an heretical element if added to Lyell's theory, "obliging him to allow that causes had in fact existed on earth capable of producing more violent geological changes than would be possible in our own day." To Adams's doubt, Agassiz and Muir would reply that one needed only to go north to Alaska or Greenland to see these agents working in their full sublime power. They needed a living glacial reality to satisfy the second tenet of Lyell's concept of uniformity.[18]

Lyell thought that "processes now operating should explain the events of the past." Muir argued in the *Studies* that the glacier was simply another, less understood agent: "The erosive energy of ice is almost universally underrated, because we know so little about it. Water is our constant companion, but we cannot dwell with ice. Water is far more human than ice, and also far more outspoken." When an agent, however strong it is, may be studied and understood, then it can be placed in the theory of uniformity. Catastrophic theory depended not so much on the power or violence of geological forces as on their inscrutability. Thanks to Agassiz's *Études*, Muir could explain the mechanism of glaciation in the Sierra. And Agassiz put his seal of approval on Muir's work, exclaiming, "Here is the first man who has any adequate conception of glacial action."[19]

The third tenet of Lyell's geological uniformity is that "Geologic change is slow, gradual, and steady, not cataclysmic or paroxysmal." This tenet is the basis for Muir's resistance to Whitney's theory that Yosemite was created by "subsidence" when its bottom suddenly dropped out. Had the "violent hypothesis," catastrophe, or subsidence been true, Muir's method of study could achieve virtually nothing in Yosemite. He could neither read Nature's book nor follow geological history with his feet. Muir echoed Lyell's argument when he satirized the catastrophic theory, "seeming to account for the remarkable sheerness and angularity of the walls . . . by its marvelousness and obscurity." But the mechanism which Muir proposed as an alternative to the violent origin of Yosemite was not considered by Lyell to be a gradual geological change. Agassiz's notion of a past ice age suggested, as did Muir's view of the Sierra, that the glaciers working in the past were not only more powerful than those one found in the Sierra's present, but represented a sudden change during the earth's past.[20]

And this in turn contradicted Lyell's fourth and last tenet of uniformity. Lyell believed that "the earth has been fundamentally the same since its formation." This was not a belief about method of study at all, but about the nature of Nature. This was where Agassiz parted from Lyell, and opened the door on a new vista. Agassiz argued not only that natural history had direction, but that there was a complete discontinuity between the pre-glacial and post-glacial earth. "Since I saw the glaciers,"Agassiz said in 1838, "I am quite of a snowy humor, and will have the whole surface of the earth covered with ice, and the whole prior creation dead by cold."[21]

If Muir were to follow the letter of the Agassizean law, his description of the Sierra after the glacial age would be a genesis indeed, but not the first genesis for the earth. Agassiz described the glacial age as a vast and sudden metamorphosis from a tropical earth to a "huge ocean of ice. . . . The silence of death succeeded to the movement of a powerful creation." Then followed a "deep seated reaction,"as "fluidal masses inside the earth boiled up once more with great intensity." In other words, the causes of the glacial age and the subsequent rebirth came from within the earth. Earth's core was intimately connected to the life on its surface. "The surface of the earth is not simply a stage on which the thousands of present and past inhabitants played their parts in turn. There are much more intimate relations between the earth and the living organisms which populated it, and it may even be demonstrated that the earth was developed because of them." This was the sort of teleology that enraptured Muir, since it suggested so much about a living geological earth which harmonized with the meadows, groves, beasts, and birds.[22]

So when Muir accepted Agassiz's idea that the glacier was God's great plow, he also accepted a set of implications which were cosmic in extent. On the one hand, he was blinded from seeing very obvious evidence that contradicts the idea of one great glacial winter in the history of the earth. From Mono Lake on the east side of the Sierra one can look up at Muir's favorite Bloody Canyon and see parallel and crosscutting lateral moraines which bear witness to a periodic glaciation that he ignored. For him a glacial era would "separate the knowable from the unknowable in geological history." On the other hand, the belief in one great glacial winter meant that the active glaciers Muir found were living remnants of a single step in the genesis of the Sierra. Men lived closer to the dawn of creation than they knew, and were linked to an earth which had been reborn during its glacial age. Even as they walked the earth, it continued toward its destined shape, an unfinished sculpture in the midst of one of its many lives.[23]

THE LIVES OF GLACIERS

When Muir thought about the glacial history of the Sierra, he did not imagine a universal ice sheet, but a system of individual glaciers. He called them by their names because he thought of them as distinct personalities. The glaciers excavated mountain mansions and lake basins which would later become meadows; they prepared places for life. They turned rock to soil and distributed this sustaining "mountain meal" high and low. They carved paths which were followed by rivers, winds, plants, animals, and men. They also sculpted monuments, a task they continued even during the Sierra's present.

As Muir wrote the life history of Yosemite glaciers, he caught them in action. He described the Tenaya Glacier, for instance, as "setting out in its life-work" and "spending its strength." In its final descent, "crushing heavily against the ridge of Clouds Rest, [it] curved toward the west, quickened its pace, focalized its wavering currents, and bore down upon Yosemite with its whole concentrated energy." As its body withered at once along its whole length, it liberated Tenaya Canyon, "exposing broad areas of rolling rock waves and glossy pavements on whose channelless surface water ran everywhere wild and free." This kind of glacial biography was necessary if one were to understand the legacy of a glacier. Muir described the Hoffman Glacier in Agassizean terms, as it crept back into the shelter of its fountain shadows and separated into its chief tributaries. It left soil, small basins, lakes, and a world of light.[24]

Thus Muir's glaciers developed the ground where life began to flourish, and he recorded their lives as a part of the dynamic history of the Sierra. However, there was another question which troubled him, especially in the early seventies before he wrote the *Studies*. To what extent could he say that the Sierra was a completed sculpture? In "Exploration in the Great Tuolumne Cañon" he wrote that the world, "not yet half made, becomes more beautiful every day." Later he revised that passage to say that the world "though made is still being made." He was strongly tempted to see the post-glacial Sierra as a finished work of art. If it was completed, it could be read as the whole story of Creation.[25]

The glacial and post-glacial history of the Sierra suggested that Nature was an organic whole, a tree with roots and branches. The plan for the tree of life was inherent in the rock, which provided its roots. The glaciers brought the plan to light, and were succeeded by the life which flowed upward from the valleys. So there was a tension between two kinds of comparisons that Muir used to describe the Sierran landscape. Perhaps he first wished to describe the Sierra as a completed book, but as he realized that Nature was flow, he began to describe the flowing landscape as a tree. The glaciers in the *Studies* are seen alternately as makers of the Book and as sculptors of the Path, but finally become the creators of a vast tree-like system of life in the Sierra.

NATURE AS BOOK

Despite its prevalence in the *Studies*, the metaphor of Nature as Book was already an artifact from Muir's pre-Sierran thinking. He would finally have to abandon it as he came to accept the implications of evolution, but it still served a purpose before it died. Rooted in medieval conceptions of Nature and heavily used by nineteenth-century scientists, it was a cliché when Muir inherited it. But its presence in his writing tells much about his debt to Agassiz.

Agassiz was the scientist most congenial to Emerson's philosophy because Agassiz believed that connections between phenomena were not material, but intellectual, or ideal. This belief had a profound effect on his method of study. When Agassiz described the Natural world as God's Book, he did not mean to speak only a metaphor. Scientists had always been the "unconscious interpreters of a divine conception" when they attempted to "expound nature." They "followed only and reproduced, in our imperfect expressions, the plan, whose foundations were laid in the dawn of creation." Indeed, he was arguing that Man's scientific classification systems were inherent in God's plan and were not products of the ingenious human mind.[26]

Muir's method of study — his trust in close observation and comparison, which led to classification — indicated that he had accepted not only the faith which underlies Agassiz's theory, but also a basic tenet of Emerson's idealism: "Books are for the scholar's idle times. When he can read God directly, the hour is too precious to be wasted on other men's transcripts of their readings." Unfortunately, neither Agassiz nor Emerson told the scholar how to translate God's thoughts. But comparison is the heart of metaphor. Agassiz's method of study led directly to a metaphor of Nature as Book.

Even while Agassiz's method of study became the standard in American schools, Asa Gray began to scrutinize its validity. Indeed, Gray was known as the American Huxley because he supported Darwin against Agassiz in this country. When he considered the Darwinian method as opposed to that expounded by Agassiz, he decided that Agassiz ultimately interpreted Nature as a theological text in which Nature's phenomena were seen in relation to the Divine mind. Darwin examined phenomena in Nature as they related to one another and as they resulted from natural causes.[27]

If Gray could not share Agassiz's faith in the relationship between God's systematic intentions and man's scientific classification systems, he still thought the method of study had value. As he explained in his own *Lessons in Botany*, the purpose of classification systems was to allow the student to ascend in a disciplined manner toward the plan of the Creator, even if he never reached it. Gray never doubted that Nature was a planned conception, he only thought that the neat chapter headings and categories of man's classification systems were approximate.

[Man] is often obliged to make arbitrary divisions where nature shows only transitions . . . to assume, on paper at least, a strictly definite limitation of genera, of tribes, and of orders, although observation shows so much blending here and there of natural groups, sufficiently distinct on the whole, as to warrant us in assuming the likelihood that the Creator's plan is one of *gradation, not of definite limitation*, even perhaps to the species themselves.[28]

For a thoroughgoing Darwinian it was no longer possible to think of Nature as a book. The chapter headings were false distinctions, because the Creator's plan flowed continuously from species to species.

Muir had ascended toward higher and wider views, as Gray recommended. He had evolved as Gray thought an ideal student ought. While he was using the metaphor of Nature as Book as he classified Yosemite Valleys in the second chapter of the *Studies*, Muir used these comparisons only as a crude introduction to his message. As he finally reached higher views, these individual canyons and particular glaciers would become part of the integrated system of life which was the Sierra.

PALIMPSEST, POLISH, AND PATH

When he described the world as a palimpsest in the journal published as *A Thousand Mile Walk to the Gulf*, he was implying that Nature was a Book. The passage itself dramatized his own aspirations to be a future translator of Nature.

When a page is written over but once it may be easily read; but if it be written over and over with characters of every size and style, it soon becomes unreadable, although not a single confused meaningless mark or thought may occur among all the written characters to mar its perfection. Our limited powers are similarly perplexed and overtaxed in reading the inexhaustible pages of nature, for they are written over and over uncountable times, written in characters of every size and color, sentences composed of sentences, every part of a character a sentence. There is not a fragment in all nature, for every relative fragment of one thing is a full harmonious unit in itself. All together form the one grand palimpsest of the world.[29]

Justice requires that we see Muir's metaphor as subtler than Agassiz's. Already he had a conception which would allow him to see the signs of the present and the signs of the past overlaid, yet interdependent. But as he came to the Sierra and evolved there, he had to change his views in order to see his environment clearly. Meanwhile he attempted to see the Sierra in pre-Californian terms. It was at first easy for him to read the glacial age as the first chapter of the Book of Nature, written on a page on which later chapters had been superimposed. When he tried to write this vision, however, he seemed to be describing the glacial history as separate and *abstracted* from the present life of the Sierra. He spoke awkwardly in his first published essay on the glacial history of Yosemite.

Two years ago, when picking flowers in the mountains back of Yosemite Valley, I found a book. It was blotted and storm-beaten; all of its outer pages were mealy and crumbly, the paper seemed to dissolve like the snow beneath which it had been buried; but many of the inner pages were well preserved, and though all were more or less stained and torn, whole chapters were easily readable. In this condition is the great open book of Yosemite glaciers today; its granite pages have been torn and blurred by the same storms that wasted the castaway book.[30]

Though Muir certainly did not intend it, his early effort to describe the glacial book of Yosemite's history bore a remarkable resemblance to Clarence King's perception of Mount Whitney as "ice-chiselled and storm-tinted, a great monolith left standing amid the ruins of a bygone geological empire." Both men suggested that the mountains themselves were ancient artifacts in a period of decay, neither alive nor essentially related to the world they nourished. The metaphor of Nature as Book seemed to go dead in Muir's hand, and he wisely left it at the beginning of his essay, turning to the life and death of Yosemite glaciers, trees, and animals. The past was not indelible, he thought in 1871, but was being written over by a new and vital present even while he studied.[31]

When he reforged the palimpsest in the *Studies,* he did so because he was prepared to move beyond a dead metaphor into a more complex vision of the Creator's Plan. Now he could see that the glacial history of the Sierra merged imperceptibly into the post-glacial era.

The ice-sheet of the glacial period, like an immense sponge, wiped the Sierra bare of all pre-glacial surface inscriptions, and wrote its own history upon the ample page. We may read the letter-pages of friends when written over and over, if we are intimately acquainted with their handwriting, and under the same conditions we may read Nature's writings on the stone pages of the mountains. Glacial history upon the summit of the Sierra page is clear, and the farther we descend, the more we find its inscriptions crossed and recrossed with the records of other agents. Dews have dimmed it, torrents have scrawled it here and there, and the earthquake and avalanche have covered and erased many a delicate line. Groves and meadows, forests and fields, darken and confuse its more enduring characters along the bottom, until only the laborious student can decipher even the most emphasized passages of the original manuscript.[32]

From this, the most elaborate and concrete version of the palimpsest, it is clear that Muir was no longer assembling the slides or comparisons which would allow him to classify glacial phenomena like Agassiz, but was traveling the path of natural history from the summits to the foothills of the Sierra. Seen through this revised metaphor, Nature was a myriad of paths. The glaciers wrote their own history, but they also carved paths of life. The *blank* pages of rock, the rich soils: these were their legacy.

Muir observed the wonderfully fresh glacial polish on the pavements in the middle Sierra. It seemed so perfect, he imagined that the glaciers had scarcely left. That "strange brightness of the ground" was their finishing touch, a sure sign of their dominant influence on the land. A mountaineer "stoops and rubs his hand admiringly on these shining surfaces, and tries hard to account for their mysterious smoothness." He noticed that "only the wild mountain sheep seems to move wholly at ease upon these glistening pavements," for only the sheep has traveled these rocks for generations. If a man wished to learn about processes which took thousands of years, he could not read them in a moment. Like the mountain sheep, he would have to live in this realm and follow its myriad paths back and forth.[33]

Muir believed that the student was obliged not only to read the blurred pages of the past, but actually to live in history. He dramatized this sense of commingling present and past by combining the central metaphor of Nature as Book with the central theme of the *Studies*: apparent destruction is in fact creation. "When Nature lifted the ice-sheet from the mountains she may well be said not to have turned a new leaf, but to have made a new one of the old . . . repictured with young life, and the varied and beautiful inscriptions of water, snow, and the atmosphere." The mountains were but one leaf of the tree of life, or one page out of the most recent Book of Nature. God had written many such texts; no doubt some had been entirely erased. But the reborn Sierra was quite young, its face scarcely aged, and its physiognomy still strictly glacial.[34]

Nevertheless, Muir did not claim that he could translate this book of mountain history fully. Instead, he directed his reader to the mountains themselves, to books on glaciology, and to the active glaciers of Alaska. He was simply admitting that his *Studies* was not to be taken as a primary text. His book represented only a brief meeting of theory with close study. He could not describe the myriad paths of natural history, but could only describe how he had found one path. The Sierra itself was multidimensional in time and space. Its path was not like the linear argument of a book, but was like a branching tree.

SACRED BOOKS

In January of 1866, Muir had confessed to Jeanne Carr that he took "more intense delight from reading the power and *goodness* of God from 'the things which are made' than from the Bible. The two books, however, harmonize beautifully, and contain enough of divine truth for the study of all eternity." Since 1866 he had left completely his dependence on the Book of Books, and would never again accept the Bible as a final authority. And if he wanted to articulate truly the vision he received, he would also have to rid himself of the limiting idea that Nature was a book. But writing the *Studies*, he immersed himself in the divine truth of the Book of Nature, and read it largely as an early nineteenth-century scientist might, with the assurance that it was a sacred book.[35]

Great danger lay in using or disposing of this working hypothesis, as I am reminded by the humanistic perspective of Murray Krieger, one of my teachers. In a defense of poetry as the highest human activity, Professor Krieger summarizes the history of the two great books — Nature and the Bible — their claims to sacredness, and their final loss of authority. The story spans the entire history of western civilization, and ends with the modern viewpoint that both books turn out to be "monumental fictional contexts" rather than "metaphysically referential texts." Consequently, "once they are revealed as fictions only, their hold as sacred books is removed. . . . In the secular and skeptical aftermath that followed the loss of sacredness of these Books, we find the retreat . . . from metaphysics to aesthetics: man's fictional power to write such books is retained, though the power of any of the books to become a literally sacred text is gone." So giving up the sacredness of the Book of Nature meant a retreat from metaphysics to aesthetics — a retreat from Nature as True, Whole, and Good, to the more limiting view that Nature is only beautiful scenery. That was why Muir willingly pruned, grafted, and replanted the metaphor of Nature as Book; he wanted to preserve its metaphysical roots.[36]

If one approaches the issue from the opposite direction — not from its metaphysical roots, but from its factual branches — then the question is: what happens when the Book of Nature is not totally interpretable and complete, according to empirical facts? To put this in concrete terms, what is the consequence of Muir's inaccurate view that the glaciers of the Sierra are remnants of the one original Ice Age? Modern geologists have uncovered evidence of at least three major glacial periods in the history of the Sierra, and the glaciers we see today are the remnants of a short and minor glacial period that began sometime around four thousand years ago. But actual ice is not a final fact; no ice now present was a part of the beginning of any previous glacial age, nor would it be even if these glaciers were remnants of Agassiz's hypothetical original glacial period. Do we devaluate Muir's vision because he is factually limited? No, because the essential spirit of his glacial theory is more important than the accuracy or completeness of his details. Living glaciers meant a living Nature to him, and the spirit of that discovery remains true.

Just as he was blinded by accepting Agassiz's glacial theory, so too he could not escape the language of a limited vision which he inherited from nineteenth-century science. Yet his attempt to see clearly and write clearly is apparent when we realize that he began to transcend the limiting and false language he had inherited. Even when I follow his errors of expression, I am assuming that his books — and behind them, his life — have an intrinsic coherence. Further, when I write this book about Muir, I must assume that wild Nature, the source of his writing, is the same source that I value, and largely for the same reasons. Nature remains the sacred text from which men take their wholeness. Like Muir, I write a flawed book. I know that Muir's thinking was more complex than any version I can present in these pages, yet I can only embody the serious meditation I have done about him in a book.

And I am reminded by Professor Krieger of the consequences of giving up the sacredness of Nature: writing itself then becomes an escape for Man, who "must create forms beyond Nature's 'given' if he is, even momentarily, to be more than a driven and determined thing, a part of Nature's 'given' himself." Humanists like Murray Krieger replace the Book of Nature with the books of Man. But Muir and I do not wish to find our identity in "forms beyond"; we wish to be a part of Nature. We do not fear to be a part of the "given," a part of Nature's bounty, and so we find the terms "driven" and "determined" totally misleading. We may fear the civilized social forces which drive and determine our needs, but we are not afraid of the reduced stature we seem to take on when we stand under El Capitan, or are dwarfed in the midst of Sequoias. It is our true self we see among the rocks and in the sacred groves.[37]

So it is that the modern humanist's attitude toward himself and Nature dramatizes precisely the consequences of giving up that clumsy and clichéd metaphor of Nature as Book. Muir was not ready in 1874 to give up this value-laden way of conceiving natural history. Certainly he began to seek alternatives when he described rocks which moved like waves and snow which drifted wave-like over them, but a western audience was not likely to attach value to such a language.

GLACIAL SOIL

If Muir's first interest was in the glaciers as sculptors, he also wished to show that the glacier was the primary creator of the *whole* landscape. He tried to fill out his picture of the Sierran landscape by speaking not only of the polished granite domes, but also of the sediment-filled valleys below them. If he was going to claim that the glaciers had removed more than a mile's thickness of granite, then he would also have to show where all the rock went. At the same time, in the chapter "Formation of Soils" in *Studies*, he seized a chance to influence an audience that might be more interested in agriculture than in beautiful sculpture. He used the language of agriculture. Glaciers, when they formed soils, were like plows, producing "soils belts or furrows." The glacier was the perfect contour plow, a model for men: "instead of disappearing suddenly, like a sun-stricken cloud, it withdrew from the base of the great soil-belt upward, in that magnificently deliberate way so characteristic of nature—adding belt to belt in beautiful order over lofty plateaus and rolling hills and valleys, wherever soil could be made to lie." One cannot help but notice that this is a sort of natural recycling. A good craftsman not only cleans up after himself, but uses everything at hand.[38]

The winds and the rains had their roles in these secondary glacial phenomena. Acting over the centuries, they "smooth rough glacial soils like harrows and rollers. But this culture is carried on at an infinitely slow rate, as we measure time." Culture, the refining process, is an afterthought. Of course Muir's notion of Nature as the Original Gardener was hardly novel, but it became the basis for some interesting lessons for farmers in his later writing. In the *Studies* he kept his attention, not on the refinement, but on the production of soil, for "notwithstanding the many august implements employed as modifiers and reformers of soils, the glacier is the only great producer." It is a democratic agent, giving "soil to high and low places almost alike; water-currents are dispensers of special blessings." The language here is so suggestive that I have always suspected a veiled social and theological argument, perhaps influenced by Henry George's plea that every man should be allowed to own land. Certainly Nature gives fertile land to high and low places alike. Unlike the social and economic system of California, which Muir's old teacher Professor Carr found so inequitable, Nature in California had spread her blessings.[39]

According to Muir, the great ice sheet had provided the soils of the Owens, Walker, Carson, Sacramento, and San Joaquin valleys, but his heartfelt interest was found in the central soil band of the Sierra. Above the gold-bearing slates and below the middle Sierra, on the great moraine, grew the great green wall of climax forest.[40]

Thus Nature as Book was slowly supplanted by Nature as Path, and as a footnote, Nature as Gardener. In all of these the glacier was the key agent who wrote the book, carved the path, and distributed the soil. Finally, Muir turned to more organic metaphors —Nature as Tree, or Nature as Cycle. At the same time he began to resolve in his own mind the paradoxical process of geological change which troubled his contemporaries.

ORGANIC GEOLOGY

When he began to classify glaciers and glacial valleys in *Studies in the Sierra,* he was still following the metaphor of Nature as Book. When he separated valleys into distinct genera and species, he seemed to be following Agassiz, for he was claiming distinct divisions —"the valleys naturally classify themselves"—where other observers might only have noted gradation. He would claim that the distinct divisions were the product of his more careful observation. Nevertheless, he recognized gradation within the species of Yosemite valleys, caused by environmental situation. Classification by comparison was part of his method. When he looked at Hetch Hetchy he tried to see how it was similar to, rather than different from, Yosemite. This was in part a matter of developing appropriate language to convince the reader that the detailis of his geological analysis made up one system — God's system — which had a conceptual unity.

When he turned to the method of classification in his second and third chapters, "Origin of Yosemite Valleys" and "Ancient Glaciers and their Pathways," Muir delighted to find five major glaciers which converged to make Yosemite Valley, in comparison to the three major glaciers which had converged on Hetch Hetchy, and the four tributaries which created the Kings River Yosemite. What he saw, then, was that Yosemite Valley was like these others, only more so. He even wrote a poem, "Nature Loves the Number Five," which Mrs. Carr convinced him to exclude from the *Studies.* After all, Agassiz, in his *Methods of Study,* reminded the reader that there were five orders of Echinoderms, which were but "five expressions of the same idea," and concluded that "the best result of such familiarity with Nature will be the recognition of an intellectual unity holding together all the various forms of life as part of one Creative Conception." In extending this idea to geology Muir was simply following another geologist, Hugh Miller, who had argued that geology is natural history extended over all ages. The Yosemite, as creative conception, could be seen as part of a family, as an example of natural history. And the number five had always held a place as a magical number in other views of a unified cosmos.[41]

Muir followed the standard textbook methods, and his classification of valleys contained an internal assertion that the categories were not his own, but belonged to the valleys themselves. He demonstrated significant qualitative distinctions between glacial and non-glacial valleys. Normally, botanical and zoological classifications depend on the plants' or animals' method of reproduction. This may not be what Muir had in mind when he named his chapter "Origin of Yosemite Valleys"; his description of species depended on "material, form and foliage." These are close to ecological categories, since the distinction between glacial and non-glacial valleys was partly between the valleys which contained meadows, lakes, and groves and those where these features were notably lacking. The glacial valleys, made of either slate or granite, were rich in life. Thus Muir took the name of the valley he knew best, and used "yosemite" as a geological and geographical term, as noun and as adjective: "yosemitic." It is a granite valley, *"branching at head, with beveled and heavily abraded lips at foot.* Bottom *level,* meadowed, laked, or groved." It is a sort of a tree with a mouth. Muir might have been more accurate if he had also used the term as an adverb or verb because it names part of a process. This is exactly the problem Roderick Nash deals with when he attempts to define "wilderness" at the beginning of *Wilderness and the American Mind.* Wilderness is not a place, but a process in Nature. The problem: is a yosemite a place, a process, or an indication of the quality of the process? Such a problem dissolves when the harsh dividing lines of our conceptions of Nature fade out. In certain philosophers such lines do fade out. The very syntax of Heraclitus, for instance, denies these divisions. The problem, then, is with human language, not with Nature. We are relearning in small particle physics that Nature does not distinguish between subject, predicate, and modifier.[42]

Muir knew botanical classification best, and his analogy between glacial systems and plant images made for a credible metaphor. "Nature manifests her love for the number five in her glaciers, as well as in the petals of the flowers which she plants in their pathways. These five Yosemite glaciers we have been sketching are as directly related to one another, and for as definite an object, as are the organs of a plant." The petal image worked nicely, since he would have liked to suggest that the flowery snowflake was somehow related to these later flowers, that the laws of the atoms were the laws of the larger masses. When he asserted that "granite crystallizes into landscapes; snow crystallizes above them to bring their beauty to the light," he was depicting the harmony of the elements.[43]

Muir absorbed and reworked images which structured the arguments of other scientists. He had been reading Darwin's *Origin of Species*, and he turned one of Darwin's key images to his own use. In the summary of the fourth chapter of the *Origin*, Darwin himself reworked the image of the Tree of Life, arguing against an Agassizean view that each species had been independently created.

The affinities of all the beings of the same class have sometimes been represented by a great tree. I believe this simile largely speaks the truth. The green and budding twigs may represent existing species; and those produced during former years may represent the long succession of extinct species. At each period of growth all the growing twigs have tried to branch out on all sides, and to overtop and kill the surrounding twigs and branches, in the same manner as species and groups of species have at all times overmastered other species in the great battle for life. . . . From the first growth of the tree, many a limb and branch has decayed and dropped off; . . . so by generation I believe it has been with the great Tree of Life, which fills with its dead and broken branches the crust of the earth, and covers the surface with its ever-branching and beautiful ramifications.[44]

The thematic import of the Tree of Life is that strife and destruction result in beauty and diversity. Muir would agree about the beauty and diversity, but about the strife he had doubts. Donald Worster suggests that even Darwin did not want to overemphasize the strife in the process.[45]

Muir's basic premise was that Yosemite expressed the workings of a divine and harmonious law, "yet so little understood that it has been regarded as an 'exceptional creation,' or rather *exceptional destruction* accomplished by violent and mysterious forces." So when he described Yosemite as a tree in the *Studies* he turned Darwin's image around. All of Muir's drawings of glacial flow looked like branching trees, and he used this image as he had used the flower earlier to suggest the organic unity of the landscape.

In Yosemite there is an evergreen oak double the size of ordinary oaks of the region, whose trunk is craggy and angular as the valley itself, and colored like the granite bowlders on which it is growing. At a little distance this trunk would scarcely be recognized as part of a tree, until viewed in relation to its branches, leaves and fruit. It is an admirable type of the craggy Merced cañon-tree, whose angular Yosemite does not appear as a natural portion thereof until viewed in its relation to its wide-spreading branches, with their fruit and foliage of meadow and lake.

First, one notices that Muir's evergreen oak is an upside-down version of Darwin's more abstract tree of strife. The branches of Muir's tree reach into the glacial past, and nourish the trunk. Then one realizes that Yosemite is really a commingling of two trees, the glacial tree which flows down from the heights, and the Tree of Life which ascends from the lowlands, bringing plants, meadows, birds, and beasts from below. They fuse in Yosemite, "things frail and fleeting and types of endurance meeting here and blending in countless forms." Then one realizes that Muir's Tree of Life is a spatial, geographical, and, finally, an economic system. The glaciers, as they sculpted the valleys, meadow and lake basins, and canyons of the Sierra created mansions which house the life of the present Sierra. Muir would never use the term "niche" to describe these places — rather, he used the terms "mansion" or "temple" to indicate the spaciousness and freedom for flowing life which his vision of the world suggested.[46]

The branches of Muir's Tree of Life distributed the sun-power stored in glaciers and gathered in snow and rain distilled from flowing clouds. There is a nice paradox here, for glaciers are created by sun-power, cold as they may seem. They are "fountains" too, supplying the summer flow of water so necessary for life in the mountains. They created the vascular system and continue to supply the water for it. By focusing on the trunk of this broadleaf evergreen Tree of Life, Muir reminded himself and his reader not of the obfuscating strife of branches, but of the sturdy life which they fed; the trunk was only a concentrated part of a wonderful system. The trunk, being the result of the long development of the branches, reminds us of the integrity of the system. Muir's image is very much like Coleridge's theory of natural organic form: "A living body is of necessity an organized one — and what is organization but the connection of parts to the whole, so that each part is at once end and means . . . [in Nature] each exterior is the physiognomy of the being within, its true image reflected and thrown out from the concave mirror." Like Coleridge, Muir was intrigued by the law within that spoke of the harmony in Nature. Every branch was important to Muir's craggy oak. Darwin may indeed have missed the organic implications of his own theory when he thought in terms of the struggle within: the very vitality of the Tree of Life was a result of the diverse limbs, as modern Darwinists see. In Muir's tree there were no extinct branches; everything in natural history was both means and end. When Muir turned Darwin's image on its head, reminding us that the branches keep the trunk alive, then "strife" becomes a consequence of a limited point of view. Just as Muir's craggy Yosemite oak is not a symbol of struggle, strife is part of an observer's limited perspective.[47]

To classify valleys as one might trees is no small task, particularly since "the greatest obstacle in the way of reading the history of Yosemite valleys is not its complexity or obscurity, but simply the *magnitude of the characters* in which it is written." Muir solved this problem by climbing up above the valley to a vantage where the harmonies could be seen, where he received the wider viewpoint Asa Gray had suggested as the aim of classification. On its surface this might appear to be an argument for aesthetic distance, but taking Muir's description of Yosemite valleys as temples, one sees that the point of view is not distant at all, but rather that of the *builder*. Because we are overawed when we stand on the floor of a temple, we should climb up and look down on it from its walls, see it as the builder saw it, take as nearly as possible a God's-eye view. Then, if we look carefully at the rock forms, we will see that "the abundance, therefore, of lofty angular rocks, instead of rendering Yosemite unique, is the characteristic which unites it most intimately with all the other similarly situated valleys in the range."[48]

Such a cosmic view gives the deathblow to catastrophic theory by showing that Yosemite is not a unique phenomenon, but rather one of many Sierran temples, a member of a large family. They are all different, of course; some are produced by three, some by four, some by five major glaciers, but their features are similar and all suggest larger harmonies.

However, Muir did not expect his reader to see as a god, but only as a glacier might see. While this perspective may put a man in his proper and rather small place, it also requires an expansion of consciousness into time and space. Muir asked a reader to come into the mountains when he concluded,

> When we walk the pathways of Yosemite glaciers and contemplate their separate works — the mountains they have shaped, the cañons they have furrowed, the rocks they have worn, and broken, and scattered in moraines — on reaching Yosemite, instead of being overwhelmed as at first with its uncompared magnitude, we ask *Is this all?* wondering that so mighty a concentration of energy did not find yet grander expression.

When we have seen from this perspective, we will have learned to suspect that phenomena which we used to call sublime are in reality neither chaotic nor beyond comprehension. Because Muir wanted his reader to judge the history and beauty of the landscape in terms appropriate to its majesty, he knew that he would have to interpret the Sierra not as a sublime landscape, but as a sacred one. He knew, as Kant knew, that those things in Nature which we call sublime are also those things which, because of their limitless power or measureless size, seem beyond man's aesthetic judgment. Muir's metaphors suggesting classification and the Tree of Life and organic unity were not meant to reduce the majesty or power of the Sierra's creation; rather, they were meant to make the size and power of the forces which created it comprehensible, harmonious, beautiful, and thus unified. He attempted to show that the Sierra was a creative conception, a part of the unity of God's creative Plan for the earth.[49]

HIGHER LAWS

Only in the middle chapters of the *Studies* which deal with the heavy glaciation in the middle region of the Sierra did Muir begin to express his most recently acquired view of Nature as process, flow and cycle. Participating in the seasonal and historical, the glacier was itself a part of the natural cycle which took its power from the sun. "Glacial denudation is one of the noblest and simplest manifestations of sun-power," said Muir, and he illustrated this with a drawing "wherein a wheel, constructed of water, vapor, snow, and ice, and as irregular in shape as in motion, is being sun-whirled against a mountainside with a mechanical wearing action like that of an ordinary grindstone." This glacial cycle is essentially the same as the seasonal cycle which continues even in post-glacial ages like our own, and "every atom . . . whether of the slow glacier or swift avalanche, is inspired and directed by law."[50]

Like a snake with its tail in its mouth, Muir's cycle, though irregular in shape as in motion, represents the continuous flow of Nature which has neither beginning nor end. The glaciers of the Sierra were the concrete material manifestations of that flow, but the cyclical motion of Nature—its ceaseless change and direction, coming and going, expansion and contraction—that flow continues forever. When we understand the central place which this Tao of Geology takes in Muir's conception of the world we begin to see that the illustrations he drew for the *Studies*, crude as they may seem, have one continuous theme; with their smooth rocks, wavelike granite pavements, and arrows showing the direction of glacial flow, they are reminders of the cycle of Nature. The snow itself, offspring of sun and sea, is only a crystallizing of one cycle of life, as the wheel of sun-power meets the wave of granite.

The paths of the glaciers, the paths Muir traveled, represented only the earthly arc of this cycle. Where the ocean of air, carrying moisture from the Pacific Ocean, meets the ocean of rock at the crest of the Sierra, Muir found the meeting of heaven and earth. So too, there at the crest of the Sierra was a place—only one of many places—where he could begin to trace the way of Nature. He could stand at the top of Fairview Dome, right at the top of Tuolumne Divide, and watch where the flow had gone.

We can better appreciate Muir's seeming preoccupation with glaciers when we too stand at the top of Fairview Dome or Mount Ritter. Around him the landscape itself seemed to flow: rock, water, and air. "The winds that sweep the jagged peaks assume magnificent proportions, and effect changes of considerable importance," he said. Invisible though they may be now, ancient glaciers have shown how much more powerful this flow could be. Slower than the winds, hidden in darkness, their work attested to the powerful ongoing way of Nature. Here is the real breakthrough Muir had achieved in writing the *Studies*—a cosmic perspective which freed him from the limiting and belittling views suggested by such tame metaphors as the Book of Nature, the Tree of Life, and the Plow of God.[51]

My friend George Sessions has been badgering me to call Muir the Taoist of the West, and there is much to support George's point of view, besides the pleasing vowel sounds. The very writing of the *Studies* suggests Muir's final emergence from a mechanistic to an organic conception of the cosmos. He did not give up fully his mechanistic way of speaking—the cycle of Nature is still compared to a grindstone—but neither did he find this way of speaking superior to the wordless insights he had arrived at by essentially mystical means. Thus he seemed able to balance tenuously—even without resolving them—contrary ways of seeing the Sierra. Maybe Fritjof Capra is right when he says in *The Tao of Physics* that "mystics understand the roots of the Tao but not its branches; scientists understand its branches but not its roots. Science does not need mysticism, and mysticism does not need science; but man needs both." This argument is essentially analogous to Emerson's in the "American Scholar": there is One Man, and One World, and only a Whole Man is capable of perceiving a Whole Nature. If Capra is right, then Muir's own struggle with the *Studies* can be understood as an attempt to see a world which contains and yet transcends opposites that are implicit in the act of human perception. The yin and yang of the world are inseparably joined; a dark period of glaciation is part of the baptism of the landscape into light. The power of the sun became the power of the ice which hid the Sierra from light, killing and creating life at the same time. Glaciers made mountains by tearing them down. All such paradoxes suggest the motto of Neil Bohr's coat of arms: *Contraria Sunt Complementa*. Beyond the metaphors of artist, tool, medium; beyond any flat maplike projection of the Sierra; beyond any mechanistic analysis, there is another way to see the world: all flow and cycle, all paradoxical, and yet whole.[52]

In a sense, the *Studies* was a book Muir needed to write to free himself. It looked back at past ideas and it looked forward to a clearer conception of the world. It was an agony to write and he was always running away from it. It failed to describe the Sierra with perfect justice, yet it began to establish the terms Muir would use when he came to write what he really felt was necessary to a proper understanding of Nature. It was his first and last attempt to write a scientific book, and his suffering over it attested to his discomfort with and final liberation from the conventions of scientific writing. He became aware of the limitations of the language he had inherited, and even while the *Studies* was motivated by his awareness of how poorly others had written of the Sierra, he must have realized that his book failed to do justice to the wholeness of the mountains he loved.

I suppose that the inconsistencies and errors in his own views of Nature were dredged up and objectified in the writing of the *Studies.* I have argued that he was aware of the tension between unsatisfactory metaphors, and that he learned much about himself, about his limitations. In the process of writing an imperfectly coherent book, he discovered cracks in the structure of his thought which do not appear again in his writing. Most important, his attention to flow became the theme of his best writing in the middle seventies; so even while he felt obligated to complete the *Studies,* he was moving in a new direction, was consolidating his energies. These burst forth in the Stormy Sermons.

Dear Mrs. Carr Do behold the King in his glory, King Sequoia. Behold! Behold! seems all I can say. Some time ago I left all for Sequoia: have been & am at his feet fasting & praying for light, for is he not the greatest light in the woods; in the world. Where is such columns of sunshine, tangible, accessible, terrestrialized. Well may I fast, not from bread but from business, bookmaking, duty doing, & other trifles, & great is my reward already for the manly treely sacrifice. What giant truths since coming to gigantea, what magnificent clusters of Sequoic *becauses*. From here I cannot recite you one, for you are down a thousand fathoms deep in dark political quagg, but a burr length less. But I'm in the woods woods woods, & they are in *me-ee-ee*. The King tree & me have sworn eternal love — sworn it without swearing & I've taken the sacrament with Douglass Squirrell drank Sequoia wine, Sequoia blood, & with its rosy purple drops I am writing this woody gospel letter. I never before knew the virtue of Sequoia juice. Seen with sunbeams in it, its color is the most royal of all royal purples. No wonder the Indians instinctively drink it for they know not what. I wish I was so drunk & Sequoical that I could preach the green brown woods to all the juiceless world, descending from this divine wilderness like a John Baptist eating Douglass Squirrels & wild honey or wild anything, crying, Repent for the Kingdom of Sequoia is at hand.

There is balm in these leafy Gileads; pungent burrs & living King-juice for all defrauded civilization; for sick grangers & politicians, no need of Salt rivers sick or successful. Come Suck Sequoia & be saved. Douglass Squirrel is so pervaded with rosin & burr juice his flesh can scarce be eaten even by mountaineers. No wonder he is so charged with magnetism. One of the little lions ran across my feet the other day as I lay resting under a fir & the effect was a thrill like a battery shock, I would eat him no matter how rosiny for the lightening he holds. I wish I could eat wilder things. Think of the grouse with balsam scented crop stored with spruce buds, the wild sheep full

122

of glacier meadow grass, & daisies azure, & the bear burly & brown as Sequoia, eating pine-burrs & wasps stings & all—then think of the soft lighteningless poulice-like pap reeking upon town tables. No wonder cheeks & legs become flabby & fungoid. I wish I were wilder & so bless Sequoia I will be. There is at least a punky spark in my heart & it may blaze in this Autumn gold-fanned by the King. Some of my grandfathers must have been born on a muirland for there is heather in me, & tinctures of bog juices, that send me to Cassiope, & oozing through all my veins impel me unhaltingly through endless glacier meadows seemingly the deeper & danker the better.

See Sequoia aspiring in the upper skies every summit modeled in fine cycloidal curves as if pressed into unseen moulds. Every bole warm in the mellow amber sun how truly godful in mein. I was talking the other day with a dutchess & was struck with the grand bow with which she bade me goodbye & thanked me for the glaciers I gave her but this forenoon King Sequoia bowed to me down in the grove as I stood gazing & the highbred gestures of the lady seemed rude by contrast.

There goes Squirrel Douglass the master spirit of the tree top. It has just occurred to me how his belly is buffy brown, his back silver-gray. Ever since the first Adam of his race saw trees & burrs, his belly has been rubbing upon buff bark, & his back has been combed with silvery needles. Would that some of you wise—terribly wise Social scientists might discover some method of living as true to nature as the buff people of the woods running as free as the winds & waters among the burrs & filbert thickets of these leafy mothery woods.

The sun is set & the star candles are being lighted to show me & Douglass Squirrel to bed therefore my Carr good night. You say, When are You Coming *down*? Ask the Lord—Lord Sequoia.

5

Stormy Sermons

THE LANGUAGE OF VISION

Sometime in the fall of 1870, Jeanne Carr received an amazing letter. Since it was headed "Squirrelville, Sequoia Co., Nut time," and bore no signature, it might have suggested some mysterious origin. But the voice! It was the eternal voice of vision, and indicated that John Muir had entered the timeless season in the soul that one might call Harvest.[1]

He was ecstatic; "I'm in the woods woods woods, & they are in *me-ee-ee*," he sang. He had been saved, healed, and made whole by taking the sacrament of Sequoia with Douglas squirrel. Drunk with Sequoia wine, he considered eating the sacred meat of squirrel, grouse, wild sheep, and bear. By partaking of these wild medicines he hoped to grow wilder, finally "descending from this divine wilderness like a John [the] Baptist," a voice from the wilderness imploring all civilized people to "Repent for the Kingdom of Sequoia is at hand."

He had learned from "Squirrel Douglas, the master spirit of the tree top," that it was possible to live truly in Nature, and had observed that the electric energy of the squirrel came from constantly rubbing against the trees in his own true home. Muir was imbued with bog juices and heather, and so he felt at home in "endless glacier meadows seemingly the deeper & danker the better." No wonder he was loath to descend from the mountain: "You say, When are You Coming *down*?' Ask the Lord — Lord Sequoia."

124

Here was a wild and true voice which revealed the most radical, that is to say the most essential and deeply rooted Muir, pantheistic, ecstatic, and possessed by the cosmic vision. It was the Muir that America needed to hear. Indeed, his letter was written to civilization, not simply to Jeanne Carr. "Behold," said Christ in the Revelation of Saint John the Divine, "I come quickly." "Behold! Behold! seems all I can say," insisted Muir. John of the mountains might become a baptist, but not yet. Muir's allusion to his kinship with the other Johns reflected the ambivalence about his own role in a cosmic drama. Would he, like John the Baptist, "descend from this divine wilderness" and preach the gospel? or would he, like the John of Revelation, write from exile? For the time, in 1870, he wished to remain in exile and send down his letters, which he did with the inestimable help of Jeanne Carr. I call them Stormy Sermons because they embody the true gospel Muir articulated in the early seventies while he lived in the mountains.

In this chapter I will be talking not about his scientific but about his expressive language, the language of his poetry and religion. He spoke two languages because he was advised, by Jeanne Carr and others, that he would have to divide his sensibility if he wanted to publish his views; so he attempted to visualize two different audiences when he wrote, pretending that the reader of a magazine like *Overland Monthly* was himself two different persons. This strategy might have been disastrous to his final goal — the full and whole appreciation of Man's need for Nature — since the distinction between science and spirit would lead to a view of Nature divided into material and spiritual aspects. This he wished to avoid.

He had arrived at his wholeness by essentially mystical means, and felt himself to be a part of a larger cosmic order when he was in the woods, in the mountains. But down in the lowlands men might fail to understand the essential unity of his linked paradoxes. "Destruction is creation," he would intone in the *Studies. Concours discordia rerum:* the triumph of cosmos over chaos would always be his principal theme. He had heard cosmic music, but by the time it reached the cities the symphony sounded chaotic. To use a historical parallel, Plato was hard pressed in the *Symposium* to explain Heraclitus's theory of music; he found it difficult to justify rationally a statement like "The One is united by disunion, like the harmony of the bow and lyre." Such a paradox might be understood by reasoning: "everything happens by strife" is the basis of universal union—as with the bow and the lyre, so with the cosmos—and it is the tension of opposing forces which makes the structure one. Muir's rock and glacier were like the lyre and the bow, and on a more fundamental level the sun, like the fire of Heraclitus, was a permanent motive force for all change. In the woods the Sequoia was a symbol of permanence attesting to the flow, being the one greatest living monument to the sun. This kind of paradoxical thinking was likely to sound a bit intricate and mysterious to any Americans who were not enthusiastic Transcendentalists.[2]

Muir's vision, gathered in earthquakes, floods, wind storms, and blizzards, would sound apocalyptic because it discovered the divine harmony within the strife and justified the good which came out of seemingly evil chaos. Society, however, takes a dim view of storms when they occur here and now. An earthquake in the Bible is one thing, but few hear cosmic music when Mount Saint Helens erupts; the newspapers, full of false gospel, call it a "killer mountain." Men are, under such circumstances, motivated by fear and thus unable to appreciate larger harmonies. President Carter, for instance, is said to have described the landscape that resulted from Mount Saint Helens's activity as making the surface of the moon look like a golf course. Yet Mount Saint Helens is part of the earth; her eruption ought to remind us that the earth is alive. "What the earth does is right," Muir would say. Divine madness? Certainly his father thought so. So Muir found it necessary to argue in terms that Christian people might understand. His text was Nature, but he could use a Biblical text if it would strengthen his argument. Just as his father used 1 Corinthians as an authority for condemning his son's activities in the wilderness, so it was the text to which many of the Biblical allusions in Muir's journals can be traced. It is characteristic that he would turn the gospel marshaled against Nature toward an affirmation of her own supremacy.

When sent a narrative of his son's adventure on the volcanic summit of Mount Shasta, Muir's father wrote bitterly: "I *wished* I had not seen it, because it harried up my feelings so with another of your hair-breadth escapes." Daniel Muir always had misgivings about his son, and importuned early and late that one should do

God's work, be like Paul, and desire to know nothing "save Jesus Christ, and him crucified." Indeed, Paul argues in 1 Corinthians that Man must redeem himself through the Spirit of God, the mind of God, to be known through the mind of Christ. In these latter days one must accept the New Testament, said Muir's father, taking Paul's argument as his model and asking his son to abjure the world: "It is no use to look through a glass darkly when we have the *Gospel* and its *fulfillment,* and when the true practical believer had got the Godhead in fellowship with himself all the time, and reigning in his heart all the time." When the son absorbed and turned the Paulist argument against his father, he simply substituted the Spirit of the Wilderness — the Spirit of Nature — for the Spirit of Christ in the Biblical text. References to 1 Corinthians 2.9 —"But as it is written, Eye hath not seen, nor ear heard, neither have entered into the heart of man, the things which God hath prepared for them that love Him" — abound in the early Yosemite journals, and the mystery to which this passage refers is, in Muir's vision, the testimony that comes from the wilderness. Thus his testament was both old and new; though Man might not know the mind of the Lord, he could know the mind of the Redeemer through natural history. She was Nature.[3]

Just as Paul spoke of "the wisdom of God in a mystery, even the hidden wisdom, which God ordained before the world unto our glory," so Muir appealed to the hidden wisdom being uncovered every day in the flow of Nature. Spirit was but thinly veiled in the mountains. (Heraclitus said, "Nature loves to hide.") Like Paul's, Muir's wisdom was unrecognized by the princes of the world, for if they had recognized it they would not have crucified the Lord of Glory, which is to say they would not destroy Glorious Nature instead of living in her. So the pattern of Paul's thought often informed the structure of Muir's arguments, even while the source of spiritual light was replaced by a living text and testimony. To Muir's "glacial eye" the mystery of Nature became a living truth and could be known by those who were willing to repeat the mystical experience of living *in* the wilderness, as a Christian would live *in* Christ. Here was his radical reason for writing, even for popular magazines. He was a fundamentalist of the wilderness, was radical in the root sense of the word, going to the foundation or source of things — a botanist who insisted that all things must grow from sturdy roots if they were to survive. The roots of the mystery, the roots of the radically enigmatic, were in his mystic experience.

When describing expressive language, Phillip Wheelwright shows that the two ideas, the *mystical* and *mystery*, are "deeply interrelated, but analytically distinguishable." Muir knew that mystical experience — the risky business out in the mountains — was a path to the mystery, while his father preferred the safer and more secure recourse to The Book. Realizing the problems he would face in explicating his radical vision, Muir knew that he would have to do two things well: he would have to recommend his transcendental experience, and then validate it by the mountains. He knew it was not enough for men to go to the wilderness; they had to see truly and live by the laws which Nature exhibited there. If men would live by Nature's gospel, they would have to be rooted in her.[4]

NATURE AND ART

Writing for the public did not come easily for him because he suspected that the understanding of a general audience was limited. He was not even certain that his message could be communicated; after all, the Tao that can be told is not the eternal Tao. An inventory of the sort of audience he might reach suggests his problem. There were his close friends from Wisconsin, like Emily Pelton, an old schoolmate. There were his brothers and sisters, his mother. There were the Carrs, who might find his vision appealing. There were geologists and botanists he met before and after coming to reside in Yosemite: they came for their own scientific purposes, satisfied themselves, and left, unchanged; they were already buttressed by their professional duties and thus not truly free to see. There were the tourists themselves, and Muir had met plenty of them; easterners and westerners, he never distinguished between them. Whatever they were doing while "doing" Yosemite, he knew that it didn't lead to anything like the spiritual rebirth he had in mind. We see them now in the novels of Henry James or William Howells, or in Thorstein Veblen's leisure class. They are not very different from present-day Americans of their class.

Muir's attitude toward this public was ambivalent at best. If his reader would be one of the tourists he had seen in Yosemite, then he held such a person in low regard, as he wrote to Jeanne Carr in May of 1870. For him, the "human stuff" which was "poured into the Valley" was only a "harmless scum" which collected in eddies at saloons and hotels. He was disgusted with its "blank fleshly apathy . . . They climb sprawlingly to their saddles like overgrown frogs pulling themselves up a stream bank through the bent sedges, ride up the Valley with about as much emotion as the horses they ride upon — are comfortable when they have 'done it all' and long for the safety and flatness of their proper homes." This grim view of the American public was not likely to be useful to an aspiring writer. And it was buttressed by a kind of wilderness elitism which assumed that the tourist would remain at the bottom of the Valley. It is echoed by David Brower in his preface to the Sierra Club's *Climber's Guide to Yosemite Valley*. Brower's attitude is as tangled and ambivalent as Muir's, since on the one hand he does not want to "overadvertize how satisfying the cliffs can be," but on the other hand he thinks it unlikely that "any mere book could lure excessive numbers from the throttle and cushion." This is a troublesome rhetorical stance; the writer of the guide invites the public to come and enjoy the wilderness, while undercutting his invitation.[5]

On a purely personal level, Muir did not wish to see more people running around in his wilderness. When he was bothered by the congestion, he simply escaped, as he wrote two months later. "The Valley is full of people, but they do not annoy me. I revolve in pathless places and in higher rocks than *the world* and his ribbony wife can reach." If he wanted to escape, then why write for the public at all? He was not at all sure that he did want to produce what he called "book-sellers' bricks." Even two years later he was still protesting about public taste and language:

I can proclaim to you that moonshine is glorious, and sunshine more glorious, that winds rage, and waters roar, and that in "terrible times" glaciers guttered the mountains with their hard cold snouts. This is about the limit of what I feel capable of doing for the public — the moiling, squirming, fog-breathing public. But for my few friends I can do more because they already know the mountain harmonies and can catch the tones I gather for them, though written in a few harsh and gravelly sentences.

This assertion indicated once again that Muir was unsure of the power of his writing, but feared more the results of its possible success.

He doubted that he could save a vulgar public, and feared that these unenlightened people would invade his realm.[6]

Not only did he distrust his audience; he was also afraid to tell his own sentimental, transcendental dreams, and did not want to include too much of his "special self" in his essays. Yet he could not account for his mystical experiences by showing only the unity and flow of the mountains, as he had in the *Studies*. He had to account for his own spiritual communion with the wilderness. He wrote in his journal, as he returned from San Francisco after finishing the *Studies*, "Winter blows the fog out of our heads. Nature is not a mirror for the moods of the mind." This was the foundation of Muir's belief that Man depended on Nature; Nature was not a projection of human needs, but the creator of a healthy mind. He wanted to blow the fog out of the public consciousness.[7]

Jeanne Carr knew that to accomplish this task Muir must not preach science. Her solution was for him to learn to depict Nature for the public, to study the craft of picturesque writing as he had studied Nature. As early as 1866 she had written, "You are a true lover of Nature. I want to know you, dear friend, many years hence when you shall have a true deep love *for art*, also." She tried to "broaden" his outlook, even while she was working to get his essays published: "Try your pen on some humans too. Get sketches at least. Then you will have to put your scientific convictions into crystalline prose for other uses." Muir did start to pay more attention to matters of artifice, and became less self-conscious, but even two years after the King Sequoia letter he remained reticent. On Christmas of 1872 he confessed, "Book-making frightens me, because it demands so much artificialness and retrograding." He contrasted the clear light of the mountains to the opaque and unsatisfactory state of language:

You tell me that I must be patient and reach out and grope in lexicon granaries for the words I want. But if some loquacious angel were to touch my lips with literary fire, bestowing every word of Webster, I would scarce thank him for the gift, because most of the words of the English language are made of mud, for muddy purposes, while those invented to contain spiritual matter are doubtful and unfixed in capacity and form, as wind-ridden mist-rags.

This complaint is not that of an escapist, but of a serious artist. He was trying to find a strategy which would allow him to write essays that would not be artificial, but would capture the essential flow of Nature.[8]

Some of these pronouncements suggest that Muir was a reluctant prophet indeed. One might account for his attitude toward the public by admitting frankly that the typical tourist is not very attractive in the eyes of the hotel employee, the guide, or the ranger. Muir no doubt suffered from the occupational hazard which affects so many who work in the parks or who wish to live in Nature, but who must deal with the public to make a living. Dealing with the public is fatiguing work, and one tends to become oppressed by the constant repetition and accumulated banality of interaction with a faceless horde. By the 1870s, Muir wasn't affectionate about the human animals he met in the mountains.

But his time in Oakland, where he finished the *Studies* and prepared them for the press, had a lasting effect on him. He did not like urban life, yet gained a certain sympathy for the plight of city-bound people. He came to realize the kind of artifice he would need to influence this audience, though he still wished to keep his personal self out of his writings. He wrote in October of 1874 that he cared "only to entice people to look at Nature's loveliness." In December of the same year he announced at the beginning of a newspaper article on Mount Shasta, "I have seen Montgomery Street, and I know that California is in a hurry, therefore I have no intention of saying anything here concerning the building of this grand fire mountain, nor of the sublime circumference of landscape of which it is the center." He was willing to put aside his interest in geological history in order to accomplish his final goal, to bring men to love Nature. This is the beginning of artifice; it represents a willingness to make certain concessions in order to reach his audience. But one cannot help noticing that Muir's tone had become slightly satirical.[9]

MODERATION

Muir still had little faith that anyone would want to hear his gospel. Even a man like Emerson, for whom he had great expectations, was a terrible disappointment. When the great Transcendentalist visited Yosemite in May of 1871, Muir failed to spirit him away from his eastern entourage. Emerson's friends, to judge by their recollections, thought that Muir was an amusing figure, perhaps slightly laughable. They thought it was absurd that the Sage would want to go camping with a young enthusiast. If Muir hoped that Yosemite would be enough to transform this sophisticated group, he was shocked to discover how little Nature affected them. "I felt lonely, so sure had I been that Emerson of all men would be the quickest to see the mountains and sing them," he said later.[10]

Worse, Emerson suggested that Muir come to New England where he could meet "better people," thus allying himself with other influential people who seemed intent on encouraging Muir to pursue writing by leaving the mountains for civilization. Their message was obvious enough; they wanted to force a civilizing influence on Muir, one that they suspected was badly needed. No wonder he was hesitant to begin a career as a writer. He did not seek a ticket out, an escape from the life he found so satisfying. He did not want to change himself. Rather, he wished to entice others to come to his world.[11]

The knot of his problem is right here. Could he learn to write for popular magazines like *Overland* or *Harper's* without unrooting himself? What we now know — that working in and through a medium, with its own conventions, has a way of shaping the mind of the creator — Muir also suspected. Popular literature and industrial tourism have this in common: they vulgarize the writer and the tour guide as well as the reader and the tourist. Muir was on the brink of a very dangerous abyss, and annihilation here was more likely than it had been when he climbed into the *bergshrund* of Red Mountain's glacier. By falling into the occupation of a popular writer he could endanger the very message he had a sacred mission to convey. He would have to stand astride the abyss between wilderness and civilization and mediate between the vision he had gained in the mountains and the expectations of his readers.

It is no surprise that he struggled with the strategy of mediation in his early essays and had difficulty controlling his tone. He was deeply troubled by the "mist-rags" of language. He seemed to pay painfully close attention to the key terms of other writers, and was equally attentive to his own diction. What becomes clear enough, through comparison, is that Thoreau's language of argument became a model for his own. If Emerson had been the mentor for a young man who had left the family farm, Thoreau was the superior craftsman to whom a serious writer who wanted to say a word for Nature would turn. This choice produced further complications for Muir, as we shall see, since Thoreau's strategy did not lead toward mediation, but toward confrontation. Rather than coax his reader, Thoreau assaulted him. So too, Muir sometimes attacked his civilized reader.

Before a choice of diction or rhetorical strategy, however, came a selection of material. Muir had to select from his journals the kind of experiences which would illustrate effectively several themes. First, he wished to present his view of Nature as Savior—a literal savior, not just a figurative one. All storms recommended themselves as concrete manifestations of a live Nature still about her business of shaping the world. But immediately Muir found it necessary to mediate with his second theme: because civilized men were house-ridden, alienated from Nature, they could not recognize that such phenomena illustrated the orderly flow of natural processes. They would have to be shown. Finally, men who were alienated from Nature could only see her more noble processes after conquering their fear. Even using himself as mediator, he could present only certain moderate experiences to demonstrate his themes.

Writing moderate essays was a serious concession to civilized conventions, especially in view of his condemnation of Ruskin's principle of Moderation in art: "Telling us most solemnly that Nature is never immoderate! and that if he had the power and the paint he would have 'Moderation' brushed in big capitals upon all the doors and lintels of art factories and manufactories of the whole world!! etc., etc." This was not the principle that Muir wished to follow in his own writing. He wished to be as wild and immoderate as Nature. In practice, he had to compromise.[12]

MOVING MOUNTAINS

Glorious as are these rocks and waters arrayed in storm robes, or chanting rejoicing in every-day dress, they are still more glorious when rare weather conditions meet to make them sing.[13]

Weather in the mountains is different from the weather that comes to the lowlands. There is something about the mountains that makes any kind of storm more real. And in winter, the season of weather for the Sierra, the mountains come alive. When Muir spent his third winter in Yosemite in 1871 and 1872, he received much of the reality he loved. A grand flood in mid December was followed by the glorious earthquake in the predawn hours of March 26. The earthquake offered Muir the most profound experience. Apocalyptic imagery indeed! A revelation. Did this earthquake announce the opening of the sixth seal, when "every mountain and island were moving out of their places"?

By the end of that day Muir had begun to write the good news of the earthquake to Emerson, using the occasion to invite the philosopher to come back for a whole summer at least. If Emerson assumed that Muir's tenure in the Valley was a "probation and sequestration in the solitudes and snows" at the end of which he would bring his "ripe fruits so rare and precious into waiting society," the young man answered with his most enthusiastic earthquake-prose. If Emerson spoke for civilization, Muir would respond for wilderness.[14]

An earthquake was an awakening and a revelation: "as the John Baptist angel said squarely, 'I am Gabriel' this storm said I am earthquake & I rumbled out to the open sky shouting 'A noble Earthquake, Noble Earthquake!!'" Muir depicted himself meeting this sublime phenomenon with sublime enthusiasm. Such an experience represented an important test for the student of Nature, and Muir was only briefly troubled by the diction he needed to describe his enlightenment. Mundane terms like "earthquake" or "shock" were clearly unsatisfactory. The tidal movement of the earth could only be described as "waving" and as "fervid passionate throbbings." It was "as if God had touched the mountains with a muscled hand or were wearing them upon him as common bones & flesh." The heavy rumblings? "These are the first spoken words that I have heard direct from the tender bosom of mother earth." The Yosemite was indeed a pantheon for a living god that day.[15]

Muir watched a pinnacle as large as one of the Cathedral Spires come down to the Valley floor. In an avalanche of rock, "firs, oaks, & spruces were snipped like thistles." The mountains moved, and yet so very little was broken — a sure sign that "Yosemite granite is well plumbed & dovetailed." The lesson was clear enough: the mountains were built on a firm foundation. He satirized Whitney's "violent hypothesis" by showing the consequences to the humans who believed that mountains were insubstantial. As in Revelation, men without faith hid themselves. Muir reported their fear and trembling to Emerson: "Vertical animals are mostly in consternation. Two or three have fled." Worse, these degraded humans taught their children to fear: "A little girl of Hutchings cried terror-stricken in the night, 'Grandma! Grandma! Pray to God to Stop it.'" Ignoring the hand of God in Nature, no wonder vertical animals lost their balance; they could not dance to the subtle music. The hand of God never *dropped* anything, but it was not influenced by human fears.

The falls sang unchanged, the frogs were not nervous, the owl continued his song, and when Muir met two violets up by Indian Canyon he stopped to ask them what they thought. Their answer, "It's all love," validated Muir's view by dramatizing the ongoing health of Yosemite. But what if Muir had been wrong and Whitney right? Despite his portrayal of himself as "not in doubt for one moment," another variant of his experience described the hard fist of fear at the pit of his stomach. Dancing under the walls in an earthquake despite his fears required that he fully believe his own theory of Yosemite's creation.[16]

As he wrote to Emerson, his enthusiasm carried him beyond fear. He repeated an invitation: "think how a whole Yosemite year would shine in the middle sky of a life like yours." The two might drift along like winged seeds, bathe in the mountains' light, drink pure mountain winds. Since all men were children of Nature, Muir ended, "I wish you were here this night to be trotted and dumpled on this mountain knee." Here was a perfect answer to the gospel of civilization, but it was not a sermon Muir could write for popular magazines.

Perhaps earthquakes and volcanic eruptions are a perfect test of one's true attitude toward Nature. Earthquake fear has always been a kind of social psychosis in California, perhaps because men do not want to believe that they are subject to powers beyond human control.

Earthquakes suggest a kind of fate, and insist that men are not the lords of creation. The way men speak of "natural catastrophes" indicates their attitude. This expression, born in the fog which enveloped civilized minds, indicated to Muir that cultured language too was born in the fog. Men called earthquakes bad because they harmed humans and human artifacts. When, nearly forty years later, Muir would respond to the San Francisco earthquake in very different terms from the ones he used in 1872, he indicated the extent to which he had become civilized.[17]

To love Nature when she did not please and paid men no mind: this, we might say, was the test of a real faith, and it was this message that George Santayana delivered in California five years after the San Francisco earthquake. He argued, in "The Genteel Tradition in American Philosophy,"

When you transform Nature to your uses, when you experiment with her forces, and reduce them to industrial agents, you cannot feel that nature was made by you or for you, for then these adjustments would have been pre-established. Much less can you feel it when she destroys your labor of years in a momentary spasm. You must feel, rather, that you are an offshoot of her life; one brave little force among her immense forces.

This was very much what Muir wished to say to Emerson, the genteel philosopher, and in addition he wanted to say that humans must transcend the selfish perspective which kept them from hearing harmonies not made for human ears. Santayana said that he had met a Californian who observed that "if philosophers had lived among your mountains their systems would have been different from what they are." Since Muir's message to Emerson was precisely of this kind, it would be nice to think that the Californian had been Muir. But California was not ready, in 1872 or in 1906 — and may still not be ready — for such a view.[18]

GOOD WEATHER

Fortunately Muir could turn to the wonderful outpouring of waters the previous December to develop his favorite stormy themes, using a slightly more moderate vehicle. Though he aptly called his essay

"Jubilee of Waters," *Overland* chose to publish his first contribution under the more prosaic title of "Yosemite Valley in Flood."[19]

Here he was better able to embody the flow of his theme — "destruction is in fact creation" — as he structured his essay around the image of Nature's throbbing heart. The Merced River was an artery, fed from the heart of Nature, and the heart beat in all storms: "Many a joyful stream is born in the Sierras, but not one can sing like the Merced . . . of sublime Yosemite she is the voice." The sound of the storm was the sound of the waters, flowing in the same joyful place, to the listener who was mindful of the deeper harmonies of Nature. In the storm one could hear the throbbing of Nature's loving heartbeat.

Rooted not in Muir's fancy, but in his scientific theory, the vision of Yosemite's watershed as a circulatory system showed that what appeared to be chaotic was in fact an organic phenomenon. The many torrents which streamed over the walls of the Valley became a "countless host of silvery-netted arteries gleaming everywhere!" A scene that would normally be taken as sublime in the full eighteenth-century sense — a war of the elements — became powerfully but lawfully beautiful as he wrote about it. No doubt he had prepared himself by coming to see the same truth in the power of Yosemite Fall.

Two years before, he had struggled to describe the rushing waters of Yosemite Fall without falling into a dualistic or gothic perspective. His journal records that exercise in spiritual and expressive discipline. After attempting to describe the falls as "infuriate waters" which roared, screamed, and hissed like "a perfect hell of conflicting demons," he realized that he spoke "after the manner of men, for there was no look nor syllable of fury among all the songs and gestures of these living waters. No thought of war, no complaining discord, not the faintest breath of confusion. One stupendous unit of light and song perfect and harmonious as any in heaven." Just as the catastrophic mechanism Whitney had proposed to account for the magnitude of Yosemite Valley suggested an illusory chaos and disunity — the bottom falling out — so the view of a flood as a fearful and exceptional event was also an illusion of chaos. In Muir's cosmos there were no singular phenomena. If men spoke of a fifty-year flood, a Jubilee of Waters, what was fifty years to Nature? Such storms merely telescoped geological history, making visible a process, a flow, which was normally too subtle for human eyes. Muir could see in one day what normally took place over many seasons.[20]

He had gained a revelation, not simply a memory, and this experience had remained alive: "Visions like these do not remain with us as mere maps and pictures — flat shadows cast upon our minds, to brighten, at times, when touched by association or will, and fade again from our view, like landscapes in the gloaming. They saturate every fibre of the body and soul, dwelling in us and with us, like holy spirits, through all of our after-deaths and after-lives." Yet even if a flood was a better vehicle than an earthquake for spreading Muir's gospel of Nature, he was still writing with conflicting purposes. He knew that few San Franciscans or "Boston wise" would wander out into the middle of a Yosemite flood to hear the beating heart of Nature.[21]

So he returned to his theme in 1875, writing a more radical argument and confronting the prevailing narrow civilized view of Nature. "Flood-Storm in the Sierra" appeared directly below *Overland's* motto, "Devoted to the Development of the Country," and it argued that men who were too concerned with their own interests ought to be mindful of Nature's. Muir observed the flood of 1875 after spending at least ten months in the Bay Area working on his *Studies*, and he had an increased awareness that he spoke to an audience whose members might appreciate his sentiment only as long as it didn't interfere with their material comfort. Though the flood of 1875 may have been particularly destructive of human artifacts, Muir argued radically that it was unfortunate so few people had enjoyed this noble storm in its home among the mountains, and that "it will doubtlessly be remembered far more for the drifted bridges and houses that chanced to lie in its way than for its own beauty, or for the thousand thousand blessings it brought to the fields and gardens of nature." That *Overland* published this essay suggests that the editors didn't realize how radical it was.[22]

In an early draft of this essay Muir attacked his audience fiercely, saying that the impressions that storms excite in individuals depended "almost exclusively upon the way in which their own small, material immediate interests are affected." He tempered this statement for publication, yet the original expressed his impatience with the limited perspective he found in the "civilized" town where he had witnessed the flood — Knoxville, or Brownsville, as it is now called. This was the home of Emily Pelton, whom he had come to visit, another friend who was concerned that Muir might need the refining influence of civilization.[23]

According to his biographer, he returned to the Pelton home soaking wet, and the homebodies took a pitying attitude toward his suffering in the rain. He replied, "Don't pity me. Pity yourselves. You stay here at home, dry and defrauded of all the glory I have seen. Your souls starve in the midst of abundance!" He had little humor or patience with these people, but when he came to write this sermon for *Overland* he tried to use a more moderate voice, and to speak to civilization using its own terms of gains and losses: "True, some goods were destroyed, and a few rats and people were drowned, and some took cold on the house-tops and died, but the total loss was less than the gain." *Goods* — he could never resist the obvious pun; dry goods one might suppose. Hiding indoors, or climbing onto the tops of houses which were hardly suitable as ships, the people themselves were spoiled dry goods.[24]

It was unavoidable that Muir would attempt this radical strategy, would attempt to shock the reader. Even though his revisions show that he toned down his sermon by focusing through the middle of his text on the beauties of the storm and by arguing that "storms are fine speakers," but "we are poor listeners," still he suspected that only storms which put men out of their houses were loud enough for men to hear: "How terribly downright must seem the utterances of storms and earthquakes to those accustomed to the soft hypocrisies of society. Man's control is being steadily extended over the forces of nature, but it is well, at least for the present, that storms can still make themselves heard through our thickest walls." He hoped to affect the reader as a storm might; his voice would be permeated with the wild wind and torrent. Thus it was contrary to his purposes that he should sympathize with human losses while the gains to Nature were so much more important. Storms were graphic reminders to men, and a necessary therapy for an anthropocentric society.[25]

THE LANGUAGE OF WILDNESS

I suspect that Muir was reading Thoreau even while visiting Emily Pelton. Certainly "Flood-Storm" used the language and strategy of Thoreau's late and most radical essays, like "Walking" (originally entitled "The Wild") and "Wild Apples."

I wish to speak a word for Nature, for absolute freedom and wildness, as contrasted with a freedom and culture merely civil — to regard man as an inhabitant, or a part and parcel of Nature, rather than a member of society. I wish to make an extreme statement, if so I may make an emphatic one, for there are enough champions of civilization: the minister and the school committee and every one of you will take care of that.[26]

So begins "Walking," and this was the tradition of rhetoric which Muir took as his model. If Muir was to be the heir of Thoreau, it was not because of ideology alone, but because he chose the strategy and the voice which could not be assimilated or acculturated. There is something of honesty and something of artifice in an insistence that compromise would violate the purity and integrity of transcendent ideals. If Jeanne Carr wished Muir to learn to love art as well as Nature, then he would study the art of Thoreau.

In the final summing up of "Flood-Storm," Muir alluded heavily to Thoreau and recorded his allegiance to Thoreauvian ideology. He too would follow the ministry of Nature, yet he didn't know how obvious his debt ought to appear; and he had trouble turning Thoreau's language to his own purposes. Muir supposed that we couldn't go to the higher mountains to appreciate wild Nature if we didn't appreciate it at home. This storm, witnessed not in the high mountains but in a town only twenty miles from and two thousand feet above the Central Valley, was a case in point. Knoxville, Muir claimed, was noted for its ministers, but Muir preferred the apple room, a place without human ministers, "a kind of church, free to all, where one may enjoy capital sermons on color, fragrance, and sweetness, with very direct enforcements of their moral and religious correlations." The apple room was part of an old ruined building called the Fox Den, because red foxes were known to "watch and plan concerning the squirrels and quails that feed beneath the trees."

It was a wild place because it had *returned* to the wild state, like the trees in Thoreau's "Wild Apples," which produced fruit that had to be "eaten in *season,* accordingly — that is, out-of-doors." Similarly, Muir's storms could only be absorbed in season, out-of-doors.

Ministers, as representatives of society, warn us against eating the apple, and against becoming too wild. But Muir thought we might return to the same wild Garden of Eden by the same door we used to leave it. His juxtaposition of sublime storm and wild apples tells us much about his attempt to absorb Thoreau's argument and to carry it further into the wilderness, further into the West. When Muir first attempted to conclude his essay he found himself using Thoreau's language:

Civilization needs pure wildness & is beginning to seek it but it is not yet ready to appreciate the best beauties of the lower Sierras, any more than that of storms. Their closely printed scriptures & still small voices, are not heard or seen.

One immediately notices the diction and themes of Thoreau in Muir's draft conclusion. In "Walking," Thoreau carefully defined his term, "wildness":

The West of which I speak is but another name for the Wild; and what I have been preparing to say is, that in Wildness is the preservation of the World. Every tree sends its fibers forth in search of the Wild. The cities import it at any price. . . . From the forest and wilderness come the tonics and barks which brace mankind. . . . I believe in the forest, and in the meadow, and in the night in which the corn grows.

Later in his essay Thoreau argued, "A town is saved, not more by the righteous men in it than by the woods and swamps that surround it." And finally, "The most alive is the wildest."[27]

Indeed, Muir's storm furnished the perfect illustration of Thoreau's thesis. The storm reminded Muir that the land was still alive. "The rain brought out all the colors of the woods with the most delightful freshness." As he sauntered through the dripping forest he saw "the woods were born again." In the final draft of his conclusion, Muir eradicated much of the language of Thoreau as well as the Biblical language, and added a little of his own Scottish, to make it his own.

The world needs the woods, and is beginning to come to them; but it is not yet ready for the fine banks and braes of the lower Sierra, any more than for storms. Tourists make their way through the foot-hill landscapes as if blind to all their best beauty, and like children seek the emphasized mountains.

Muir's lesson was an extension of Thoreau's. You couldn't have trees without the storms which fed them. Muir had drawn the line, the frontier of Man's dominion over Nature, and was making his first tentative stand for the preservation of the wild natural landscape wherever it was found.[28]

WIND FROM THE WILDERNESS

Perhaps the most famous of Muir's Stormy Sermons was published in 1878 in *Scribner's* as "Wind Storm in the Forests of the Yuba." It is a companion to "Flood-Storm in the Sierra." Here, however, Muir only wished to show what might be learned from the wind. "After one has seen pines six feet in diameter bending like grasses before a mountain gale," after one has seen the power and destruction of the north wind, one must remember, said Muir, that "the manifest result of all this wild storm-culture is the glorious perfection we behold; then faith in Nature's forestry is established, and we cease to deplore the violence of her most destructive gales, or of any other storm-implement whatsoever." Sierran forests, "the most beautiful on the face of the earth," were grown and governed by weather. The wind, in Muir's view, culled out the forest, even as a farmer's hand might.[29]

Muir received another, more subtle message from the wind storm. He found that "we all travel the milky way together, trees and men"; trees too make journeys through the world. And "the countless hosts of the forests" heard God's message after the storm; as Muir's essay ended, "the setting sun filled them with amber light, and seemed to say, while they listened, 'My peace I give unto you.'" The setting sun, then, bore Christ's message from the Gospel according to John: "Peace I leave with you, my peace I give unto you: not as the world giveth, give I unto you. Let not your heart be troubled, neither let it be afraid." If Man wanted to hear this blessing given to the trees by wind and sun, then he would have to go to the trees. Christ also said, "I am the true vine, and my father is the husbandsman. Every branch in me that beareth fruit, he purgeth it, that it may bring forth more fruit . . . I am the vine, and ye *are* the branches." Translated into Muir's gospel, the message of the sun is the message of the son, the vine is the complex web of life in the wilderness, and the trees, like men, are really only branches of that vine. Once again Muir argued through his metaphor that the wilderness was a Savior. It did its father's business on earth and man could only be redeemed if he lived in its spirit. This required that a man literally climb the trees.[30]

If woods were the saviors of towns, then pines and spruces were the "best interpreters of the winds." So Muir climbed a Douglas spruce to get the full experience of the storm. Perhaps he was following Thoreau's example. In "Walking," Thoreau had noticed that the thoughts of men, like the forests of New England, were laid waste. "We hug the earth—how rarely we mount!" he said, as he climbed a white pine at whose top he was repaid with far vistas, "new mountains in the horizon." He also discovered the "minute blossoms of the forest" which were too high and too subtle for most men to notice. Muir's winds, like Thoreau's blossoms, were "above men's heads and unobserved by them." Said Muir, "Most people like to look at mountain rivers, and bear them in mind; but few care to look at the winds, though far more beautiful and sublime." Climbing a tree in the midst of a gale was also a test of faith, a necessary risk which led one to the "Aeolian music of its topmost needles." Mind you, the climber chose his tree carefully, for under the circumstances that was a serious matter. But from the lithe bushy top of a young tree, rocking and swirling in wild ecstasy, Muir's outlook became that of the branch, and he finally began to participate in the cosmic as his "eye roved over the piney hills and dales as over fields of waving grain."[31]

A grown man climbing into the branches and spending a day aloft "like a bobolink on a reed"? Child's play, of course. He closed his eyes, absorbed the sounds, until he could hear the different trees talking in their own voices. He smelled the spicy tonic of the wind, steeped with trees. He enjoyed himself thoroughly.

Do we really need to be reminded? I go out of my office and go into the wind. I am in the midst of the trees of our campus. The sounds! The smells! They flow around and through me. It is all right here. What shall I do? Return to my office, under my roof, and write about Muir who tells me to experience this wind? Or shall I climb a noble blue spruce which advertises so well the winds of Utah? I know the answer, yet I return to my office. Muir was a year older than I am when he climbed his tree.

Apparently we need to be reminded. So Yosemite National Park has planted a series of signs along the asphalt trail which leads from Happy Isles to Vernal Fall, telling the walker to stop, look, listen, smell. That is how estranged we are. On a spring day, how many hikers turn back on the Mist Trail above because windblown spray from the falls will bathe them? Perhaps the wonder is, how many hikers do not turn back.

FOUND IN A STORM

There are some storms which test men to the limit of their endurance. If you spend enough time in the mountains you know that sooner or later you will have your turn with this kind of weather. For some, it is enough to survive. For Muir, such an occasion offered new possibilities for expansion of consciousness. Just as he could not resist entering a glacial womb or climbing a tree in a gale, so he could not resist experiencing the stuff out of which glaciers were made — the winter storm. He got his wish on Mount Shasta in November of 1874, and again on the last day of April in 1875. These storms must have seemed to him to betoken the beginning and the end of winter. Laved in snow on both occasions, he sat out the first slightly below timberline after climbing the summit, and in April he met his storm on a summit bivouac. He wrote separately about these excursions in the 1870s, and finally included both in one narrative for *Picturesque California* in 1888.[32]

The two storms were one in his mind; they embraced the snowy months. They suggested the sense of winter that he wanted to experience, a winter perhaps like the one that Thoreau spent at Walden, a deep winter when a man could measure the depth of his soul.

In a hand-written note at the top of a version of one of the essays, Muir reminded himself of the place this experience might take in a future book; the note "Vide Rain Storm on Mount Yuba" places "Snow Storm on Mount Shasta" in the canon of Stormy Sermons. This is the narrative his father read and found so reprehensible. No doubt Muir felt a need to justify this kind of primitive experience to others as well, and the later, more complete versions of his adventure justify the risks by delineating the rewards.[33]

After climbing the summit in November, he made camp below timberline, where he had the company of an occasional Douglas squirrel or mountain sheep. He wrote that he enjoyed this storm-bound position for a week, "lying like a squirrel in a warm, fluffy nest," busying himself with his own affairs "and wishing only to be let alone." Sought by the people of Sisson's resort, who feared that he had perished, he was compelled to return to the lowlands, his winter incomplete. "But the next spring, on the other side of this eventful winter, I saw and felt still more of the Shasta snow. For then it was my fortune to get into the very heart of a storm, and to be held in it for a long time." The spring storm was narrated most carefully for *Harper's* in 1877. Not willing to say that he would deliberately expose himself to the danger of a summit bivouac, he explained that the expedition was ostensibly for the purpose of measuring by barometrical observations the summit of Shasta. Science made him do it? No, the real lesson in altitude was heard from the words of the storm that he met, after the mechanical devices were packed away.[34]

Muir portrayed himself as living through the whole geological history of Shasta while the storm sang. On the summit Muir and his companion, Jerome Fay, were in the very place, at the very time of Shasta's creation, on a patch of volcanic climate at what seemed like the beginning of an ice age. The mountain awakened in the storm. At Shasta's summit, it was as if "the fires of the old volcano were breaking forth again." Muir and his companion felt as if they had "lain castaway beneath all the storms of winter." Thus an overnight bivouac became a geological excursion from the beginning of Shasta's history through its glacial age, dramatized as the men warmed themselves at the hissing fumaroles of the summit, which Muir regarded as "the last feeble expression of that vast volcanic energy that builded the mountain." He could link his own life to that of the dormant volcano: "The ordinary sensations of cold give but faint conceptions of that which comes on after hard exercise, with want of food and sleep, combined with wetness in a high frost wind. Life is then seen to be a mere fire, that now smoulders, now brightens, showing how easily it may be quenched." The night passed like history, slowly, "like a mass of unnumbered and half-forgotten years, in which all our other years and experiences were strangely interblended."

Through the whole mystical night Muir portrayed himself as losing faith in neither the fair play nor the beauty of Nature — unlike Jerome, who, though an equally competent mountaineer, Muir portrayed as lacking certain inner resources. Muir could only comfort him, promising that the next day they would go a-Maying, and "all that would be left of the trying night would be a clump of unrelated memories he would tell his children." These memories would be not unrelated to Muir, who satirized Jerome's wish for a minister; Muir even tried to convert the piteous freezing fellow to the out-of-doors gospel: "The snow fell on us not a whit more harshly than warm rain on the grass," Muir said.

When they trudged down the next morning to "God's country, as Sisson calls the Chaparrel zone," Muir might have asked, "God's country? Then where had we been?" He had described a kind of journey to the underworld at the top of the world. By participating in the fire-and-ice history of Shasta he had learned something about the God of Nature, and embodied much of the lesson in his description of the snow itself. He spoke of its lavishness: "The marvelous lavishness of the snow can be conceived only by mountaineers. The crystal flowers seemed to touch one another and fairly to thicken the blast. This was the blooming time, the summer of the storm, and never before have I seen mountain cloud flowering so profusely." Winter became a strange summer. He contrasted the snowflowers to the bloom of the manzanita on the lower slopes of the mountain. The climbers were laved, washed, baptized in flowers.

This is the final irony of Muir's message. Men appreciate the flowers under their feet, the flowers on the lower flanks of Shasta, but they have great difficulty — as did Muir — appreciating the snow-flowers of May. If the chaparral was God's country, so was the summit of Shasta. If, on the next day, "the storm on the mountaintop vanished like a dream," it was just as real as the life below. There are flowers and there are flowers: all are part of the flow.

"Snow Storm on Mount Shasta," the most extreme of Muir's published Stormy Sermons, is also his purest and most intricate. Born out of his mystical temperament and his scrupulous attention to geological history, it is an elaborate and subtle allegory. In a world of fire and ice, a world which can be understood and appreciated only by the exercise of great discipline, a world which seems to have nothing of humanity in it, Muir found beauty. Yet it was a strangely beautiful world, where the man who sat close to the noxious gases which kept him alive dared not breathe deeply, where a man who wanted to enjoy the snow dared not let himself be drifted over. This was a place where becoming "part and parcel of Nature" entailed great risk.

If the whole adventure was like a dream, Thoreau had concluded *Walden* by comparing our lives to dreams: "The light that puts out our eyes is darkness to us. Only that day dawns to which we are awake. The sun is but a morning star." Only in the storms of the mountains could a man be sure that he had awakened to reality. All below was illusion. This was the gospel of the Stormy Sermons.

THE OUT-OF-DOORS GOSPEL

There may be a certain deception behind my analysis of Muir's Stormy Sermons. A good many of his attitudes come not out of his abstract, or thesis statements, but out of the ironic juxtaposition of concrete details and incidents. Thus in his letter describing the earthquake to Emerson, he did not call the Hutchings bad parents, but simply described the fear in their child. No wonder his friends worried that his writing was too polished, too slippery, too subtle. His subtlety was a consequence of close attention, of his focus on the ideas in things, and the depth of his own meditative temperament. Yet this constant attention to concreteness, which was Muir's single most powerful literary virtue, causes the critic problems when he looks for a theory, philosophical or ecological. As a writer, Muir was more interested in how he saw and in the marvelous radiance of natural objects than in a reified conception of Nature.[35]

Once he realized that his own process of enlightenment embodied the wholeness of his vision, he became more comfortable writing narratives and began to include more of himself. One wonders about the rhetorical power of these essays. Did he expect his reader to emulate him? No, that would turn attention away from Nature and onto the hero of the story. Besides, it is hard to imagine enthusiastic hordes of citizens running through the wilderness, seeking out floods to dance in, climbing trees in wild storms, celebrating earthquakes. There are a few of us, but not many. What seems clearer is that Muir could only expect his readers to recognize the possibility of the wilderness, if they would open themselves up to it. In fact, that comes to be the definition of wilderness as it gradually takes shape in Muir's Stormy Sermons: it is the realm of possible insight. Its meanings are infinite, and since it is all of one piece, every experience partakes of more of it than the explorer can tell. All he can report are isolated visions and how he arrived at them. Perhaps Muir knew, though he never stated it explicitly, that the audience would be satisfied with an awareness that there was someone out there climbing the high mountains and getting their good tidings, that someone was following the ideal life which was not for everybody; perhaps this was what Emerson signified when he added Muir to a list entitled "My Men." A chance for Muir to rejoice in the glorious might be for the uninitiated an occasion for fear, terror, and later sorrow.

Muir himself was not born to the out-of-doors gospel. On his Thousand Mile Walk he guiltily reminded himself that he had promised his mother or friends that he would not lie out-of-doors if he could help it, and then found excuses for doing what his mother would censure. Yet when he did sleep out, he felt anxious and lonely. He needed to enforce the discipline upon himself. Later he wrote in his journal, about the course of his life, "Not like my taking the veil—no solemn abjuration of the world. I only went out for a walk, and finally concluded to stay out till sundown, for going out, I found, was really going in." Such was simply not the case. He was abjuring the world when he went out, and those who cared about him were constantly trying to bring him back in. His condemnation of the "house habit," the "strange dread of pure night air" which he discovered in the Emerson party in 1870, was the result of his many nights spent out in the mountains. He had learned to live in Nature and to see the glory.[36]

Commentators have noticed Muir's abundant use of the word "glorious," a habit which later was an object of criticism by his editor, Robert Underwood Johnson. Yet "glorious" was exactly the term which Muir meant, glory being an Old Testament term signifying God's presence. Muir used the term in very much the same way that Jonathan Edwards, in his *Personal Narrative,* used it to describe the increasing sense of the divine, the appearance of divine glory in every thing. Indeed, Edwards used it in a description of a thunderstorm which became a source of delight: before his senses were altered. Edwards had been terrified, but now he was rejoiced as he "felt God's presence, so to speak at the first appearance of a thunder storm"; like Muir, Edwards would

fix myself in order to view the clouds and see the lightnings play, and hear the majestic and aweful voice of God's thunder, which oftentimes was exceedingly entertaining, leading me to sweet contemplations of my great and glorious God. While thus engaged, it always seemed natural to me to sing, or chant for my meditations; or, to speak my thoughts in soliloquies with a singing voice.

This is a kind of archetypal experience, but one which can be had only by an individual who has begun to know that he is saved, or redeemed. The fear disappears when the faith becomes strong.[37]

There is, however, a notable difference when we return from Edwards's vision to Muir's. Muir did not choose to fix himself in the landscape. In "Wind Storm" he took up the term "saunter," which replaced the word "drift" used in his earlier writing, to describe his own movement through the landscape. He sauntered through the flow, climbed the tree and waved in the storm; he emphasized his own dynamic approach to Nature and the element of thought in his walking. "Saunter" is rooted in Middle English, and means "to muse."

In his Stormy Sermons he was constantly on the move, and well he might have been. His own life during the seventies, when he refused to settle down, consisted of a kind of cycling through the mountains, from the base of the Sierra to the summits and back down to the city, then up into the mountains again; it was a process he recommended to all men. Weak animals that we are, we must be continually reminded of our place in creation, must be cycled through her meditative structure, over and over again.

In this process is our hope for redemption and salvation. Muir took himself seriously, and so shall I. His Stormy Sermons are to be taken quite literally as a gospel. He meant that Nature was the only church where his religion could be practiced. Go indoors on Sunday and listen to the man tell you about the Scriptures? That was absurd. Better to go outdoors and listen to the Scriptures which are plain enough in the sun, wind, waters, earth, plants, and animals. Any book but the Book of Nature is a graven image. Any path but the Pathless Way of the wilderness is a rut which leads downward to Man's fall. And one must wander, saunter, take time for such a transformation.

I suppose I have, for a long time, implicitly accepted Muir's faith, but have been embarrassed to express it in explicit terms as a faith or gospel. What right but that of experience do I have? I remember a moonlit night, the flowing waters, the flowing clouds — but it's Nature I remember, and I believed. There was no *human* voice, only silent assent. I had been taught to expect something less subtle, perhaps a voice in English. If we wish a vision from Nature, we must listen to her voice, hear her language.

The trouble is that Muir's religion is by its very nature a solitary one, in its practice and in its revelations. It may be that there can be no church of the wilderness. Perhaps there can never be more than one worshipper, since two people create a society. Maybe this is a consequence of our Judeo-Christian civilization, but I find it at present inescapable.

6

wwwww

Sacred Animals:
Ecological Consciousness

A standard college textbook on ecology announces that an ecologist is a scientist who studies, models, and manipulates the pattern of relations between organisms and their environment. The same text argues in its concluding chapter that the lessons the ecologist learns become philosophical imperatives if Man is to have any future at all. Other ecologists write that ecology is much more than a scientific discipline: it is a resistance movement, a subversive science. A recent history of ecology argues that the ecologist is a new prophet of science who proposes to mediate between Man and Nature. But there is also something about the "ecology movement" which suggests a religious awakening; it is with this sense in mind that a sociologist has asserted that ecological consciousness, as distinguished from the scientific specialty, is "a radical form of consciousness in contemporary, urban-industrial North America." In other words, the ecologist who only serves the contemporary social structure has not necessarily acquired ecological consciousness. The ecologist who follows the philosophical consequences of his discipline begins with the study of the interrelatedness of things in the world, as Muir did, but ends, if he follows the implications of his perceptions, with a philosophical, religious, and radical attitude toward human culture. While true ecologists may differ over technical issues, they share a similar consciousness and similar values. Theirs may not be a new consciousness, but only a renewed world-view, built on a new foundation. Today the ecologist often wears the clothes of a scientific specialist; he was putting on this costume when Muir was developing his own philosophy in the Sierra. As I have argued, Muir did not dress himself in the austere finery of the scientific specialist because he was not asking society to sanction his role in the wilderness. However, photographs show that his attire did become more conventional over the next two decades as he gradually became a public figure.[1]

In this chapter and the next I follow the evolution of Muir's ecological consciousness, considering it in the nineteenth-century context where it evolved, but also placing it in a more modern context. Like other nineteenth-century ecologists, Muir faced his greatest difficulty when integrating Man into the larger pattern of organism and environment; I shall hold off a full discussion of that problem until next chapter, for first I wish to investigate his interest in the biotic community, or ecosystem, as it is now called. What did he find in this web of life that could form the basis of a new set of human values? How did he attempt to integrate the more obdurate theories of the Darwinists with his own mystical mountain joy, his own pantheistic leanings, and his trust in Nature? This was a necessary task because ecology has been, since its nineteenth-century origin, a Darwinian science in which the relations between organisms and environment have been perceived in terms of the evolution of those relations.

I have been pursuing Muir's studies as if they were purely geological, but from the beginning he was also observing a geographical Nature. Linnaeus, Humboldt, Lyell: the writers on botany, geography, and geology who were powerful influences on Darwin also figured heavily in Muir's education. Further, Muir was engaged in a Sierran study like that which C. Hart Merriam would conduct ten years later in Arizona: geography perceived from an ecological rather than a taxonomic model. Muir observed the communities of life in the Sierra, and sometimes noticed the interpenetration between alpine and lowland plants. He thought about the microclimates of Yosemite Valley, where it was often winter on the south wall and summer on the north wall. Once he had immersed himself in glacial history he was prepared to imagine the flow of life into the Sierra as a succession — lake became meadow and meadow became forest. He began to think of each species as a part of the changing community of organism and environment.[2]

All of these observations were prerequisite to ecological thinking. Yet Muir would not make outstanding contributions to the science of ecology. He continued to write standard taxonomical notes about Alaskan botany, for instance, in the eighties. But in his more popular essays he began to present essentially ecological arguments about the community of the Sierra. These were implicit in the Stormy Sermons, though I have not dwelled upon them. Muir looked at rain pouring off the trees during a flood storm and saw the microcosm of a watershed. In fact, many of his near views constitute ecological visions. Merriam would present a theory of "life zones," as they are called, in an engaging theoretical way, but such an idea was implicit in Muir's view of the communities of the Sierra and in his diagram of concentric zones on Mount Shasta. So I begin with a paradox: Muir was a practitioner of ecological thinking when he wrote about the Sierra in the 1870s, even though he was not a theorizer about ecological themes such as "life zones," "diffusion," "climax communities," "symbiosis," "succession," etc. Muir did not speak ecotalk; his ecology was implicit in his vision and writing.[3]

Perhaps the way he studied was more important than what he saw. His decision to immerse himself in the flow, to soak himself in rain and freeze himself in snow, to become part of the landscape "like a bobolink on a reed"—this method of study guaranteed an ecological perspective. Paul Shepard has argued that the human skin is "not a shell so much as a delicate interpenetration." And ecological thinking takes cognizance of this interpenetration, revealing that "the beauty and complexity of nature are continuous with ourselves." Muir had known this from the beginning of his days in California. He was to be a contributor to ecological consciousness, even if not recognized as an ecological scientist.[4]

DARWINISM

As a serious student of Nature, Muir found the jungle of Darwinian thought in his path. How different it was from the flora and fauna of the Sierra. It is reported that he condemned, as early as 1864, "the dark chilly reasoning that chance and the survival of the fittest accounted for all things." But even Darwin did not like to think of evolution in such dismal terms. During the 1860s almost no American scientist became a pure Darwinian, if there was such a thing. But neither could any scientist avoid the tangled implications of *The Origin of Species.* Muir entered this jungle when he literally walked toward the tropics during his Thousand Mile Walk, but he probably did not start to think about the complexities of accounting for evolution until he came to the Sierra. This is not surprising. Evolution was in the air before the *Origin* was published, and it was probably in Muir's mind before he thought about it.[5]

Just as the process of evolution can be thought of as challenge and response — challenge of the environment met by response of the organism — so the evolution of Muir's thinking can be seen as a response to the challenge of the Darwinian view of Nature and Man. Muir was meeting the challenge of two jungles when he walked through the tropics. His journal was a response to his education, and a response to a wild and seemingly violent biological community. The meditations on these internal and external intellectual forces continued when he reached the Sierra, but became more specific. By 1873, Muir was sometimes thinking in explicitly Darwinian terms.

More important than measuring Muir's adherence to or rejection of Darwinian theory is seeing how he threaded the jungle of implications which he perceived in evolution. One must recognize that he resisted the language of Darwinism, but did not reject evolutionary theory. It is possible for a man to accept an unpleasant thesis when it is restated in more congenial terms. And Muir was not alone in resisting some of the implications of evolution. Certainly the rest of the scientific world had been trying for more than fifty years to avoid the revolution that Darwin would catalyze. The *Origin* precipitated a crisis in the scientific world because it offered a radical and complex scientific theory which questioned the assumptions of science itself.

The main issues raised by Darwin pertained first of all to the processes of Nature. Was biological change the result of a cold law of chance and necessity? This perspective had much in common with the analysis of glacial evolution Muir had written. Did one see "survival of the fittest" as a struggle among individual organisms, or among species? The question had more powerful implications than might at first be obvious. Many Darwinists, for instance, would decide that a struggle was waged in all societies, man against man, or bear against bear — not just men against bears. This was social Darwinism. Was the struggle waged for food only, was it largely economic, or was the struggle territorial, for "niches" in the environment? Or did species struggle against their environment, as Marsh believed men did? Depending on the attitude of the observer, either the most adaptable or the most ferocious species might appear fittest. Or was there no struggle at all? Did the process through which species diverged into a waiting landscape lead to a more varied and numerous family of life on earth?

As a consequence of such questions about process, the direction of evolution began to trouble scientists. Did it have a goal? Was it a means to some higher or better end? Social Darwinists wondered if strife in society was an inescapable law; did it lead to a better society? Was the final goal of Nature that each species would find its "niche" in a stable, rich, self-perpetuating biological realm? Or was the order of things unceasing change? What about Man? Was he the goal of evolution, or just one more species which would one day pass out of existence?

Many of these questions arose from Darwin's own consideration of Man, but other evolutionists could not help focusing on Man, his freedom, his death, his future. Did Man ascend or descend as he evolved? Was he a part of Nature, or dominant over it? Could he hope to control his own evolution in the future? Was he now evolving as an organism, or as a society, or both? These are questions which still bring hot debate from scientists who are supposedly masters of this theoretical realm. Muir could not hope to answer all of them, yet he found himself worrying about these issues because they challenged a faith he did not wish to abandon.

Darwinism seemed to explain the laws within Nature. Muir was certain that such laws did exist, but he suspected that they went deeper than the visible mechanism a scientist might discover or isolate. Muir was sure that the subtle interblending of life and death in the mountains was a "mystery of harmony." Each cause was an effect, because everything had its own inner life and was hitched to everything else. He came to Darwinism already convinced of the wholeness of Nature.[6]

FAITH

There have always been spirits in the American air, and our hidden faith may be pantheism. In the back of our minds — though we have never liked to admit it — in the back of our landscape we have always suspected immanent gods, or at least spirits. At the same time we have always felt an impulse to "unify and thereby sanctify the total natural world, of which we are," as Gregory Bateson puts it. Lately, several writers have been trying to follow mystical American pantheism back to its roots, hoping that this faith may save us if only we will accept and live by its dictates. One might begin this search with the romantic Wordsworth, with "a sense sublime / of something far more deeply interfused," or with the words of Emerson, "The first in time and the first in importance of the influences on the mind . . . the inexplicable continuity of the web of God." Both of these writers saw the spirit of God as a "circular power, returning to itself" as it "rolls through all things." As I have tried to show, this was the view Muir had come to when he finished the *Studies*, though he went deeper into a kind of animism which ascribed consciousness to the rocks themselves.[7]

But it would be a terrible oversimplification to assert that we Americans have always been mystics when we approached the whole and cyclical creation. From the outset we have never fully accepted our own insights. It has frequently seemed to us that we have to choose this faith against the evidence scientists offer. We do not want to appear willful and perverse, or unrealistic. This choice has been a plight particularly of what we call "nature writers." Loren Eiseley dramatized his personal crisis in his essay "The Star Thrower": when he admitted in a whisper to an empty room, "But I *do* love the world," he knew that he had renounced his scientific heritage.[8]

Why would a man fear to love the world? Because he might receive nothing in return, or because it was not worthy of him? Muir wondered in the journal of the *Thousand Mile Walk:* "How little we know as yet of the life of plants — their hopes and fears, pains and enjoyments!" Thus he indicated his trust that plants would be worth knowing and loving. Late in life he wrote unashamedly in his journal, "It is my faith that every flower enjoys the air it breathes. Wordsworth, Professors Wagner, French, and Darwin claim that plants have minds, are conscious of their existence, feel pain and have memories." This surprising statement indicates that he had found a way to reconcile his essentially pantheistic faith with Darwinian theory. Such a divergent group of men, all testifying to Muir's own faith! One wonders at first whether Muir hadn't simply avoided the implications of evolution. I do not believe that was the case. Apparently he had weathered the Darwinian age without losing his mystical certainty. But during the seventies he rarely made such bold statements in public. He knew that he would provoke laughter rather than belief.[9]

A sense of embarrassment attends pronouncements of faith in Nature. In *The Sun Also Rises*, which takes its name and theme from Ecclesiastes, Hemingway's characters fear to be caught "talking rot." Bill Gorton, a nature writer, parodies himself by claiming that he is only a purveyor of stuffed animals. And when he expresses a real pleasure in the mountains, he can only do it jokingly because he is ashamed of being soft-headed. He is deep in a Darwinian crisis:

"Let us not doubt, brother. Let us not pry into holy mysteries of the hencoop with simian fingers. Let us accept on faith and simply say — I want you to join with me in saying — What shall we say brother?" He pointed the drumstick at me and went on. "Let me tell you. We will say, and I for one am proud to say — and I want you to say with me, on your knees brother. Let no man be ashamed to kneel here in the great out-of-doors. Remember the woods were God's first temples."

The reference to the great out-of-doors and God's first temples may allude to Muir's first call for the preservation of the forests. One wonders about poor Bill. Even drunk in the mountains of Spain, with only his close friend Jake to hear, he is embarrassed to admit that he loves Nature.[10]

We may finally have to accept Bill's out-of-doors gospel, though it cannot be justified by the terms we learned at school. Doing so, we may reveal romantic and primitive selves, and may be vulnerable to our skeptical brothers. Have we constructed an elaborate fiction which hides us from the void? If so, it is because we wish to be more human and whole. "The expression of love projected beyond the species boundary by a creature born of Darwinian struggle" — the great paradox of humanity — this is the unexpected yet overwhelming responsibility that Muir, and later Loren Eiseley, accepted and chose to champion. One can call it a biocentric outlook, but it is really a faith.[11]

THE SNAKE IN THE GARDEN

It has never been easy to acquire a biocentric outlook. One thinks of Herman Melville, who was enraptured by the loving kindness of mother whales suckling their young, and who was horrified by the stupid, violent Maldive shark, "pale ravener of horrible meat." He could never decide whether a man needed to reevaluate himself or his vision of Nature. In *The Encantadas*, Melville looked upon the Galapagos and decided that "in no world but a fallen one could such lands exist." Desolate, solitary, unchanging, the world of the Galapagos seemed like the aftermath of a penal conflagration. "Little but reptile life is here found . . . the chief sound of life here is a hiss," he said. In Melville's nightmare, there were many snakes in the Garden of the World, and Man would either have to take dominion or be reduced to a horrible existence in an unredeemed Nature.[12]

Muir said he was "naturally" repelled by alligators and snakes as he wandered into a realm of reptiles in Florida. But he was also sure that these beasts were "beautiful in the eyes of God" and were not mysterious evils. The alligator was present more in his imagination than in person as he walked through the tropics. So when he tried to reconcile himself with this saurian in the Garden he was wrestling with inherited ideas and fears.

While guessing that men were naturally repelled by these creatures, he decided that he would need to transcend his natural limitations if he were to become whole. There was a certain paradox in a man denying his nature so that he could improve his consciousness, but Muir pressed his thoughts toward their limit, celebrating the appetite of alligators: "Honorable representatives of the great saurians of an older creation, may you long enjoy your lillies and rushes, and be blessed now and then with a mouthful of terror-stricken man by way of dainty." He continued to discipline himself by rejecting the anthropocentric point of view and entertaining the alligator-centric and bear-centric. In his journal he sketched an alligator eating a man. "Men and other bipeds were made for bears, and thanks be to God for claws and teeth so long," he prayed in his animal mood. "Why," he asked, "should man value himself as more than a small part of the one great unit of creation?"[13]

Given the post-Civil War South as the context for this journal, the ravenousness of Nature seemed essentially cleaner and more healthy than the profitless slaughter of men. Muir noticed in passing that "Man and other civilized animals are the only creatures that ever become dirty." In point of fact, he had more trouble with humans who preyed on humans — highwaymen, if you will — than he did with natural predators. He was unimpressed with the conversation of southern gentlemen, and noticed the heavy pall which hung over human life in the South, where "fallen parents" like the burned landscape bore "in sad measure the ineffaceable marks of the farthest-reaching and most infernal of all civilized calamities."[14]

Though he could do nothing about this social calamity, Muir could resolve his internal conflicts, his fears of alligators, and re-focus his view of a landscape that seemed "very sickly, entangled, overflowed, and unwalkable." Through conscious effort he forced himself to give up an anthropocentric outlook by the end of his journey. Yet there is something almost miraculous in his transformation as it is written in the journal — an abrupt conversion followed by preachy biocentric conclusions which suggest that he had not fully transcended his early prejudices. Nevertheless, he knew he would have to, and began the readjustment of his consciousness.

Seeing as an alligator might was the end of a process and the beginning of one as well. First he had to detach himself from certain limiting human perspectives. What was for him a sickly environment he knew was edenic for alligators. A man could not walk on water. Man had grown out of the environment where he had evolved, and was not likely to return and conquer it. He had become Nature's jack-of-all-trades, but was still master of none, despite his so-called "divine aspirations." Because Muir knew this when he began to puzzle over evolutionary problems, he would not easily fall into an opinion like Thomas Huxley's: since Nature's world was a Darwinian jungle, Man would have to extend his own ecological transformation, the English Garden, ever outward to replace Nature's realm.[15]

On the title page of a volume in Muir's library, Bancroft's *History of the United States*, one finds the words of Emerson: "Man is fallen — Nature is erect and serves as a differential thermometer, detecting the presence or absence of sentiment in Man." Emerson expressed the need for Man to redeem himself by mystical communion with Nature. But that process might have its limits. Melville carried such mystical communion to absurdity in chapter 36 of *The Confidence Man*, "In which the Cosmopolitan is accosted by a mystic, whereupon ensues pretty much such talk as might be expected." Melville's mystic was Emerson; he spoke about rattlesnakes of a Miltonic species:

"When charmed by the beauty of that viper, did it never occur to you to change personalities with him? to feel what it was to be a snake? to glide unsuspected in the grass? to sting, to kill at a touch; your whole beautiful body one irridescent scabbard of death? In short, did the wish never occur to you to feel yourself exempt from knowledge, and conscience, and revel for a while in care-free, joyous life of a perfectly instinctive, unscrupulous, and irresponsible creature?"

So said the Emersonian mystic. And why not? If one launched into this kind of thinking about Nature, one had to believe in the innocence of lethal snakes. As Melville described it such a mystical stance was passionless and pitiless, and the mystic finally said, "Don't you think, that for a man to pity where nature is pitiless, is a little presuming?" Muir had arrived at the very perspective that Melville parodied. Had he gone too far?[16]

Muir too was troubled to find an appropriate attitude toward rattlesnakes. In 1869 an almost comic episode was recorded in the journal, dramatizing the difference between the theory and practice of a biocentric outlook: "Killed a rattlesnake that was tranquilly sunning himself in coiled ease about a bunch of grass. After dislodging him by throwing dirt, I killed him by jumping upon him, because no stones or sticks were near. He defended himself bravely, and I ought to have been bitten. He was innocent and deserved life." Clearly, Muir wasn't easily charmed by the viper, though in later years he took a live-and-let-live attitude, even writing about a rattlesnake with a "bashful look in his eye." He finally decided to kill snakes only in self-defense, and found that was never necessary since rattlesnakes were eager to get out of the way of men. Late in life he said, "I would rather brave Gila monsters, and rattlers, and wild Indians, and tarantulas than life in the city."[17]

Others found Muir's sympathetic view of snakes and other crawlies to be quaint. Gifford Pinchot noted, "When we came across a tarantula he wouldn't let me kill it. He said it had as much right there as we did." If Pinchot had truly understood what Muir was saying, the history of conservation in America might have been different. But western conservationists saw the eradication of Man's enemies as a duty, and pursued their duty with zeal. A major work on the history of national parks in America uses an anecdote to show Secretary of the Interior Albert Fall proving his stuff as a real westerner: in Yosemite, Fall drew his six-shooter and killed a rattlesnake from horseback. There was no heroism in Fall's shooting, nor was Muir's attitude quaint. If there was a snake in the Garden, it was there for reasons that men were not likely to understand. If men were capable of appreciating Nature they would have to accept, first of all, her own ways, which included alligators, tarantulas, and rattlesnakes.[18]

THE EVIL IN NATURE

How could a man place his trust in Darwin's Nature? What if Nature was not so benevolent as men had always hoped? These questions were sources of tremendous uncertainty. Emerson was very little help because his version of Nature was so much a mirror of the poet's mind. As his colleagues in Concord knew, Emerson frequently saw himself when he looked at Nature. It was no longer possible to believe that things were so simple in the more complex version of the cosmos that Darwin proposed.[19]

Herman Melville had traveled further from Concord than Emerson, and that had only made him less sure of the benevolence of the creation. When he considered the Galapagos he was appalled not only because they suggested a diabolical world, but because they also destroyed his faith in Providence. Years later, he seemed a broken man to his friend Nathaniel Hawthorne.

[He] informed me that he had "pretty much made up his mind to be annihilated"; but still he does not seem to rest . . . until he gets hold of a definite belief. It is strange how he persists — and has persisted ever since I knew him, and probably long before — in wandering to and fro over these deserts, as dismal and monotonous as the sandhills amid which we were sitting. He can neither believe, nor be comfortable in his unbelief; and he is too honest and courageous not to try to do one or the other.

Melville was only one of the doubters. In the 1890s, Stephen Crane satirized a young soldier who "conceived Nature to be a woman with a deep aversion to tragedy." How could a modern enlightened man continue to place his trust in Nature when he could no longer justify that trust?[20]

Joseph Le Conte, Muir's companion at Tenaya Lake, was an enlightened man who influenced the thinking of his age more than might first be imagined. He taught evolutionary theory to Frank Norris, and the result was fiction as evolutionary argument. Le Conte also wrote a book called *Evolution and its Relation to Religious Thought*, which answered the widespread belief that evolution was "synonymous with blank materialism" by proposing that in reality God was operating in Nature "in a more direct way than we have recently been accustomed to think." Yet he did not mean to preach pantheism — that God was "only the soul or animating principle of Nature." He was afraid to give up the belief in a personal, providential God, and was more afraid of the possibility that "God is naught else than an abstraction, created like other abstractions or general ideas wholly by the human mind, and having no objective existence." Because he did not think of himself as either a pantheist or an atheist, he finally insisted on a fundamental antithesis between "spirit and matter, or mind and brain, or God and Nature." He disassociated the two sides of himself, separating the inner, spiritual person from the scientist. The first acted as if God were personal, and the second acted as if God were immanent in Nature, while denying pantheistic implications. Thus he argued that "The only rational view is to accept both immanence and personality, even though we cannot clearly reconcile them, i.e., immanence without pantheism, and personality without anthropomorphism."[21]

No wonder Muir was evasive on the confrontation between pantheistic faith and scientific skepticism. He neither wished to split his consciousness nor deny that there was some organic principle within Nature. Late in life he spoke of evolution in an interview, criticizing the theory if it meant that the harmonious processes of Nature were understood as only "the blind product of an unthinking abstraction." "No, somewhere before evolution was, was an Intelligence," he insisted. "You may call that intelligence what you please; I cannot see why so many people object to call it God." He would not involve himself in a debate about ideas abstracted from Nature; when they were abstracted, they were dead. In the same interview he asserted that creation was not an act, but a process, a process men needed to witness. No amount of theorizing would change the basic issue: men who abstracted themselves from Nature could not reason about her or enjoy her beauty. He told his interviewer, "You say that what I write may bring this beauty to the hearts of those who do not go out to see it. They have no right to it."[22]

Only a man in Nature had a right to meditate on her spiritual blessings, Muir thought. A man like Le Conte, who saw immanence without pantheism, could treat Nature as if she were only material. In such men ecological consciousness had not advanced beyond the theories of George Perkins Marsh. Marsh thought that Man realized himself by rebelling against Nature's commands, and so finally did Le Conte. That was the thesis of Le Conte's last chapter, which related evolution to the problem of evil: "Man also is surrounded on every side with what at first seems to him an evil environment, against which he must struggle or perish. Heat and cold, tempest and flood, volcanoes and earthquakes, savage beasts and still more savage men. What is the remedy—the only conceivable remedy? Knowledge of the laws of Nature, and thereby acquisition of power over Nature." If this was the evolutionary scientist's answer to the Nature Muir had celebrated in his Stormy Sermons, then things had changed very little since Darwin. All the phenomena which proved to Muir that Nature was alive became, in the eyes of Le Conte, only more evidence for Man's need to ascend above Nature into an abstract and empty realm of power.[23]

Men like Marsh and Le Conte pointed the way to a program of "Resource Conservation and Development." Perhaps this was a form of ecological consciousness, but it ran in a shallower stream than Muir's. If Le Conte thought that Man could elevate his plane of life by using rational knowledge to make the laws of Nature his servants, then Muir thought in 1871 that this abstraction from Nature was likely to be disastrous. A case in point involved a dead bear Muir found in Yosemite Valley. Men killed bears because they did not respect God's other children. Men felt that they were above bears, but Muir knew bears were "made of the same dust as we, and breathe the same winds and drink of the same waters." It was evil to kill beings who were part of the same Nature as we. Muir was led by this incident to consider the permanence of Nature and the transitory existence of civilization: "Our tidal civilizations will ebb and flow, we will continue, heaven only knows how long, to choke our minds in moulds of our own making, and discover discord in Earth's simplest harmonies, but God's creation as a whole is unchangeably pure, unfallable, undepravable — one of his own expressions, one thought, one spoken unalterable word." When men perceived evil in Nature, they were simply creating an excuse to follow their own selfish ways.[24]

A BITE FROM THE ANT

Muir was too careful a naturalist to ignore the violence in Nature. He saw the signs which others interpreted as a struggle for existence, but avoided their language when he could. In fact, the phrase and conception "struggle for existence" was a legacy from Lyell, who challenged the Linnaean notion of peaceful coexistence in the plant and animal communities. Like another famous phrase, "survival of the fittest," which can be attributed to Spencer, most of the popular language of evolution was not invented by Darwin. Marsh, for instance, had depicted Man as the imperialistic species who continued to displace other creatures in his march toward dominion. One did not have to be a Darwinian to see a struggle in Nature.[25]

Muir did not think of his excursions in the Sierra as a part of Man's imperialism or as a part of a struggle for existence, but the issues were unavoidable. He worked as a shepherd in the Central Valley and in northern Yosemite, replacing wild animals with sheep. His employer willingly killed bears and coyotes. In the mid 1870s Muir himself recommended Tuolumne Meadows as a campground for tourists; as a result, the bears he wanted men to leave alone would someday be shot, not because they had a taste for sheep, but because they wrecked vacationers' automobiles in their search for food.

Muir wondered about territorial imperialism. Certainly Man was not the first organism to expand its realm and become aggressively yang. The death of many species in the past testified to a passive yin side of natural history. The harmony of this flow could be imagined as incorporating strife, as Heraclitus had conceived: "Opposition brings concord. Out of discord comes the fairest harmonies." Nevertheless, it required some ingenuity to arrive at this point of view. Visualized as a food chain, the harmony of strife may have had its origin in the eighteenth-century metaphor of the "great chain of being." Man might stand at the top of this chain, or pyramid, as it is now visualized. Or he could stand at the bottom of the chain, waiting with an open mouth while all of Nature's concentrated energy flowed into him. Muir tended toward the latter view, imagining that Man was in a sense the sum total of all species that preceded him, and which he now consumed. Contemporary genetic and brain research tends to confirm this view in principle, with some reservations.

Or one might see the opposition among species as a competition for food. In such a case each species would occupy a "niche," so no two species could occupy the same position; one would survive by "competitive exclusion." Muir must have been aware of this phenomenon as he watched his employer's sheep destroy the forage which bear and deer had eaten in the past. He spoke of the bear as king of the forest, but witnessed the regicide Man committed. When a man killed a bear, he was involved in an act of imperialism. He was guilty of the same act when he brought domestic sheep into the meadows of the Sierra. Wild sheep did not naturally compete with deer; only Man's domestic sheep did that, and only because men led them.

I recall skiing high on a plateau in Utah and coming across a domestic sheep in the snow. He was clearly starving, and it was only February. Unlike the deer, he didn't have the sense to walk five miles off the mountain on his own; he had missed the herder's truck five months earlier. What a stupid animal, I thought. And so Muir thought when he herded sheep. Yet it was really Man who usurped the niche which deer occupied. Why should men be angry when a coyote or a bear decided to eat the more easily captured sheep who replaced the deer? There is no safe place in Nature.

All concepts of natural selection that depend on competition for food sources eventually have to face the so-called "Malthusian death struggle," in which "balanced order, according to [Malthus], must rest on the most unfortunate imbalance, created deliberately by God, between population and resources." Muir had trouble facing this prospect in his own life, as bread was often scarce; he refused to see it as a law of Nature. Instead he suggested that scarcity was a problem which obsessed Man more than animals, "although tame men are slow to suspect wild sheep of seeing more than grass." Muir's blindness was great in this regard. He never showed any full understanding of population dynamics, or of the role of predation in stabilizing the relationship between population and food source.[26]

In a passage from *First Summer in the Sierra*, Muir continued a meditation on Nature's violence which had begun when he considered the alligator. Although *First Summer* is an edited and rewritten version of forty-year-old journals, the pattern of his thought in the entry for June 13, 1869 seems characteristic. He considered the struggle in Nature and then chose not to deal with it. Absorbed by the day, he thought that "Life seems neither long nor short . . . This is true freedom, a good practical sort of immortality." So his meditation began as he looked around at herbaceous plants which had "come this far up the mountains from the plains." He was enchanted by the rich seven-foot growth of ferns under Pilot Peak. They reminded him of a tropical forest. At times they even hid the sheep, which is to say that they eradicated his worldly cares. Surrounded by this "fairyland created out of the commonest fern-stuff," Muir began to observe lizards. He admired their "beautiful, innocent eyes," their bright colors, and their "soft, sly ease and grace of a snake." He thought of them as "gentle saurians," descendants of a mighty race, who were as lovable as creatures covered with feathers, hair, or cloth. Perhaps he was reminded of the alligators he had seen in Florida; in any case he began to consider extinct elephants, mastodons, and finally the fierce beasts of the present Sierra. Surprisingly, he was "almost tempted at times to regard a small savage black ant as the master existence of this vast mountain world."[27]

Had the ferociousness of life diminished? Under the surface of his meditation, he seemed to be led almost unconsciously in this direction. The smallest of creatures was the fiercest hunter. Ants, whose bodies were mostly jaws, who attacked without visible cause: they were ubiquitous and inexplicable.

I can't understand the need of their ferocious courage; there seems to be no common sense in it. Sometimes, no doubt, they fight in defense of their homes, but they fight anywhere and always wherever they can find anything to bite. As soon as a vulnerable spot is discovered on man or beast, they stand on their heads and sink their jaws, and though torn limb from limb, so they will yet hold on and die biting deeper. When I contemplate this fierce creature so widely distributed and strongly intrenched, I see that much remains to be done ere the world is brought under the rule of universal peace and love.

So Muir was awakened to reality by the bite of an ant. "A quick electric flame of pain flashes along the outraged nerves." Muir's oceanic mood was shattered. It is reasonable to see a sense of humor here, also a fine sense of irony. One was never so likely to be bitten as when lying in the June sun of the Sierra, dreaming. But there was also a real sense of disenchantment.[28]

In a more serious mood, Muir considered how bears and Indians ate the "tickly acid body" of ants "with keen relish. Thus are the poor biters bitten, like every other biter, big or little, in the world's great family." He was satisfied with this theory of dialectical retribution as he deliberately and abruptly changed the theme of his thinking. He considered "how many mouths Nature has to fill, how many neighbors we have, how little we know about them, and how seldom we get in each other's way!"[29]

He suspected that gratuitous violence was an exception, not a rule, and that it was part of a larger plan which Man did not understand. He finally refused to judge the ethics of Nature in human terms. In his refusal was the personal recognition that seeing "Nature red in tooth and claw" would disrupt his own peace. After all, he began his meditation by claiming that he was satisfied with a "good practical sort of immortality." To think long on death and destruction was also to deface this pleasing, if somewhat dreamy, illusion. I am reminded of Melville's masthead. Muir chose to go through life a dreamer rather than spend his time clutching at the mast. He suspected, in any case, that he had precipitated the violence by invading the ant's realm. An imperialistic animal like Man was constantly intruding on environments which were already satisfactorily occupied, sometimes without even knowing it.

STRUGGLE AND ADAPTATION

Muir was not alone in his blindness to population dynamics. The expanding America of the late ninetenth century was not receptive to Malthus's thesis that population increased faster than food supply. As a result, American Darwinists did not like to emphasize the struggle for an insufficient food supply when they considered the process of natural selection. Writing from his staunch Catastrophist viewpoint in 1877, Clarence King claimed that Darwin's theory was rooted in Uniformitarianism, and that "biology as a whole, denies catastrophism in order to save evolution." King suspected that the law of selection would not be determined by the food supply in a rapidly changing environment, where "the companion law of adaptivity, or the accommodation to circumstances, is one which depends half upon the organism and half upon the environment; half upon the vital interior, and half upon the pressure which environment brings to bear upon it." This law was the basis for "plasticity" as he called it, which determined the ability of an organism to adapt to a changed environment: "Moments of great catastrophe, thus translated into the language of life, become moments of creation, when out of plastic organisms something newer and nobler is called into being." Despite King's insistence on catastrophe, this argument harmonizes with the one Muir had written in the *Studies.* Destruction is in fact creation, and the fittest in Nature's biosystems are those who can adapt.[30]

Similar to John Dewey's idea of flexibility, King's plasticity suggested that the genius of creation lay in adapting the creature to the environment. This did not mean that animals evolved by intelligent need and impulse, as Lamarck had argued. Neither King nor Muir would take that position in the 1870s, even if they sympathized with it. Just as Muir claimed in his King Sequoia letter that the wilderness had transformed him spiritually, so he also claimed that animals had been shaped by their environments. The wonder of Nature was how well-adapted wild animals were in a changing environment.

In a revealing analysis of Darwin's thinking, Donald Worster points out that the great evolutionist slowly committed himself to competition as the law of Nature. There was a second major theme in Darwin's thinking, that of divergence and tolerance, but competitive replacement dominated this theme so much that it was not noticed. If one followed the principle of divergence, one could imagine offspring working out new occupations for themselves, "diverging from their parents and siblings and exploiting untapped resources and habitats." If evolution worked by divergence, it worked toward a constantly increasing diversity of life. And so Darwin's tree of life need not have required that "branches overtop and kill" competing branches. It was possible for him to imagine an open-ended future of a divergent system of life, as long as he ignored Malthus's thesis.[31]

Muir's geographical tree in the *Studies* seemed to suggest just such a process, through which a new landscape was peopled by plants and animals who followed the retreat of the glaciers. Those that adapted found new and appropriate environments. Muir's essays about the inhabitants of the Sierra imply an optimistic view of divergent evolution, perhaps governed by a principle like King's plasticity.

Further, there was the relationship between cause and direction in natural selection. If, as Muir believed, there was a cause which operated "behind" natural selection — some abstract quality not identical with events but disclosed by them; some power or efficacy by which change was produced — if there was such a cause, then there might be direction as well. Lyell wondered about this, and Asa Gray carried on a correspondence with Darwin which one commentator calls "frankly theological." Gray could not give up a heartfelt belief in design, and even though Darwin admitted to being inclined in that direction, he concluded that "the whole subject is too profound for the human intellect. . . . Let each man hope and believe what he can." As Muir admitted in his interview, he chose with Gray to believe that a final cause ruled behind natural selection, and he had no problem calling it God.[32]

BIRDS AND SQUIRRELS

But Muir was not ready to enter the realm of abstract speculation in 1873 when he prioritized his program of writing. He was going to write about the creation of the Sierran landscape and its metamorphoses from canyons to lakes, to meadows, and finally to forests. And he also thought that he would write some portraits of "Birds, bears, etc." As it turned out, the portraits of animals and birds would win him an audience, and much more. They would be instruments he would use to discuss the superiority of Nature's breeding program; but they would also gain sympathy for his own plan to reintroduce Man into Nature. He would use great care in writing, making sure that scientists would not attack his observations as inaccurate or fanciful.[33]

His animal portraits have one continuous theme: each species is perfectly adapted to its own environment. So the animals and birds act as guides for human visitors. Muir had favorite, perhaps totemic animals. His three most famous portraits — of the water ouzel, the Douglas squirrel, and the mountain sheep — dramatized the perfectly adapted life in three major ecological communities of the Sierra: the river canyons, the forests, and the alpine heights. He considered writing about bears and coyotes as well, but did not in the 1870s. Clearly he did not want to confront the issue of predation, or deal with the violent aspects of Nature in his public utterances. His animals were wild, but peaceable.

By 1873 he knew what he would say about the water ouzel. He would describe its life as "an echo of the mountain streams." One could find no such "complete compliance to glacial conditions in the life of any other mountain bird, or animal of any kind." Muir believed that the flights of these birds, if charted, "would indicate the direction of the flow of the entire system of ancient glaciers." Their ability to ascend the flowing canyons had allowed them to disperse throughout the Sierra. As for their origin, Muir fancied that "The Humming-Bird of the California Water-Falls" was a spontaneous creation: "Ouzels seem so completely part and parcel of the streams they inhabit, they scarce suggest any other origin than the streams themselves; and one might almost be pardoned in fancying they come direct from the living waters like flowers from the ground." A careful naturalist knew better, of course, and found the nests where birds lived and reproduced, but "our ouzel, born on the brink of a stream, seldom leaves it for a moment."[34]

The ouzel was a model of adaptation. He was bothered neither by cold nor wet. He could fly under water as well as through the air. And he always sang, though his song was sometimes indistinguishable from the song of the cataracts. Unlike the "frost-pinched sparrows, on cold mornings," the ouzel never seemed pitiable to Muir, "not because he is strong to endure, but rather because he seems to live a charmed life beyond the reach of every influence that makes endurance necessary." No doubt there were severe tests in the life of the ouzel, but Muir could see no sign of them. Thus the ouzel was a living answer to those who viewed all of Nature as struggle. He offered Man a spiritual lesson about adaptation and divergence in Nature.

For similar reasons, the Douglas squirrel was one of Muir's favorites, the wildest animal he had ever seen, birdlike, "this bright chip of nature,— this brave little voice crying in the wilderness." The squirrel entertained Muir endlessly, but was "far too self-reliant and warlike ever to be taken for a darling." Although Muir could not analyze the familial relationships among the Douglas and other squirrels, and admitted that he did not know for sure what evolutionary forces had acted upon them, the result was the largest and most beautiful of the furry foresters.[35]

Douglas squirrel seemed created on the spot and "enduring as the trees," since he was master forester and played a significant role in Nature's economy. He was like a "condensed . . . piece of sun-fire" because he lived on his harvest from the sun-filled trees. Muir thought he handled half of the cones ripened in the Sierra. Since many of the seeds Douglas hid germinated and became trees, he was planter and harvester. Muir contrasted this naturally symbiotic relationship between animal and tree with the coarser relationship of men and trees. Men chopped down evergreens for their seeds, or stole from the stores of Douglas. Men became pitchy in the process, unlike Douglas, who was a clean eater and a bright spirit. So Muir's squirrel cast a shadow on Man's more solemn pretentions as tree farmer. Douglas fled when Muir whistled a solemn hymn.

Here then were two simple lessons for men. The ouzel and the squirrel were the master spirits of the waters and woods of the Sierra. In harmony, living parts of their communities, they were the evolutionist's version of the mythical Ariel and Caliban. They were spirits in the wilderness, but not mysterious. Muir realized the meanings of their lives one day when he walked to the canyon of the Tuolumne. "How blessed it would be to be banished to the Canyon!" he wrote. "There are many witches, say the Indians of Yosemite. Blessed witches! Even banishment to the lonely tundras of Siberia would be a blessing to many."[36]

WILD SHEEP AND TAME MEN

The wild mountain sheep provided the best example for Muir's theory about the adaptability of wild animals in Nature. He pursued his study of these inaccessible and "noblest of animal mountaineers" in the Sierra and around Mount Shasta. But when he began to write about them he entered a controversy which had been flowing west since 1860, when Asa Gray reviewed *The Origin of Species* for *Atlantic.* By 1868 the Darwinian issue had followed the railroad as far as Antelope Station, Nebraska, and it became a major part of what one historian calls the rediscovery of the West by the scientists. O.C. Marsh had identified in Nebraska the fossil bones of *Protohippus,* a primitive horse; he published his findings in 1874, and Darwin acknowledged that Marsh's paper "constituted the best support for evolution appearing in the two decades following *The Origin of Species.*" Marsh reconstructed the genealogy of the horse from fossil bones; but Muir had a different method of study and a different purpose in writing; he wanted to say a word for living evolution in Nature by celebrating the living inhabitants of the wilderness.[37]

Muir's "Wild Sheep of California" was convincing evidence that he was no ignorant shepherd. He conducted a serious investigation into the evolution of sheep, and praised Nature's breeding techniques. One of his chief claims to authority echoes that of the *Studies.* He had lived in the alpine world of the mountain sheep and had observed the inhabitants in their homes. He was familiar with their environment, but perhaps it was more important that he had some idea of the pleasures of their lives.[38]

Nevertheless, he began his essay with a survey of research, and reviewed the theories of Cuvier and Darwin on the origin of wild sheep. He asked whether all sheep came originally from the same species and adapted to different environments, or whether they were of different origin. He gave a careful physical description of the Sierran sheep, and used Audubon's data on the Rocky Mountain sheep. He could play the scientific game as well as anyone, but his attitude became crystal clear when he compared the wild sheep to the domestic variety: "The domestic sheep is expressionless, like a round bundle of something only half alive; the wild is elegant as a deer, and every muscle glows with life. The tame is timid; the wild is bold. The tame is always ruffled and soiled; the wild is trim and clean as the flowers of its pasture." This is the distinction he had made so many times between dirty men and clean wild animals. He knew why he didn't like tame sheep or tame men; now he could counterpoint his attitude with a careful and accurate portrait of one of Nature's best products.[39]

Man's domestic product inherited Man's problems, while wild sheep were "more guileless and approachable than any of their tame kindred." This would seem a paradox until the reader realized that wild sheep represented conditions before the Fall. Muir admired their muscular beauty and watched them "scaling cliffs for pleasure." He sympathized with them because they were so beautifully suited to their mountain environment, but "anxiety to observe accurately on so rare an opportunity checked enthusiasm." When he described them, they appeared as flowing parts of Nature. He marked the "flowing undulations of their firm-braided limbs; their strong straight legs, . . . their graceful rounded necks, the upsweeping cycloidal curve of their noble horns." Their image was remarkably similar to the hardly veiled fictional Muir in Thérèsa Yelverton's novel,

Zanita: "a lithe figure . . . skipping over the rough boulders, poising with the balance of an athlete, or skirting a shelf of rock with the cautious activity of a goat, never losing for a moment the rhythmic motion of his flexible form." He had much in common with these sheep, but he did not intend to write a heroic self-portrait. The sheep were the heroes of his mountains.[40]

Nature's hand was open to her mountaineers. They chose their meals from alpine gardens, relishing spicy leaves and shoots for "both their taste and beauty." As Muir described the conditions of their lives, he was attacking the narrow Darwinism which saw Nature as only a process of consumption and survival. When he said "tame men are slow to suspect wild sheep of seeing more than grass," he was making the same point that Henry James would later insist upon: that the "modern deification of survival *per se* . . . with the denial of substantive excellence in *what* survives . . . is surely the strangest intellectual stopping place ever proposed by one man to another." Men had been seeing their animal neighbors through the dark lens of a doctrine which blinded them to the higher qualities of life in both Nature and themselves. Muir's portrait may have been anthropomorphic, but at least it did not suggest the vulgar and simplified version of evolution that deified survival for its own sake.[41]

He was pleased to discover the "strong self-reliance and noble individuality of nature's sheep," and "exulted in the boundless sufficiency of wild nature displayed in their invention, construction, and keeping." Unlike domestic sheep, of which each one was "only a fraction of an animal," wild sheep were "capable of a separate existence." They seemed to have few enemies. Even Man, "the unsatisfiable enemy of all nature," could not reach them because, "like stars and angels, they dwell mostly above his reach in the sky." This was such a close echo of his attitude toward himself and society in the early 1870s that one recognizes a dual meaning in his conclusion.[42]

When he reminded his readers of the many wild animals Man had driven to extinction, Muir hoped that "all lovers of wilderness life will rejoice with me in the rocky security of *Ovis montana,* the bravest mountaineer of the Sierra." He was arguing that wilderness life was the reality of a mountain sheep and a possibility for Man. Humans would have to return to Nature if they wished to continue their own evolution. Otherwise they would become domestic animals like their own sheep, for whom survival per se was the highest value.

THE USES OF WILD WOOL

Muir was not done with the subject of wild sheep. A year later he wrote "Wild Wool," probably the best ecological argument of his career. Its subtle and intricate strategy was the result of serious wrestling with Darwinian issues, as the heavily revised manuscript shows. The theme of the essay, stated squarely in its middle, had been foremost in Muir's consciousness for nearly ten years: "No dogma taught by the present civilization seems to form so insuperable an obstacle in the way of a right understanding of the relations which culture sustains to wildness as that which regards the world as made especially for the uses of man." Now he could begin to discuss this issue in Darwinian terms, and his early draft shows that he carefully integrated his own view of Nature as flow with hard-headed Darwinian theory.[43]

When he attempted to account for the combination of hair and wool on the hide of a wild sheep, he found himself swept into cosmic issues. He wrote in an early draft: "The entire universe is in a state of change — flowing like a river. The circumstances of a sheep's life — food, climate, the mountains over which it roams, its friends, & enemies, etc., change imperceptibly from generation to generation & from day to day; & so of course Mother Nature must ever have her fingers in wild wool making corresponding changes in the maintenance of perfect harmony." As he considered evolutionary change in a uniformly evolving environment, he realized the extent of Man's ignorance: "Most of the world will always be wild, the sky is — so is the sea and the . . . kingdom of crystals beneath the mass surface of the ground. Not one in a thousand of the family . . . are ever seen by men & innumerable animals enjoyed life and became extinct before present greedy man came into existence." He removed these passages from his final draft. These were not to be the issues he discussed, but they indicate the kind of thinking that lay behind his argument.[44]

Between the writing of "Wild Sheep of California" and "Wild

Wool," he had not only watched men hunt mountain sheep at Mount Shasta, he had also spent nearly a year in San Francisco. He had gathered valuable experience writing for the *San Francisco Bulletin*, and tested his ideas on a number of educated urban folk. He was prepared to write about the relationship between Nature and civilization. In particular, he was ready to attack the pastoral ideal, Man's desire to turn earth's household into a farmyard, to substitute domestic animals for Nature's own.

Domestic sheep, after all, were created by Man and represented his best attempt at artificial evolution. What a sorry thing a domestic sheep was when compared to the original article, Muir thought. Apparently men were in great danger when they cast their lot with the work of their own hands. If the quantity of wool on a domestic sheep was more important than the quality, if the different qualities of life represented by domestic and wild sheep were ignored, then Muir suspected that men were defrauding themselves. He would write an argument that cut through social Darwinist issues straight to the center of Man's true relationship to Nature. What men did reflected upon themselves, and in the end they were creating themselves when they meddled with Nature. If a domestic sheep was any indication, Man's work had been degrading for himself and his charges.

Darwin praised sheep breeders in *The Origin of Species* — "what English breeders have actually effected is proved by the enormous prices given for animals with a good pedigree"— but this was hardly Muir's criterion of worth. The highest pedigree would always be owned by the wildest animal. Nevertheless, Muir used a Darwinian argument when he put a value on Nature's ability to create and maintain the attributes needed in a changing environment. Doing so, he followed many of Agassiz's students on the path away from their first master. Agassiz had insisted to the end that "wild species remain, so far as we have been able to discover, entirely unchanged — maintained, it is true, in their integrity by the circumstances established for their support, but never altered by them." Thus Agassiz and all pre-Darwinian thinkers could not show the value of Nature to Man's agriculture. Muir could. The secret of successful agriculture would be the principles of adaptation, which scientists understood only in very general terms. Men would need to preserve the vast unspoiled realm of Nature and study the laws exhibited there.[45]

"Wildness," Muir would conclude, was the "one great want, both of men and sheep." That meant that any "higher culture" should be concerned with the production of high-quality men and animals. This was very close to the argument Henry George presented in "Our Land and Land Policy." The influence of George on Muir has interested critics because John Swett, one of Muir's closest friends during this period, was also a close friend of George and helped edit *Progress and Poverty.* George believed that men were "children of the soil," and he attempted to remind his fellow Californians that simple dominion over or ownership of the soil, did not constitute wealth. Out of this soil, George felt, "our greatest product is a crop of men." Muir agreed with George about the goals of agriculture, though he took a different view of the means to those ends. They both doubted that a "gross national product" was a worthy goal for a culture. Men needed to grow from Nature, not aspire toward independence from it. They needed to recognize that quality, not quantity, was the hallmark of a fine culture.[46]

Muir was aware of the modern consciousness which held that the world might not be made for men, but men could use it anyway. He would try to answer this godless argument, and to meet the resource-conservation-and-development consciousness on its own ground. He would write a kind of Socratic dialogue between himself —"the wild man" of his first draft—and his friend, "a man of grass and fruit." In this way he could expose the "enormous conceit" that his friend's dogma represented. "Wild Wool" was an unusual essay for Muir since it was a human drama about human values. A man spoke of his conflicts with other men. It was also a humorous piece, filled with Thoreauvian puns.

Muir's opening lines called into question the possibility that men might "improve" or "redeem" Nature: "Moral improvers have calls to preach. I have a friend who has a call to plow, and woe to the daisy sod or azalea thicket that falls under the savage redemption of his keen steel shares." At first Muir thought he would make this passage more obvious by giving his friend a "divine call to plow" and by saying that the "old man devotes all his days to the destruction of the fine wilderness of his mountain home." Later he decided to characterize this anthropocentric activity as "reclamation" and "subjugation." "Not content with the so-called subjugation of every terrestrial bog, rock, and moorland, he would fain discover some method of reclamation applicable to the ocean and the sky." Because Nature was already claimed and needed no improving, Muir assumed the role of a preacher who wanted to redeem men and improve society. His language bristled with ironies. "Keen steel shares" were hardly a suitable tool for a man who wanted to share Nature's bounty, and "moorland" contained a pun on Muir's name. The zealous farmer might have been a sodbuster, like Muir's own father, who had wandered from place to place, establishing a farm and then selling it. The farmer's philosophy was simple: "Culture is an orchard apple; Nature is a crab."[47]

Men who suspected "in the manufactures of Nature something essentially coarse" were limited by their own lack of finer senses. This had been the message of Thoreau's "Wild Apples" and "Natural History of Massachusetts." Only the godlike among men might appreciate the ambrosial qualities of wild fruit, and "a deeper and finer experience" of Nature was the true aim of science. So the wild wool came into Muir's dialogue. "Wild wool is finer than tame," he said, "finer than the average grades of cultivated wool." Such a discovery was the result of Muir's wilder senses.[48]

The quality of Nature's product could be considered in terms of use "because fine wool is appreciable by everybody alike." When Muir's friend responded that a wild sheep was deficient in quantity of wool, Muir could respond that wild wool wasn't made for socks, but for the sheep who wore it. "I have never yet happened upon a trace of evidence that seemed to show that any one animal was ever made for another as much as it was made for itself," he insisted. Wild species were designed to take care of themselves, unlike orchard apples and domestic sheep. We all know what happened to the domestic varieties when they were abandoned; nature "would throw the one to her caterpillars, the other to her wolves."

Were it not for the exercise of individualizing cares on the part of Nature, the universe would be felted together like a fleece of tame wool. But we are governed more than we know, and most when we are wildest. Plants, animals, and stars are all kept in place, bridled along appointed ways, *with* one another, and *through the midst* of one another — killing and being killed, eating and being eaten, in harmonious proportions and quantities. And it is right that we should thus reciprocally make use of one another, rob, cook, and consume, to the utmost of our healthy abilities and desires. Stars attract one another as they are able, and harmony results. Wild lambs eat as many wild flowers as they can find or desire, and men and wolves eat the lambs to just the same extent.[49]

This was the pattern of use created by Nature, and it was a better plan than the one Man substituted when he created plants as bland and stupid as an orchard apple and a domestic sheep.

In his final draft, Muir suppressed the image of himself as wild man. He chose instead to be a Thoreauvian scientist, counting the hairs on a sheep, and demonstrating the seriousness of his research by its fineness. Consequently he ended up playing a civilized role, not arguing against Man's uses of Nature but only that Nature's plan contained a better pattern of use and a better pattern of value. As for human culture, "we should be careful not to ascribe to such culture any improving qualities upon those on whom it is brought to bear." It would be better to reconsider the quality of wild life and to make a "new departure."

Here was a utilitarian argument that the twentieth-century ecologist would begin to use insistently. The wilderness was a place where natural processes continued to function unimpaired. Wild areas and wild life would always be important to Man as standards and as sources of virgin stock for "fresh starts." Without wildness, the quality of life on earth would continue to decline until it was hopelessly "felted together."

SACRED ANIMALS AND THE STRIFE IN NATURE

"Wild Wool" is such a well-written and ingenious argument that one tends to forget that it is hardly a complete statement of Muir's response to wildlife. In trying to create an effective argument he had omitted much of his own vision. What had happened to his essentially sacred bond to animals? Is it possible that the man who spoke of eating the sacred meat of Douglas squirrels, grouse, mountain sheep, and bears, who wrote of beasts and birds filled with essences of Sequoia lightening, of spruce buds, meadow grass, daisies, pine burrs, and wasps—is it possible that this man did not recognize the full animism of his own vision?

His way of understanding animals followed an essentially sacred path toward ecological vision. He studied wild sheep and squirrels as Eskimos studied the wolf, yet he failed to recognize the kinship of his own thinking with that of the Indians he met. As reasoned and rational as his rhetoric might have appeared in "Wild Wool," his unstated allegiance was to the sacred animal—other, whole, complete, and part of its own world.

One wonders about the portraits of animals he didn't write in the seventies. If he did write about the alligators, bears, and coyotes, he did not publish his work. In the John Muir Papers there is one page of a manuscript about Coyote, in which Muir began to sing the praise of this favorite. He never published the essay, though he once promised to send his thoughts on "poor persecuted, twice damned Coyote" to Jeanne Carr. Perhaps the climate of opinion about predators was so extreme that he dared not raise his voice, fearing to produce an effect opposite to the one he intended. Perhaps America was not ready for a discussion of sacred animals in 1875. Muir kept his peace through those years, and when he did begin to write about animals in his last years, the results were disappointing.[50]

I think there is something deeply and seriously flawed in Muir's own vision. His sheep, squirrels, and deer were all herbivores, and dainty feeders at that. He preferred for himself to eat only bread in the mountains. He seemed essentially frightened of looking too closely into the hunter in Nature or the hunter in himself. He believed that meat soiled. Indeed, he did not want to think of any struggle in Nature at all. He even seemed put off by the appearance of the Sierran juniper, which reminded him, with its rocklike rigidity and fortitude, that life was tenuous on the granite slabs above Tenaya Lake. Somehow he missed the jewel in a whorl of twisting weathered branches, shaggy bark, and bristling foliage. In other words, he was unable to look fully at the struggle or the pattern of eater and eaten which he commended to his reader in "Wild Wool."

Let us consider the strife in Nature. This summer, without consciously looking for it, I have seen several striking incidents, many right outside the door of McCauley cabin. I watched a red-shafted flicker chase and attack a weasel as it ran down the hill through the talus. If that wasn't enough, the weasel had problems with men who interfered with its hunting. I have seen conflicts between juncos and ground squirrels. Down at the river, the gulls were constantly raiding the nests of the Brewer's blackbirds, and the blackbirds were constantly harassing the gulls. Trying as that was, the river rose high this July, flooding and submerging the willows where the Brewer's blackbirds built their nests; the birds were very distressed during the flood. I remember how unexpected and surprising it was when a Clark's nutcracker killed a mole while I sat under a tree a few yards away. One day near Wawona I watched a coyote carrying a new fawn at a run through the woods, followed by a doe. If a deer can be imagined as forlorn, then that doe was. But of course the coyote too had a family. Now I know that one is not supposed to think in terms of individuals when practicing ecological consciousness, but all of these examples were, as I say, unlooked for. When Muir avoided talking about such incidents, he indicated something about his own predispositions.

7

‖‖‖‖‖‖‖

Sacred Groves:
Man in the Woods

THE EATERS

Perhaps the greatest problem with American defini-
tions of ecology, and consequently with American definitions of wilderness, has been finding Man's place in the landscape. Muir shared
this problem, and we need to examine his own life in the wilderness
to appreciate the origin of his incomplete analysis of Man's life in
Nature.

When he traveled in the Sierra, Muir never lived off the land.
Since he wasn't a hunter or fisherman, he was frequently hungry.
But when he considered the men who were hunters, he was disgusted.
A constant refrain in his journal was, "Man seems to be the only
animal whose food soils him." Though he was right that "meat of
any kind is hard to carry, and makes a repulsive mess when jamm-
ed in a pack," that was not his real objection. He found the need
for meat a "depraved appetite" and an indication of Man's lack of
true independence. If someone wanted milk or butter in the
wilderness, Muir said that person was "never weaned." His journal
suggests that he was influenced strongly by Thoreau's view of Man
as a gross feeder when in a larval state. In "Higher Laws" Henry
asked, "Is it not a reproach that man is a carnivorous animal?"[1]

Muir did not grow beans in Yosemite, nor did he eat pine nuts
as did the Douglas squirrel. He did not learn from the Indians how

to eat acorns. Nor, apparently, did others; there was a minor controversy in 1869 when Galen Clark, Yosemite Guardian, tried to keep Yosemite Indians from cutting branches off oaks, which was their way of gathering acorns in early fall. The Indians could not understand why Americans could cut down large numbers of oaks for their ranches, but natives could not remove a few branches from their own trees. Muir ate bread made from wheat, the wheat a product of the monoculture which eradicated the gardens of the Central Valley. At one time he asked Jeanne Carr about the possibility of obtaining concentrated bread and meat; he thought he might be able to carry a whole year's supply with him and purchase total independence in this way. In more than practical terms this was a false hope, and indicates how little Muir was either a hunter or a gatherer.[2]

He sought to avoid the violence in Nature by doing no violence himself. This was a serious concern for him and explained why he would not kill his meat. But it was a strangely unexamined issue. What was the difference between the bear who raided beehives and killed sheep, and the man who did the same? Unlike Thoreau, who admitted feeling a strange thrill of savage delight when he was tempted to seize a woodchuck and devour it raw, Muir either did not feel that thrill, or repressed it. In *Walden* Thoreau spoke of an essential tension in the human soul between the savage primitive and the spiritual instincts; he could only say, "I love the wild not less than the good." He knew wildness included the passion of the hunt.

Muir's wildness too included the lure of hunting, but he was not able to accept it as an appropriate or necessary part of himself. In 1874 he observed a hunt for wild sheep near Mount Shasta, and was surprised that he who had "never killed any mountain life, felt like a wolf chasing the flying flock." He tried to explain this "ferocity" in evolutionary terms: "We little know how much wildness there is in us. Only a few generations separate us from our grandfathers that were savage as wolves. This is the secret of our love for the hunt. Savageness is natural, civilization is strained and unnatural. It required centuries to tame men as we find them, but if turned loose they would return to killing and bloody barbarism in as many years." His language revealed a major contradiction in his own thinking. If he was pleased by the savageness of alligators who lived by their natural inclinations, then why would he praise men who de-

nied this savageness in themselves, becoming unnaturally tame or
Christian? Elsewhere "tame" was an epithet he used to describe dull
and disoriented animals. But his language became tangled when he
spoke of hunting because he did not examine closely the anthropomorphic assumptions about predator and prey that he had inherited.[3]

He was never aware of the significant bond forged between
hunter and hunted, when a man became a part of the flow of energy
in Nature. When it came to man's hunting, he could not see that
the predator was not savage or ferocious and the prey not sweet
or docile. He did not recognize the alertness, the sharpening of the
senses that someone like Ortega y Gasset found admirable in primitive hunters. For Muir, hunting simply had "no religion in it." Just
as he never talked about sexual reproduction, so he chose to ignore
the meaning of this essential and perhaps mystical activity of man.
His alertness was redirected. Where the primitive man focused much
of his consciousness into the process of keeping body and soul together, Muir hoped to be free of social and economic duties so he
could seek purely spiritual truth. He was a geologist, botanist, mountaineer, and to the extent that he pursued those activities in a single-
minded way he became a specialist, an example of the split between
primitive and spiritual approaches to Nature which Roderick Nash
sees at the root of American attitudes toward wilderness.[4]

Muir's lack of insight into violence was simply a Victorian trait,
according to one commentator. Perhaps it was this lack of insight
which kept Muir from ascending to the "tower beyond tragedy," as
did Jeffers. Part of Muir's blindness resulted from his lack of interest
in hunting. On the other hand, it may have been an interest in hunting that made Aldo Leopold aware of the role of predators in ecological communities. Despite frequent contact with Indian culture,
Muir did not think about hunting as an enlightening activity. After
he went to Alaska in 1879 he began to show more interest in the
Indian's view of Nature, but not much. His first encounters suggested
that "the wild Indian power of escaping observation, even where
there is little or no cover to hide in, was probably slowly acquired
in hard hunting and fighting lessons while trying to approach game."
He admired this art of the primitive, which was "vaguely called instinct," but he did not cultivate it himself by using the means of
the Indians.[5]

WILD MEN AND TAME

One would suppose that Muir's essential philosophical differences with speakers for civilization like Marsh and Le Conte would have sharpened his attitude toward Indians. Both Marsh and Le Conte believed that "savages," as they called them, were a part of wild Nature and so should be conquered by Lord Man, who had risen above them. Muir seems to have accepted this view, even though it conflicted with his larger philosophical assumptions. If Muir believed that wild animals deserved an undisturbed, happy, harmonious life in Nature, and further that they were necessary to civilization, then why did he not speak of Native American cultures as wild cultures, as essential resources for civilization? Just as he tried to learn something about living in the wilderness from animals who had adapted, so he might have learned from the primitive cultures of North America. Such an attempt to learn has been pursued by Gary Snyder; if one wants a more scientific scholar, the geographer Carl Sauer has argued that civilization needs to understand the ways so-called primitives found to live in the world by adapting to its rules. As Thoreau said, "The Natural History of Man is yet to be written."[6]

Muir criticized the civilized men who hid from Nature in their houses, but rarely seemed to understand that primitive societies living close to the changing conditions of their environment came to respect those conditions. Perhaps Muir's personal experience with Indians was limited to the observation of decaying or degraded cultures. The state of anthropology in the 1870s, when Muir formed his own attitudes, had not approached the kind of cultural relativism it has now achieved, so Muir's reading could have helped him little. One doesn't have to be sentimental about this issue or talk of "noble savages"; but one must notice with surprise that Muir didn't look seriously at the possibilities of life suggested by Native American ways. The Old Ways, as Gary Snyder calls them, are not really very old at all, in the context of the natural history of man.

In purely practical terms, even if Muir had wanted to introduce the Indian culture as heroic he would have faced great difficulty in breaking the stereotyped usage of "savage," "wild," and "degraded" as synonyms for "Indian." Such language was part and parcel of the consciousness Muir wanted to change, and indicated the fear that colored so much of the Victorian attitude toward wilderness. Yet he had experienced fear of Indians himself as he grew up in Wisconsin.

If one compares Darwin's portrait of the inhabitants of Tierra del Fuego with Muir's portraits of the Sierran Indians, one sees the consequence of this Victorian fear. Both were appalled by the appearance of natives, Darwin to the point of repulsion, and Muir not quite so far. "Perhaps if I knew them better, I should like them better. The worst thing about them is their uncleanness," Muir said in *First Summer*. For Darwin, physical appearance indicated a difference between savage and civilized men which was greater than the difference between wild and domestic animals. For Muir, filthiness was shared by sheepmen, lumbermen, and all who took their living from Nature. Their spiritual alienation could be measured by their dirtiness. Thus he may have felt that Indians were more like white men than they were different; all were degraded by their economic lives.[7]

Both writers had difficulty identifying Indians as individuals. In *The Voyage of the Beagle*, Darwin attributed the plight of "miserable degraded savages"—the Fuegans—partly to their social condition. He thought they were too equal, too communistic, too sharing ever to improve themselves. He argued that "perfect equality among individuals composing the Fuegan tribes must for a long time retard their civilization." Similarly, Muir imparted more individuality, self-reliance, and personality to the animals he portrayed than to men of any kind. Only humans he *wished* to learn from had any reality to him.[8]

Beneath the issue of individuality was a key question for evolutionists about the influence of environment on men. Darwin guessed that Nature circumscribed the Fuegan's aspirations toward nobility when she placed him in a degrading natural environment. However, Muir's world was never the "miserable country" that Darwin described, so he would be hard pressed to explain why Californian Indians had not been ennobled by their surroundings. Indeed, he argued consistently that Man was redeemed by spiritual commerce with Nature. Did he believe that only an educated man like himself was capable of absorbing the spiritual wealth of California, as did a typical California intellectual, David Starr Jordan? If he did, then he wasn't fully convinced that Man should be come part and parcel of Nature, and he may have let the concept he called "Lord Man" influence the direction of his thought. Darwin, for instance, had not denigrated the human abilities of the Fuegans; when he looked at their sooty faces he believed that they were men who could not or did not improve themselves. For Darwin, Le Conte, or Marsh, Lord Man was not simply a biological species. He was the result of socialization, cultural progress, and civilization which fostered individuality. Lord Man was the animal who chose to take dominion. Men who could not take dominion might be despised, as Darwin despised the Fuegans. Men who chose not to take dominion might be seen as frivolous, hedonistic, or worthless. Muir sometimes described himself as a tramp. But was he serious? David Starr Jordan grouped Digger Indians with hobos, pointing out that the latter seemed even less able to absorb anything from the scenery and climate of California than the former. From the perspective of Palo Alto, an Indian was not a man because he did not improve his condition. This was the very issue Muir had struggled with in "Wild Wool." Wasn't it enough for any species to live in harmony with Nature?[9]

Muir wanted civilized Man to improve his spiritual condition by immersing himself in the flow, not by transcending it. Was that even possible? He had occasional intimations that Indians expressed a spiritual communion with the mountain spirit. Listening to their death chants in the Sierra one night, "the wild wailing came with indescribable impressiveness through the still dark woods." He imagined that "falling boulders and rushing streams and wind tones caught from rock and tree were in it." He was entranced, and "wondered that so much of mountain nature should well out from such a source." Yet several months later he wrote of the defeated Modocs in the stereotyped language of the time. He spoke of them as "panthers," "unsavory," and "not very amiable looking people." If he was repulsed by wild Indians, he was also disappointed when he met an Indian who had become a shepherd and lost his wildness.[10]

Muir chose not to see poetry in the Indian soul, and that was at least consistent with his view of most men. He wrote to one friend in Oakland: "I don't agree with you in saying that in all human minds there is poetry. Man, as he came from the hand of his maker was poetic in both mind and body, but the gross heathenism of Civilization has generally destroyed nature, and poetry, in all that is spiritual. I am tempted at times to adopt the Calvinistic doctrine of total depravity." This was the sort of reasoning which failed to reach any clarification.[11]

An anthropologist might point out that the Native American had more leisure, more time for contemplation and meditation, than the representative of European culture who chased him off the continent. Thoreau thought that civilized Man might become a "more experienced and wiser savage," unless he foolishly "employed the greater part of his life in obtaining gross necessaries and comforts merely." Man might become more philosophical to the extent that he simplified his life. Yet Marsh had argued a position diametrically opposed to Thoreau's: the moral weakness of natives in the southern climes was the result of the *ease* by which they got their living. Muir was not sure whether a man was better off if he was underdeveloped or overdeveloped. He observed the Europeans who came to the Sierra for the Gold Rush and compared them with the Indians who had long wandered in the mountains.[12]

Patrick Delaney, Muir's employer during the First Summer, had come to California for gold, but had been worn down by that harsh period. His character had been sculpted, but in the end the overtaxing and frenetic industry had eroded his character and caused him "to become a gentle shepherd, and to literally lie down with the lamb." This man had been overdeveloped to the point of exhaustion. Muir contrasted his character and countenance with that of the Mono Indians he saw during the same summer. Their faces seemed "mostly ugly, and some altogether hideous," but the problem was superficial and might be remedied by washing. Unlike the abraded character of his employer, the Monos seemed "as if they had laid castaway on the mountains for ages." They were underdeveloped men. Upon his first encounter, Muir thought of them as "dirt-specks in the landscape," and was glad to see them fade out of sight. Later, however, he saw them in their own home, gathering wild rye by Mono Lake. He couldn't help catching the humanity of the scene, the women "coming through the rye." He thought "their incessant laugh and chatter expressed their heedless joy." He realized they were youthful and hopeful people, unlike the European Americans who had been worn out by excess industry. He concluded his thoughts about the Mono Indians and their world in 1874 by stating simply,

"I never believed the doctrine of deserts, whether applied to mountains or men."[13]

When he reconsidered the doctrine of deserts in 1888, he knew more about Indians from his travels in Alaska. The Mono Indians had acquired an infamous reputation among whites because they ate with relish the larvae of flies that bred on Mono Lake. Muir observed that they also ate a caterpillar which grew on the yellow pines on the south shore of the lake. They gathered caterpillars and pine nuts, thus acquiring meat and bread from the same tree. For the Indian, the "gray, ashy wilderness" was "a paradise full of all the good things in life." Muir had apparently developed this perspective by conversing with an Indian who worked in Yosemite Valley as a hotel servant. In the Valley the Indian "enjoyed all the white man's good things in abundance," but nevertheless vacationed every year in the Mono desert. The Indian explained his taste, and drew "a picture of royal abundance that from his point of view surpassed everything else the world had to offer."[14]

This is the most suggestive of Muir's writings on Indians. That an Indian would go to Mono Lake for a vacation from a resort hotel in Yosemite was a fine irony indeed. And the man's view of the desert as paradise was also suggestive. But Muir never pursued this insight, and in fact eliminated the passage from the revised version of the essay that appeared in *The Mountains of California.* It is hard for me to understand. Did he get unfavorable comments about his description of the Indian's diet? Did he decide that Americans were incapable of acquiring a sense of place from Native Americans? Did he think that there was no point in trying to fight the American fear and hatred of "savages"? For whatever reason, Muir never managed to integrate completely the figure of Native Man into his ecological vision of the American wilderness, though he mourned the passing of Alaskan cultures in the newspaper articles collected as *Cruise of the Corwin.*

Even the Wilderness Act indicates that in wilderness "man is a visitor and does not remain." Since the Indian has always been more than a visitor to the American continent, legislators had to draw a line between "European man" and "indigenous cultures." In this symbolic act they separated white Americans from a true and complete relationship with wilderness lands. It was a practical and perhaps politically necessary distinction, but was also the result of a history filled with prejudice and ignorance. The Wilderness Act is certainly not a document meant to further a deeper understanding of Man's relationship with the earth. As long as we continue to pretend that wilderness represents the *illusion* that a man is alone, we will not get to the heart of the matter. The only long-term solution to our problem of preserving wilderness will come when we have learned how Man can be more than a visitor, without destroying the earth. Perhaps it is too late.[15]

So I end this section of my meditation with a paradox. Despite his desire to see Man as a part of Nature, Muir's actual view of Man's effects on Nature was predicated on the thesis Marsh had argued in the previous decade: Man was a disturber of Nature's harmonies. When Muir decided to perceive Man as either a visitor or an abuser of the earth, he was forced into the dualistic perspective characteristic of many nineteenth-century ecologists. It was but a short step to his perception of only two alternative human activities in the wilderness — tourism or resource development. Perhaps this perception was a result of his own style of mountain travel. Since he never attempted to live self-sufficiently in the mountains, he never investigated seriously the possibility of a harmonious economic existence in Nature. In the late 1870s, when he began to be mentioned more frequently in the newspapers, he was called John Muir the Geologist, or John Muir of San Francisco. His own link to civilization and the city had been forged, even while he was wandering in the mountains.

ECOLOGICAL CONSCIENCE

A harmonious relation to land is more intricate and of more consequence to civilization, than the historians of progress seem to realize. Civilization is not, as they often assume, the enslavement of a stable and constant earth. It is the state of *mutual and interdependent cooperation* between human animals, other animals, plants, and soils, which may be disrupted at any moment by the failure of any of them.
Aldo Leopold, "The Conservative Ethic"

Aldo Leopold was heir to the kind of thinking Muir established in the mid 1870s.[16] Certainly Leopold was more knowledgeable than Muir about many aspects of the ecological community in American forests, and he thought long and hard about the significant relationship between predator and prey. Leopold had the advantages of more than sixty years of research by ecologists. And he knew in addition that the discipline of forestry as practiced in Europe did not offer the hope of restoring forests to their primeval wholeness, as Muir had hoped it would in the 1870s. But Leopold followed the spirit Muir had begun to articulate. When he concluded his essay on "The Conservation Ethic" by saying that "the stampede is an attribute of animals interested solely in grass," he was echoing language and attitudes Muir had expressed nearly sixty years earlier. What could one expect of tame men "who are slow to suspect wild sheep of seeing more than grass?"[17]

The stampede had been going on for nearly thirty years in the West when Muir witnessed it. At first Americans stampeded for gold and silver, but by the mid 1870s they were destroying the forests of the Sierra at an amazing rate. Muir had argued well that Man's attempt to redeem Nature for his own uses was doomed to failure, but men in the woods did not seem to be involved in any kind of moral quest. They were not farmers, but rapists, and if they attempted to justify themselves, they scarcely covered their greed with the rationalization that Nature's day was over in any case.

When he began to write about the forests, and the Sequoia forests in particular, Muir attempted to demonstrate that Nature's realm was self-perpetuating and worth protecting. Men needed forests for water, lumber, and more. Their health depended on the well-being of an entire community of life. Muir's thinking about Sierran forests began with theories Marsh had argued, but also included themes which would be worked out in theoretical detail during the next twenty years by men like C. Hart Merriam, Frederic Clements, and Eugenius Warming. Muir was creating an ecological model of the Sierran forests at least fifteen years before such models were introduced to scientific theory in the 1890s, yet he has rarely been recognized as a pioneer ecologist because he spoke of forests in such personal terms. When he saw the impending destruction of the Sierran forests and meadows, it was a personal tragedy for him. This is the nature of ecological conscience.[18]

Late in the seventies Muir dramatized the kind of conversion he had undergone when he discovered that his own sacred places were be-

ing desecrated. It was a surprisingly personal revelation. Shadow
Lake, now called Washburn Lake, had been his own special "High
Altar." He secluded himself in its basin many times, and wandered
into the Clark Range from there, notably when he made his first
excursion into the glacial womb. This was probably the place where
he dedicated himself to baptizing "all of mine in the beauty of God's
mountains." When he returned from meditations one day late in
the fall of 1874, he wrote to Jeanne Carr, "I care to live only to entice people to look at Nature's loveliness. My own special self is
nothing."[19]

For years he had reserved Shadow Lake as his own retreat, keeping it a secret, an "unlooked for treasure that is bound up and hidden away in the depths of the alpine solitudes of the Sierra." He
had hoarded its beauty as Indians before him had saved its sacred
hunting grounds for times of hunger. They knew that "hunting in
this lake-hollow is like hunting in a fenced park," and respected its
special status. Muir had assumed that he could protect this sacred
place by keeping his silence. He had "told the beauty of Shadow
Lake only to a few friends, fearing it might come to be trampled
and improved like Yosemite." But on one visit he discovered new
tracks, and after an excursion to the higher mountains he returned
to find his worst fears realized: "all the gardens and meadow were
destroyed by a horde of hoofed locusts, as if swept by a fire. The
money-changers were in the temple."[20]

He had been afraid of the tourist's trail, and by his silence had
allowed the stampede of sheep. So he learned that it would not be
possible to hide in or escape into the wilderness for long. If a place
were to remain sacred, it would have to be sanctified by the society
of men who threatened it. Even while Muir was attempting to show
how well Nature's economy worked, men were ransacking her realm
indiscriminately. He needed to find a powerful social means to fight
this tide of destruction.

The problem must have preyed on his conscience while he stayed
at the Swett home in San Francisco and nursed the frozen feet he
had acquired on Shasta in April of 1875. Living with John Swett,
he came in contact with serious talk about California's most pressing social problem, land monopoly. As his biographer says, Muir
was "awakened to the monstrous evils that would have to be sub-

dued if the forest and the water resources were to be conserved."
He may have read in college Spencer's *Principles of Biology*, with
its implicit social Darwinism. But he was exposed to a more hu-
manitarian view of social relations by his acquaintances in San Francisco. Certainly from this date he began to condemn in print the
changes men were making in the forests. He began to argue that
sheepmen, cattlemen, and lumbermen were appropriating the land
for their own uses with no goal except a fast profit. He began to
document the new wave of destructive civilization which was breaking over the Sierra, perhaps like the Gold Rush.[21]

THINKING LIKE A FOREST

He had visited the southern Sierra in the summer of 1873, following the Kings River Canyon and climbing Mount Whitney. Several
months after he had written "Wild Wool" he returned to this area
with an altogether different perspective. On his first return he guided
a couple of men through the region and led them to the summit of
Mount Whitney. During this excursion he began to use his influence with the *San Francisco Bulletin*, sending letters that documented
the destruction of the forests and meadows. He met woodsmen who
were proud of felling a giant Sequoia. He read a notice posted by
"land grabbers" who claimed the valley of the South Fork of the Kings
River for raising stock. He advised his readers to "visit the valley
at once while it remains in primeval order." He announced that "all
the destructible beauty of this remote Yosemite is doomed to perish
like that of its neighbors, and our tame law-loving citizens plant
and water their garden daisies without concern wholly unconscious
of loss." But this was only the beginning of his rhetoric. He now
knew that he would have to make rapid progress in his own writing
if he were even to keep up with the destruction that was going on
in the Sierra.[22]

He feared most for the Sequoias, and set out again in September to inventory the groves. He was alone. It was typical of him
that he would accumulate the necessary data first—though not slowly
this time—and present a careful analysis of the actual condition of
the Sierran forests; then he would call for reform. He knew what

he wanted to say, but he wanted to make a substantial and unimpeachable statement.

Asa Gray had addressed the American Association for the Advancement of Science on "Sequoia and its History" after visiting the Sierra in the summer of 1872. Gray thought of the trees as pre-Tertiary, a remnant of an older botanical era. He said that they were probably dying out, since he saw few young trees and noted that the groves he visited were small. He compared them to the redwood, and concluded that they would not be wiped out as rapidly as the redwood, which was "too good to live long." Muir wished to re-evaluate not only Gray's scientific thesis, but also his fatalistic attitude about the future of Californian forests. He would revise Gray's assessment of the Sequoia's history, but would be more deeply troubled by the social assumptions Gray had made.[23]

It is no wonder that Muir was deeply troubled about the relationship society would bear to wilderness in the future. His friends in San Francisco were worried about the inequalities within society, but they did not consider the impact of progress on Nature, or the final result of even moderate economic development. Henry George, for instance, believed that competition was the necessary means by which economic life led toward social progress, even if he was not an extreme social Darwinist like William Sumner. Muir was tempted to accept this historical necessity too.[24]

As he traversed the rich forests of the Sierra, he looked at the trees and wondered about Man's future. He wrote copiously in his journal: "Will he cut down all the trees to make ships and houses? If so, what will be the final and far upshot? Will human destructions like those of Nature — fire and flood and avalanche — work out a higher good, a finer beauty? Will a better civilization come in accord with obvious nature, and all this wild beauty be set to human poetry and song? . . . What is the human part of the mountains' destiny?" Was Man's role in the evolution of the North American continent to be destructive? Was this all part of the Plan? Muir had listened to the arguments of the social Darwinists, and entered a dark night of the soul. His journal seems to express the pure archetype of tragedy, as described by Northrop Frye: "The sunset, autumn, and death phase. Myths of fall, of the dying god, of violent death and sacrifice and the isolation of the hero." It was a long climb out of those canyons of despair, just as it was a long climb out of the many canyons he traversed between Sequoia groves as he headed south. He heard "a sound of ah-ing in the woods."[25]

It is a sound I have heard in late fall, once when walking in Yosemite Valley among trees marked to be cut so a new wing could be built on the Yosemite lodge. My friend Dennis rescued me from despair that day. But Muir was alone and rescued himself by finding the magic. "Where the crowns of five or six trees come together is the spot for a camp bed," he wrote. As he began to feel once again a part of the flow, he asked about the uses of the woods. Were they made for healing and consolation? No, he realized, "the woods are made for the wise and strong. In their very essence they are the counterpart of man." They represented perfectly the freedom civilized man vaguely remembered.

The forest buried her own in peace, while "we read our Bibles and remain fearful and uncomfortable amid Nature's loving destructions, her beautiful deaths." "In contemplating some lovely grove, I have wondered how if this dead stump or white mast were removed, would it be bettered. But I never could see room for even such paltry improvement. . . . Pollution, defilement, squalor are words that never would have been created had man lived conformably to Nature." Even the death of trees by fire seemed surpassingly beautiful. "Sequoia fire is more beautiful in color than that of any other species I ever noticed"; in his journal he wrote of "old prostrate trunks glowing like red-hot bars . . . rills of violet fire running up the furrows swiftly, lighting huge torches flaming overhead two hundred feet, on tops of pillars dried and fractured by lightening strokes. . . . Smoke fragrant like incense." He witnessed the death of gods. Sequoia fire was the same stuff from which Buddha's Fire Sermon was made. If it was set by human hand, though, it was more deplorable than the torching of fine buildings, for these forests were "majestic living temples, the grandest of Gothic cathedrals."

He passed a lumber mill which moaned "like a bad ghost," and observed the natural death of Sequoias. Struck by lightning, "being very brash," a tree "breaks up like blasted granite." Felled by men, the Sequoia broke like glass. The most enduring of Nature's living creations was too fragile to withstand Man. Pausing from his botanical studies, Muir thought of "the weary in soul and limb, toilers in town and plain, dying for what these grand old woods can give."

Our crude civilization engenders a multitude of wants, and lawgivers are ever at their wits' end devising. The hall and the theater and the church have been invented, and compulsory education. Why not add compulsory recreation? . . . Our forefathers forged chains of duty and habit, which bind us notwithstanding our boasted freedom, and we ourselves in desperation add link to link, groaning and making medicinal laws for relief. Yet few think of pure rest or of the healing power of Nature.[26]

Compulsory recreation was a way to save the trees and men as well. "Of all the upness accessible to mortals, there is no upness comparable to the mountains." He regained his vision and was ready to write his argument.

LIFE IN THE FOREST

Muir was like the strolling Indian in *Walden*; he had woven a basket of delicate texture in his journal, but he had to consider how he would sell it. He would have to unravel the strands of his experience and offer parts of them to three different audiences. His argument about Sequoia forests appeared in three different publications, but was essentially one.

He sent "God's First Temples. How Shall We Preserve Our Forests?" to the *Sacramento Record-Union*. Because it was aimed at Californian legislators, it was practical-minded and emphasized the value of forests as watershed. Muir's argument was based almost entirely on the theories of George Perkins Marsh, though he considered the particular history and ecology of the Sierra. He tried to appeal to the self-interest of Californians who would be appalled to discover that they were losing an important economic resource, and who would be ashamed to admit that they were not keeping up with the Europeans in practicing efficient, economic forestry. He talked about wasteful lumbering methods and the great ravages of fires, ninety percent of which he attributed to sheepmen who wanted to "improve" pasturage.[27]

"On the Post-Glacial History of Sequoia Gigantea" was published by the American Association for the Advancement of Science, and contained a more sophisticated analysis of the ecological condition of the Sequoia forest. Muir spoke of the ecological integrity of the climax forest of the Western Sierra, using the same Darwinian language he had tried in a letter to the *Bulletin*: "Species develop and die like individuals, animals as well as plants; and man, at once the noblest and most conceited species on the globe, will surely become extinct as the mastadon or sequoia. But unless destroyed by man sequoia is in no immediate danger of extinction." He was reexamining Gray's assertions of 1872 that the Sequoia was an archaic species and that Man would of necessity destroy it.[28]

Muir wrote "New Sequoia Forests of California" for *Harper's*, trying to appeal to the sentiments of an eastern audience. This may have indicated a change in his strategy, since he was turning away from the western utilitarian consciousness and addressing eastern aesthetic sensibilities. He was asking for federal intervention, probably because he knew that the state government could not or would not act. In *Harper's* he dramatized his own conversion to the gospel of King Sequoia, while depicting the multidimensional living community of the Sierran forest.[29]

He wanted to recommend "compulsory recreation," so he narrated his own free-roaming way through the forest wilderness into the universe. Wildlife was important in this unshackling process. The "mammoth brown bears harmonizing grandly with the mammoth brown trees," the "perfect jets and flashes" of energetic Douglas squirrels, and of course the songs of the birds — all were attractive to Muir. But the key to his conversion came from the deer he found eating near him one morning, "eating breakfast with me, like gentle sheep around a shepherd"; he "only wanted to run [his] hand along its beautiful curving limbs." Muir saw deer as the "perfect embodiment of poetic form and motion."

No wonder he was increasingly repelled by anything that wasn't wild. He met an Indian who was working as a shepherd of sheep. "Unfortunately, however, he made pretentions to civilization, and spoke contemptuously of *wild* Indians; and of course the peculiar instincts of wildness belonging to his race had become dim." Muir's irony worked nicely. He became wilder by the day, plunged into the wilderness, and finally even set free his mule, Brownie, "for no mountaineer is truly free who is trammelled with friend or servant, or who has the care of more than two legs."

Once he was wild, he could see the wilderness in its own terms and could begin to answer the scientific questions about the Sequoia which were the basis of "Post-Glacial History." These were questions about area, distribution, relations with the environment, and possible changes in those relations. Muir was not using the catchwords of ecological writing that we have come to look for, but he was engaged in a high order of ecological thinking. For the sake of convenience and clarity, I will outline his argument about the natural history of Sequoia forests as it appears in all three articles, using the terminology of later ecologists.[30]

1. The climax forest of the Sierra is the Sequoia forest, built in a specific life zone on the "oldest and warmest portions of the main glacial soil-belt." It is growing on an ancient moraine, like the Cedars of Lebanon. Its life zone is defined by altitude, climate, moisture, and exposure to the sun.

2. Though divided into groves by intervening canyons, the Sequoia forest is really all of one piece if viewed, not spatially, but in accordance with environmental or life-zone conditions. These groves are not remnants.

3. The Sequoia forest evolved by a process of succession and dispersion of species. There are places where new seed beds are exposed on new avalanche soil, and "in this instructive illustration of the struggle for life among the rival species" young Sequoias gain a marked advantage over others. Muir's evidence supports his theory that the sugar pine came down the range from the north, while the Sequoia migrated up from the south. Where they met and harmonized, the Sequoia became King and the sugar pine became priest. They both came to occupy niches, as did other species that arrived and flourished in a favorable environment. The result is a rich and diverse ecosystem.

4. Although the result of struggle, the Sequoia forest is now in a climax state — stable, well-balanced, self-perpetuating. There are a number of kinds of evidence to support this claim.

A. That the Sequoia is "enduringly established in concordance with climate and soil" can be understood when one realizes that the tree can grow on dry soil. Its presence in well-watered areas results from its own presence, which "*creates* those streams." (Muir admits that he had confused cause and effect at first, but finally realized that the forest creates its own environment when it conserves water.) Thus the tree's incredible longevity is a result partly of its own creation of a cordial environment.

B. Because of its monumental size, men assume that the Sequoia is a monument from a bygone era. "There were Giants in those Days," Emerson had said. Not true. The Sequoia is an example of "irrepressible fruitfulness." Part of the false notion that it is archaic is a result of science's ignorance of the more vigorous southern groves. The forest is ripe, yet growing. Since men measure time in such short terms, they cannot appreciate the cycle of a species which is measured in thousands of years.

C. In the climax forest, "fire, the great destroyer of Sequoia," also furnishes one of the conditions for its renewal, though "the main supply of fresh soil is furnished by the fall of aged trees." Indeed, the branches of the Sequoias are themselves "faithful" and repair damage done by such mishaps as lightning strikes. In the cycle of life and death, the forest maintains itself.

5. The climax state of the Sequoia forest cannot be understood in terms of the trees alone. Not one Sequoia seed in a million germinates. This is not because Nature is "inefficient," but rather because the Sequoia is part of a larger forest community.

In a passage he removed from the final manuscript of "New Sequoia Forests" Muir reasoned about Lester Ward's complaint that Nature was uneconomic. By human standards, the waste of reproductive powers in Nature appeared fantastic, yet Muir saw a kind of "mutual aid" in the seeming overproduction of Sequoia seeds. His thinking reveals that he was trying to change the ecological consciousness of his reader:

The fact is not however a gloomy one nor does it indicate the slightest imperfection, for just sufficient are developed for the purposes of the highest cosmic beauty + then nature has a big family to feed while the rest are given as food to the birds + squirrels + insects . . . Besides we must not in our own childish outcry of *Cui Bono* overlook the simple fact that a seq[uoia] seed is in itself a most beautiful consummation, + whether [the] colossal tree which it contains is to be called up out — into the light — or be doomed to lie buried in eternal sleep, is a question that only nature can decide.

But Muir's thinking went well beyond the purpose of his article, which was to make people love Sequoia forests.[31]

Instead of arguing his ecological theory he portrayed the life in the forest, where the animals were all part of a harmonious pattern of use. The squirrel was both harvester and planter. The deer were "dainty feeders" who did not destroy life, but kept the garden in order. Life fed on life, but not destructively. This answered a question which had troubled Muir throughout his excursion in the Sequoias. For weeks that fall he had traversed the desolation left by the summer's sheep herds. He had walked through areas where there was not enough forage for his one mule. He wondered about the natural condition of the Sequoia forests, when they were unmarred by Man's flocks: "I have often tried to understand how so many deer, and wild sheep, and bears, and flocks of grouse — nature's cattle and poultry — could be allowed to run at large through the mountain gardens without in any way marring their beauty." The answer was of course that a natural community allowed each species to feed on what its tablemates didn't want. Muir's answer was the one Warmer would make popular in 1895: there was a communal life of organisms in an ecosystem.[32]

This was the way Nature had managed her realm before Man began to disrupt it. Muir had developed a symbolic argument about ecology in his work on the Sequoia forest. The forest was not a specialized or a unique environment, but typical of the communities of life existing throughout the wilderness. If one could understand that these were communities of interrelated species, one could find the same truth in all living landscapes and recognize their perfect adjustment of means and ends. The Sequoia forest indicated the diversity and complexity Nature aimed at, in which every effect was also a cause. Because everything was connected to everything else, when men interfered they could not do any one thing without changing the entire dynamic of the system.

A MAN'S ROLE IN NATURAL HISTORY

All three articles about the Sequoia forest argued that Man had radically disrupted the natural community of the forest: "unfortunately *man* is in the woods, and waste and pure destruction are already making rapid headway." Muir could prioritize the seriousness of various methods of destruction men used. Indians set fires to "improve" deer hunting, but their fires were less frequent than those of the "muttoneers" who tired to burn over the range each fall in order to "improve" it. The Sequoias were fire-resistant, but repeated burning and the added fuel left by the slash of the lumbering operations became too much for them to withstand.[33]

Nor could Muir understand the pointless and wasteful methods used by lumbermen. When a giant Sequoia was felled much of it shattered into useless fragments. The long cycle of life in the Sequoia forest — the almost eternal life-span of the Sequoia itself — would make even modern plans such as tree farming absurd and simpleminded. The logger's notion that a forest attained ripeness and then tended toward "senility" was simply not the truth. Climax was a state of dynamic renewal. Sequoias were thousands of years old, and even the highly marketable lumber of the sugar pine came from trees which were hundreds of years old. These forests could never be replaced. Further, when men took any species out of a forest they usually destroyed the whole community in the process and destroyed the watershed altogether, and so destroyed their own material and spiritual future.

Muir was ready to challenge civilized men to remedy the abuses of the past and present. He assumed that scientists were interested in the Sequoia itself, so his strategy for his scientific audience was to argue that "unless protective measures be speedily invented and applied, in a few decades at the farthest, all that will be left of *Sequoia gigantea* will be a few hacked and scarred monuments." He did not argue as directly with the readers of *Harper's*, but pointed out the role of the Sequoia forest as watershed, concluding his essay by explaining that there had been little decrease in the volume of water carried by post-glacial streams since they had come into existence. He was suggesting that any theory which claimed that the Sierra was drying out could only conclude that Man was responsible. When he spoke to the legislators in Sacramento, he encouraged more careful and thorough research on the actual condition of the Sierran forest, and recommended that the state consider scientific methods of forestry. "Whether our loose-jointed Government is really able or willing to do anything in the matter remains to be seen," he commented. But if Californians wanted their good life to last, they would have to take responsibility.[34]

He had come out of his meditative excursion to the Sequoias with more than a challenge to civilization. He also had decided upon two strategies which he would use to improve the relationship between Americans and their environment and to change the course of natural history on the North American continent. The first was his out-of-doors gospel, with its cornerstone of compulsory recreation. The second was his call for government to protect the natural resources of America. They were separate strategies, and would require separate campaigns which would take much of his energy for the rest of his years. The first was a matter of educating people, of convincing them to expand their consciousness and change their way of life. Muir's journal suggests that he had in mind some kind of institutional program like compulsory education. The second strategy would require that government take firm control over the natural resources of the states, and by logical extension, of the continent. This was a call for institutionalized stewardship.

Both of Muir's programs challenged the prevailing trend toward social Darwinism in America. The more vulgar form of this movement was represented by William Sumner, who developed a kind of "Naturalistic Calvinism" based on the image of the "industrious, temperate, and frugal man of the protestant ideal" who would be the model citizen capable of winning the hard struggle against Nature. This kind of man was the hero who could rise in a system of laissez-faire capitalism. The social Darwinist thought that Man's duty was to work, and that leisure was suspect. When Muir looked at civilization and the "multitude of wants" it engendered, he denounced the "chains of duty and habit which bind us, notwithstanding our boasted freedom." A philosophy which advertised in public that "hog, root, or die" was the only logic of life! Muir found it abhorrent. So he tended to sympathize with dissenters from the "social gospel" like Henry George, who believed that Man's problems were a result not of the hardness of Nature, but of the inequalities of society. Compulsory recreation, or what we now call ecological education, was Muir's program for the spiritual redemption of the individual citizen.[35]

Muir was also appalled at the economics of the social Darwinists. He called it the "gobble-gobble school of economics." With Henry George he believed that blind progress was a dead end, since "what has destroyed all previous civilizations has been the conditions produced by the growth of civilization itself." George Perkins Marsh had argued a similar thesis in *Man and Nature*, when he considered the destructive exhaustion of national resources. Agreeing, Muir found it necessary to speak against the narrow view of government held by people like Sumner. If a social Darwinist believed that government was responsible chiefly for defending only "the property of men and the honor of women" against crime, Muir believed that public good was intimately associated with Man's natural environment. And government would have to protect that communal resource.[36]

This meant much. Muir would find some of his best allies in the coming decades in the ranks of the Progressives, despite many deep philosophical differences. They at least wanted to reform state and national government.

It would have been a sign of naïveté if Muir had expressed very much faith in the corrupt legislature of nineteenth-century California. He didn't. He believed that men were most governed when they were most wild, and so by logical extension must have felt that men who lived closely enough to Nature did not need social structures at all. The author of "Wild Wool" might be characterized as a "Naturalistic Anarchist." But that kind of thinking could not be exported to the cities. Like Thoreau, he may have decided that there was no point in asking for no government, and instead took the stance that government was a necessary expedient by which the quality of life could be preserved. In other words, when he spoke in his public voice he was a reformer, not a revolutionary.

In retrospect, it is easy to see where that strategy would lead. The public Muir would be a man who worked for political solutions to ecological problems. But in private he was deeply repulsed by politics. Thus he became an enigmatic and problematic figure. Politicians could never understand what Muir hoped to gain by preserving wilderness. They assumed that he planned to acquire something material from his public campaigns. On the other hand, his decision to work within the political and governmental realm caused him personal agony and would have tragic implications. He could never achieve complete realization of the deep values he held while working in a system so shallow in motives and means. He imagined a rebirth of American consciousness, but would never be able to bring it about in the political arena. These were the long, tragic themes in his public life. There would be significant victories along the way, but the tide of civilization prevailed. As hard as he would work to publicize the benefits of recreation and as hard as he would lobby for the preservation of native American ecological systems, he would finally live to see the very government that might have aided his cause become the chief destroyer of American men and American wilderness.

8

Tourism
and the Pastoral Life

THE MODEST PROPOSER

If the American government was to protect the resources of the West, public approval would be required. Americans
would need some encouragement, would need to know not only
what they possessed, but why it was worth protecting and how this
could be done. So might have gone Muir's optimistic reasoning. The
public required the service of a guide. Muir had been a tour guide
for several seasons in Yosemite, yet he had not thought of this activity as "real work." (Perhaps it isn't "real work," but until we all
live in Nature again someone must remind us of what living in Nature means.) Before the completion of his glacial studies he had been
immersed in geological research, and after that in the painful task
of writing the *Studies*. When he was reminded of his duty to preserve the live part of Nature—he had no inkling at first that the
rocks and fountains of rivers in the mountains were in danger—he
came to see the value of the role of tour guide. What did the guide
know? He knew the tourist, and if the tourist was a representative
urban citizen, the guide knew just how alienated urban America
was from Nature.

Though a guide often satirizes the pitiful tourists when speaking to his close friends, he must find some value in the people he
serves. Muir felt his difference from the public he wished to influence

and would justify his job only as a way to get bread, but he felt a deep ambivalence. The conflict between his satirical view of the tourists and his stated aim to "entice people to see Nature's beauty" remained with him throughout his career as a writer. He never wanted to become a humanist, yet he had to appeal to human needs and values for the sake of the forests and for the future of men. The view that the critic of humanism hates men is as false as it is popular. Muir merely wanted civilized men to recognize their limitations, and thus become better men.

If he wanted to save the forests, he would have to propose a human use for them that might compete with the plans of the timber, agricultural, and sheep interests. The sheep flocks were reaching their peak populations in California in about 1875, but Muir could see no end to this destructive increase. Muir thought that a growing tourist business might drive the more exploitive users out of the mountains. Despite his suspicion that the path of moderation was not the best way to a true vision of Nature, he attempted to write moderate articles which would bring urban tourists. His allies in his fight for preservation would be moderate progressives too, from the eastern and western urban centers. When he objected to Ruskin's "uninspired" view that "nature is never immoderate" and linked such a perception to limited taste —"The heavy masonry of the Sierra seems immoderate to some"— Muir was saying that such "taste" for scenery was subjective, man-centered, and inaccurate.[1]

He would appeal to a moderate audience, take the role of tour guide seriously, become more than an entertainer of the public; he would attempt to radically re-create public attitudes and taste, hoping to lay the groundwork for an ecological conscience in America, a reevaluation of the management of Yosemite, the desire for new parks, and wise use of agricultural lands and forests.

The series of letters he wrote for the *San Francisco Bulletin* between 1874 and 1878 might seem to be straight tourist-trade material, yet he spoke there to the most general of audiences. Further, when he encouraged travel he involved himself in a subtle evaluation of Californian society. There is a deceptive innocence about these letters from the "travelling correspondent," these "Notes from a Naturalist." Writing from his campfire, seemingly about the mundane questions a traveler might want to entertain, he was trying out his ecological perspective on the public.

"What's worth seeing and how shall I see it?" These are no simple questions, since the answers require that one consider who the traveler is, what his journey should do for him, what he will do to the places he visits, how his visit will change his view of himself, and how differently he will see his home when he returns. One might see in these considerations a complicated ecology of tourism that leads to the overwhelming question: "Oh, do not ask, 'What is it?' / Let us go and make our visit."[2]

Certainly the tourist to Yosemite already had a choice among writers and artists to guide him. He may have learned to see through the eyes of Bierstadt, Thomas Hill, or Muir's friend William Keith. He may have learned of Yosemite through the photographs of Muybridge. He might come to the Valley with his copy of Ruskin's *Of Mountain Beauty*, or with a copy of Tyndall's *Hours of Exercise in the Alps*. More likely, Whitney's guide and Hutchings's articles had provided the tourist with a specific itinerary. In a sense, all of Muir's writings were for the tourist, since they involved the question of how to see. Most tourists did not want to hear philosophy, but wanted to know exactly where to stop and look.

Muir hesitated to enter this field, and his two most obviously tourist-directed essays for Benjamin Avery's *Overland*, in 1872 and 1874, recommended that the tourist enjoy scenes normally passed on the way to Yosemite, or that the tourist pass Yosemite in order to seek out the more "condensed" landscape of the high Sierra. The two essays reveal Muir's early awkwardness at the task. The most reasonable strategy, Muir thought, would be to initiate the tourist as he himself had been initiated at Twenty Hill Hollow in the Central Valley or at Bloody Canyon at the crest of the Sierra. Was his experience the same as that which the average tourist might be expected to have? He would assume it was. As a result, these articles were public versions of Muir's own growth of consciousness. "Twenty Hill Hollow" became an analysis of his own complex attitude toward a pastoral landscape, and "By-Ways of Yosemite Travel. Bloody Canyon" dealt with his initiation into high cold solitudes and hot desert plains.[3]

THE TOURIST AND A MODERATE SCENE

Why send the tourist to Twenty Hill Hollow, a little valley lying in the plain of the Central Valley, between the Merced and the Tuolumne Rivers, five miles from the Sierran foothills? Because Muir said it was the scene of his own baptism into the "plant gold" and "sun gold" of California? Because it was left out of the "descriptions of California scenery, by the literary racers who annually make a trial of their speed here"? Because tourists "who are hurled into Yosemite by 'favorite routes,' are not aware that they are crossing a grander Yosemite than that to which they are going"? Perhaps Muir suspected that those who were traveling for "peace and health" might find them more abundant off the tourist's route than on it. Here, he indicated, was a place wild and yet moderate: "Here are no Washington columns, no angular Capitans, to bring doubt upon Ruskin's 'Moderation.'" Fortunately, he said, "our proper arithmetical standards are not outraged by a single magnitude of this moderate, comprehensible hollow."[4]

He inadvertently revealed his opinion of the tourist's actual wants and needs in this essay. He had told Mrs. Carr that he hoped it would be a "lawful article fit for *outsiders.*" A place like Twenty Hill Hollow permitted satisfactions within the reach of the average tourist's sensibilities. Here was a pastoral landscape, "a charming fairy-land of hills, with small, grassy valleys between" where one might "drift away confidingly into the broad gulf-streams of Nature, helmed only by Instinct." Muir recognized the limits of the average tourist's taste. I don't believe he was satirizing the poor fellow, who only wanted to have fun, relax, and be happy.[5]

One need only stand at Glacier Point on a pleasant, warm July afternoon and watch the crowds respond to the overpowering scene — witness their fear, their confusion. They have not come to a place that will make them feel relaxed or peaceful. Most are awestruck, excitable, unable to sit still or be quiet. It is simply too much. So one might ask what these people hope to accomplish by their journey. Perhaps they have come to the wrong place. If they are "choked in the sediments of society," as Muir described tourists in his essay, then they should not simply join a new social group of tourists. As

Muir saw it, if such people were truly seeking their own re-creation or resurrection, if they wanted their souls to "breathe deep and free in God's shoreless atmosphere of beauty and love," if they wanted to "blend with the landscape, and become part and parcel with Nature," then these moderate people needed a moderate landscape.

Why should they come to Yosemite when they were so obviously not ready for it, when their experience would only be alienating, when they would believe that such a fierce and gothic place must have been caused by cataclysm? How could they learn to love a Nature they couldn't get close to? Better they should witness the "annual genesis of plant and insect life" in the Central Valley. As he argued in "Flood Storm," we need not begin reading the Book of Nature with the alpine capitals.

There was no special reason, thought Muir, to lead tourists to Yosemite. They would get there by virtue of the wide-ranging and already energetic tourist trade, run by "agents" and industry. Instead, he attempted to say a word for places the tourist was likely to miss, places whose interest was too subtle for the tourist to notice without help. Because he wished to destroy the myth that Nature was made up of a collection of "scenes of wonder and curiosity," Muir argued that Yosemite was but one slice — more concentrated, but still a part of the whole. The Central Valley was a "garden wild," not a "sort of Sahara" to be traversed as quickly as possible; it was an appropriate part of the gradual ascent to the high mountains.

Just as the January spring in the hollow led to a later spring higher in the Sierra, the "plant gold" of the hollow was the clue to brighter possibilities than Californians envisaged for their state. The "summer flood of tourists" passed the Central Valley well after its bloom time, and so took it to be a desert. No wonder they did not complain when agriculture and sheep herding stripped the bloom from their lowland valleys. Muir suspected correctly that he was writing an elegy; as he wrote to Jeanne Carr, "Plant gold is fading from California faster than did her placer gold, and I wanted to save the memory of that which was laid upon Twenty Hills." In this and other early articles for tourists he was encouraging visits to threatened areas. He would use this strategy for the rest of his life. Is there a better one?[6]

He also had personal reasons for beginning with Twenty Hill

Hollow. Muir had earlier described with enthusiasm the wealth of flowers in the Central Valley: "Florida is indeed a 'land of flowers,' but for every flower creature that dwells in its most delightsome places more than a hundred are living here. Here, here is Florida. Here it is not as in our great western prairie, flowers sprinkled in the grass, but grass in the flowers; not as in Cuba, flowers piled upon flowers, heaped and gathered into glowing masses, but flowers side by side, raceme to raceme." Yet Twenty Hill Hollow was at that very moment making its transition from land of flowers to land of sheep, and for Muir the meaning of the place was at least twofold. The land itself was edenic, a botanist's paradise. His own work there for Smokey Jack involved him in its destruction. No wonder he was ambivalent when he attempted to describe his own state of mind while living there. His joy in the flowers and his disillusionment with the industry of sheep herding were indissolubly mixed, one coloring the other in his memory.[7]

In the summer of 1868 he had still been able to write with enthusiasm to his brother David of "sheep, wild as antelopes" and deeds of romantic daring "equal to those of knights of old." But by the end of February, 1869 his early romantic illusions were passing, though he tried to write in a pastoral vein to his sister, referring to Old King David who had called herding "following the sheep," and describing "the rich mellow light . . . laid on plain and mountain without a tinge of haze." The later author of "Wild Wool" awoke. In the hollow he had learned to despise the pastoral conventions, the "*patriarchal* business," as a fabric of lies.[8]

Love of flowers and pastoralism could not coexist in the same Californian scene. Either one sat in a meadow or one sat in a pasture. After he knew better, Muir would follow Pat Delaney's sheep for a summer in the Sierra only because he needed bread. Following the sheep meant quite literally being led up a trail of shit by stupid beasts over stubble fields where the flowers had been eaten or trampled.

Though sheep are not mentioned in "Twenty Hill Hollow," Muir's disenchantment with the pastoral is barely under the surface of a central incident, his encounter with an eagle. The eagle first came into his journal on January 2, 1869. Muir immediately felt a close personal identification with this visitor.

At first I could not guess what could bring this strong sailor of the sky to the ground. His great wings, seven or eight feet broad, were folded as he stood, dim, motionless, and clod-like as if all excelsior instincts – all of cloud and sky – were forgotten, and that, lark-like, he meant to walk about in the grass hereafter, or stand on a hillock like a little burrowing owl. . . . Food, which brings both eagles and men from the clouds, was a-wanting – he hungered and came down for a hare.

After describing the bird's hunt for a hare, Muir allowed his eagle to "satisfy his hunger, wipe off all marks of grossness, and go again to the skies." He felt that there was something unseemly about the eagle's descent to the earth and meat. The "strong sailor of the sky" was, like Muir, compelled to leave the heights in winter and come to a hillock to get his bread. Naturally Muir hoped that he too would be able to "wipe off all marks of grossness, and go again to the skies." The "real incident" of his journal was equally the coming of the eagle and the mental state of Muir; they were inseparable. The eagle's departure represented his own aspirations to be rid of all material needs and earthly problems, and one can see why he would oppose all pastoral "improvements" to landscapes, which represented the feeding, clothing, and housing of men.[9]

Yet three years later, in 1872, he asked the tourist to stop in the hollow rather than aspire to the skies. If this was a place which Muir and the eagle had come down to, it was a place which the public needed to come up to, a sort of middle ground that Muir could share with the tourist. This is the very definition of "pastoral" – a middle ground between the wilds and the city. To seduce the public Muir would attempt to speak with the voice of a lark, not that of the eagle. So in his revised version of the incident he eliminated the dim and clodlike aspect of his eagle, did not mention any "excelsior instincts," and consequently presented neither a discontented eagle nor a discontented Muir. Such a revision allowed him to present unambiguously the much-admired conclusion of the essay:

It may be asked, what have mountains fifty or a hundred miles away to do with Twenty Hill Hollow? To wild people, these mountains are not a hundred miles away. Their spiritual power and the goodness of the sky make them near, as a circle of friends. They rise as a portion of the hilled walls of the hollow. You can not feel yourself out-of-doors; plain, sky, and mountains ray beauty which you feel. You bathe in these spirit-beams, turning round and round, as if warming at a camp-fire. Presently you lose consciousness of your separate existence; you blend with the landscape and become part and parcel of Nature.

Muir *wished* for such an oceanic experience, even in a sheep camp, and his essay was a kind of acceptance and even a rationalization; it allowed him to make peace with the "power [which] could fetch the sky king down into the grass with the larks." To "wild people" like Muir, for whom Nature is all one piece, the mountains should always be in mind.[10]

Still, there remained a central contradiction. As Muir had described him the traveler was not wild, though he might become extravagant, at least as Thoreau defined the term: "The migrating buffalo, which seeks new pastures in another latitude, is not extravagant like the cow which kicks over the pail, leaps the cow-yard fence, and runs after her calf, in milking time." Even a moderate traveler could hope to find his own Nature near his own home. But the hollow did not represent extravagance to Muir, who needed larger fences to leap. The strategy of the essay is clear enough, yet there is a significant difference between the aspirations of the narrator and those attributed to the tourist. Muir's awkwardness in the face of this difference is apparent in his blunting of the personal significance of his encounter with the eagle, in his clumsy use of pronouns, and in quick transitions between private and public points of view. His conclusion, written as a direct address to the reader, meant one thing to Muir and another to the traveler, since the lonely traveler did not feel that going to the mountains was going home. For the reader who might become a traveler, Nature was *not* home; he still felt out-of-doors, and was not as extravagant as Thoreau's cow.[11]

This barrier to communication would return as Muir began, in the same year, to attack the pastoral "improvements" of Yosemite Valley. If one looks at the photographs taken in the late 1860s, early 1870s, and later during state administration of the Valley, one realizes that the scenes might well have been perceived by a cultured American audience to be perfectly and pleasantly pastoral. The rail fences, haystacks, orchards, and other changes would be accepted as a humanizing part of the landscape, a much more moderate combination of Man's and Nature's work than the "industrialized version of the pastoral ideal" which had become popular by the middle of the century, and which included factories and railroads as part of the ideal landscape. In these Yosemite scenes the agricultural improvements often formed the unifying aesthetic element, making Yosemite comprehensible for the viewer. A fence row directed the eye, a cow in the foreground gave a peaceful tone to the scene. Later, of course, the automobile would become an integral part of the twentieth-century scenic snapshot.[12]

Like the English professor I once met who thought the Grand Canyon needed improvement by more human creations, who bewailed the fact that the only human improvement he could see from the South Rim was the small and distant hotel on the North Rim, the pastoral viewer desires some sign that humans have made something of this wild land. It was this attitude that Muir fought in his objections to "improvements" in the Valley, and it is interesting that he usually did not find such improvements distasteful when he looked at the farms of Utah or Nevada, the orange orchards of California, Mrs. Carr's Carmelita in Pasadena, or his future father-in-law's spread in the Alhambra Valley. Perhaps he was briefly lulled into such acceptance in the late seventies, only to be reawakened at the end of the decade.

It was not at all clear in the seventies that a distinction needed to be made between national parks and other scenic areas. The notion of a national park as partly "wilderness" is a more modern public ideal, held in the nineteenth century by only a few extremists who believed that Man's work did not improve the landscape.

Frederick Law Olmsted was one of those extremists, and had recognized in 1865 that Yosemite should remain, as nearly as possible, in its "original" condition. As my quotation marks indicate, this was a problematic issue. If "original" described the processes which had shaped the landscape, then there was good reason to believe that Indians had been burning and removing brush by hand in the Valley long before white men had arrived. Thus men had been a major ecological force in Yosemite for quite a while. Further, as a modern geographer points out, the ecological notion of "climax" implicit in the desire for a permanent, unchanging park like Yosemite Valley is at best an ideal. All over the earth from before the dawn of written history men have been a dominant ecological force, a part of the processes of ecological change. In Yosemite Valley many changes effected under the stewardship of men have had contradictory results. And the same men who disapproved of grazing would approve of fire suppression, yet both acts encouraged forest succession on the Valley floor.[13]

Muir wanted to describe a pastoral scene without a human component. Thus he left the sheep out of his literary version of "Twenty Hill Hollow." Was it possible to change public tastes to such a radical extent? If he would leave Man's works out of the picture, then he would compensate by describing wild Nature in tame human terms, risking the charge of anthropomorphic description when he humanized the wilderness.

THE TOURIST IN THE WILDERNESS

Perhaps Muir had tried to humanize sublime scenes for himself so that he would be comfortable. Certainly he did so for the reader in "By-Ways of Yosemite Travel. Bloody Canyon." He must have decided it was an appropriate strategy, since he was attempting to convince his audience that the high passes and the east side of the Sierra were not deserts.

Muir's reason for visiting Bloody Canyon and the Mono Basin was perhaps similar to that of his reader. His first excursion took place during his First Summer when he was working for Pat Delaney, the man who had become a "gentle shepherd" content to "lie down with the lamb." Discontented with following the sheep or with the life of a sheep camp, Muir took Delaney's suggestion and sought wilder places within reach of Tuolumne Meadows, one of which was Bloody Canyon. Muir assumed that his reader too wished to get beyond the improved, degraded, and accessible features of Yosemite Valley, since "lovers of clean mountain wildness must therefore go up higher, into more inaccessible retreats among the summits of the range." He assumed too that his reader would learn to accept the intimidating landscape, and come to love it in spite of his first impressions "under the gaze of [Nature's] coldest rocks."[14]

By definition, an "impression" is vague and inaccurate. The tourist's impressions might be too weak or too strong, the first temporary, and the second producing fear. Muir wanted the tourist to get a more lasting response, which he called vision.

Though Bloody Canyon hardly seems a gothic place to contemporary visitors, it apparently did to the nineteenth-century traveler, and certainly did to Muir on his first visit. Perhaps his uneasiness resulted from the close proximity of a group of Mono Indians when he camped for the night, or perhaps it was a result of his own mood. For a horse-mounted tourist the dangers were more tangible. As Whitney's guide proclaimed — Muir concurred — the name of the canyon probably came from the bloodstains on the wounded legs of mules and horses "compelled to slip and shuffle awkwardly over its sharp cutting rocks." Muir could not resist mentioning the possibility of animals falling headlong to their deaths during the descent. All of this was likely to be discouraging to the tourist. First impressions would be likely to turn him away.

In compensation, Muir's essay humanized the landscape and the Indians who resided in it. Muir was recreating his initiation. If his first impression of the Indians was that of wallowing bears, by the next morning they appeared in a more pastoral aspect near Mono Lake, "coming through the rye." So too the strange voices of the night yielded on the next morning to the songs of the creek, which became "more human and lovable at every step" during the descent. As he reiterated when describing his own initiation in the morning light, "The world seemed wholly new; young beauty appeared at every step." The lesson learned, in spite of possible fears, came in his concluding sentence: "Nature's love is universal, and nowhere have I heard it proclaimed in more understandable terms than in the hot plains of Mono, and in the rocky and storm-beaten mansions of Bloody Canyon." It seems that the fears and doubts of the traveler only make his final awakening that much stronger, if he is open to the true message of the mountains.

In a casual, yet significant way the two essays in *Overland* attempted to redefine the means and ends of tourism by reconsidering where the tourist went and why. Knowing that the American was programmed to appreciate certain kinds of scenes, and for the wrong reasons, Muir tried to expand the range of popular taste by recommending places which were either less dramatic or more intimidating than those normally considered worthwhile by the sightseeing public.

Perhaps I have slighted one element of both essays. Through his descriptions, Muir wanted to help the traveler to see with the informing accuracy that scientific understanding could provide. Both essays relied on more than sentiment and devoted considerable space to the specific flowers, the kinds of plant communities, and the geological history of the areas. For Muir the scientific viewpoint was a significant tool in attempting to see Nature in her own terms. Yet neither botany nor geology, Muir hoped, would be cold and passionless. As he later argued in "The Glacier Meadows of the Sierra," an Emersonian kind of transcendence that allowed the tourist to "become all eye, sifted through and through with light and beauty," and which "gave inexpressible delight," was also educational:

> The influences of pure nature seem to be so little known as yet, that it is generally supposed that complete pleasure of this kind, permeating one's very flesh and bones, unfits the student for scientific pursuits in which cool judgment and observation are required. But the effect is just the opposite. Instead of producing a dissipated condition, the mind is fertilized and stimulated and developed like sun-fed plants.

Muir humanized Nature but did not become fanciful. Perhaps his use of anthropocentric and anthropomorphic language was a concession to Emerson's dictum that "the artist must employ the symbols in use in his day and nation to convey his enlarged sense to his fellow men."[15]

Muir was using the symbolic language of the garden pastoral because it seemed to be the only language accessible to his readers. He was right. In the American outlook a modern critic has seen a split that is entrenched in the language of the earliest commentaries on the American scene:

> To depict America as a garden is to express aspirations still considered utopian — aspirations, that is, toward abundance, leisure, freedom, and a greater harmony of existence.
>
> To describe America as a hideous wilderness, however, is to envisage it as another field for the exercise of power. This violent image expresses a need to mobilize energy, postpone immediate pleasures, and rehearse the perils and purposes of the community.

This kind of polar view was fixed strongly in the symbolic consciousness of America, and Muir knew that he could only fight the destructive exercise of power by using the language of the garden. It was rare for him, in the seventies, to even use the word "wilderness." Instead he would speak of "wild gardens" or "the wildness of Nature."[16]

THE TRAVELING CORRESPONDENT

In the fall of 1874 Muir was happy to be on the road again, after more than three hundred days in San Francisco. He wrote to Jeanne Carr that he had escaped from the work of bookmaking, and wrote to the readers of the *Bulletin* that he was free of the "characteristic processes and vicissitudes of civilization." His journal indicated a more serious concern with the poisons of the cities and the "death exhalations" that brood there. His condemnation of urban life was categorical: "All are more or less sick; there is not a perfectly sane man in San Francisco." Even when he wrote a report on salmon breeding on the McCloud River he remained preoccupied with the pollution of civilization. He spoke of the destruction of the fish's habitat that resulted from mining, but was more concrete when he referred to the poisoning of fish by "those strangely complicated filths for which our civilization is peculiar." One did not make direct reference to sewage when speaking to the readers of a middle-class newspaper in San Francisco.[17]

Certainly a good part of Muir's disgust with city life came from the changes he observed in himself during that year. So LeConte had prophesied about him: "I think he would pine away in a city or in conventional life of any kind." However, the underlying assumption in Muir's journal and in his articles for the *Bulletin* was that all men were immersed in invisible poison when in the cities. Only those who stood above in the clean and healthy air had the sense to pull the dying ones out. He compared city life to his own near disaster in "choke-gas" while digging a well for his father. The comparison worked nicely. Urban people were digging their own graves, but didn't know it.[18]

Muir had undergone a significant change in his attitude toward the city dweller as prospective tourist. Such a person, as Muir saw him, was an innocent, trapped by an environment beyond his own control. Only a year before Muir had claimed to be tempted to "adopt the Calvinistic doctrine of total depravity." Now he thought that even if he could not send them to his own kind of radical baptism on Ritter or Shasta, men would awaken to Nature if only given a moderate chance. "Of all the overworked and defrauded toilers of California towns, only about twenty came to the daylight of Shasta last season. . . . there is no daylight in towns, and the weary public ought to know that there is light here, and I for one clear my skirts from the responsibility of silence by shouting a cordial *come*." This enthusiastic invitation is ever-present in Muir's letters to the *Bulletin*. It is based on a philosophy very similar to that which Olmsted had articulated nearly a decade earlier in his report to the California legislature on the management of the Yosemite Grant.[19]

Olmsted wrote in his early report on tourism in Yosemite that "the power of scenery to affect men is, in a large way, proportionate to the degree of civilization." Savages, for instance, were not much affected by beauty. But the appreciation of scenery required mental exercise, and paradoxically the city dweller was so mentally fatigued by concern for his future, "laying up wealth" attending to "small and petty details," that he was dulled to any interest in the present moment "for itself and at the moment it is enjoyed." Thus Olmsted believed that the appreciation of scenery was necessary to the civilized person as a release from cares which civilization had thrown upon his shoulders, and was necessary to the sanity which would advance civilization in the future. Mind you, Olmsted knew that the farmer and his wife suffered also. He stated, as Garland did twenty years later, that the asylums were filled with the wives of the "Independent American Farmer." Like Muir, however, Olmsted was most fearful for the urban citizen.[20]

There are two unavoidable paradoxes here. First, it troubles me to think that the only person who could appreciate scenery is the individual most alienated from Nature. Typically, the nineteenth-century champion of tourism seemed tied to the assumption that *only* the civilized man was capable of appreciating Nature. It is the twentieth-century ecologist who tells us that the primitive's "life is so profoundly in transaction with nature that there is no place for abstractions or esthetics or a 'nature philosophy' which can be separated from the rest of his life." The second paradox is more troubling. If the urban dweller is in danger of losing his sanity, then there is something wrong with urban life which must be remedied, rather than put off by a temporary therapy that takes the urbanite out of his city and then returns him to it. Why use the wilderness to save the insane system which works to destroy Nature? Why feed the monster?[21]

Muir had reason to suspect the idea that only civilized men could appreciate the power of scenery, and had attacked the idea when he read it in Ruskin's "Mountain Gloom": "We must not dwell in contact with Nature, he tells us, else we will become blind to her beauty, which is the vulgar gross old heresy that familiarity with God will produce contempt of him. He would have us take beauty as we do roast beef or medicine." Muir clearly disapproved of Ruskin's distant appraisal of Nature, but he was still willing to argue, with Olmsted, that scenery could be taken as a kind of medicine.[22]

He could argue to his readers about the "utility of rest," propose that the many "slaves, duty bound, business bound, in ways wholly unnatural and unpardonable" could increase their output of work as a result of compulsory recreation. Yet such an argument troubled Muir, as it didn't Olmsted, because it made recreation the handmaiden of a growing urban industrial civilization. Men made happy by their commerce with Nature might have more energy to destroy her, as Muir thought later when depicting the shake maker whose happy, healthy life in the woods only made him destructively industrious. What was the value of saying a word for the wilderness if the upshot was that men were refreshed by their experience to do more duty, more business? What if encouraging travel was only a kind of philanthropy? He wondered whether he wanted to join the profession of man-loving: "Ho weary town worker, come to the woods and rest! I wish it were possible to compel all to come; not that I am just at this moment filled with a fit of Quixotic philanthropy, for with Thoreau, I am convinced that the profession of doing good is full." Nevertheless, he went on to point out that the Calavaras Grove of Sequoias was only a day and a half away from San Francisco, thus appealing to the haste of the city person. Throughout this period, and perhaps throughout the rest of his life, Muir would have conflicting feelings of pity for the poor men who were trapped in the cities and fear for the Nature they were destroying. He was never comfortable in the role of philanthropist.[23]

Yet, like Olmsted, he recognized that the class of people who could enjoy Nature also had to be changed. The rich always had a monopoly on recreation, a fact he recognized while in San Francisco during the year he spent there. The poor children of Tar Flat needed a chance at something brighter in their lives. So his long-range mission *was* philanthropic: "No matter into what depths of degredation humanity may sink, I will never despair while the lowest love the pure and the beautiful and know it when they see it."[24]

When Muir's invitation went out from the front page of the *Bulletin*, when he said "Come to Yosemite, where all places and seasons are fine," he was in practical terms not speaking to the poor. Though he had thrifty recommendations on how to "do" the Valley, and thought it would be better still to ride up into the forests where "perfect was the oblivion that fell upon the fever-work of the far off town," where even Yosemite "was almost forgotten," he appealed mainly to the tourist with leisure — leisure only possible to the moneyed. If "Going to the mountains is going home," as he claimed, then Tuolumne Meadows was the central camping ground "for those who have a summer to spend." Who had a summer to spend? Only the leisure class, Muir knew, and he said it: "Let those contemplating health journeys to fashionable Bethesdas bear Tuolumne in mind."[25]

But the beauty of the mountains could not be exported to the towns. In an article which announced the interesting scenery of the Kings River Yosemite, Muir mentioned that he and his companions had seen a Sequoia being cut down for exhibition at the Philadelphia Centennial. He commented, "Many a poor, defrauded town dweller will pay his dollar and peep, and gain some dead arithmetical notion of the bigness of our Big Trees, but a true and living knowledge of these tree gods is not to be had at so cheap a rate." Maybe it would be possible for the poor to come to the forests in the future; in 1875 Muir was appealing to those who could afford to pay for their rest.[26]

If there was rest in the woods, there was forgetfulness in the waters. On the east side of the Sierra, he found Mono Lake to be "as translucent as Tahoe. . . . And the Mono desert is a desert of flowers the beauty of which the most loving pen will never describe." In these articles, every lake and canyon seemed the finest of them all. Tahoe in winter was "King of them all" and a "fine place this to forget weariness and wrongs and bad business." But several months later he was wondering why everyone went to Tahoe when Pyramid Lake was the "most singular and beautiful sheet of water" he had ever seen, surpassing "anything on the face of the earth for picturesque grandeur." After bathing in the Great Salt Lake, he said that the railroad had made it "as accessible as any watering place on either coast," and that it would lure thousands "were its merits but half known."[27]

The clear message was that westerners who could afford it had the answer to their problem of overwork near at hand. He spoke in Thoreauvian terms when he told his fellow citizens that in the American West they had "Laplands and Labradors, . . . rivers of mercy as sacred as the Himalaya born Ganges"; the "Pah Ute Indian . . . Bedouin of the California deserts," roamed the Great Basin. Muir seemed to have caught the spirit of Bryant's *Picturesque America,* and was bringing out a western version. Yet westerners did not come to their wonderful scenic areas. Of Yosemite, Muir noted, "Not quite 33 percent of all the visitors to this famous place are Californians." Was it "because so many from this state can go at any time that they never go?" Or maybe, he reconsidered, it was easier for a New Yorker to visit England than for a Californian to visit Yosemite. Yosemite needed free roads. "There is too much Niagara," Muir said, referring to the destructive commercialization of that scenic area, which was just gaining national attention. America had the scenic resources, but she needed to appreciate them.[28]

Despite the downturn in tourism to the Valley during the summer of 1876, a result of the Centennial expositions, there was an increase in family camping, which pleased Muir because he saw this as a more leisurely method of enjoying Nature. But then he seemed pleased by any kind of tourism he saw. He was capable of indiscriminate praise for tourism: "The regular tourist, ever on the flow, is one of the most characteristic productions of the present century; and however frivolous and inappreciative the poorest specimens may appear, viewed comprehensively, they are a most hopeful and significant sign of the time, indicating at least the beginning of our return to nature, for going to the mountains is going home." Since he wanted to channel this flow into truly productive experiences, he had much to say about how a tourist might get the most from his excursion. Beneath such advice was his real strategy, I think: people would resist the destruction of places they had visited. So also one might see why Muir directed his letters toward the upper middle class, which could contemplate a trip to Bethesda. These people could become influential allies, as the children of Tar Flat could not. Later, when a battle was won for a new park, Muir would usually see it as a victory for the trees, not for the people. Tourism of any kind was a development Muir would applaud during these years.[29]

He continued, however, to recommend a pastoral sort of tourism, appropriate to the view of Nature as garden, not wilderness. "I would advise sitting from morning till night under some willow bush on the river bank where there is a wide view. This will be 'doing the valley' far more effectively than riding along trails in constant motion from point to point." Muir's kind of recreation did not require strenuous exercise, and for good reason. He did not want to encourage those activities in which men tested their powers over Nature. Although he wrote about the abundance of "wild life in the form which hunters call *game*" in the area of Shasta, and recounted his experiences with a group of hunters, he had a better way. "Regarding Mount Shasta from a bee point of view," he advised, "if you like hunting there is game in abundance. But better let blood alone and come purely a beeing." By "beeing" he meant, aside from eating honey, aimless flitting about in flowers and woods. He encouraged more peaceful family activities, not manly sport, and was happy to report that Shasta was "speedily becoming a family resort." So too, he was pleased to see young couples "dabble away their hot holidays in the cool pool" under the falls of Eaton Creek, in the "Yosemite of San Gabriel." This kind of pastoral recreation was an exercise in letting things be, but it would not be able to compete with the Teddy Roosevelt brand of the Strenuous Life which was soon to come.[30]

Though Muir also advertised the virtues of swimming in the Great Salt Lake, skiing near Lake Tahoe, and climbing Mount Whitney, he was greatly concerned lest sacred places become only playgrounds. He feared too that the mountains and forests would be seen only in dead statistical terms. Both fears suggest that Muir understood well a real danger that the tourist would not give himself up to Nature, but would find himself the center of the scene. He had early been suspicious of the highly urban ways of visitors to the Valley, and was particularly troubled by what I might call anthropocentric tourism. When he noticed that tourists seemed obsessed with curious comparisons, when they said that one attraction was better or more impressive than another, when they admired one Sequoia because it was bigger than another, when they persisted in judging falls by the quantity of water rather than by their individual character, Muir responded,

As far as the falls are concerned, it seems to be pretty generally believed that the greater the quantity of water the greater the beauty, and it certainly seems pathetic that at this stage of evolution it should be necessary to state that every waterfall has an individual character, and that each possesses a series of beauties changing with the seasons, and all the various types of beauty blending with one another inseparable and incomparable.

He sometimes despaired of finding the end to such anthropocentrism from the tourist at a place like Kings Canyon:

The waters of the new valley effect their descent by a series of comparatively short leaps and inclines, which, according to the vague classification in vogue in these dark pretentious days, would mostly be brought under the head of cascades. . . . Nevertheless, it may be long ere waterfalls have their beauty measured in any other way than by plumb lines and tape-lines.

The American preoccupation with the biggest, oldest, and tallest was offensive because it assumed a false standard of judgment. Thus he pointed out that Mount Whitney had "no special geological significance" and possessed "little appreciable individuality." Just because it was the highest, it was not necessarily the most sacred mountain in America.[31]

He knew that people tended to avoid seeing Nature in and of itself, and preferred abstractions to the real thing. The desire not to miss any scenic turnout, feature, or point of interest could be traced, perhaps, to the same vulgar following of crowds which created a cluster of people around the Mona Lisa at the Louvre. In a place like the Sierra such behavior was a crime against Nature, who was inseparable and incomparable.

Muir felt, justifiably, that recreation was not the same thing as entertainment. After being shown two rooms in Cave City Cave near Murphy's camp, and being told that one was used as a chapel and the other as a dancing hall, he became impatient. The stream of satire, which rippled somewhere below the surface of all these articles, surfaced:

Mass-saying is not so generally developed in connection with natural wonders as dancing. One of the first conceits excited by the giant Sequoias was to cut one of them down and dance on its stump. We have also seen dancing in the spray of Niagara; dancing in the famous Bower Cave above Coulterville; and nowhere have I seen so much dancing as in Yosemite. A dance on the inaccessible South Dome would likely follow the making of an easy way to the top of it.[32]

Social games and entertainments turned the tourist's attention away from Nature, and were clearly linked to his insensitive and destructive behavior. Although there may be nothing wrong with partying in the national parks per se, Muir noted that partiers tended to forget where they were and soon fouled the wilderness as they had fouled their own cities. Why else do people leave beer cans on the trails and wine bottles in the meadows? Do they perhaps suppose that these constitute pastoral improvements? Now, of course, the national parks go to great pains to provide entertainment in the hope that occupying the tourists' time will keep them out of trouble. A full social round keeps the tourist busy, and keeps his mess localized.

Power games also came under his attack. The anthropocentric notion of conquest always seemed wrongheaded to Muir, particularly when it came to men standing on the summit of Half Dome; "as well say a man is conquered when a fly lights on his head," he growled. "I have always discouraged as much as possible every project for laddering South Dome, believing it would be a fine thing to keep this garden untrodden. Now the pines will be carved with the initials of Smith and Jones, and the gardens strewn with tin cans and bottles." Even though he later made peace with the idea of a ladder on the Dome, he insisted that the view from the summit was less impressive than views of the Valley from elsewhere because the walls on both sides "seem comparatively low and shrunken," and the Dome itself, "the most sublime feature in all Yosemite," was below one's feet. Men often lost their proper perspective when standing too high in a landscape.[33]

He scrutinized closely the behavior of two men he guided to the summit of Mount Whitney. They became caricatures in an article on the climb, types familiar to most mountain guides. He wrote about them with a subdued and ironic sense of humor. Bayley, the inveterate whooper, didn't think of consequences, frequently lamented the absence of danger, but nearly killed his fellow climber by loosening and dropping a rock. Washburn, the young student, was cautious, undemonstrative, and wiser. He climbed the mountain "like a child clinging timidly to its mother." To Muir, the determination and persistence of a Washburn was preferable to the rash enthusiasm of a Bayley, who said he "could or at least *would* follow" Muir anywhere. On the summit, Muir noted Washburn's "becoming satisfaction" when he said "I'm the first and only student visitor to this highest land in North America." All men who climbed the mountains should behave as students and visitors, Muir thought; Washburn's care and decorum were appropriate. As is clear from his journal, Muir's chief concern as a guide, in the mountains with friends or in the pages of the *Bulletin*, was to help people to forget themselves, escape from the anthropocentric poisons of the cities, and live in the eternal moments which could be theirs in Nature.[34]

THE MEANING OF RECREATION

When one comes out of the woods everything is novel. . . . even our fellow beings are regarded with something of the same keenness and freshness of perception that is brought to a new species of wild animal.

John Muir, November, 1875

Few tourists spend all of their time contemplating wild scenery. Even if Muir himself was primarily interested in the "original" condition of the West, he still found himself thinking about the way the landscape was being recreated and re-created by men.[35] The direction this re-creation might take troubled him deeply because he knew it was inescapable. Agriculture certainly offered the best hope for the future, if only it would take a careful and moral direction, but there was little evidence of that happening. Agriculture as a way of life might be the least of evils if conducted on a reverential and scientific basis which led to a harmonious and lasting relationship between men and the land. Muir flirted with agriculture as a pastoral compromise.

Like the narrator of Thoreau's "Where I Lived and What I Lived For," Muir seemed to contemplate every place he visited in the late seventies as a possible site for permanent residence. He sent his observations along to the *Bulletin* — sketches of the inhabitants of La-Grange, Pasadena, Salt Lake City; all thought they had found a good thing. An old friend who had settled in Pasadena told him, "[There] is a block of land that is for sale; buy it and be my neighbor; plant five acres with orange trees, and by the time your last mountain is climbed their fruit will be your fortune." Muir responded with sympathy and appreciation to this and other offers. He appeared generally pleased to see the growth of agriculture in southern California in 1877: "Travel-worn pioneers, who have been tossed about like boulders in flood-time, are thronging hither as to a kind of terrestrial heaven, resolved to rest. They build, and plant, and settle, and so come under natural influences. When a man plants a tree he plants himself." Seduced by such a vision of spiritual plenty, the man who did this kind of work produced "grander miracles every day than were ever written." Muir thought that the development of agriculture in California was a *comparatively* good thing. The prayers of the farmer, expressed in seeds, slips, and rootlets, were far superior to the miners' singleminded prayers for wealth, when "in the search the seekers too often become insane, and strike about blindly in the dark like raving madmen." Muir believed he saw a serious attempt by his fellow westerners to re-create a more lasting, healthy, and harmonious life in their land, after what he called the "fever" or "the disturbance of the gold period."[36]

When portraying a sharp contrast between the old mining ethic and the new agricultural ethic he wrote as an optimist, because he wished to foster the hope that a new and better life was coming to the West. After meeting John Nelder in Giant Forest, he commented with sympathy on the forty-niners; he had met many. "How sad the tones of the invisible undercurrent of many a life here, now the clang and excitements of the gold battles are over. What wrecks of hopes and health, and how truly interesting are those wrecks. Perhaps no other country in the world contains so many rare and interesting men." Yet he would not cater to the sentimental lies about gold periods in California or elsewhere; he spoke of "Nevada's dead towns" with clear and cold authority. These were monuments to the failure of wasted effort, "monuments of fraud and ignorance — sins against science. . . . like prayers of any kind not in harmony with nature, they are unanswered." And this judgment applied to more than just mining. It applied to all get-rich-quick schemes. Of the rural homesteads near Murphy's camp he said, "In spite of all the rustic beauty of these dell cabins, they can hardly be called homes. They are only a better kind of camps, gladly abandoned whenever the hoped-for gold harvest has been gathered." In these places Muir sensed an air of "profound unrest and melancholy," which could be contrasted to the happy communal life of Grangers in Tulare County. He assured his readers that like wildcat mining, "wildcat farming is dead." He hoped for a more permanent life in the land. He saw room for more farming in Nevada through the use of wells and limited but unused surface water, which still "reached old deathbeds in the desert." He was pleased by the gardens, orchards, and flowers surrounding the houses in Salt Lake City and Pasadena.[37]

He reported the reclamation, redemption, and recreation of men who turned from get-rich-quick schemes to the steady work of agriculture. These individuals sprinkled his narratives. He admired the aims of Livingston Stone of the United States Fish Commission, who worked on the McCloud River restoring wasted waters and extending the range of food fishes. Mono Joe Boler had decided to raise hay instead of mining at the foot of Bloody Canyon, and was now worth thirty thousand dollars. The children of Utah were "Utah's best crop," and certainly her most plentiful; they seemed "remarkably bright and promising." But in all this praise there remained an attitude of waiting; Muir respected the energy of these home builders, but wondered about their future; he was compelled to articulate their prayers, but reserved judgment.

Like John Wesley Powell, he knew that the prayers of men were not always answered. He warned in 1877 in Nevada that he did not want to give the impression that agriculture was, or ever would be, of major importance in the Great Basin, and that the limit had already been approached. Lumber in Nevada was also limited, and "of an inferior kind." Nevada's largest crop was pine nuts, "perhaps greater than the entire wheat crop of California," though "fortunately for the Indians and wild animals that gather around Nature's board, this crop is not easily harvested in a monopolizing way." This reference to California's agricultural monopoly shows that Muir knew the Homestead Act had not succeeded in creating the family farm in the West, but his critical attitude took a different direction from Henry George's.[38]

When Muir guessed how little of Nevada would "be made to blossom in grass and wheat," he turned this disappointing fact to an unexpected advantage: "If tillers of the soil can thus be brought to see that possibly Nature may have other uses even for *rich* soil besides the feeding of human beings, then will these foodless 'deserts' have taught a fine lesson." Like Powell, he felt the need to cast a skeptical and scientific eye on the Myth of the Garden which had been the basis of the Homestead Act. A case in point was provided by a character he satirized in his article on the San Gabriel Mountains, a fellow he described in allegorical fashion. This "strange, dark man of doubtful parentage" talked to Muir in the dark of his cabin because he was out of candles. He hoped to settle among the boulders at the mouth of Eaton Canyon, "make money, and marry a Spanish woman." He was busy mining for water: "People mine for irrigating water along the foothills as for gold." He already envisioned an orange orchard in "a small irregular patch of gravelly detritus," and knew where he would plant his vines; and where he would put his bee boxes. "All this propsective affluence in the sunken, boulder-choked flood-bed of Eton Creek!" Muir marveled. No wonder Muir preferred to say a word for wild Nature; he was appalled by the unreasonable expectations of civilized men.[39]

He even had doubts about Jeanne Carr's Carmelita, which seemed to him a foolishly artificial, and therefore unlikely, project. Mrs. Carr hoped to grow a little Eden in Pasadena, and occasionally asked Muir's help as she collected new plants and researched the trees of California. Said Muir, "I suppose nothing less than an *Exhaustive* miniature of all the leafy creatures of the globe will satisfy your Pasadena aspirations. You know how little real sympathy

I can give in such play-garden schemes." The best Eden was planted by God. How near Muir was in 1879 to disobeying his own advice. A few years later he would be planting gardens on his ranch in Martinez, and grafting trees while he cultivated cash crops.[40]

It is doubtful that Muir ever wanted to write about the romance of farming, but when Robert Underwood Johnson of *Scribner's* requested an essay on farm life, Muir tried to oblige him. He collected his material, and tried to create a unified picture of the state of agriculture in the West. Probably this attempt is a manuscript called "California Agriculture," which was never published. It is a suspiciously humanistic and optimistic document, and perhaps its viewpoint was created by Muir's desire to meet the expectations of *Scribner's*. In any case, Johnson first tried to get him to condense it, and then finally rejected the essay.[41]

Never was Muir more wrong about the direction of history. He observed, for instance, that the farm monopolies in the Central Valley were a thing of the past: ". . . fortunately farming on so collossal a scale even with improved implements and good cultivation seldom pays, and therefore the big grants are being subdivided into comparatively small lots and sold to true husbandsmen." Clearly he had missed the larger reality which would destroy the hopes of "true husbandsmen" in the West. Muir predicted an agrarian utopia in the Central Valley; his vision of "the most foodful and beautiful of all the lowland valleys of like extent in the world" would result from a preserved forest watershed, storage reservoirs, and other practices he had learned about from Mormon water-rights systems and Nevada farming.[42]

He failed to consider the economic forces which were already shaping the American landscape. Henry Nash Smith explains:

The agrarian utopia in the garden of the world was destroyed, or rather aborted, by the land speculator and the railroad monopolist. These were in turn but expressions of the larger forces at work in American society after the Civil War — the machine, the devices of corporation finance, and the power of big business over Congress. The Homestead Act failed because it was incongruous with the Industrial Revolution.[43]

Perhaps Muir had deceived himself to please a hypothetical audience, or did not fully consider what he was saying. As his other articles for *Scribner's* make clear, his perspective of agriculture had not really changed; as long as he viewed the farms *from the mountains* all of man's improvements appeared as blots on the landscape.

It is fortunate that *Scribner's* did not publish his essay on farm life. When, in 1882, he rewrote the material after working as a farmer for several years, he expressed his true and complex attitude toward the developing agriculture of California. Today, walking through what is left of the Strenzel ranch in the Alhambra Valley, surrounded by suburban sprawl, one can appreciate the vision of a desolate future which Muir projected in "Bee-Pastures of California." This essay was his final and dystopian view of the Californian Pastoral.

BEE PASTORAL

Wild animals were always the best guides to the harmonious working of Nature's economy. If the water ouzel inhabited the canyons, the Douglas squirrel was master forester, the wild sheep traveled the alpine peaks, then the bee was the gardener of California's flora.[44]

Surely Muir would sense the ironic connection between the symbolism of the free, happy Shasta bees he wrote about in 1874 and the insignia of the State of Utah — a great hive of bees with the motto "Industry" printed below. The bee could be seen as a symbol with more than one meaning. Muir thought the industry of Utah's men was most unbeelike. Polygamy, he thought, "exerts a more degrading influence upon husbands than upon wives. The love of the latter finds expression in flowers and children, while the former seem to be rendered incapable of pure love of anything." The men were beaten down by too much business, and had a "sort of Uriah Heep manner." Although he did not oppose industry as a human trait, he was appalled by the blind or joyless work which produced "humble" tradesmen and dutiful husbands. The Douglas squirrel was the very image of industry and energy, but of a cheerful sort: a harvester who was also a planter. So too, the bee, the great pollinator, became Muir's image of the industrious gardener of flowers. Industry ought to produce a better, more peaceful life. The bee's kind of agriculture made more flowers, not fewer.[45]

Muir wrote to Jeanne Carr that his "last efforts were on the preservation of the Sierra forests, and the wild and trampled conditions of our flora from a bee's point of view." He would use the symbolic strategy that he had first used to emphasize the pastoral aspect of tourism. His viewpoint would be the same as that found in modern books which attempt an ecological perspective –"Red Winged Blackbird" in *An Island Called California,* for instance, or *Track of the Grizzly,* which presents the reader with the Yellowstone ecosystem from the bear's point of view. Humans, like the grizzly, are used to a view from the top of the food pyramid, but what does a bee see? What is it like to live on flowers without destroying them?[46]

Muir was not simply interested in a view of the state's "original" condition, but also in what men had done to it. Like Raymond Dasmann's *Destruction of California,* Muir's essay was a vision of progress from an ecological perspective. "When California was wild, it was one sweet bee-garden," Muir began; but not any longer, not since the coming of the plow and sheep: "Culture thus far has given no adequate compensation, at least in kind — acres of alfalfa for miles of the richest wild pasture, ornamental roses and honeysuckles around cottage doors for cascades of wild roses in the dells, and small, square orchards and orange-groves for broad mountain-belts of chaparral." From a bee's point of view it appeared that agri-culture had destroyed a boundless garden and replaced it with circumscribed plots. The culture of the fields was better, thought the bee, when the state was under a wild cultivation, when the fields were the cult of the bee. The root of "culture" indicates not only tilling and care, but worship and dwelling. So agriculture could be worship and dwelling in the fields.

The strategy is similar to that of "Wild Wool," where Muir contrasted fine wild and coarse tame culture. The bees themselves were solar-powered, "impelled by sun-power, as water-wheels by water-power," like the flowers they fed on and pollinated; they were "dainty feeders" who "hug their favorite flowers with profound cordiality, and push their blunt, polleny faces against them, like babies on their mother's bosom. And fondly too," Muir continued, "with eternal love, does Mother Nature clasp her small bee-babies, and suckle them, multitudes at once, on her warm Shasta breast."

If the reader wanted sentiment, here it was in sweet abundance. If Shasta was a breast to the bees, then their honey was a kind of spiritual food, "exactly delicious," Muir had thought in 1874, "and no wonder, inasmuch as it was in great part derived from the nectal bells of a huckleberry bog by bees that were let alone to follow their own sweet ways." In apparent seriousness, Muir considered the possibility of a domesticated bee culture, which had never gained much attention in the great Central Valley, where honey and wax consumed at home was "scarcely taken into account among the coarser products of the farm." Here the contrast between coarse and fine was taken a step further toward a condemnation of all coarser agricultural practices.[47]

If commercial bee culture began in California in 1853, it had made little progress; "sheep, cattle, and grain raising are the chief industries, as they require less skill and care, while the profits thus far have been greater." Muir knew that agriculture as fortune-seeking —"wildcat agriculture," as he called it—had destroyed the Central Valley, its ranches becoming centers of desolation, not truly homes. Though he foresaw the time when the whole valley would be tilled like a garden and irrigated "giving rise to prosperous towns, wealth, arts, etc."—when there would "be few left, even among botanists, to deplore the vanished primeval flora"—he saw at present only waste, and in 1882 he was disgusted.

His complex and ambivalent attitude toward agriculture was clear, and may have indicated the difficulty he was having in adjusting to the prospect of life as a farmer in the Alhambra Valley. He found the prospect of a Central Valley "tilled like a garden" not an adequate compensation for the wild garden lost, yet he also found such a future inescapable, even as he became a planter of tame Tokays and Bartlett pears. As a result, he could only condemn in explicit terms the waste occasioned by hasty, profit-motivated development. If people would make homes and learn to dwell in the Central Valley, he would have to make peace with the losses of wild Nature.

It was too late to save the Central Valley. More than even Muir knew, its wild bloom was long gone. He had never seen the perennial glory which the Spanish shepherds had destroyed. He mourned only the passing of the valley's annual glory. He was led in his search for bee pastures out of the valley and into a survey of the bee resources of the whole state. He worried that "before long the wild honey-bloom of the mountains will vanish as completely as that of the fertile lowlands." He began to envision a pastoral buffer zone of bee culture between the heavy farming of the valleys and the forest wildernesses above. Since "the plow has not invaded the forest region to any appreciable extent," he proposed that "thousands of bee ranches might be established" in the foothills. Further, the more arid region, normally regarded as desert, might be utilized as it was rather than being "reclaimed" through impossible schemes. If men saw no use for such an arid region, "very little of it, however, is desert in the eyes of a bee."[48]

Such a program, taken seriously, would require that bees be protected from droughts like the one of 1877. The "small winged cattle" would need supplementary feeding, or pehaps bee farmers could save their hives "by cutting roads back into the mountains, and taking them into the heart of the flowery chaparral." Advocating this practice, Muir pointed out that "the Santa Lucia, San Rafael, San Gabriel, San Jacinto, and San Bernardino ranges are almost untouched as yet save by wild bees." These mountains, all named for saints, were of course spiritual resources; when Muir attempted to quilt together the ragged edges of the remaining Californian landscape, he was making one last attempt to repair a pastoral dream, a place where one could "drift away confidingly into the broad gulf-streams of Nature, helmed only by Instinct."

The neglected mountains of California indicated Californians' false perceptions about their state. At the conclusion of his essay, as Muir stood at the top of Mount San Antonio, he had a sort of vision from the summit of Pisgah. He had not expected a view of the promised land from the San Gabriel range—"from base to summit all seemed gray barren, silent, its glorious chaparral appearing like dry moss creeping over its dull, wrinkled ridges and hollows"; but strangely, he found water on his excursion, and a flowery "impenetrable growth of honey bushes." From the summit he saw the "sage brush country . . . far as the eye could reach, the landscape was one vast bee-pasture." As promised land, it was not milk and honey by human standards, but "very little of it . . . [was] desert in the eyes of a bee."

A most interesting twist. If Muir began his essay by describing the Central Valley garden which California had turned into a desert, he ended by pointing to a so-called desert which was really a garden. If Californians persisted in turning their flowerlands into agricultural lands which were, paradoxically, deserts, then they still dismissed most of their lands, not realizing that these too were promised lands.

As a proposal, Muir's plan for bee culture cut two ways, into both false vision and foolish practices of his fellow Californians. If they took him literally as making a plea for bee culture, he told them that bee keeping was in its infancy and the domestic bee an immigrant. But then California was in its infancy, and the population largely immigrant. Perhaps the human immigrants were the least mature and least perceptive of all visitors to California. Like Moses, Muir was permitted to see the promised land, but his brothers would be the ones to take stewardship. So the prophet was unable to "measure the influence on bee interests likely to follow the destruction of the forests, now rapidly falling before forest fire and axe." Surely, as he said earlier in the essay, the effects of sheep and the attendant fires set by shepherds who hoped to "improve" the range would set "in motion a long train of evils which will certainly reach far beyond bees and beekeepers." Hence he became a satirist when he ended the essay with a sentence that would become, twelve years later, the conclusion of *The Mountains of California*: "In short, notwithstanding the wide-spread deterioration and destruction of every kind already effected, California, with her incomparable climate and flora, is still, as far as I know, the best of all the bee-lands in the world." The California of the future might be a suitable land only for bees.[49]

Few readers recognized the full impact of these words; after a decade-long attempt to make Californians see that much of their state was not a desert, Muir was suggesting that they might just as well cultivate a taste for wastelands. That was what they were making of their state. Perhaps because Muir's own feelings were tangled, ambivalent, and too embittered with the losses he had seen, he ended up writing a satire which was too subtle. Certainly *Scribner's* seemed unaware of his message, since they illustrated "Bee-Pastures" with a romantic etching of shepherd and sheep, just as they had earlier illustrated Muir's "Glacier Meadows of the Sierra" with a similar sketch. Muir objected to such a picture, but his answer from Johnson, his editor, was that the illustration "was praised as a piece of sentiment."[50]

Perhaps Muir had moderated his position too much in the seventies. In trying to make peace with the society in which he would have to live, he had chosen to accept Man's right to find a home in Nature, his right to make improvements in order to make a home. Even while he attacked the myths that represented the American West as either desert or garden, even while showing that Nature did not divide her realm so simply, he had accepted the image of the American farmer reposing on the bosom of the American Earth. He found it difficult not to believe in a generation of "hardy and virtuous yeomen," in an agriculture which would be better than the urban or mining cultures. Perhaps, as Henry Nash Smith argues, the agricultural utopia was doomed by the Industrial Revolution. But from Muir's point of view, Californians claimed to be living in a democracy where the will of the people determined the future of the landscape. He wondered about the American people and their government—about their intelligence, their strength, their will. He wondered if they could learn.[51]

Toward the end of 1881 he had reason to wonder about American democracy. He had been involved in legislative efforts to enlarge Yosemite and the Mariposa Grove, and had also helped draft a proposal for a park in Sequoia and Kings Canyon. Both proposals failed to get through congressional committee. Perhaps because he was so disheartened, he turned to private affairs for the next seven years. The tone of "Bee-Pastures" suggested such a turning away: Muir viewed at an alienated distance the affairs of California, and then washed his hands of the matter. Even eight years later he wrote to Robert Underwood Johnson, "The love of Nature among Californians is desperately moderate; consuming enthusiasm almost wholly unknown." He must have recognized that moderation was the worst enemy to his cause, that his campaign of the seventies was, finally, a failure.[52]

9

The Genteel Wilderness

Many years ago, the writer, in company with an accidental
party of travellers, was gazing on a cataract of great height,
breadth, and impetuosity, the summit of which appeared to
blend with the sky and clouds, while the lower part was
hidden by rocks and trees; and on his observing, that it
was, in the strictest sense of the word, a sublime object, a
lady present assented with warmth to the remark, adding—
"Yes! and it is not only sublime, but beautiful and absolutely pretty."
Coleridge, "On the Principles of Genial
Criticism Concerning the Fine Arts"

What does it matter whether the scene was beauti-
ful, sublime, or picturesque? The lady liked it, and even in Coleridge's
version of the conversation she showed more enthusiasm than the
genial critic, more cordial sympathy toward Nature. She, at least,
was moved. In her excitement she failed to make significant distinctions, to recognize aesthetic categories, perhaps because she did not
stand at a sufficient distance from the scene for proper judgment.[1]

Muir thought of aesthetic distance, which is synonymous with
disinterested aesthetic judgment, as a reprehensible habit of mind in
Ruskin, whom he characterized as superintending and reporting on
Nature "with the conceit and lofty importance of a factor of a duke's
estate." "You can never feel that there is the slightest *union* betwixt
Nature and him." Just as beauty was what mortals called something
that was really eternal, so too all aesthetic categories told one about

236

humans, about Man's limitations rather than about Nature. When men began to organize their observations of Nature into categories, they ceased to wonder. Emerson had said as much to Muir while they wandered together in Mariposa Grove: "The wonder is that we can see these trees and not wonder more!"[2]

This is a philosophical position directly opposed to that of the humanist, particularly the new humanist, who argues (1) that philosophical assumptions are unavoidable, (2) that the essential quality of experience is not natural, but ethical, (3) that there is a sharp dualism between human beings and Nature, and (4) that human will is free. Unlike Emerson, the humanist could not say enough for Man's wonderful capacity to wonder. For a humanist there is a real distinction between what men call sublime and what men call beautiful in Nature. For him, the aesthetic categories of men are more important than the seamless whole of the universe. When applied to a landscape, such categories become part and parcel of man's desire to dominate Nature, since they divide and conquer by reducing Nature to human-sized pieces.[3]

Perhaps I am being too dogmatic. For the present, it may be enough to say that aesthetic categories tell us more about men than about nature, and so Muir's use of aesthetic categories tells us about him, or about his assumptions about the audience he directed them toward.

The most anthropocentric of aesthetic categories was certainly that called the picturesque. Falling between what could be called beautiful (that which was lawful, understandable, and unified in Nature, and which could be appreciated because of its inherent form — a daisy, for instance) and the sublime (that which seemed infinite in size or power, and thus could not be comprehended or fully understood by men because it transcended human judgment), the picturesque was devised as a kind of "wild civility," a way to create an aesthetic whole, or to make a moderate scene out of sublime elements. Essentially, the observer who looked for the picturesque tried to see Nature as it conformed with the rules of painting. Nature is seen as picturesque in the paintings of the Hudson River School and in the literary descriptions of James Fenimore Cooper. The picturesque also took on a more vulgar form, however, in which everything that was interesting to the tourist could be described in con-

ventional terms. Thus one had books called *Picturesque America,
Picturesque California Homes,* and the collection Muir edited in
1887–88, *Picturesque California and the Region West of the Rocky
Mountains, from Alaska to Mexico.* The archetype for such a book
was Bryant's *Picturesque America,* published in 1872, which aspired
to prove that American scenery was as wonderful as Europe's. It
used the combination of "pen and pencil," writer and artist, attempting to see Nature as if it were art.[4]

These were the forerunners of the Sierra Club Exhibit Format
Books, which have even been used to explicate Muir, as in Brower's
edition of Muir's *First Summer in the Sierra,* called *Gentle Wilderness.* Such a book assumed that the reader could not "see" Nature
unless it were interpreted through the eyes of a pictorial artist; such
a book replaced the viewer's perceptions with a pictorial artist's perceptions, with two-dimensional flat projections, paintings, etchings,
or photographs. The editor of *Gentle Wilderness* said in effect that
Muir, even after all his "pathetic fallacy" had been edited away, was
not objective enough. For true objectivity, for us to really appreciate *First Summer in the Sierra,* we needed the eye of the camera.
Although Kauffman's photographs have their own charm, the result of reading such a book is a strangely mixed response. Somehow, the reality of the Sierra is formed not so much by Muir's words
as by the more dramatic and impressive color photographs; they
create the image of the Sierra presented in the book. Most readers,
I think, would assume that those photographs are truthful and objective; they tell what the Sierra "really" is. An audience which has
accepted the conventions of the picturesque expects, even demands,
that Nature be portrayed in aesthetic terms, that Nature follow the
rules of pictorial art. The camera doesn't lie, the twentieth century
says. In the nineteenth century, the illustrator, whatever his medium,
had the same tremendous power to create the "reality" presented in
a picturesque book. One might even go a step further and ask if
Picturesque America or *Gentle Wilderness* used their written texts
to fill the interstices between paintings, etchings, or photographs.
A picturesque book is finally a picture book, designed for display
on a parlor table, just as certain paintings are no more than decora-
tion for parlor walls. (I must say that film brings in a new element.
DeWitt Jones, for instance, tried to capture in a film about Muir's

Sierra not scenes, not just individual images, but the larger conception of Nature as flow — the flow of sunlight and seasons.)[5]

One must remember that Muir himself invited this kind of approach to his writings. When he began to use the language of the
picturesque, when he began to play an active part in selecting and
editing the illustrations for his essays, when pictures began to play
a larger part in his own exposition, he was allowing that a picture
really was worth a thousand words. This descent to the picturesque,
which sacrificed a sense of place for aesthetic sensibility, was no
doubt a yielding to the exigencies of public taste. Just as he could
become moderate and learn to use the language of the pastoral ideal,
so too he could use the humanistic language of the aesthete, the language which placed natural scenes in human categories.

One trouble with Coleridge's lady was that she could not see
herself. Further, she did not want the direct experience of Nature,
but rather something which was "absolutely pretty." She wanted her
experience to be limited by a mediating influence, to convert it into
an image or a souvenir. Susan Sontag has recently pointed out that
the twentieth-century tourist who carries a camera is on essentially
the same quest. Taking photographs, she argues, is not only a way
of certifying experience, it is also a way for the tourist to refuse it,
by putting the camera between himself and whatever he encounters. Thus Coleridge's lady hid from her own possible disorienta-
tion by throwing a veil of words over the scene.

But there is a deeper philosophical issue here, which Susan Sontag also lays bare. Again, her critique of popular photography, of
snapshots, indicates that a twentieth-century tourist has only a more
sophisticated technology available. It may not matter whether one
frames a scene with one's hands or with a camera; either way, the
observer is attempting to comprehend what he sees: "Photography
implies that we know about the world if we accept it as the camera
records it. But this is the opposite of understanding, which starts
with *not* accepting the world as it looks. All possibility of understanding is rooted in the ability to say no." When the readers of Muir's
essays said, "Make it pretty, John, make us feel at home and comfortable in the wilderness," they were asking him to mediate for them.
They did not want to expend the necessary effort to understand.[6]

For years he had been warning his friends and readers to beware of first impressions, since a real understanding of Nature came from disciplined contemplation, from suspended disbelief. But from the late 1870s on he was writing for an audience of easterners who would get their wilderness at home, in the parlor. He would provide through art the immediate pleasures they had not received through their lives, so that they might be converted to a belief that wilderness was important. He was beginning to aim at a strategy which Wallace Stegner picked up in 1960; the view of "wilderness as opportunity and idea." He wanted his easterners to recognize that wilderness, even if they never entered it, was part of their "geography of hope." Muir knew that the genteel audience would not be coming out to California in winter to get a firsthand look at the "Snow Banners of the California Alps."[7]

But in the article by that name he could try out, as a tentative experiment, the role of a mannered, civilized, and cultured narrator. Such a role seems so out of character that one wonders what led Muir to this kind of conventional artifice. Perhaps he was trying to show himself that he could do it; perhaps he was yielding to a challenge offered by his friends in San Francisco; perhaps he was even saying to William Keith, "If you can paint a picture of the Sierra, so can I." In any case, *Harper's* bought Muir's article: it worked. By accepting such material, the editors suggested that Muir continue to write in the same vein for an eastern audience. And so he did continue to write picturesque essays in the late seventies, and he would do so again as he returned to writing in the late eighties. One looks for a sharp transition from the wild Muir of the early seventies to the mannered Muir of the late eighties, and finds instead that he gradually accommodated himself to the exigencies of writing for eastern publications. His articles in *Harper's* and *Scribner's* established his reputation in the seventies as a master at describing picturesque scenery, and when he came back to writing he found that his reputation limited his possible publishers. He would have to work within the excessively mannered conventions of a publication like *Picturesque California*.

THE PICTURESQUE SCENE AND THE NEAR VIEW

It is important to remember that Muir the writer was very self-conscious and always knew what he was doing. Just as he invited the public to a moderate landscape at Twenty Hill Hollow, so too he invited the reader in "Snow Banners" to stand on a ridge with him while he pointed to a scene which was, "in the strictest sense of the word," sublime. The aesthetes claimed that a sublime scene could only be appreciated from a safe distance which allowed the viewer to contemplate what would otherwise be a distressingly powerful impression. Muir provided his reader with a safe and comfortable place where the violence of the wind could not be felt, "looking through a calm sheltering opening in the woods, as through a window."[8]

More important, Muir provided aesthetic distance by using the language of art. He was speaking of God's art, asking how God created such scenes, but he spoke with the language of human artifice. The purpose, it seemed, was to turn a scene which might normally be taken as "the war of the elements" into something lawfully beautiful. He was working with a strategy contrary to that of the humanist since he wished to make men see that a sublime natural scene contained an inner law and didn't require men to give it form. Snow banners were the lawful result of snow, a north wind, and the glacial forms of the Sierra, Muir argued. If the banners he saw streaming off the "Crown of the Sierra" seemed "in every way perfect," that was not only because God Himself was an artist, but because beauty was the natural result of His creativity, a diminished though humanly understandable consequence.

The essay fairly drenched the reader in the language of artifice. The banners were "as regular in form and as firm in texture as if woven of fine silk." Such "imposing spectacles" were "like a clear painting on the sky." At his forest window, Muir too was artificial as he said, "And now, reader, come with a clear mind for a few moments and fancy yourself . . . looking with your own eyes." He constantly reminded his companion readers of their comfort, and of their distance from the wild gale and the tempestuous roar: "They are twenty miles away, but you would not wish them nearer, for every feature is distinct, and the whole is seen in its right proportions, like a well-hung picture on a parlor wall." Muir himself, in creating this "picture on a parlor wall," was responsible for the diminished sense of Nature's glory it provided. The unstated lesson of the essay was that an attempt to describe a sublime scene must diminish natural glory so that a cultivated reader might see its beauty.

Even while he described the "chief features of the picture as seen from the forest window," even while he asked that the reader mark the lines and textures of the scene, he revealed his impatience with an aesthetic view which required foreground, middleground, and background. For him, it was not as important to view the scene as to be *in* it: "It would still be a surpassingly glorious [view] were the whole of the fore and middle grounds, with their domes and forests, obliterated altogether, leaving only the black peaks, the white banners, and the blue sky on which they are painted." "Snow Banners" is a nice enough piece until one thinks about the Muir who had always believed that the only true experience of Nature required getting out of one's self and into Nature.

On a late fall afternoon, after the season's first storm, I wander out through the hills near June Lake, California. The aspens are turning, a new cold light streams over the ridges of the Sierra, and the wind pours through the passes. I can smell winter coming. On a day like this, on a walk like this, I remind myself that Nature is no picture on a parlor wall. But Muir must have known that very well. He must have also decided that such pictures could and would appeal to an audience he couldn't reach with an ecological argument — the cultured people, the ones who might have the power to act on Muir's ideas. And it did work on readers like Robert Underwood Johnson, who became Muir's most important ally in the nineties. And it did work on David Starr Jordan, who was much too conservative to like Muir's wilder sort of writing.

With Muir's picturesque writing in mind, it is worthwhile to reread his essay on the ascent of Ritter. In chapter three I read it as a parable about his method of study, a method that taught him more than any aesthetic view of Nature could provide. Now I will reverse my reasoning and read it as an attempt by Muir to create an essay structured by aesthetic language.

When he stepped through the foreground and middleground while narrating his ascent of Mount Ritter in the essay "In the Heart of the California Alps," the scene he entered was precisely the one which still remained in the distance in "Snow Banners": "a deep chasm drawn between the divide and the glacier separated the massive picture from everything else. Only the one sublime mountain in sight, the one glacier, and one lake; the whole veiled with one blue shadow—

rock, ice and water without a single leaf." He was literally entering his own string of pictures as he proceeded to climb the mountain and survey the scene, and as he discovered far-reaching harmonies which were not available to the artist's distant perspective. He described them quadrant by quadrant. The whole narrative, in fact, was structured in order to allow the reader to appreciate some of the significance of his climb: "The lessons and enjoyments of even a single day would probably weary most readers, however consumingly interested they might be if brought into actual contact with them. Therefore, I am only going to offer some characteristic pictures, drawn from the wildest places, and strung together on a strip of narrative." The lessons and enjoyments were not really discrete, as his characteristic pictures make them appear. The picturing itself, which stopped movement and put the experiences into frames, was an artifice which Muir knew distorted the true nature of his revelation. Even though he tried to break such a rigid structure with the flowing rhythm of his prose, distortion was the price he would have to pay if he were to turn his intense mountaineering insights into a vehicle for public participation in wilderness. Though his essay defended mountaineering and the near view as a way to vision, it also provided the kind of word-pictures the audience could enjoy at home. Thus Muir really sent out two messages: one for those who really wanted to know, and the other for those who wanted to sympathize, but would never know.[9]

The *Scribner's* articles of the late seventies were, then, written in the conventions of the picturesque. And they show how easily Muir made his transition into the fashionable language so loved by the eastern press. He was writing genteel material for a genteel press. Here was the origin of the "genteel wilderness."

When he replaced the "evergreen oak . . . craggy and angular as the valley itself . . . an admirable type of the craggy Merced cañon tree" with an elm tree in "The Mountain Lakes of California," Muir was well on his way toward a toned-down version of the Sierra, and one is not surprised to find descriptions of landscape that accord with the conventions of the picturesque. "Picturesque junipers," "venturesome dwarf pines," and "graceful fringes" of oaks stood out in contrast against "unflinching rockiness" as Muir redrew for easterners his image of the Sierra. All through his *Scribner's* articles his imagery took on the anthropocentric conventions of the picturesque. A lake was born "when, like a young eye it first opens to the light," and lakes were described as "strung together like beads."[10]

Muir hoped that this kind of artifice would make sentimental readers love the mountains they had never seen. Speaking to his eastern friends, he said, "Everything about you is beating with warm, terrestrial, human love, delightfully substantial and familiar." He began to attempt scenic pictures of certain types of lakes and meadows to "give a hint of the fine beauty that lies hid in the wildernesses of the California Alps." Even his use of the term "California Alps" was a clue to his concession to the expectations of the picturesque tradition; Nature looked like art, and the Sierra looked like the Alps which the genteel audience had experienced in the prints and paintings of Europe. After all, the American painters had all taken an obligatory trip to Europe and had learned to paint landscapes there before they had returned to paint the landscapes of the American West.[11]

But Muir was not totally lost to the importance of his own vision during these years. He resisted a morbid version of the picturesque, a gothic view of wilderness, knowing it could lead to the gothic of Ruskin; Muir wrote, "And I know something about 'the blasted trunk, and the barren rock, the moaning of the bleak winds, the solemn solitudes of moors and seas, the roar of the black, perilous, merciless whirlpools of the mountain streams;' and they have a language for me, but they declare nothing of wrath or of hell, only Love plain as was ever spoken." Though his language was in danger — grave danger — his undiminished appreciation of the extravagant and the exuberant was apparent when he wrote of the trees and the falls of the Sierra. Yet here he fell into a habit which he frowned upon when speaking of the works of Nature: the habit of comparison and contrast, the judgment of relative merit when speaking of living trees and waters — all equal in the eyes of their creator.[12]

THE GREEN DANCE OF TREES
AND THE WHITE PLUNGE OF WATERS

If Muir was going to provide readers with a picture of Sierran conifers, he was also going to warn readers that any instant enlightenment about these forests was unlikely. Few, he thought, had "gone far enough and lived long enough with the trees to gain anything like a loving conception of their grandeur and significance." The real appreciation of Sierran forests went beyond a momentary aesthetic appreciation; "For knowledge of this kind one must dwell with the trees and grow with them, without any reference to time in the almanac sense."[13]

Further, he was suspicious of the very kind of essay he was writing, which would give static portraits or fixed classifications of individual species of Sierran conifers. He was displeased with the books by other authors he consulted while working on his articles, and said to Jeanne Carr, "How a tree book can be exhaustive when every species is ever on the wing from one form to another with infinite variety, it is not easy to see." Yet his own judgments were based on fixed notions of the different species. His articles on pines really comprised a portrait gallery.[14]

For him, "the noblest pine yet discovered" was the sugar pine, and for good reason. Admitting that in most pines there was "a sameness of expression, which, to most people, is apt to become monotonous," he applauded the individual character of the sugar pine, "as free from conventionalities of form and motion as any oak. . . . No two are alike, even to the most inattentive observer; and, notwithstanding they are ever tossing out their immense arms in what might seem most extravagant gestures, there is a majesty and repose about them that precludes all possibility of the grotesque, or even picturesque, in their general expression." The juniper, however, he found less pleasing because it seemed an aged relic, "reminding one of the crumbling towers of some ancient castle scantily draped with ivy." The tree was too picturesque: "Its fine color and odd picturesqueness always catch an artist's eye, but to me the Juniper seems a singularly dull and taciturn tree, never speaking to one's heart." I think there is something perverse in this judgment—Muir seemed to dislike the juniper precisely because it was judged by men to be picturesque. Thus he was still trapped by conventional aesthetic standards, even while rebelling against them.[15]

He continued in the same vein when he dealt with waterfalls in *Picturesque California*, preferring the extravagant to the regular, and disliking that which is conventionally picturesque. Thus, he did not prefer Vernal Fall: "It is the most staid and orderly of all the

great falls, and never shows any marked originality of form or behavior." Perhaps Muir devalued Vernal because it was "a general
favorite among the visitors," or perhaps he preferred Nevada Fall,
because it was so impetuous. Later, in "Treasures of Yosemite," he
complained that Vernal was "proper and exact . . . with scarce a hint
of the passionate enthusiasm of the Yosemite or the Nevada." Such
anthropocentric comparisons, then, were becoming stock-in-trade
despite Muir's desire to avoid the conventional picturesque. Even
when he asserted himself against the stereotyped aesthetic categories, he used their unconscious assumptions in making his judgments.
This was a hard habit to break, once he had begun.[16]

While praising Illilouette, he found himself embroiled in the
kind of abstractions that such comparisons brought on: "It is not
nearly so grand a fall as the Upper Yosemite, so symmetrical as the
Vernal, or so nobly simple as the Bridal Veil; nor does it present
so overwhelming an outgush of snowy magnificence as the Nevada,
but in the richness and exquisite fineness of texture of its flowing
folds it surpasses them all." As if Yosemite Valley were a theater or
convention stadium in which the falls competed in some kind of
beauty contest! Once Muir had been elected judge, he had to make
his decisions in terms the audience could understand. One must grant
that he was trying to make his reader see the wealth of beauty in
Yosemite, trying to speak for neglected rights; but such a strategy
became a trap.[17]

As his comparisons stretched out, he found himself linking Hetch
Hetchy to Yosemite, and Alaska to Yosemite, using the language of
Yosemite for other landscapes. Perhaps because many of his essays
in *Picturesque California* were hastily written summaries of earlier,
richer narratives, he was writing about too much, with too little compass, and of course his experiences were flat when reduced to the
bare bones; they appeared almost superficial. In his essay "Yosemite
Valley," for instance, he hustled the reader through Sierran forests,
Sequoia groves, all the major falls in the Valley, the source of Yosemite Creek, lunar rainbows, the views from Sentinel Dome and
Glacier Point, an ascent of Half Dome, the seasons in the Valley,
avalanches, snow banners, wildlife, the Hetch Hetchy Valley and
its falls, and finally ended up in the Kings River Yosemite. He was
beginning to sound like one of those literary racers he had once
laughed at.

On the other hand, *Picturesque California* allowed Muir to manage some good syntheses of materials which had been spread in various publications during the seventies. His essay on the Shasta region unified previously dispersed material. This was the best article he ever wrote on Shasta, and gave a nice sense of the wholeness of the region which surrounded the grand fire mountain. In a separate chapter about Yosemite he was beginning to discover that he could bring together a collection of near views, as he did when dealing with Yosemite Fall. In this section of an otherwise rambling essay, he put together his views from behind and from the top and bottom of Yosemite Fall in a thorough narrative of one man's attempt to approach a sublime and powerful natural phenomenon. Such an approach would lead to his more effective use of the near view two years later in "Treasures of Yosemite." But he failed in his first attempt because he only vaguely reconsidered his own experiences. His near views seemed blurred because he was reluctant to dramatize his own experiences. Most of his shots were scattered, and his arguments were lost in a chaotic collection of observations.

Undoubtedly, Muir's problems were partly a result of the ambiguous nature of the project. He was employed by the J. Dewing Company of New York and San Francisco to edit and contribute essays to a loosely organized group of illustrated publications, to be issued serially, which would attempt to portray the United States west of the Rockies, from Alaska to California. The project lasted from 1887 to 1890, and Muir became increasingly impatient with his own role in it. His writing was far from lively, and the writing of other contributors was hardly more inspired. More than anything else, *Picturesque California* demonstrates that San Francisco's literary renaissance did not live past the middle seventies. It is hard to say what the thesis of the series was. Muir wrote to Jeanne Carr that the object of the publication was amorphous; "What a bright appreciative traveller would like to see and hear is what is wanted as near as I can make out." The publishers had neither thesis to offer nor direction to give, and Muir found himself unable to give his own direction to the finished copy. No wonder he was not happy about his commitment to the serialized structure of *Picturesque California*.[18]

Meanwhile, the conditions under which he was writing were unpleasant. As his father-in-law was approaching death, Muir had to isolate himself in San Francisco in a hotel to get anything done at all. Even though he was editor of the project, his publishers seemed to have the final word about his decisions. Haste in his writing produced a kind of telescoping of experience which led to repetition. His visions of sunsets and alpenglow on Mount Ritter, on Mount Hood, and in Alaska were either described as "effects"—which is to say impressions—or as "terrestrial manifestations of God." The latter phrase, after being used several times in the series, began to lose its interest and became a cliché.

He seemed to wonder why he was writing a book called "picturesque" anything. In his essay on Alaska he said, "To sketch picturesque bits definitely bounded is comparatively an easy task—a lake in the woods, a glacier meadow, a cascade in its dell, or even a grand mountain landscape. . . . But in this web of scenery embroidering the northern coast there is such indefinite expansiveness." Illustrations didn't help much. There is a nice painting by Thomas Hill of the Muir Glacier, but in the book it loses the luminescence of the original. As one senses, even in a recent book on Glacier Bay, many pictures of ice cubes on beaches do not really give a sense of being there. The illustrations for *Picturesque California* seem as washed out as Muir's own style. They were vague, insubstantial, and represented the antithesis of the sharp focus of a near view.[19]

He became downright irritable, and in desperation described the squalid and littered streets of Wrangel in Alaska as filled with "picturesque obstructions." The whole idea was ridiculous. How had he gotten into it? By 1888 he didn't need the money. He was writing presumably because it was still important to say a word for the wilderness.

He had accepted the project with his eyes open, and had known that he would be involved in a book very much like Bryant's *Picturesque America*. As Bryant claimed in the introduction to his book, such an enterprise was occasioned by a desire "for the elements of natural beauty in new combinations, and for regions not yet rifled of all that they can yield to the pencil," and because "Art sighs to carry her conquests into new realms." Such books brought a kind of artistic imperialism to the West, and were an aesthetic version of Manifest Destiny; *Picturesque America* was not so much about America's wild landscape as it was about what Americans could do with it, as artists or as the bringers of culture. It was natural, then, that *Picturesque America* and *Picturesque California* did not confine themselves to "the natural beauties of our country," but included "the various aspects impressed on it by civilization." Wonderful. Muir was working on a type of book which used Nature as raw material for art, and which found cities like San Francisco and New York equally good material for art. He could not, given the character of the project, turn such a collection into a plea for wild Nature.[20]

Still, he was making a new beginning. Like an old patriarch grizzly, he seemed to be awakening in the spring after a long winter. His growling could be heard here and there in the woods, as throughout these essays he awoke. Sometimes he grumbled in spite of his better judgment.

For instance, his attitude toward tourism was not as optimistic as it should have been for such a book. At one place he thought he saw tourism as "at least a beginning of our return to nature," with people "travelling to better purpose than they knew." But elsewhere he saw tourists as merely ridiculous —"the weak and the strong, unable or unwilling to bear mental taxation." He growled about the noisy gun-shooting and hallooing crowds who returned from the wilderness, who reported "no birds in the woods or game animals of any kind larger than mosquitoes." Muir wanted to reenter the fray and remind his fellow Americans of a right view of Nature.[21]

Further, his disgust with the development of the West was becoming more consolidated, and he could not repress a cynicism that had been present earlier in "Bee-Pastures." When he summarized the "discovery" of North America, he depicted the search in brutal terms:

During the last few centuries, when the maps of the world were in great part blank, the search for new worlds was a fashionable business, and when such large game was no longer to be found, islands lying unclaimed in the great oceans, inhabited by useful and profitable people to be converted or enslaved, became attractive objects; . . . Those early explorers and adventurers were mostly brave, enterprising, and after their fashion, pious men. In their clumsy sailing vessels they dared to go where no chart or light-house showed the way, where the set of the currents, the location of sunken outlying rocks and shoals were all unknown, facing fate and weather, undaunted however dark the signs, heaving the lead and thrashing the men to their duty and trusting in Providence. When a new shore was found on which they could land, they said their prayers with superb audacity, fought the natives if they cared to fight, erected crosses, and took possession in the names of their sovereigns, establishing claims, such as they were, to everything in sight and beyond, to be quarrelled for and battled for, and passed from hand to hand in treaties and settlements made during the intermissions of war.[22]

This violence, Muir saw, was what the settlement of the West was founded on, and such a view must have gravely colored his own explorations in Alaska, where he played a role filling in the blank places and laying claim to at least one island for the United States. The discovery and consequent development were crude and warlike affairs all told, and he knew that they still continued, especially on the north coasts of Oregon and Washington.

He reported on the fur trade in less than romantic terms; its "hairy harvests" were the skins of our "poor earth-born companions and fellow-mortals." He found the residents of Washington "hacking, burning, blasting their way deeper into the wilderness, beneath the sky, and beneath the ground." The homesteaders of western Washington seemed equally abhorrent, "gnawing like beavers, and scratching for a living among the blackened stumps and logs, regarding the trees as their greatest enemies — a sort of larger pernicious weed immensely difficult to get rid of." He left the defense of culture to the other writers whom he commissioned for *Picturesque California*. Jeanne Carr, in her essay, spoke of the "love of the freeholder for his home." He wouldn't. In spite of his best intentions to restrain himself, he was once again grumbling about the destruction of the West. Such was not the stuff out of which volumes called *Picturesque California* were made.[23]

In almost all ways the whole book was out of Muir's control. When he helped the young Charles Howard Shinn to write an essay on "The Land of the Redwood," things went wrong. First of all, Shinn took a practical view of the cutting of coast redwoods, speaking of scientific forestry and the timber crop. But worse were his opinions that the redwood was "a striking but not altogether a picturesque tree," that the Sequoia forest had a "monotony of coloring in reds and browns of the soil and bark," and that it contained a "scarcity of animal and bird life." Shinn made factual errors as well, not recognizing the difference between the cones of the Sequoia and the redwood. He committed his most heinous crime when he asserted, "There is nothing in California that is more picturesque than one of these redwood logging camps." Apparently the tree wasn't picturesque, but the killing of it was.[24]

This sort of thing from the pen of a writer whom Muir no doubt helped. Shinn referred to Muir's article on Sequoia forests, as well as one written by Asa Gray in 1872, and I have little doubt that this material was supplied to him by Muir. But then, what could one expect from a San Francisco journalist who thought the Gold Rush was a "classical and heroic background for modern life"? It is true that Muir was so far ahead of his fellow Californians, so far removed from the self-centered view held in the rising civilization they thought they were producing, that he simply could not depend on a group effort when it came to writing about the state of the West.[25]

PICTURES AND PARKS

But he tried. He proposed, in brief paragraphs, that Shasta and its environment be made into a national park, that the forests in Oregon be "protected for public use forever" as parks. He continued to complain about the improvements in Yosemite, railing against the so-called "mending" of Nevada Fall. He pointed to the disastrous effects of predator extermination in Oregon, which led to the extinction of many noble animals. He was aided by Joaquin Miller's contribution on Yellowstone Park; Miller's enthusiastic appeal for the preservation of parklands and wild game seemed to echo Muir's. Both men argued that America would need wildernesses for her future; they would be needed, just as some representative grizzlies would be, to "declare to man that he is not yet God." "The railroads have enough. Spare this one spot of this vast continent," said Miller.[26]

But Man was becoming God. With the creation of national parks, he was fencing in his little Edens. It was a short step from picture books to the idea of national parks; all one needed to do was fence off the places where there were possibilities for pictures. This was not what Olmsted had meant by the need for national parks, and certainly not what Muir had in mind, but the language used to describe the first national parks was a predictable result of the taste for picturesque description. The idea of a "public Park or pleasuring ground for the benefit and enjoyment of the people" was perfectly anthropocentric. The idea of a park was also perfectly antithetical to Muir's ideas of a wilderness, since a park was an enclosed area within artificial boundaries. The creation of parks suggested that "natural attractions" and "scenic wonders" could be framed in a painting. The whole idea denied Muir's view of Nature as shoreless, boundless, and infinite.

Muir's first response to Yellowstone National Park gives a clear view of his own attitude. For him, there were virtues in the idea of "The National Park as a Camping Place," but he realized that the experience of Yellowstone was educational at center. "One needs a big faith to feel at ease in a shop like this," he said, for first impressions were likely to suggest that "Divine Government were at an end and the world given over to utter chaos and ruin." But a true appreciation of the park was to be had in seeing it as a fountain of rivers, where the beauty of water could be seen in its origin. "To everybody over all the world water is beautiful forever," Muir argued at the conclusion of his letter to the *San Francisco Bulletin.* Yellowstone was a place of origins; thus he recognized that the significance of the park — its spiritual significance — whatever its proposers might have thought of it, did not lie in the collection of scenic curiosities, but in its true and rightful wholeness as the mother of great rivers.[27]

This was a view that went beyond the idea of national parks as the nineteenth century conceived of them. Muir knew that artificial boundaries set by Man would always mean that only a fragment of the whole would be set apart, though perhaps a central fragment.

A truly sublime scene, as Coleridge had suggested, was infinite in extent, blended with the heavens above and was lost in the foreground. One recognized that it was always part of a larger whole. All of Nature was a sublime scene, and in that sense the only national park which could encompass such a scene was the whole of the earth. Any park which was less than the whole earth was a fragment, however great that fragment might be.

Thus Muir grew tired of the arbitrary nature of such books as *Picturesque California*, which tried to capture and enclose picturesque scenes here and there. He was suspicious of parks like Yosemite Valley that tried to do the same thing with the land itself. Yet he knew that the language of the picturesque was the only language Americans were likely to understand. He would use their language, but still try to tell his own truths. He would write such books and would encourage the kinds of park-making they led to. He would try to preserve fragments of Nature because they were at least better than nothing.

THE RESURRECTION OF JOHN

Writing for a publication like *Picturesque California* was a dead end. Muir needed a hearing in the East, but not the audience of picture-book tourists he described in a letter to Jeanne Carr. He wanted to speak to more than just "a bright appreciative traveller." He needed to associate himself with a crusading magazine, and he got his chance with Robert Underwood Johnson and *Century* magazine, the successor to *Scribner's*. In the association between the two men was born a mythical figure of Muir which saunters through the American consciousness even today.

Johnson had the means to turn Muir into a national hero, and to that end he used the forum of *Century* effectively in the early nineties. Though the idea of Muir as prophet was not new, it needed polishing. Much of what Muir had said in the seventies was prophetic, but that was not what William Keith had in mind when he said, "We almost thought he was Jesus Christ. We fairly worshipped him!" Muir had a certain stature in the estimation of his acquaintances in San Francisco, the power of his presence coming from his moral uprightness, which seemed not to need culture at all. In fact, people like Keith—artists and writers—were more likely to think of Muir as a Jeremiah who warned that men who "worshipped the works of their own hands" were doomed to failure. As an Old Testament figure, Jeremiah–Muir did battle against men who tried to re-create Nature in their own image.[28]

This warning was particularly evident in his message to artists. While Muir admired a good deal of Keith's work, he favored those paintings that showed geographical accuracy. They had always argued about art, but when Keith began to move away from "realism" in the eighties, the battles over aesthetics increased. Muir liked the work of Thomas Hill, while most people today find him to be too "realistic." Even while Muir worked on *Picturesque California*, a dark voice rumbled beneath the surface, ready to burst forth as it had in "Bee-Pastures." Nature could not be improved by art any more than Nevada Fall could be mended by men; "as well whitewash the storm-stained face of El Capitan or gild the domes," growled Muir.[29]

Johnson preferred to think of Muir as a bronze John the Baptist, perhaps by Donatello. A Muir carved in such a New Testament image was not to be confused with the speaker of the Stormy Sermons; he was to be softened and made reasonable: "He was not a 'dreamer,' but a practical man, a faithful citizen, a scientific observer, a writer of enduring power, with vision, poetry, courage in a contest, a heart of gold, and a spirit pure and fine." This assortment of virtues, designed to portray Muir in modernized and smiling aspect, resulted from Johnson's own genteel predisposition. It suggests Johnson's idea of the necessary and appropriate qualities of the late nineteenth-century progressive conservationist. It became a most effective persona for Muir precisely because he could be presented in New York and Washington circles as the poetic scientist, as the practical visionary, and most important, as the faithful citizen.[30]

Here was an image that could work, as the Jeremiah image never could. Just such an image could harmonize with the programs in environmental education represented in our national parks today — programs that require federal approval. The Yosemite Institute, for instance, proclaims its mission in New Testament terms: "To foster concern for the environment we emphasize a positive approach, feeling that a 'doomsday' tone is not effective for our program." Johnson knew that Americans did not want to hear bad news, so in the nineties he encouraged Muir to become John the Baptist, to bring good news for the future.[31]

Muir was quite capable of playing that role, and had tried in the early seventies to baptize his fellow citizens in the beauty of Nature. But he would have to change his tone for *Century* if the strategy was to work. Muir did accept Johnson's advice, and even attempted to convince certain allies to follow the same course, to depend on what Johnson called the "power of understatement" when dealing with such issues as the California state administration of Yosemite Valley. Muir would try not to attack government, civilization, or culture; the explosive fire of youth would yield to the constant flame of maturity. A genial prophet would replace Jeremiah.[32]

Muir's image as cultural hero became a tool, to be used in the campaigns for a large national park surrounding Yosemite Valley, a similar park in the Kings Canyon region, and the creation of national forest reserves in the West. Later the Sierra Club would use Muir's stature in its fight to save Hetch Hetchy from the dam proposed by San Francisco. Johnson tried to buttress this powerful image by soliciting autobiographical material from Muir. He was probably instrumental in getting Muir an honorary degree from Harvard. He would use anything that made Muir a popular figure in the East. The power of the image can be judged by the magnitude of later efforts to destroy Muir's reputation. John P. Irish of California was the most effective of Muir's attackers, speaking of him as a "pseudo-naturalist" and accusing him of cutting live trees in Yosemite Valley in the early seventies. As will be seen, making Muir represent the wilderness put a heavy burden on him personally. Soon those whose interests were impinged on by park and forest movements vented their spleen on Muir himself.

Johnson's memoirs indicate that he had so accepted his illusion, his myth of Muir, that it became a reality. When we see the first meeting of these two men through Johnson's eyes, we see in fact the images they were creating of themselves as they courted each other's favors.

Johnson came to San Francisco looking for someone to write material on what he thought of as the romantic gold-hunting period in California. Because Muir did not see the gold rushes in California, Nevada, or Alaska as romantic, the two men's expectations conflicted. As it turned out, Johnson got his articles, but not from Muir. Muir, he saw, was another kind of beast altogether. Here began the parable of the preacher and the politician. When Muir arrived in the wilderness of the Palace Hotel, Johnson had him playing his role to the hilt: "'I can't make my way through these confounded artificial cañons. There is nothing here to tell you where to go. Now, if you were up in the Sierra, every tree and mound and scratch on the cliff would give you your direction. Everything there is plain as a signpost, but here, how is one to know?'" This innocent naturalist, lost in the city, is both fictional and authentic. Certainly Muir was not really lost. He had been a farmer for six years, not a mountaineer, and had lived in San Francisco off and on while writing during the last two years. He was a member of San Francisco's cosmopolitan Bohemian Club, and spent many evenings with fellow journalists, smoking and talking in parlors. On the other hand, there is a spiritual truth here; Muir had lost his way in attempting to foster civic righteousness. The Muir who understood a wilderness of Nature better than the one made by men needed Johnson to help him through a decade of legislative activity.[33]

If Johnson had plans, so did Muir. He knew that *Century* magazine offered a chance for a national campaign for national parks. To impress *Century* with the need for such a campaign, Muir would have to take Johnson out of the artificial canyons and into the Sierran wilderness. A few weeks later they were in Yosemite, and Muir wrote to his wife that he was "getting into a sort of second youth." They were off to Tuolumne Meadows and Tuolumne Canyon. "But how much we will be able to accomplish will depend upon the snow, the legs, and the resolution of the Century." Muir knew what he was after, and was using the strategy he made a part of his later program, when he lured Taft, Roosevelt, and other influential easterners into the woods where Nature could speak. When he referred to Johnson as "the Century" he indicated his real target on this excursion.[34]

Johnson's legs didn't hold out, but his resolution did. At the same time, Muir learned more than he thought he would. On their excursion down the Tuolumne River he learned to appreciate the plight of a sympathetic intelligent man whose resolution was strong, but whose legs were weak. Johnson, who was fifteen years younger than Muir, had a rough time after eight miles of trailless walking into "the wildest region ever haunted by the God of Silence." It was difficult, he claimed, to keep up with Muir; "if he ever became tired nobody knew it." Nevertheless, Johnson got his genteel baptism, and described his own bewilderment in the natural canyon of the Tuolumne:

The detritus of the wall of the gorge lay in a confused mass of rocks, varying in size from a market basket to a dwelling house, and the interstices were overgrown with that objectionable shrub, the manzañita, the soft leaves of which concealed its iron trunk and branches. . . . When at last I was obliged to rest, Muir, before going on alone for an hour's exploration, sought out for me one of the most beautiful spots I have ever seen, where the rushing river, striking pot-holes in its granite bed, was thrown up into a dozen water wheels twenty feet high!

Johnson's anthropocentric view of "confused" rocks and "objectionable" shrub tells us about his distance from Muir's appreciation of the wholeness of Nature. But the human drama here, Johnson's relationship with Muir, the relationship between tourist and guide, established their complementary roles in the fight for Yosemite.[35]

This alliance between a tenderfoot sitting by the river and a hardy mountaineer who penetrated deeper into the wilderness became the bond between the eastern reader and the narrator of Muir's essays of the early nineties. Muir had learned to be a gracious host, as Johnson was at pains to show. Apparently Muir had changed his style, since Keith had complained that Muir was always a poor provider. But now there would be a place in the canyon of the Tuolumne for both Johnson's and Muir's activities; they could appreciate it according to their tastes and abilities. The appreciation of wilderness according to taste and ability would become essential to Muir's conception of a national park and would become basic to his rhetorical technique when he wrote of national parks. A park would be partly a wilderness accessible to those who could appreciate it, but it would be created for the good of Nature, not Man. In it, the manzanita could flourish. But a park would also be a place where a man like Johnson could receive his own baptism, tenderfoot though he might be. Parks needed tourists, even if Nature didn't need Man. Tourists *were* better than sheep.

Muir carefully planned Johnson's baptism into the wilderness; at the same time he planted seeds of discontent. When Johnson asked about those beautiful mountain meadows Muir had described for

Scribner's in the late seventies, the answer was ready: "'No,' said Muir, 'we do not see any more of those now. Their extinction is due to the hoofed locusts.' This was the first time I heard him use this graphic expression for sheep." Thus Muir converted Johnson, and allowed him to discover the solution: "Obviously the thing to do is to make a Yosemite National Park around the Valley on the plan of the Yellowstone." Believing that this was his own plan and that Muir was skeptical, Johnson had the enthusiasm a man entertains for his own ideas. Certainly Muir had always hoped for such a plan, and had helped propose such a park in 1881. Now Johnson persuaded Muir that it was a political possibility. If Muir would do the writing, Johnson would handle the political end of things in Washington. Thus Muir would write two articles, the first to attract general attention, and the second to propose boundaries. Johnson would get a new campaign for *Century*, while Muir gained a highly effective ally in his battle for preservation of the wilderness.[36]

Johnson's impact on Muir's writing was significant. He encouraged Muir to use first-person narration, and worked to keep him from the habit of repeated superlative adjectives. But those were jobs any editor might accomplish. He went beyond his professional duty with constant encouragement, ensuring that Muir kept at work. At the same time, he criticized Muir's work. And Muir's letters indicate that he did not take criticism well at all. He became cranky and irritable; he complained like a mule with a heavy load.

As a direct result of their association, Muir wrote with renewed force and direction. Now he had a specific goal, the creation of Yosemite and Kings Canyon national parks. His three essays for *Century* were significant literary and historic pieces. Not only did they represent the first effective and popular arguments for the creation of national parks in America, but they also made significant contributions to the public idea of a national park. Further, as a result of these articles Muir was encouraged by Johnson to reconsider and revise his earlier essays, which took new form in *The Mountains of California*. There were also political implications in their association, as we shall see. Johnson was instrumental in the formation of the Sierra Club, and in making John Noble, Secretary of the Interior, a key ally in the fight for national parks.[37]

Muir would speak to the tourist as he had to Johnson. He would take the tourist as far down canyons and up mountains as Johnson had been able to go. In this spirit he would acknowledge the difficulties of wild terrain in places like Tuolumne Canyon. "Any one accustomed to walk on earthquake boulders, carpeted with cañon chaparral, can easily go down the cañon as far as the big cascades and return to camp in one day. Many, however, are not able to do this, and it is far better to go leisurely, prepared to camp anywhere, and enjoy the marvelous grandeur of the place." Muir's rhetoric echoes the lesson he learned with Johnson. If a tourist wanted to climb a mountain, Muir would take his reader up Mount Dana, not Mount Ritter. Dana is a gradually sloped peak, one of the highest but at the same time easiest climbs in the proposed Yosemite Park. Muir became conscious of his new necessity — selling the parks — and seemed actually comfortable for a while as a publicizer. His truce with such a role would only last for a few years.[38]

For the present, Muir's role as narrator was designed on the ideal of John the Baptist, and he realized aspirations recorded in his journal twenty years before. "Heaven knows that John the Baptist was not more eager to get all his fellow sinners into the Jordan than I to baptize mine in the beauty of God's mountains." The tourist might still be a sinner, but John tried to enlighten him:

Then it seemed to me the Sierra should be called, not the Nevada or Snowy Range, but the Range of Light. And after ten years in the midst of it, rejoicing and wondering, seeing the glorious floods of light that fill it — the sunbursts of morning among the mountain-peaks, the broad noonday radiance on the crystal rocks, the flush of the alpenglow, and the thousand dashing waterfalls with their marvelous abundance of irised spray — it still seems to me a range of light.

If a reader learned anything from this narration, it was not what to see but how to see. Behind Muir's exuberance was his carefully thought-out method of study. He tried to make his readers powerful and enthusiastic observers, like himself. They would believe in the divine beauty; they would accept his metaphor of light and water. Muir was neither the light nor the water, but he was clean like them in his exuberance; he had baptized himself in the light and water of the Sierra and Americans could do the same. He would show his readers where and how to look, but not the magical thing itself.[39]

He was developing a public image of the trustworthy guide. What does the good guide do for us in the mountains? He does more than show us where to go or how to climb. He does more than ensure our safety. If he is a real guide, he himself becomes our example. For Muir to do this he had to make himself the hero of his own narrative, in spite of his natural inclination toward self-effacement. Johnson had made him see that his "own personal private self" could be a useful device in making the public see the value of the wilderness.

Yet Muir's aim always had been to make the reader come to his own discoveries. Just as he had seduced Johnson into making his own observations, so he tried to show the reader that the primary teacher, the hidden teacher, was Nature. Muir learned by careful observation, and so must his reader. So he tried to draw attention away from himself to the phenomena worth seeing.

THE WATERS OF YOSEMITE

Johnson's political strategy required two essays, one visionary, the other practical. The first article, "to attract general attention," really did a good deal more than publicizing, since Muir had to teach his readers how to see the wilderness. By constantly drawing their attention to the waters of Yosemite, he showed how important was the whole watershed surrounding the Valley. His knowledge of Yosemite's geography could serve him admirably in "Treasures of Yosemite." He would seem to be taking the reader of the "Midsummer Holiday" issue of *Century* on a tour of the Valley, organized by points of interest. This was the sort of thing he had tried with so little success in his essay on Yosemite for *Picturesque California.* But everything Muir had failed to do in *Picturesque California* he succeeded in doing when he wrote "Treasures." His style became sharp and precise as he began to reveal his own baptisms in the wilderness, using near views of the falls. He made a clear distinction between views that were "wild but not safe" and those he recommended for the tourist, yet he nevertheless returned to serious consideration of the full creative possibilities of wilderness. Because the points of interest to the reader were waterfalls and Muir's chief interest was the watershed, he could reconcile his own intentions with the expectations of the tourist.

Muir saw with the eyes of the waters. He described Yosemite's riches, her treasures, as they were mirrored in the Merced River, "peacefully gliding, reflecting lilies and trees and the onlooking rocks, things frail and fleeting and types of endurance meeting here and blending in countless forms, as if into this one mountain mansion Nature had gathered her choicest treasures, whether great or small, to draw her lovers into close and confiding communion with her." The riches of Yosemite, magnified by the reflecting lens of the Merced, were the best evidence that the real beauty of the park was part and parcel with the flow of waters through it. The temple was open at both ends, and was only a special part of a larger whole. If the reader focused with Muir on the flow of Yosemite, then he began to see that contrasts were the soul of Yosemite—"things frail and fleeting and types of endurance meeting." Muir tried to show all scenes in this manner, blending forests, flowers, and rocks into a harmonious landscape.[40]

Century did its part by dispersing through the essay illustrations with forests and reflecting pools in the foreground. In ironic contrast, Johnson carefully included pictures of plowed meadows, trimmed trees, and a stump forest. So too Muir undercut the edenic vision which might be in Yosemite by making sad comments on the actual state of affairs under California's administration: "But no terrestrial beauty may endure forever. The glory of wildness has already departed from the great central plain. Its bloom is shed, and so in part is the bloom of the mountains. In Yosemite, even under the protection of the Government, all that is perishable is vanishing apace."[41]

The question of endurance was central to his argument because it pinpointed the real "treasures" of Yosemite. From a distance, the whole Sierra looked like a celestial city surrounded by "a wall of light, clear as crystal, and ineffably fine, yet firm as adamant." Yet in such general views there was nothing to suggest the "wonderful depth and grandeur of its sculpture." Was the sculpture the treasure? Yes and no. From a distance, no particular part of the range could "publish its wealth. . . . No great valley or river is seen, . . . [no]

group of well marked features of any kind standing out as distant pictures." So too first impressions of the range were wrong. The canyons were "not raw, gloomy, jagged walled gorges, savage and inaccessible"; in closer views they became "mostly smooth, open pathways conducting to the summit; mountain streets full of life and light, graded and sculptured by ancient glacier." The light and life, the flora and fauna of the Valley, were essential and destructible treasures. "Yosemite, presenting such stupendous faces of bare granite, is nevertheless imbedded in magnificent forests," Muir pointed out. Without the light and life of forests and meadows, the Sierra would be desolate.

So the preservation of Yosemite required that men care for the flora of the canyons and protect the watershed:

For the branching cañons and valleys of the basins of the streams that pour into Yosemite are as closely related to it as are the fingers to the palm of the hand — as the branches, foliage, and flowers of a tree to the trunk. Therefore, very naturally, all the fountain region above Yosemite, with its peaks, cañons, snow fields, glaciers, forests, and streams, should be included in the park to make it an harmonious unit instead of a fragment, great though the fragment be.

America would need to preserve the whole to have any of the parts, because the life of Yosemite depended on the flow of living water through it.

Living vision animated Muir's essay as he dramatized near views of Yosemite's waters. There are many narrated visions in the essay, but their progression can be indicated by a series of three. Muir's first near view was from a small ledge near the top of Yosemite Fall: "Here the view is perfectly free down into the heart of the bright irised throng of comet-like streams into which the whole ponderous volume of the fall separates a little below the brow. So glorious a display of pure wildness, acting at close range while one is cut off from all the world beside, is terribly impressive." This airy view was only a beginning. Closer still, he ventured out onto Fern Ledge at the base of Yosemite Fall to observe what he called lunar rainbows, made up of "moonlight and spray, silent interpreters of the heart-peace of Nature in the stormy darkness." Here he could clarify the relationships among his themes of light, water, and baptism.

Muir ventured too close, and got a lesson in power he had not come looking for. Risking such a "wild scene but not a safe one" was part of his own price for vision, and the labor as well as the risk involved seemed to him necessary everywhere in Nature, although he did not recommend them to his reader. After climbing up to Fern Ledge in the night, he attempted to observe the moon from behind the falls. The view was "enchanting," drew him closer— when the wind shifted, and the falls shifted, and Muir, in what he thought was fairyland, suffered sudden disenchantment.

Down came a dash of spent comets, thin and harmless-looking in the distance, but desperately solid and stony in striking one's shoulders. It seemed like a mixture of choking spray and gravel. Instinctively dropping on my knees, I laid hold on an angle of the rock, rolled myself together with my face pressed against my breast, and in this attitude submitted as best I could to my thundering baptism.

Muir did not recommend such an experience to the tourist, yet it yielded a lesson the tourist needed to understand. Somebody had to get close enough to Yosemite Fall to learn with his whole body about the power and substance of falling water. Otherwise, the reader could not feel the power and substance of the forces pouring into and drifting through Yosemite. But Muir approached still closer to the cosmic vision.

The third near view was all-encompassing. Muir revised his early "Jubilee of Waters," describing the Valley as it became one great waterfall in the "full bloom of flood":

This was the most sublime waterfall flood I ever saw—clouds, winds, rocks, waters, throbbing together as one. And then to contemplate what was going on simultaneously with all this in other mountain temples: the Big Tuolumne Cañon—how the white waters were singing there, and the winds, and how the clouds were marching. In Hetch Hetchy Valley also, and the great King's River Yosemite, and in all the other cañons and valleys of the Sierra from Shasta to the southernmost fountains of the Kern— five hundred miles of flooded waterfalls chanting together. What a psalm was that!

This was the great vision of watersheds he had depicted in the Stormy Sermons. Here was the argument of the sublime, the God's-eye view of the power of Nature which jerked one out of one's self, a vision which explained the truth about "things frail and fleeting and types of endurance meeting" in Yosemite. This kind of rhetoric came naturally to Muir, and represented a quantum leap in consciousness from the picturesque. The essay was perhaps the best Muir ever wrote about the function of national parks, because of its drama, its clarity, and the moral certainty implicit in his slow but steady ascent toward the wild and holy power of Nature. It was, finally, a sermon.

Muir did not expect the congregation to duplicate his experience. Like Father Mapple in *Moby Dick,* he drew up his ladder behind himself. But the intensity of his own baptism still seduces one, and suggests that unsafe experience should be available to those who are capable, who are hearty enough to seek it. In showing his reader how he had discovered himself as a part of the power of the wilderness, Muir presented the strongest possible argument for national parks as wild places where each man could seek, according to his ability, direct, unmediated intercourse with the elemental forces of Nature. For Muir, a national park had never been the sum of exceptional features, but rather a place where a man might seek and find exceptional, extravagant experiences, a place where men were immersed in the flow. Yosemite was a place of worship, and was necessary for nourishing the pastor as well as his flock.

Would this strategy work, or would the public misunderstand what Muir was trying to do? Would they take Muir as their hero, rather than following his advice and seeking out the waters of Yosemite for their own baptism? Would they idolize him because they preferred the shepherd to the fields he led them to? Would they refuse to leave their Moses behind, to enter the promised land? Or would they take Muir's promise of freedom?

Maybe such hero worship was an unanticipated consequence of Muir's public personality. After all, Johnson never fully understood what Muir was doing. He became preoccupied with the "adventure" for its own sake and played on the dangerous side of Muir's excursions, later giving Muir's "Stickeen" the title "An Adventure with a Dog and a Glacier." Muir felt this was a "vulgar, catchy title." Later, Johnson published excerpts from *The Yosemite* as "Three Adventures in Yosemite."

There was a great danger in making himself into the adventurous hero, and Muir knew it. He wasn't out for thrills, and he didn't want to lead anyone astray on the point. Further, he was in danger of becoming not the publicizer of parks, but the product being sold. Even while the strategy seemed to be working in Congress, it carried a price to be paid in the future.

THE BOUNDARIES AND CONTENTS OF PARKS: "FEATURES"

In principle, Muir thought the whole Sierra should be preserved, preferably as a national park. But in practice he and Johnson were proposing as a park a large rectangle which included the watersheds of Yosemite Valley and Hetch Hetchy, as well as the headwaters of the San Joaquin, including Mount Ritter. A year later, Muir would propose a similar plan for a different park that would include the Middle and South forks of the Kings River and the Kaweah and Tule river watersheds. In the seventies Muir had tried to justify the preservation of watersheds in terms of the agricultural benefits which would accrue to the Central Valley. Now, however, he was going to argue from the position that the mountains themselves were worth preserving. In the Yosemite proposal, the most obvious issue was the inclusion of an entire wild and trailless area that took in Tuolumne Meadows and Hetch Hetchy.

Thus he would have to publicize the recreational possibilities of the entire northern half of the park. It was crucial that his second article for *Century* persuade the public, and perhaps even more important, persuade Congress, that northern Yosemite was an available new recreation area — that the public could follow in his footsteps, could use and appreciate this part of the park. The division of the park into two halves — the inclusion of Hetch Hetchy — indicated an ideological duality in Muir's concept of a national park: the tame Yosemite for the tame tourist, and the wild canyons of the Tuolumne for the wild people like himself. He saw the necessity for conceding the front country, and even allowing it to be "improved" by landscape architects and road builders, if only Congress would include the wild half of the park and protect it unimpaired for future wilderness.[42]

Johnson pushed for an article "not sentimental but descriptive." The park was already being considered in committee in Congress. So Muir could not be visionary in his second effort, "Features of the Proposed Yosemite National Park." He would have to defend the specific boundaries of the two hundred and fifty square-mile reservation he had proposed, and in addition justify his concept of a national park which would be mostly wilderness. He would try to make preserving the drainage of the Tuolumne seem like good business. This entailed two arguments: first, that tourists could enjoy the wild parts of the park, and second, that America could and should afford more than one Yosemite Valley.

Thus the first half of the essay was largely devoted to a guided tour of the northern drainage, beginning at its center, Big Tuolumne Meadows —"the wildest, smoothest, most serenely spacious, and in every way most delightful summer pleasure park in all the Sierra." One must remember that this was a description of a place which could only be reached after two days of riding. Now, of course, it is one of the most popular camping spots in the Sierra, being only an hour and a half from the Valley by car, or five hours from San Francisco. Until recently it also contained the most populous public campground in the national parks system. In 1890, such recreational possibilities seemed a long way off. Muir devoted considerable space in his article to four "capital excursions" from the Meadows to peaks, passes, and canyons, all of them described with painstaking care as reasonable, enjoyable journeys. This essay was largely an enumeration of features and points of interest. But it worked, and for the present that was sufficient. Congress would accept Muir's proposal in October, 1890.

The second part of the essay dealt with Hetch Hetchy. Muir felt that the American public, the public which had been taught to marvel at one dead Sequoia tree at an exhibition, required reeducation about the need for more than just one of anything. One tree did not constitute a forest, and one Yosemite did not constitute a full sample of the Sierran canyons. His rhetoric echoed that of the *Studies*: "Most people who visit Yosemite are apt to regard it as an exceptional creation, the only valley of its kind in the world. But nothing in Nature stands alone. She is not so poor as to have only one of anything. The explorer in the Sierra and elsewhere finds many

Yosemities, that differ not more than one tree differs from another of the same species." So Americans had to learn that seeing one Yosemite didn't mean seeing them all. If Nature wasn't poor, then neither need America be. And the Hetch Hetchy Valley had virtues which Yosemite Valley lacked. It was still wild and untrampled. If the whole Sierra was like a forest of Yosemities, Muir was only asking for two of them, one of which had already been harmed. The park would contain two parts of the larger whole of the Sierra — really two parks, one wild and the other "improved"; two trees, one trimmed and the other still whole.[43]

Thus Muir hoped to save Hetch Hetchy by making it a wild and inaccessible hinterland of a larger, improved park. While he realized that there was no such thing as large-scale recreational use and wilderness in the same place, he was willing to sacrifice Yosemite Valley if he could preserve Hetch Hetchy. This kind of bargaining has become, by our age, a standard preservationist strategy. It didn't work for Hetch Hetchy, and it hasn't worked elsewhere. The sanctity of Hetch Hetchy was not assured by its inclusion in the park.

Poor Muir had no idea of what was to come when the developers would try to divide and destroy the park. In May of 1890 he wrote to Johnson, "The Tuolumne Cañon is so closely related to the Yosemite region it should also be included, but whether it is or not will not matter much, since it lies in rugged rocky security, as one of Nature's own reservations."[44]

KINGS CANYON, AND WRITER'S CRAMP

The political success of the proposed Yosemite National Park depended on Johnson's influence in Washington. Johnson believed he had some sway with the House Committee on Public Lands, and apparently he did. He gave himself considerable credit: "The members had never heard of Muir, though they knew of the Muir Glacier, but they responded with commendable unanimity to my presentation of the scheme, and a bill was drafted on the lines of Muir's boundaries." Muir's role, in absentia, was that of technical advisor. Johnson had to establish credibility with Congress, though Muir's writing was his primary evidence. Particularly in "Features," Muir was really writing for legislators as much as for the public pressure he could put on them. Johnson would take the proof sheets of Muir's articles to Congress, and when the committee acted favorably it would appear that the article published in *Century* reported new, nearly enacted legislation. Congress looked good because it was acting on the far-reaching needs Muir outlined, and *Century* gained by reporting so quickly on Congress's progressive action.[45]

With the success of the Yosemite scheme, Johnson had the means necessary to press for more national parks. Not only had he established Muir's credentials with Congress, but he had met Secretary of the Interior John Noble. So he wrote to Muir, asking for a map and a written proposal, to be made in the pages of *Century*, for a Kings Canyon National Park. This was the second of the two proposals Muir had supported in 1881, and he was anxious to help as much as he could now that a favorable opportunity presented itself. At this point, however, there was a subtle change in the relationship between Muir and Johnson. Johnson was pressing Muir very hard, and was even outlining writing strategy: "I think you might call the article 'A Rival of Yosemite,' and you might begin by referring to the criticism upon you as a traitor to California because of your mention of other Yosemites." The criticism of Muir as a traitor to California was not a joke. Muir's patriotism as a Californian was a growing issue, precisely as he knew it would be. Californian politicians led by John Irish wanted to defend their own park from federal encroachment, and they resented Muir's insistence that Yosemite was not the one and only incomparable valley. Muir's alliance with Johnson had set him against the entrenched state interests. He and Johnson would have to counter state appeals to Congress. Muir had to protect his credibility from the violent attacks appearing in the California newspapers.[46]

Now he was writing to order, and with considerable haste. He did neither of these tasks well, and knew it. But the time was right, and he tried. Since he felt compelled to preserve his credibility, he wanted his article on the Kings River region to be accurate with regard to geographical detail. Yet he wasn't working quickly enough to suit Johnson, who wanted to get the advance proofs to Noble as soon as possible. As months went by, Johnson pressed harder and harder, finally outlining possible articles for Muir. Meanwhile, Muir began to despair, complaining that "my stock of cliff and cascade adjectives are used up and I am too dull to get new ones." When he did finish the article and had sent it off to Johnson, he apologized: "I fear you will find the article dry and geographical — lean, scrawny but I assure you I have worked to cover the ground and keep each part in proper subordination . . . if it has no flavor of the region I will be disappointed." Muir was chafing under the pressure of deadlines, and had much personal pressure as well. His father-in-law had died the previous October and left all of the Strenzel lands under Muir's management. The load was too much. He was not even able to return to the Kings River region, and for the article had to rely on notes taken fifteen years earlier. No wonder his essay lacked the life and immediacy of his Yosemite writings.[47]

Muir's essay shows the signs of his discontent and conflicting responsibilities. The title —"A Rival of Yosemite" — was a good indication of his planned strategy. Muir was going to sell Kings Canyon by comparing it to the Hetch Hetchy and Yosemite valleys, thus building on his previous success. The comparisons which filled the article were sometimes only statistical. Though Muir frequently used the adjective "grand" to describe the new region, his language had little freshness. To say that these mountains were grander meant only that they were higher than those surrounding Yosemite. In pointing out that "this new yosemite is longer and deeper, and lies embedded in grander mountains," or asserting that the waterfalls "of the new valley are far less striking in general views, although the volume of falling water is nearly twice as great and comes from higher sources," Muir was making mechanical comparisons.[48]

Seeing the Kings Canyon area in terms of Yosemite and using the language of Yosemite were hindrances. The architecture of the region was of a different style from Yosemite's, so any exposition based on points of interest was doomed to failure. The names of the main landmarks were still not fixed by common usage, and were not as familiar as those of Yosemite had become. In fact, no one landmark was as impressive as those in Yosemite, though Muir argued that the valley contained "the highest, most elaborately sculptured, and the most beautiful series of rocks of the same extent that I have yet seen in any yosemite in the range." When comparing the Palisades to El Capitan, he was forced to confess that "neither in bulk nor in sublime boldness of attitude can it be regarded as a rival of that great rock." The closest he ever came to catching the flavor of this area's architecture was in describing the Glacier Monument, an analogue to Half Dome: "It is upward of a mile in height, and has five ornamental summits, and an indescribable variety of sculptured forms projecting or countersunk on its majestic front, all balanced and combined into one symmetrical mountain mass." Muir needed a baroque style to describe the Kings Canyon region, but he was locked into the more severe and monumental language of Yosemite. The language of Yosemite would be a handicap in the future as well; it would not translate to places like the Grand Canyon or Yellowstone. He had spent years creating a language based on the natural harmonies of Yosemite, but now he was in a hurry and used the same language for different landscapes.[49]

Illustrations made up half of the essay on Kings Canyon, as *Century* published it; most were taken from sketches by Charles Robinson or by Muir himself. This was the most elaborately illustrated of Muir's essays, and perhaps he felt pictures were necessary to acquaint legislators with a region they had never seen or heard mentioned. Muir commissioned the illustrations, and spent much time with Robinson trying to get accurate sketches of the region. It would seem that he had at last accepted the political reality that pictures were more likely to impress the eastern congressmen. Even though these were not photographs, they were a way to certify Muir's experience. As the reader went through the article, he was presented with a page of text facing a page of illustration which gave reality to the vague words that were more elusive and more difficult to test. Such profuse illustration was an admission by Muir that his own essay had limitations.

The essay was also poorly organized, and lacked a clear direction. Despite this weakness, one can see two important, linked issues which were beginning to plague Muir. The Kings Canyon region was wilder than Yosemite, yet paradoxically it was being destroyed at a much faster rate because it was less well known. The only solution Muir could see was to improve public access. For the first time, Muir was arguing that a wilderness should be opened up to improvement. But if easier access would solve what Muir called "Destructive Tendencies," he was not delighted with the prospect of the "Game and Sport" which would follow. The direction of his reasoning is not very pleasant, but it is instructive to follow.

Muir knew that the flora and fauna of the Kings region were being threatened most, and that his eastern audience needed to be reminded that the rocks were not the whole attraction of the area: "At first sight it would seem that these mighty granite temples could be injured but little by anything that man may do. But it is surprising to find how much our impressions in such cases depend upon the delicate bloom of the scenery, which in all the more accessible places is so easily rubbed off." On the other hand, the possibility that the area might be made into a reserve or park was a motive for accelerated destruction of the wonderful Sequoia groves. The lumber companies were cutting and even blasting Sequoias in great haste, fearing restrictions in the future. This was a source of immediate concern. Muir was worried not only that the lumber companies might get wind of the proposal and thus increase their activities, but also that they would bring pressure to bear on Congress and stop the creation of a park. They did both, as he had feared. The proposal never got out of committee, despite Noble's recommendation for "favorable consideration and action."[50]

The alternative to lumbering or sheep herding was tourism, of course, so Muir had to recommend that the tourist visit this place: "notwithstanding its tremendous rockiness, it is an Eden of plant-beauty from end to end." But the ways of this wilderness were not easy, although Muir tried to make them seem accessible. On its mountain trails one was "seldom compelled to travel more than two miles to make an advance of one, and less than half of the miles are perpendicular." These were not the easy highways of Yosemite. Though he argued that "almost *every one* able to cross a cobblestoned street in a crowd may climb Mount Whitney," he also knew that few could enjoy the direct route over the Sierra's crest from the east, which entailed a nine thousand-foot climb. So he recommended that "soft, succulent people should go the mule way." The mule way! This was the very way he had found so unpleasant on his excursion of 1875. But he was not writing to mountaineers; he was trying to persuade politicians.[51]

Consequently he was forced into recommending that a road be built into the region, thus destroying its appeal as a wilderness, as he knew. Making this proposal, he was conceding to the needs of soft, succulent people. But he made the best of it: "But if instead of crossing every ridge-wave of these broad boulder basins a good carriage-road were built around the brows and headlands of the main river cañon, the valley could be reached in less than half a day, and with the advantage of still grander scenery." He also knew that increased access would lead to increased hunting and fishing. He described both activities with distaste. Fishermen "bagged the glittering beauties as fast as sham flies could be switched to them, a hundred trout of a morning being considered no uncommon catch." Hunters, he thought, would simply continue the work of shepherds, who had tried to exterminate the bears of the region: "Pity that animals so good-natured and so much a part of these shaggy wilds should be exterminated." Muir remembered his own encounter with a grizzly in Tehipite Valley, when the area was still wild; then, the bear had "good-naturedly turned away and wallowed off into the chaparral." He knew the future would not allow such encounters.[52]

Thus the tone which churns under the surface of "Rival" indicates that Muir was becoming apprehensive. He knew that America was not ready for a truly wild park, but he saw no other human use as an alternative to the energetic work of the lumbermen and shepherds. His conclusion was defensive rather than enthusiastic, practical rather than visionary. He fancied the time when a road would be built, and pointed out that the region did not offer much hope to agriculture and mining, that "even the lumber industry need suffer no unreasonable restriction." Under the surface of such a defense was his suspicion that America might make the region a park only if it wasn't good for anything else. He was tired of compromising his philosophical ideals, just as he was tired of writing advertisements for parks. There was no such thing as a genteel wilderness, he knew. He wanted the Kings Canyon to remain as wild as it had been in 1873, when he had first wandered in its gardens and groves. And he wanted to be as wild and lawless as he had been in those days, before he had become civilized. It was too late in the century for either possibility.

Something was wrong. The process I have narrated represents a devastating consolidation and limitation of aims for Muir. Having accepted certain ground rules, he found himself terribly confined by them. Learning to use the language of the picturesque, even while carefully bending this language to his own uses, had allowed him to achieve a kind of initial success. He was able to preserve a good portion of the Yosemite region, though he would see even that diminished during the next twenty-five years. But a closer look at his success reveals a starker picture. The wildest parts would be stripped from the Yosemite Park, including Mount Ritter, the Minarets, and Muir's favorite, Hetch Hetchy. The Kings Canyon region, on the other hand, could not be handled within the conventions Muir had chosen. He had been able to save only those wild places he had revealed as picturesque. He had appealed to the prejudicial standards of his eastern audience, and in the process had reinforced its limited tastes. Those places which transcended the neat and pleasing categories that Americans had already learned from their parlor-room collections, those wonderful wild regions of the West—those places were not appealing to Americans. In this regard, Muir's writing in the late eighties and early nineties had not succeeded. His compromises had been costly. He had saved only that wilderness which could be made to appear genteel. But he was now a public figure, a national figure, and at least he was back to work.

10

Forest Reserves

Since this book is about Muir and his career, it is neither possible nor desirable to attempt a complete history of the growth of conservation in the 1890s and the first decade of the twentieth century. There is a good library of books documenting the developments of that period. Muir's role was significant and far-reaching, yet is often superficially understood, or misstated. He brought to politics a consciousness quite different from that recorded in the standard histories of the period, and though he had a strong influence on major figures like Roosevelt, Pinchot, Mather, and Albright — and even on minor figures like Theodore Lukens of Pasadena or Enos Mills of the Rocky Mountains — Muir's approach to conservation was more mature and more carefully considered than the dominant approaches of the time.

Part of the difference was a result of Muir's own non-anthropocentric background. Unlike the Pinchots, Mathers, and Albrights, he was not an inveterate joiner, and certainly never nurtured the abilities that these men cultivated in themselves — the abilities which made them great bureaucrats. While Muir had been urging government control of forests and parks since 1875, he had never thought of himself as a potential government employee. He would not follow the path that Powell fell into and become a resource manager. He wished to remain outside the government, to speak as a concerned citizen, though there was always the danger that he would become simply a "consulting expert." He could say a word for good government when he found it, but his real praise was for the land itself, not for the men who made parks. He did not, except to save Hetch Hetchy — and what a tragic exception! — get bogged down in the "political quagg." Rather, he remembered that the issue he could best deal with was the issue of consciousness.

SECONDARY SOURCES AND SCHOLARSHIP

A great danger awaits the student of the environmental movement in America: he may be too good a student, too well-read. Emerson had to remind the American scholar that "books are for the scholar's idle times. When he can read God directly, the hour is too precious to be wasted in other men's transcripts of their readings." So we are in danger of that failing today. I, for instance, have had to put on my pack and spend several days in the Grand Canyon of the Tuolumne to remind myself of what I am talking about. Even late in the season, when the oaks are flaming and the aspens are dropping their yellow leaves, one needs to sit by a campfire and remind oneself that the real research library of Yosemite lives in its canyons, rivers, lakes, meadows, forests, and mountains. It seems to me, now returned, that the chief difficulty we experience as humans is that we forget too easily.

There are many good books about the history of conservation, but they are all books about a *social* movement, about the cultural changes in America. None of them attempt to immerse the reader in that deeper flow, which sings quietly all the while in Pate Valley and Glen Aulin. All of these books are, in the nature of their origin and significance, anthropocentric. They are perhaps not secondary sources, but tertiary — twice removed from Nature — being neither about the real issue of conservation or preservation nor about the impact of Nature on the men who went to Washington, but primarily about the interactions among these men. Sometimes this focus produces a discussion of personalities. If it was true of Pinchot and Mather that "it was natural that each of these men, so devoted to the promotion of his own domain, should fight hard for it, and therefore against the other," then the whole history of conflict between the Forest Service and the Park Service might be reduced to power games between egotists. I would rather believe that there were real transcendent issues involved. But biographies of Mather, Albright, Lukens, and others, and even Wolfe's biography of Muir when it reaches the nineties, seem particularly inadequate reminders of the true spiritual significance of the struggle between preservation and conservation in the nineties and beyond. Muir always knew that a true understanding of issues required going to the mountains themselves. His best work was done when he was fortunate enough to confer with Taft, Roosevelt, Johnson, Lukens, and others while in Yosemite. This seems hardly surprising. The Text was written there, in characters plain enough for anyone to read.[1]

Thus I am dismayed to see so many otherwise good books being written which seem to be founded on false, because humanistic, principles. They are books about men — as all books are about men — but they fail to remember that mountains are "fountains of men," and so they become books only about men. It is probably impossible to think like a mountain, but it is possible to think like a man *in* the mountains, and the environment makes all the difference, even in little things. Muir knew the importance of a campfire, for instance. It matters a great deal that two nights ago, in the shadows of towering canyon walls, I was cooking my dinner over a fire made of oak and cedar; their taste got into my tea, and into my dreams. It matters a great deal that I slept by the Tuolumne River and heard the sound of its water. And even now, when embarking on a discussion of Muir's politics at the end of the nineteenth century, it is important that the primary source be always in mind.

I do not wish to attack my fellow students. I wish only to say a word for wildness, even while immersing myself in this most civilized game of writing. As I repeat the homework assignments of the past, reviewing the significant books on this period by Hans Huth, Leo Marx, Roderick Nash, Robert Shankland, Henry Nash Smith, Donald Swain, Kevin Starr, John Ise, Elmo Richardson, Holway Jones, and Joseph Sax, I need to remind myself that these are only secondary sources. And I find that these writers committed their own errors when they forgot that they were creating secondary sources. This becomes most obvious in their references to Muir himself. These books, and others like them, form a significant and powerful tradition. They rely on each other, and a student reading them forgets very easily that he is studying the map, not the territory.

The Muir they present is the persona who appeared in his own essays and in articles and books about him. It is the Muir who has been edited. For instance, *The Wilderness World of John Muir* is a fine book, but it is Teale's version of Muir's works, selected to present a handsome and acceptable Muir. It is a secondary or tertiary source.[2]

Why all this soul searching? Why should we be suspicious of the very tradition which has allowed us to think seriously and accurately about the relationship between man and environment in American history? Precisely because the tradition carries in it the same assumptions which flawed the conservationist movement, assumptions of a man-centered world. And those who are most interested in replacing the conservationist way of thinking about the world need to break the chains tying them to those assumptions. Just as Muir needed to walk through the South and free himself from the assumptions embodied in Marsh's *Man and Nature* — though he would later use Marsh's arguments — so we need to free ourselves from nineteenth-century assumptions about conservation which keep us from acquiring a coherent ecological perspective. Otherwise we will be enslaved by other men's thinking, without even knowing it.

So one comes to this period with great trepidation, aware that the issues Muir involved himself in were part of the larger whole, the making of twentieth-century America. When focusing on Muir one is always in danger of placing him at the center of the conservationist movement, or even suggesting that his causes were the central issues of the day. Neither was true, yet there is a certain truth about our present which can be revealed through these perspectives. Americans were thinking about more pressing issues than national parks and forest reserves, or so it seemed to them. And today we still are likely to believe that those issues are not the pressing issues of our lives. But Muir himself had focused a much more encompassing and more complex vision of life on parks and reservations because he could at least do something concrete in that realm. As previous chapters document, he was never interested in preserving only scenery.

What he believed should be abundantly clear by now. Here I ask how he planned to accomplish some of his aims. What may be most significant about the style he adopted during this period was that it embodied his own ethical standards. What kind of role could he take with good conscience, now that the time seemed right for creating real embodiments of the utopian realm, the wild America given to him in his youth? How radical a stance could he take, while still being effective? How much of a politician could he become without destroying or effacing his own integrity? How far could he go in appealing to prejudices and assumptions of Americans which he did not share? Edge-work of this kind was harrowing for Muir, yet it led to his greatest victories. Much of the wild land and many of the parks in America which we hold dear today we owe to Muir, and owe to his own self-effacing work. The canyon of the Tuolumne that I walk through with pleasure cost him much pain, and was born of compromise. Even though I must drop down into that canyon by descending a long series of switchbacks and must begin my journey along the Tuolumne River on a trail above Hetch Hetchy Reservoir, I catch glimpses of the dark waters impounded below. Even though I walk upstream next to a singing river toward Tuolumne Meadows, I must think about the dark waters below. In other words, the story I have to tell is neither tragic nor comic. Muir neither realized his dreams nor lost them altogether. He simply did the best he could under the circumstances.

His most effective tool during these years was still his pen, though he found himself increasingly placed in the public eye. Many of his friends had argued that he was a more effective speaker than writer. Traveling with the Forestry Commission, guiding Roosevelt and Taft in Yosemite, speaking to members of the Sierra Club at meetings and on annual outings — these kinds of activities tested his social abilities as well as his talents as a public speaker. His record suggests that he more than passed the test.

THE EMERGING POLITICAL MAN

The alliance Muir and Johnson forged in the late eighties became more and more significant after their initial moves for Yosemite and Kings Canyon national parks; at the same time it became strained. By the end of those campaigns Muir thought he had reached the limit of what he was capable of giving, as a writer at least. He grew tired of writing to specifications. He was tired of being rushed, being a popular writer, being a public figure. He never wanted America to love him. He only hoped for a kind of mutual respect. Indeed, he did not want to be "the best loved of Nature writers"; such accolades could go to others who had the time for them. Increasingly, Muir was writing to Johnson about his hopes for other kinds of books, scientific books, which he would in fact never write. His discontent was expressed over Johnson's reception of the essays on Alaska he submitted to *Century*, which the magazine was slow to publish. Muir had countered the responsibilities to the farm and to the movement for parks with his own escape to Alaska. He had hoped that his journeys to Alaska were still his own realm, his last remaining creative field; consequently he had voiced reservations about writing any more essays for *Century* when it came to the Alaskan materials.

These were complaints he had been nursing all along. Johnson tried to turn Muir to new tasks, the most significant being the formation of the Sierra Club. This was only part of a program which required that Muir become a public and political figure.

Muir had earned himself an audience by making concessions, by giving the public the picturesque descriptions it expected and by living up to an entirely artificial public persona. He had used the same kinds of artifice in the conduct of interpersonal relationships. But he went well beyond artifice with Johnson; the correspondence between the two men indicates that they felt genuine concern for each other. Still, the aesthete of *Century* who devoted himself to projects like a Keats–Shelley memorial in Rome was perfectly representative of Muir's eastern audience. And Muir, though willing to play the role Johnson expected, was a good deal more sophisticated than he appeared. He had been a successful fruit farmer and businessman for many years. He wasn't likely, in the nineties, to be lost or dazzled by the lights of civilization, as he had been in the early seventies. Just as his strategy allowed Johnson to believe that he had originated the idea of a Yosemite Park, so Muir realized that it was not important who got credit for good works. If the public wanted Muir to be John-O-Mountains, Kenmuir, Saint Francis, a western Thoreau, or John the Baptist, that was fine. If it wanted to hear the "life and adventures," he could on occasion provide a thrilling narrative of a ride on an avalanche.[3]

So he learned to live his own mythical role when in public—a role as real to the public and to the Sierra Club as his picturesque descriptions had seemed when printed in *Scribner's* and *Century* — taking a pose and speaking a language his audience wanted to hear. Many still believe that in the end Muir was crucified by his defeat at Hetch Hetchy, and died of a broken heart. Perhaps we should not destroy that fiction; history ought to remember the damming of Hetch Hetchy as a crime, ought to be reminded that such a scheme could break hearts. After all, building the Hetch Hetchy dam was a step toward death.

I find nothing fanciful or vulgar about Muir's artifice, in his writing or in his public demeanor. The California he described was constructed increasingly as a mirror for an America which wanted to believe it had a future. And the persona he established might be a useful kind of model. Just as today most Americans consider themselves environmentalists, and a presidential candidate who once said "If you've seen one Redwood you've seen 'em all" can now call himself an environmentalist, so too the urban citizens of the 1890s read Muir's adventures because they wanted to believe that their Frontier had not passed away. Muir would feed these appetites for a beautiful, wild, and exciting America if they would be consummated in a movement for preservation of wilderness. "We are all mountaineers," he said in *Picturesque California*. Did urban America really believe him? Apparently it wanted to.

So in his public life the real Muir of the nineties and beyond was a shrewd businessman and nobody's fool. He was a man who could talk to presidents as equals. He was undaunted by the position, wealth, and prestige of worldly men. The Harrimans and Roosevelts of the world came to him, came to his mountains and glaciers for recreation; these men were not objects of wonder, but possible allies who might help Muir's cause.

THE SIERRA CLUB AND SECULAR PANTHEISM

When Johnson proposed that Muir help form an organization on the West coast which would be primarily a "defense association" to watch over and protect Yosemite National Park, a long chain of events began which would lead to the present status of parks and wilderness and to contemporary American ideas about Nature. The Sierra Club was founded in 1892, and as a result of the composition and nature of the organization the so-called "preservationist" movement began to develop a character which could be concretely identified and defined. It was different from the Forestry Association of the seventies, or the eastern Civic Improvement leagues.[4]

The composition of the Club was predictable. Most of the members were from the urban Bay Area — San Francisco, Oakland, Palo Alto. Primarily they were men, although there were several women among the charter members. By far the most recognizable group was comprised of college professors from the University of California and Stanford, but other professional men were also represented in the ranks. These were the kind of men who would be likely to call themselves "progressives" a decade later. They were growing increasingly suspicious of a railroad-dominated California. Though not rich, they were likely to be "well fixed," and they demonstrated rigid allegiance to their middle-class values, even while denying that California's problems stemmed from a class struggle. They were well educated and saw that their own future depended on a reaffirmation of traditional individualistic values in the political, economic, and social life of California. Though they were the heirs of the Grangers and Populists, they were basically urban in their outlook. The country and the mountains were places where they sought a vacation, not a living. They wanted to clean up the cities, the politics, and the environment of California. The Sierra Club drew members interested in an alpine club as well as those who were primarily interested in defending Yosemite, and this dual interest characterizes the Club today as it did then. It seemed like a useful combination of interests; both recreation in Nature and political activity would create a better California in the future.[5]

Though Muir was elected as president, the purposes of the Club, as expressed in its bylaws, reflected the interests of other members: "To explore, enjoy and render accessible the mountain regions of the Pacific Coast; to publish authentic information concerning them; to enlist the support and co-operation of the people and the government in preserving the forests and other natural features of the Sierra Nevada Mountains." These secular aims suggested a strong emphasis on the Club's public role as a trailblazer in the wilderness, a role which would promote recreation and help to make it a popular pastime. The Club would build trails and encourage the building of roads. It would advertise the parks and publish guidebooks. It would be responsible for taking people into the mountains on summer outings. The Sierra Club encouraged a "secular religion," as Joseph Sax characterizes their cult.[6]

It was to be a secular movement indeed. And that would be its greatest weakness. When these men came to be recognized as "preservationists" they would find that, though they were almost all professionals, they had no formal professional standing as "spokesmen for the tradition of man-in-nature." And since they had established themselves as a secular organization, they could not call themselves spiritual leaders. How could you be a secular pantheist? As Donald Worster recently has argued, their real spiritual roots were Protestant, as were their values: ascetic discipline, aesthetic spirituality, and egalitarian individualism. Their movement suggested, then, a redirection of religious reforming zeal into the secular realm. Thus today Roderick Nash, one of the most influential of modern speakers for wilderness, is forced to deal with the question "Can We Afford Wilderness" by introducing the accepted *fact* that "we gave up our belief in a god of the mountains and sea and crops and harvest." Though a man like Nash might wistfully fantasize a history in which our reverence for Nature had not vanished, he must finally justify our need for wilderness in modern and diminished, subjective terms: "It follows that to obtain wilderness, all one has to do is produce wilderness feeling in a given individual."[7]

Something central to Muir's philosophy was lost as "preservation" took on an institutional and organizational form in the Sierra Club. The speaker of the King Sequoia letter was left behind. Somehow the miraculous and authentic conversion he believed in — the vision which came out of extraordinary everyday experience in Nature — was reduced to a kind of behavioral or subjective experience. The Sierra Club and other organizations like it would represent, at least from the perspective of young Muir in the early seventies, a sacrifice of spiritual truth for political power. They would be serviceable tools when it came to dealing with government and bureaucracy; but they would also create, in the persons of Steve Mather and others, exactly the flat, tasteless bureaucrats who would shape the National Park Service in the early twentieth century.

The ideals subscribed to by the Sierra Club in its Articles of Incorporation became the ideals of a utilitarian kind of recreation. By 1912 the Sierra Club *Bulletin* would publish with approval the words of Horace McFarland: "The primary function of the national forests is to supply lumber. The primary function of national parks is to maintain in healthy efficiency the lives of the people who must use that lumber." This position was a return to Ruskin's attitude toward mountain enjoyment, his belief that the mountains could be best appreciated from the places where all could view them—the child, the old person, the cripple. This was a kind of Benthamite aesthetic which endorsed "the greatest good for the greatest number." Though Muir knew that grandma could appreciate a great deal from her lawn chair, he did not wish, as Ruskin did, to drag the mountaineer down from his mountain. Neither did he wish to see everyone able to "sing excelsior in safety." He thought that a wilderness was for those who were willing and able to seek it. Not a right, but a privilege given by Nature to those who worked for it.[8]

A utilitarian and democratic aesthetic—the aesthetic of moderation—became the basis for national parks policy, premised upon a belief that wilderness experience was an inalienable right. This policy was called "facing political and economic realities." Yosemite and Yellowstone became "Our National Parks." If one were not for the greatest number, one could be accused of economic discrimination, just as today it is a mark against wildernesses that they seem to be utilized primarily by well-educated professional people, not by blue-collar workers. The trouble with this aesthetic utilitarianism was that the spiritual value of wilderness might be judged, even by its champions, by men of the Sierra Club like Warren Olney, to be less important than other, "greater" goods. The aesthetic spirituality of Hetch Hetchy would have to compete with the aesthetic spirituality of San Francisco, on the assumption that a new Jerusalem was at least as important, and probably more important, than Nature's temples. Hetch Hetchy could be utilized for a higher good it if were the source of water for San Francisco. The Protestant's mission had always been to change the world, not to accept it. So it was that San Francisco could argue that a reservoir would make Hetch Hetchy more valuable. The Sierra Club could not answer this kind of argument, having already subscribed to the terms in which it was couched. The Club could never say that San Francisco was not as important as Hetch Hetchy, but could only argue that San Francisco's greater good did not need the sacrifice of Hetch Hetchy. But I am getting ahead of myself.[9]

THE MOUNTAINS OF CALIFORNIA

The first service Muir did for the Sierra Club was to publish *The Mountains of California*. It became the Sierra Club's chief text, a political book. Muir wrote it at a time when it could do the most good as a guide or a new testament for preservationists. He wrote it instead of working on many other projects which were perhaps more dear to his heart. As an early outline of the book suggests, Muir at one time wanted it to be a mountaineering book on the order of Whymper's *Scrambles Amongst the Alps*, and the title he wrote above this outline was "The California Alps." Later, when Johnson cut a large portion of Muir's glaciology out of the second chapter, Muir could only comment wistfully that sometime he hoped to "write a hard geological book." Unlike some of the other material he was writing for Johnson "to order," of which he was even willing to let his editor "take what you want & leave the balance," *The Mountains of California* was Muir's book, and he was quite defensive about it. It was more than the "charming collection" Johnson took it for. Muir sent a copy to Jeanne Carr with the comment, "You will say I should have written it long ago." Finally he had captured, in one volume, a sense of his whole experience in the Sierra and California during the seventies.[10]

There was little new in the book, except its structure. Muir's language had undergone a gradual change since the seventies, and so the revised version of his essays had become more genteel and polished. All the craggy corners were rubbed off, and the Yosemite oak had become an elm. No doubt Muir had written his classic at the expense of spontaneity. Because its origin was in the vision achieved in mountaineering and in the substance which came from Muir's careful method of study, the whole is informed by the soul of the wilderness, despite the picturesque language so noticeable to a modern reader. The richness of Muir's years in the Sierra could not be hidden by a patina of genteel language, and the richness was triumphant.

Muir felt the necessity of craft in this book perhaps more than in any other he wrote. He justified the book's structure and language in a letter to Johnson, explaining that he had leaned chapters carefully against each other, and had killed "adjectives and adverbs of redundant growth." His most revealing statement was about the relationship between poetry and science: "In it I have ventured to drop into the poetry that I like but have taken good care to place it between bluffs and buttresses of bold geological facts." Like Yosemite, *The Mountains of California* had a living and sacred river running through it. Despite the picturesque language, despite the significant substitution of "Nature" or "Beauty" for "God" and "the Lord," Muir's pantheism flowed, from the top of Mount Ritter to the Central Valley. And since he had been to the European Alps in the summer of 1893, Muir wisely realized that the Sierra had its own wholeness and did not need to be buttressed by language which referred to it as the California Alps. He had learned not to make this false comparison.[11]

What was left out of the book was as significant as what was included. Although Muir's tentative outline had not included the ouzel or the Douglas squirrel, it had included "Wild Wool." But the actual contents of the 1894 book focused on the more moderate and pastoral landscape of the Sierra, and stressed, with the exception of "Bee-Pastures," Muir's more moderate arguments. Further, this book was not really about all of the mountains of California, but about the Sierra, and even then it did not devote much space to describing what Johnson called "the three great gorges, the Hetch Hetchy, Yosemite, and the Kings River Cañon." Muir knew that he was writing neither a guidebook nor an argument. He was compiling a symbolic version of his own spiritual journey in the seventies, a volume which might give the general reader an insight into the path to vision.[12]

Thus the structure of his book: the reader was drawn into the glacial history of the Sierra, into the womb of the glacier, up the North Face of Mount Ritter to the fountains of life, and then was allowed to saunter with Muir down through the passes, lakes, meadows, and forests where he could observe the life in the mountains, the storms, and the foothills and valleys fed by the mountains. *The Mountains of California* was structured to present an anatomy of California's spiritual watershed. In this sense it could become the new testament of the Sierra Club, being the narrative of its president's — its prophet's — sojourn in the wilderness. One wonders: did Americans, or even Club members, appreciate the difference between the text Muir presented and the speeches of "conservationists" they were hearing with increasing frequency? Maybe they didn't, because they didn't want to be faced with the choice between the two versions of their future.

BEFORE THE FORESTRY COMMISSION

The political history of conservation in the United States during the 1890s is most chaotic and tangled. Muir entered the political megamachine with great hesitancy, but by mid-decade he was fully engaged in the struggle. The most significant governmental actions, from Muir's perspective, were President Harrison's reservation, in 1891, of thirteen million acres of watershed, primarily on the Pacific slope; the formation of a Forestry Commission by the National Academy of Sciences in 1896; and President Cleveland's executive order of February, 1897, which set aside thirteen more reservations totalling an additional twenty-one million acres, and which was issued after acceptance of the Forestry Commission's report.

The establishment of forest reserves by executive order was under constant attack, particularly in the West. In the ensuing battles Muir's role would not be that of creator, but of defender. Since he thought that federal control was the only way to preserve the remaining forests of America, he felt obligated to help give direction to these pioneering actions. On the other hand, he felt his best efforts could be made as a private citizen and an independent writer. Johnson, who remained in the midst of the fray in the East, continued to push Muir into the public eye, and when Charles Sprague

Sargent, head of the Forestry Commission, invited Muir to travel as an ex-officio member during the summer of 1896, Muir's public role was assured. Muir could not refuse.

The Forestry Commission seemed to presage a giant step in American policy making. A group made up of scientists rather than politicians, commissioned by the National Academy of Sciences, would embark on a thorough and comprehensive study of the forests of the West and then present its recommendations to Congress. Johnson and Muir immediately recognized the possible significance of this event. If the Forestry Commission was successful, it would set a precedent and lead the way toward rational, scientific management of the nation's resources. Men of intellect and good sense might gain a voice in government.[13]

Many of the distinctions we now take for granted — the difference between a national park and a reservation, between a national forest and a wilderness area — had yet to be made in the 1890s. These artificial distinctions would be made only as a result of the increasing power and complexity of the bureaucracies which would administer federal lands. The Forest Reserve Act of 1891 did not specify that reserves were to be set apart for specific uses. Just as Olmsted had seen that the creation of Yosemite Valley State Park thirty years before was the occasion for formulating a philosophical base for creating state and national parks, so Muir saw, in the potential creation of a national park surrounding Yosemite Valley and in the reservation of vast forested lands across the western United States, a chance to formulate a policy for preserving the wild lands of America.[14]

I believe that Muir prepared himself for the coming battles during a journey in the summer of 1895, when he drifted through the Grand Canyon of the Tuolumne, alone in his old wild way, and then continued his outing with Theodore Lukens and a party of young women he met along the way. On this journey Muir was impressed with the army's administration of the Yosemite National Park, which contrasted to state control of the badly trampled Yosemite Valley. He was in despair about the Valley, as he wrote to Johnson, but about the national park he was hopeful, and he was also pleased with the people he met in the wilder parts of the park. He must have thought deeply about the preservation of wild flora, and about the recreation of young Americans. The first issue came out when he spoke to the Sierra Club late that fall: "The preservation of specimen sections of natural flora — bits of pure wilderness — was a fond, favorite notion of mine long before I heard of national parks." In a letter to Johnson he indicated that a specimen section had to include a whole watershed, had to be a natural ecological unit: "As I have urged over and over again, the Yosemite Reservation ought to include all the Yosemite fountains." For him, a reservation, as a specimen section, as an ecological whole, was a living organism, and it didn't matter whether it was called a wilderness, forest, reservation, or park. The point was to save its flowing life.[15]

When Harrison reserved vast tracts of timber in 1891, their function and administration were not at all established and their defense was not assured. So when Muir joined the Forestry Commission in 1896 he hoped, along with Sargent, to establish a policy of administration and protection which would benefit the already established reserves and create new ones as well.[16]

Muir knew that the policies which the government would enact would depend on the kind of men who made those policies. Thus he began to realize that he might not only write about forests, but also about the kind of men who loved forests. His article on Linnaeus, written in 1896, and his 1903 review of Sargent's Silva should be seen in the context of the work of the Forestry Commission. He knew that policy making in conservation would require special men, men who realized that the first and best use of forests and flora in general would always be spiritual. The measure of a great conservationist would be that same vision.

For Linnaeus, the creator of botanical classification who had "found botany a chaos and left it a cosmos," Muir's highest praise was that he "loved every living thing as his friend and brother." Muir was willing to judge the character of Linnaeus from evidence given by the plant that the botanist had loved enough to give his name, the plant that he had married. Linnaea Borealis, "the wildest and gentlest, the most beautiful and loveful of all the inhabitants of the wilderness," was the living proof of the botanist's own soul. Muir knew that the world in which Linnaea grew was the world where he would always "feel willing to encamp forever and forgo even heaven." The message was simple and eloquent: a man could be

judged by the natural environment he loved, not by his love for science, or his love for other men.[17]

Muir's review of Sargent's *Silva* made essentially the same point.
The weakness of Sargent's fourteen-volume work was that it was
too technical, that Sargent too frequently hid his heart: "Had the
bright lines outside the technical parts been doubled or trebled, they
could have done no harm any more than lights and flowers on mountains, or on the trees themselves." A man's contribution to forestry
could be measured by how much he loved the trees; Muir's highest
praise for Sargent's volumes was that they breathed the peace of
the wilderness, that they made the reader long for the presence of
the forests themselves. Next to this, the technical and scientific questions of botanical names or distinctions among species paled to
nothing. What mattered was that Sargent had gone out into the
woods to see all these trees in their living relations. What had qualified Sargent to be chairman of the Forestry Commission was his de-
votion to the trees themselves, as indicated by the twelve years he
had spent preparing the fourteen volumes of the *Silva*.[18]

When Muir stood up at the annual meeting of the Sierra Club in
November, 1895, he half-humorously suggested that he was not really
qualified to carry on the work of protecting the Yosemite National
Park, that it should be left to lawyers and younger men. But there
was also some seriousness in his suggestion. He knew that the task
would be ongoing: "The battle we have fought, and are still fighting, for the forests is part of the eternal conflict between right and
wrong, and we cannot expect to see the end of it." The problem
he focused on was that of administration and enforcement. Speaking to the Sierra Club, he was giving its members their own direction. He knew that he would always be a theoretician, but the Club,
he hoped, might always watch the protective fences. His analysis
of Yosemite's problems anticipated the protective problem that he
expected would plague all reservations in America. It was an ancient problem, as one of his favorite anecdotes suggested: "The very
first forest reserve that I ever heard of, the most moderate in extent,
was located in the garden of Eden & included only one tree. The
Lord himself laid out the boundaries of it, but even that reserve was
attacked & broken in upon. The attacks then of sheepmen & lum-

bermen, unregenerate sons of Adam, on the Yosemite National Park are in the natural course of things." If God could not prevent the first humans from violating His Reserves, how much harder it would be for men to make decisions for permanence. Fences always seemed to fail when it came to preserving bits of pure wilderness. Muir claimed that he had tried to preserve a small pond and meadow in Wisconsin, and had later tried to protect a quarter-section of the "flowery San Joaquin plain." But such things could not be accomplished by individuals. For that reason, Muir said to the Club, he "did not take up a timber claim in the sugar-pine woods." Neither barbed wire nor moral prohibitions could guarantee the safety of the wilderness.[19]

Because Muir saw the conflict between Man and Nature as a war, it was natural that he would like to see an army protecting the reserves. Along with Sargent, he thought that the army might offer the only changeless administration in the face of changing politics. "And always it is refreshing to know that in our changeful Government there is one arm that is permanent and ever to be depended on," he told the Sierra Club. His distrust of political solutions to eternal problems would be likely to find sympathy among Californian Club members who knew firsthand what it meant to have a government bought and paid for by railroads, monopolies, and the underworld.[20]

The need for a changeless administration for the reserves had bothered Muir since the creation of Yosemite National Park. If the Valley were to continue under state control, he hoped at least that the commissioners might include stable nonpolitical members like the presidents of the University of California, of the State Board of Agriculture, and of the Mechanics Institute. He thought an army officer should also serve. "Republicans and Democrats — what names to write after considering the lillies," Muir muttered in his beard. Nevertheless, he had seen in 1890 that the railroads were, and likely would continue to be, the most powerful political ally the Club could cultivate —"even the soulless Southern Pacific." Like the army, the railroad monopolies seemed to be an unchanging fact of western life.[21]

Men who wanted to preserve forests would have to take help where they could get it. And there was a terrible paradox in linking the fate of the parks and reserves to the railroads, which had been among the chief destroyers of the forests since the 1860s, burning tremendous quantities of wood in a pre-petroleum economy. Even during the depression of the nineties, railroads continued to support themselves by selling timber from the vast land grants they had obtained three decades earlier. They could afford to support the creation of parks and reserves precisely because they had already taken such a large and unearned bite out of the public domain. They had already violated the Garden.[22]

It was going to be a dangerous game, depending on vested interests like the railroads, and hoping that the army might be made to protect the growing reserves in the West. Looking backward, we can see that industrial tourism and national defense were to become two of the greatest enemies of wilderness. (A third, of course, is "energy development.") Was Muir aware of this twin threat? And the question still remained, what role would he play in the forests' future? This was the same question he had asked himself twenty years earlier. But now he was prepared to work within the system.

He would try to become a mediator. And he saw immediately that his credibility with the Forestry Commission and others would depend on his ability to take neither the narrowly botanical position of Sargent nor the use-oriented position of Pinchot. Even before he traveled with the Forestry Commission, he said in *Century*,

> But it is impossible in the nature of things to stop at preservation. The forests must be and will be not only preserved but used, and the experience of all civilized countries that have faced and solved the question shows that over and above all question of management of trained officers, the forests, like perennial fountains, may be made to yield a sure harvest of timber, while at the same time all their far-reaching uses may be maintained unimpaired.[23]

And even to the Sierra Club in 1895 he ended his speech by declaring, "Forest management must be put on a rational permanent scientific basis, as in every other civilized country." It would be hard for him to subscribe to these policies when it came to actual implementation. One suspects he hoped that it was somehow possible to have a productive forest as well as a wild one. Perhaps, like Aldo Leopold, Muir needed to be confronted with the actual process of managing a forest as a crop-producing field before he would realize how offensive he found the idea that "Timber is a crop." Aldo Leopold was shocked when he went to Germany and discovered what German professional methods did to the landscape. Only after his experience in Germany would Leopold say, in "The Land Ethic," "A thing is right when it tends to preserve the integrity, stability and beauty of the biotic community. It is wrong when it tends otherwise." Muir had always subscribed to this kind of land ethic, and he never thought of the reserves as tree farms, mining claims, fields for regulated grazing, or anything other than whole, complete, healthy forests. He knew that a second-growth forest wasn't a real forest. And as the decade progressed he became less able to give any voice to the language or values of "wise use."[24]

THE FORESTRY COMMISSION'S REPORT

Though Muir apparently didn't want to be a member of the Forestry Commission, he was initially interested in its work. Johnson and Sargent were less interested in his membership in the Commission than they were in the good he could do with his pen. How much he actually influenced the Commission's report is in some question. One historian believes that Muir was responsible for the Commission's taking a position against grazing in reserves. Pinchot substantiates this theory in *Breaking New Ground*. Certainly Muir's position on grazing was significant, and he was most adamant on the point: no grazing should be allowed in reserves. One must remember that grazing was the primary commercial use of forests. The fact remains that it was not Muir's report but the Commission's, and it was largely the result of Sargent's leadership. When Muir traveled with the group through Montana, Wyoming, Washington, Oregon, Arizona, and New Mexico, as well as the California coast, he was with them because through articles in the popular press he would be able to bring public support for the Commission's recommendations.[25]

The Commission was divided on both its aims and the issue of use. Part of the group wanted to survey the forests' economic values; this faction was led by Pinchot, of course. But Muir, Sargent,

Alexander Agassiz, and Henry Abbot felt that the Commission should attempt a rapid survey which would lead to early withdrawal from sale to the private sector of as much forest as possible while Cleveland remained in office. These factions were symptomatic of the deeper philosophical division between the champions of economic forests and the champions of botanical forests.

Yet Muir was delighted to be traveling with even a divided Commission. It was always a pleasure for him to be in the company of scientists. Sargent, Abbot, William Brewer, and Arnold Hague were "good forest fellows." But by the end of a month he admitted that Sargent was "the only one of the Commission that knew and loved trees as I loved them."[26]

Although Muir did not mention Pinchot in his letters, Pinchot's recollections in *Breaking New Ground* show that he was pleased with Muir's company early and late. He found Muir a "most fascinating talker" and "took to him at once." Pinchot commented that Muir and Merriam "had seen what they looked at; and they were full of facts I needed in my business." On the other hand, he took an immediate dislike to Sargent, finding him "curiously deficient in ability to see things in a forest." In fact, Pinchot thought Sargent "couldn't see the forest for the trees — individual botanical trees." One wonders if Pinchot was afraid to attack Muir, and so found Sargent his most strategic enemy.[27]

But Muir was obviously the sort of fellow people liked, in spite of their differences. Though Muir and Pinchot were to quarrel about grazing again in 1897 when the issue caught fire, and Muir was to oppose Pinchot once more over Hetch Hetchy, he could still be charitable; as late as 1910 he would write, "I'm sorry to see poor Pinchot running amuck after doing so much good hopeful work — from sound conservation going pell mell to destruction on the wings of crazy inordinate ambition." And Muir knew that Sargent was a crusty and bad-tempered fellow, and so tried to take it upon himself to remain reasonable and friendly. Muir seemed always able to distinguish between his respect for a man and disagreement with the man's ideas. In the nineties he seemed to get along with almost everyone he worked with, even on the road with the Forestry Commission, when the living accommodations were anything but comfortable. I'm sure he liked Pinchot partly because the young man was willing to sleep outside, even in the rain. That was the sort of behavior which would go a long way toward making Muir forget other indiscretions.[28]

Despite the fact that he was not an official member of the Commission, Muir gained tremendous power when he began to interpret the report of the Commission in *Harper's* and *Atlantic*. It was the Muir–Sargent view that appeared in these magazines, and the essays Muir wrote would have to present the Commission's case to the public in lieu of any proclamation by the government. Cleveland had passed out of office, and President McKinley's Secretary of the Interior, Cornelius Bliss, suppressed the Commission's report. There was very little arboreal bliss in Bliss, Muir wrote to Johnson. And shortly thereafter Congress passed the McCrae–Pettigrew Bill, celebrated by Pinchot, which went against the Commission's report and opened the reserves to use. Even while Muir and Sargent had won the first battle, they had lost the war. Reserves and national parks would become very different from wildernesses, and would be administered as commercial enterprises — reserves for lumber, forage, and water, and parks for public playgrounds.[29]

So Muir's support of the Forestry Commission was published too late to change the course of congressional action, as he knew. Though in his first two articles in *Harper's* and *Atlantic* he revealed his hope for the future of government-sponsored conservation, in his third, published by *Atlantic* in January of 1898, he realized that an appeal for tourism was the only strategy left. Muir's steady shift away from the position of the Commission's report and from government action and toward tourism indicated his growing disaffection with the political machinations surrounding the reserves.[30]

THE LANGUAGE OF CONSERVATION

Muir has normally been called a preservationist, as opposed to a conservationist; he has also been called an aesthetic, or scenic, conservationist; and his enemies have called him a misinformed nature lover or a scenic friend. But he shared these labels with allies who were often oriented very differently than he was. His actual position was significantly different from that of a Sargent, who was interested in trees but had little concern for the ecology of forests; Muir also differed significantly with men like J. Horace McFarland of the American Civic Association, who took a humanistic view of forest preservation and saw forests as a "scenic" or "recreational resource." Perhaps Muir was closest to C. Hart Merriam, who of all the Commission members was most knowledgeable about ecology. Generally given credit for introducing the theory of "life zones," Merriam later came to direct the Department of Agriculture's Biological Survey — an appointment which served as evidence that Roosevelt gave aid to preservationists. Nevertheless, Muir, Sargent, Merriam, McFarland, and Johnson all wanted to see wild forests preserved, so it is appropriate to group them together. All that is meant when we speak of preservationists, then, is a political coalition of people with diverse philosophical positions. It is a serious mistake to assume that Muir had the same reasons as his allies for political actions in the nineties and later. When he attempted to spearhead a broad-based coalition of groups, he necessarily began to articulate views which he hoped would appeal to these groups. And while he was no longer an introspective young man, he did not intend to compromise himself while playing the public role in which Robert Underwood Johnson had cast him.[31]

It was easy to become a practical man and a faithful citizen; it always has been easy. Muir could do it as well as the next man — could buy himself a three-piece suit and go to Washington. It would have been easier, though, if he had possessed a little less moral integrity, since politics was a matter of appearances only. When men like William Kent tried to discredit him, he must have felt the pain of betrayal, but he knew enough about politics by then not to worry about such bothersome, though trivial, distractions. His allies were not to be mistaken for soul mates.

William Kent was a perfect example. The man who donated the Muir Woods, "the best tree lover's monument that could be found in all the forests of the world," could decide three years later, after becoming a congressman, that "real conservation meant proper use and not locking up of natural resources." By 1913 Kent was attacking Muir for lacking the social instincts of an average man, for being "entirely without social sense." Yet Kent was considered a preservationist too.[32]

For the East, wilderness had to be clothed in pastoral language, language of the middle distance, humanistic language. That language has become petrified in the late twentieth century; easterners interested in wilderness still call themselves conservationists. More to the point, the eastern language of conservation gave false connotations to Muir's ideas. "Park" — its origin is the same as that of "paddock," "enclosure" — suggests domesticity. What an unsatisfactory term, then, considering Muir's chief complaint about Yosemite Valley as a park: it was being used as a paddock, he said. The term was too tame, and failed to distinguish between the significantly different actions of men who wanted pastures and men who wanted wildlands. "Reserve" was a term Muir was likely to prefer; it implied a command to make an exception for future use. Making reserves suggested a willingness to stop the rampant rape of the West. Muir must have been appalled by the change in terminology when "forest reserves" became "national forests."

As the movement toward conservation took direction under Roosevelt and Pinchot, it began to cultivate its own language and values. This was a movement toward nationalistic, rationalistic, technocratic efficiency which would have appalled the young Muir who had left machines in order to learn the news of the universe and to pledge allegiance to the earth. The older Muir could see it coming in the language; the ecological future of the West would be won or lost in the field of semantics. The way men perceived Nature would be heavily determined by the language they used when they described her, as well as by the actions they engaged in at her expense.

By the middle of the first decade of the twentieth century Pinchot and Roosevelt had defined conservation as the process by which America would attain dominion over Nature by utilizing efficiently the resources of material wealth in the West. Conservation might include rational planning, but it only offered a more systematic plan for lumbering, mining, and grazing on the public domain.

Muir could see through the humanistic and paternalistic double-talk of the western rapists. Could he make the American public see through its own destructive habits of expression, which clothed real motives in a tissue of self-congratulating lies? Or would Muir, like many of his eastern allies, find himself able to speak to America only by using her language, and would he thus fall into misstating his own case, finally forgetting what he had to teach? For years he had spoken in parables. If he descended to the language of the political world, wouldn't his message become as banal as the world of technology which encroached on the wilderness?

THE FORESTRY ESSAYS

Muir's "National Parks and Forest Reservations," published in *Harper's* in June of 1897, made the case for forests which "should be reserved, protected, and administered by the Federal government for the public good forever." In this article he set forth the conclusions of the Forestry Commission, as he and Sargent perceived them: (1) "immediate withdrawal from entry and sale of all that is left of the forest bearing lands still in the possession of the government, as the first necessary step and foundation for a permanent forest policy"; (2) protection of the reserves — particularly from fire — by the United States Army; and (3) "after careful study . . . [establishment of] a permanent, practical rational forest management . . .[to] make [the forests] grow more beautiful, productive, and useful every year." As Muir expressed them, these priorities — preservation, protection, and careful management for beauty — were largely preservationist in spirit. He hoped that Congress would make laws to buttress these aims.[33]

Primarily, Muir's purpose was to defend the reservations in the face of the vocal opposition he expected. Even friends, he thought, were objecting that the president had created too many reservations at once; but the Forestry Commission's real enemies were those who wanted to profit from the forests: "Gold stings worse than the wasps of the woods, and gives rise to far more unreasonable and unexplainable behavior," he said. Lawyers and lumbermen — Muir called them patriotic thieves — were complaining, "for the good of the nation, for the sake of the dear people, and to clear a path for prosperity and progress, these trees must come down." As he had never done before, Muir took great glee in satirizing the rhetoric of his western enemies, while appealing to a silent majority —"probably more than ninety percent"— who were in favor of reservations.

"All of our precious mountains," they screamed, "with their stores of timber and grass, silver and gold, fertile valleys and streams — all the natural
resources of our great growing States are set aside from use, smothered
up in mere pleasure-grounds for wild beasts and a set of sick, rich, daw-
dling sentimentalists. For this purpose business is blocked and every current of industry dammed. Will our people stand for this? No-o-o-o!" Which
in plain English means, "Let us steal and destroy in peace."

As such language attested, Muir saw the arguments of "states' rights,"
"progress," and "good business" as the window dressings of greed.
His own argument, buttressed with many illustrations, brooked
almost no compromise with use. Wise use might come later, but
he saw the work of the Commission as precisely what its vocal
opposition said it was, a locking up of huge tracts of wild country, forever. "The greatest good for the greatest number," looked at
from the perspective of future generations, could be attained only
at the sacrifice of present gain and the acceptance of being. This
was what Muir hoped the creation of forest reserves meant. Of
course, they were important as watersheds — but primarily as spiritual watersheds.[34]

Muir was engaged in what Robert Underwood Johnson called
"Spiritual lobbying." He was trying to articulate a national policy
on forests before one had been enacted. He was defending a policy
of preservation when no policy like it existed. While Roderick Nash
thinks that "Muir, Johnson, and their colleagues were able to create
a protest [over Hetch Hetchy] in 1913 because the American people
were ready to be aroused," in point of fact Muir, Johnson, Sargent,
and their colleagues were preparing the protest, were creating the
taste for wilderness, in the nineties. It began with Muir's argument
that people wanted wild forest reserves, but that their crooked representatives had been bought by special interests; and this deep suspicion took root in the public consciousness. Though the movement
for wild forest reserves failed in 1897, there were still reserves, and
Muir tried to plant in the public mind a suspicion that the groups
who wanted to use resources contained in reserves were motivated
by greed, not national interest. As much as literature like *The Vir-
ginian* would try to hide the fact, the war in the West, like the Johnson County War of 1892 in Wyoming, pitted the interests of profit-
eers against those of settlers and citizens. Since the Civil War the

federal government had been encouraging the profiteer, the monopolist, but not the squatter.[35]

After his opening sally in *Harper's*, Muir was more comprehensive and careful in *Atlantic*. Though he spoke to the issues raised by the Commission's report, he no longer felt it was necessary to speak for the Commission. "The American Forests" was essentially Muir's definitive statement about the history and future of conservation in America. It began with a view of the whole continent as God's garden, where He grew the best forests He ever planted; it ended with Muir's plea for the trees, which could not escape the stupidity of men. But in the middle of the essay Muir analyzed the history and significance of Americans' destruction of their own environment, and from that analysis drew a picture of the current friends and foes of forests, and the prospects for the future. This was not an optimistic essay, and Muir had little reason to be optimistic. He wrote to Johnson two months before his essay was published, "Those Western Corporations with their shady millions seem invincible in the Senate." And of course he was right.[36]

While he grudgingly accepted progress, Muir referred even to settlers as "an invading horde of destroyers." He found that the doom of the forests was sealed when the stone axes of the Indians were replaced by the steel axes of the white men. All of this was in the past. But he wondered how it was possible, at such a late date, that the United States government was acting "like a rich and foolish spendthrift who has inherited a magnificent estate in perfect order." As he quickly noted, Prussia, France, Switzerland — even Japan and India — were far ahead of America in the management and care of forests. What was wrong in America, that it had never grown up and acquired a mature perspective toward Nature?[37]

Perhaps, he thought, the issue was one of law. The Timber and Stone Act of 1878, "which might well have been called the 'dust and ashes act,'" allowed wealthy corporations to obtain fraudulent title to ten or twenty thousand acres or more of the public domain. The large capitalists were more to blame than the small ones, since "it cost about as much to steal timber for one mill as for ten, and therefore the ordinary lumberman can no longer compete with the large corporations." Muir did not complain about the vast holdings the railroads had acquired, although he found them guilty of inadvertently setting fire to hundreds of square miles of forest each year. He thought they might honestly advertise, "Come! travel our way. Ours is the blackest. It is the only genuine Erebus route."[38]

But the real cause of all the desolation in the West was a moral one: "Timber thieves of the Western class are seldom convicted, for the good reason that most of the jurors who try such cases are themselves as guilty as those on trial." In the "practical West," pioneers still believed that forests were boundless and inexhaustible. They would never fight a fire "as long as their own fences and buildings were not threatened." They would never fight a corporation as long as their own interests were not threatened. "Even in Congress a sizable chunk of gold, carefully concealed, will outtalk and outfight all the nation on a subject like forestry, well smothered in ignorance, and in which the money interests of only a few are conspicuously involved." Muir was coming to know this truth as he paradoxically relied heavily on Harriman's influence when it came to affairs in Yosemite. If money could talk *for* the forest reserves, Muir would have been happy to hear it speak.

On a lower and subtler moral level, the real culprit, Muir suggested, was the American attitude toward work: the best work provided the easiest, quickest way to money, where "you're your own boss, and the whole thing's fun." The shake maker who said this had used ten or twenty feet of a three-hundred-foot-tall sugar pine he had killed, and was at one with the happy fellows who killed ducks, doves, quail, deer, and bears (but not grizzly: "they want a cannon to kill em"). Shoot 'em, tie 'em, and send 'em to San Francisco, where the poets could eat 'em without a qualm. That, Muir thought, represented an American parody of individual initiative. Living off the land was an odious enterprise, but it was American as hell. "They buy no land, pay no taxes, dwell in a paradise with no forbidding angel either from Washington or from heaven." This had always been an American Dream. Muir called this attitude insanity. Men had become the tools of their lust for gain: "The axe and saw are insanely busy, chips are flying thick as snowflakes." Muir was right. In the summer of 1897 a blizzard of destruction continued in the West, made possible by the technological progress of the American Dream. He knew as well that the petty greed of the little man made him turn his head and ignore the massive destruction effected by the wealthy, who stole wholesale.

Missing in this argument was any deep analysis of railroad wrongs. Though Muir attacked the waste railroads created, he failed to mention their wrongful gains or their abuses of land grants. This suggests that he was already making certain concessions. The writing was already on the trees: he would have to concede the reserves to users, and for preservation turn to the parks, with railroads as allies. By 1905 he and the Sierra Club were willing to show the economic benefits of tourism to the western states. Legislatures, state and national, simply didn't listen to arguments which weren't measured in economic terms. The preservation of wilderness required another strategy, the encouragement of tourism. The national parks would have to be the last places where wilderness could be preserved. The Sierra Club's Outings Program was essential to the creation and defense of those parks.

11

𝖳𝖳𝖳𝖳𝖳𝖳𝖳

National Parks

GETTING PEOPLE INTO THE WOODS

The excursion Muir took to Yosemite in 1895 was in many ways as significant as the one he had taken seven years earlier with Robert Underood Johnson. He was in the region for more than a month, first descending the Grand Canyon of the Tuolumne alone, following his own austere style, walking along bear trails. Then, traveling in a much more elaborate style along the Tioga Road with T. H. Lukens, and meeting in addition the party of young women, whom he immediately liked, Muir had a social excursion to Tuolumne Meadows. With this diverse group Muir climbed Mount Conness and Mount Dana, apparently having a fine time. That he enjoyed his own kind of excursion as well as the fine social time he had with the other travelers suggests that he was no longer very critical of others in the mountains. In a letter to his wife he contrasted his own outfit to that of Lukens; but he did not refuse the trout Lukens fed him, and probably he also ate his portion of the marmot served by the women, who called themselves the Plum-duffers.[1]

There is good reason to believe that with regard to others his own rigorous standards for the "right manners of the wilderness" had been gradually tempered during the eighties and nineties. A letter to his eldest daughter Wanda in 1884 was a delightfully humane and humorous account of his wife's difficulties in adjusting to Yosemite. He had seen firsthand how the strong, healthy woman he loved could become fearful, disoriented, and uncomfortable in what he thought was a garden park. He had learned more of the same with Robert Underwood Johnson. And so by 1895 he seemed particularly enthusiastic about young people and the "girl mountaineers," who represented a "hopeful beginning." He learned what happened to people who did not have the "University of the Wilderness" as a part of their early education, and was pleased to see the positive effects such an education had on those who could acquire it.

The next year, 1896, he met Gifford Pinchot while traveling with the National Forestry Commission. Though Pinchot hardly was likely to appreciate Muir's idea of "right manners of the wilderness," he remembered, when he wrote *Breaking New Ground* more than fifty years later, that Muir had not fished —"He said fishing wasted too much time"— and that Muir wouldn't let him kill a tarantula at the Grand Canyon, because it had its own rights. Still later Muir enjoyed the company of Theodore Roosevelt, despite the obvious differences in their concepts of wilderness manners. If Robert Underwood Johnson's memoirs are accurate, Muir even lectured Roosevelt on the "boyishness of killing things," though it is unlikely that he unleashed the full fury of which he was capable. One can imagine Muir laughing and teasing Roosevelt, "Now just because you're a short fellow, there's no reason to go around with a big gun killing stronger and wilder citizens of the universe, Teddy." Maybe he did just that. But Muir got along well with Roosevelt, and was favorably disposed toward the man as a result of their three-day camping trip. Muir had great faith in the powers of Nature to redeem even presidents, and he was willing to put that faith to the test.[2]

All of this suggests that Muir was thoroughly sincere when he told the Sierra Club in 1895, "Few are altogether deaf to the preaching of pine-trees. Their sermons on the mountains go to our hearts; and if people in general could be got into the woods, even for once, to hear the trees speak for themselves, all difficulties in the way of forest preservation would vanish." His faith became the principle of the Sierra Club's Outings, and it also informed the tone of most of the essays that became *Our National Parks*, in which Muir would be "inciting people to come and enjoy" the parks "and get them into their hearts." The trouble with Muir's optimistic outlook, and with the tone it took in the late nineties, was that in his great faith he failed to make distinctions: "The tendency nowadays to wander in the wildernesses is delightful to see. Thousands of tired, nerve-shaken, over-civilized people are beginning to find out that going to the mountains is going home; that wildness is a necessity; and that mountain parks and reservations are useful not only as fountains of timber and irrigating rivers, but as fountains of life." Who could object to this kind of sentiment? Yet these are the words of a man who had once been disgusted by the ways of tourists. When Muir became not so much the defender of wilderness as the champion of recreation and the booster of parks, he was failing to heed his own distinction between a right relation to Nature and a wrong one: "Even the scenery habit in its most artificial forms, mixed with spectacles, silliness, and kodaks; its devotees arrayed more gorgeously than scarlet tanagers, frightening the wild game with red umbrellas,— even this is encouraging, and may well be regarded as a hopeful sign of the times."[3]

In 1981 it is easy to be frightened by this expansive and optimistic voice. Yet Muir did distinguish between uses when he got into the body of his argument. He satirized modern travel by railroad in his articles about Yellowstone and the Grand Canyon; he urged in words reminiscent of his first *Overland* article that "Nothing can be done well at the speed of forty miles a day." He insisted that one must take more time. "Walk away quietly in any direction and taste the freedom of the mountaineer." Said Muir, "Climb the mountains and get their good tidings. Nature's peace will flow into you as sunshine flows into trees. The winds will blow their own freshness into you, and the storms their energy, while cares will drop off like autumn leaves." These have become the most frequently quoted of all Muir's words, but have rarely been read for what they certainly were in context: a response to the rush and superficiality of industrial tourism. It is unfortunate that these words are most often read by the tourists who stop their autos briefly at the parking lot of a national park Visitor's Center, and then reenter their autos to drive about the park.[4]

If one looks for it, one finds that Muir was trying to make Americans see the parks and reserves as valuable for their own sake, without considering questions of use; thus he hoped to appeal to the heart of the tourist. He said of the Sierra Reserve that he was sure, "if every citizen could take one walk through this reserve, there would be no more trouble about its care; for only in darkness does vandalism flourish." As this statement and his preface to *Our National Parks* indicate, Muir's message to the American public was essentially the same as the one he voiced to the Sierra Club before the Forestry Commission was formed. He could hardly be accused of elitism. If the Sierra Club came to see the wilderness as its own special reserve, as has sometimes been suggested, Muir was not guilty of that kind of patronizing and exclusive attitude. Instead, he suggested that all Americans learn in the wilderness, as he had, a right relation to Nature. In such essays as "Among the Animals of Yosemite" he subtly led his reader toward a right relation with wild animals. He recounted his first interview with a Sierra bear, and admitted that the bear's behavior was better than his own. He learned this lesson: "I was then put on my good behavior, and never afterward forgot the right manners of the wilderness." He could even approve of what he saw as the "rather trivial business" of fishing, since "in most cases it is the man who is caught." Muir had grown to have a gentle understanding of men, and had come to appreciate the needs they brought from the cities. By the turn of the century, he thought they needed only to be exposed to Nature.

As a strategy for getting support for the already created but still highly vulnerable parks and reserves, this optimistic sort of publicity seemed to be the right tactic. It represented a gradual shift in Muir's published writing from trying to enlist the support and cooperation of the government to enlisting the support and cooperation of the people. Muir's appeal to the people was still based on the language and spirit of the Sierra Club's Articles of Incorporation, but also suggested his disenchantment with the direct influence one man was likely to have on an impersonal government. The parks and reserves would have to appeal to a wide range of visitors, and Muir was willing to soften his standards in order to influence a wide variety of humans, like members of the present-day Sierra Club.

RECREATION: ACCESS AND DEVELOPMENT

A modern commentary must make distinctions among the kinds of recreation which might have been encouraged, even if Muir avoided drawing sharp lines. At issue is the phrase "render accessible" in the Sierra Club's Articles. Buried in this phrase were the relationships among roads, developed accommodations in parks and reserves, and "styles" of recreation. After all, ease of access, the comfort of accommodations, and the kind of recreational trails and facilities would determine the kind of ecological consciousness produced by the parks and reserves. From the beginning the Sierra Club involved itself in decisions about access and development, advocating roads and trails in Yosemite and elsewhere, later encouraging private means of access by railroad and lobbying for improved and more extensive public roads. And the Club itself would become a means of access when it published information and organized outings. On the 1895 excursion, Muir, Lukens, and a San Francisco lawyer named Mountford S. Wilson had discussed securing government ownership of what were still privately owned Yosemite toll roads.[5]

Decisions about access and development should have been based — but were not — on a hierarchy of uses, since there would eventually have to be "master plans" to decide the kinds of trails, paths, roads, and highways needed to accommodate recreation. And if it was to mean anything, such a hierarchy of uses itself would have to be based on a decision about relationships between people and parks. Though Muir insisted that a landscape architect would be necessary if Yosemite were to be rescued from its downtrodden state; though he could see the necessity for comprehensive planning, he was unable to create a master plan as Olmsted had in 1865. Yet roads in a park were an integral part of planning the visitors' recreational experience. It was never a question simply of more or fewer roads and trails, and where to put them. The further issue was, how would a visitor advance through the hierarchy toward more spiritual recreation?

Muir's recognition of this growing issue, which would explode with the advent of the automobile, was at first casual. Long before accessibility became an integral issue in the debate over damming Hetch Hetchy, long before the critics of wilderness areas would complain that nobody went there anyway, Muir realized that it would be difficult to preserve places that nobody knew. Before the formation of the Sierra Club he had advocated in Kings Canyon a loop-shaped carriage road, an "improvement" of major proportions, "up the South Fork of the King's River through the sequoia groves, into the great cañon, and thence across the divide and down the Middle Fork Cañon to Tehipitee; thence through the valley and down the cañon to the confluence of the Middle and South Forks, and up to the sequoia groves to the point of beginning." Such a major highway would be necessary, he thought, because the terrain was so intimidating to an ordinary tourist. Muir was willing to make a concession of this kind if it was necessary for the creation of a national park. He looked hopefully upon the roads inevitably built by miners in Alaska, which would "lead many a lover of wildness into the heart of the reserve, who without them would never see it." And even while he bewailed the destruction that followed in the wake of railroads, even while he suggested that they resembled the work of the Devil, he could use their presence as a pretext for arguing that the Grand Canyon ought to be national park. But it was another thing to condone the building of roads as an *ongoing program of improvement* in parks. Yet he finally argued that "in the presence of such stupendous scenery [trains] are nothing." He compared them to beetles and caterpillars, using demeaning language, which he repeated when considering, in 1912, the impact automobiles were likely to have if they were admitted to Yosemite Valley. While Muir depicted the technological modes of travel in deprecating terms, his language revealed a grudging willingness to accept the beginnings of industrial tourism. He would not actively oppose the iron and asphalt ways of the future. One wonders what he would say now if he saw that the Tioga Road, with its aluminum "exhibits," was constructed for the same level of recreation as the trail to Vernal and Nevada falls, paved with asphalt, and posted with etched metal interpretive billboards. And what would he say, seeing today's typical backpacker planning a trip on the basis of convenience? The *roads* determine his itinerary; they shape his experience, preordain the direction of his travel. Which are the popular roadheads, and why? Which the popular rockclimbs? They are determined by ease of access.[6]

I think people have not talked about Muir's attitude toward autos because they feared that it would turn out to be an embarrassment. But his attitude, in the period 1908–12, reflected the views of a man already more than seventy years old; at the same time it dramatized an unfortunate weakness visible throughout Muir's late career. As the Park Interpreters who work at Muir's home in Martinez are fond of pointing out, Muir certainly made his peace with the railroads when it came to their proximity to his own farm. A train station is named for him. Further, his youngest daughter was a great railroad buff, and Muir seems to have encouraged her interest. Whether he would look with equal fondness on the John Muir Parkway, as the highway which goes by the Muir home is called, I would not like to guess. Perhaps he would have been pleased by it in 1912, but if so one can only shake one's head in sorrow, as one does when reading a letter he wrote in 1912 which advocated not just trails, but roads all across the wilds of Yosemite. Muir should have known better.[7]

And so should the members of the Club who followed him. Worrying so much about the access which was necessary not just for creating, but for saving Yosemite National Park, they forgot about the mountains themselves. Muir's belief that there were certain places which would remain "natural reserves," his opinion that certain places would remain inviolate because men could not touch them—these are flatly contradicted by a plan Muir approved to blast a trail up Tenaya Canyon. Had he forgotten his Milton? Didn't he remember who invented explosives and why? Had his fellow Club members missed completely what his earlier writings argued?

Indeed, the issue of access can scarcely be separated from the Sierra Club's increasing commitment to development and its focus on the national parks in the first decade of the twentieth century. To render accessible came to mean render comfortable for Stephen Mather when he became the first director of the National Park Service. Mather learned at least some of his attitudes on Sierra Club Outings. It did not require a fine distinction to see that Muir's idea of a wilderness experience — the following of a Pathless Way, of Nature's own highways into her own reserves — was in direct contradiction to the Mather plan for improved access and accommodations. By the mid 1950s the Sierra Club had come to oppose the unrestricted building of roads by the Park Service under Conrad Wirth's Mission '66 program, but by then it was already too late; at stake was the difference between the public's learning to follow Nature's ways in the parks and a federal agency providing "a rather wide range of outdoor recreation experiences graduated to the range of demands it perceives in its clientele." In *Mountains Without Handrails,* Joseph Sax considers the critieria for choosing public policies, based on a hierarchy of public needs. In his most concrete example of decisions made by federal agencies, he enumerates the kinds of camping facilities the United Sates Forest Service provides. Sax thinks that "people want illusions that provide the comfort of familiar services while suggesting self-reliant adventure, and that the Forest Service is calculatingly giving them exactly that." We have slid into this view of the responsibilities of government agencies that administer parks and forests. These are not, I think, the responsibilities Muir hoped for, or that Sax desires.[8]

By 1908 Muir, and Colby of the Sierra Club — sometimes it is hard to separate their views during this period — were advocating considerable development of trails and roads in Yosemite and elsewhere. Some of these were not just minor improvements, and the hierarchy of their suggestions, printed in the Sierra Club *Bulletin* as a letter to the secretary of the interior, called for improved permanent roads in Yosemite Valley, a new road to Hetch Hetchy, and the purchase and repair of the Tioga Road, as well as trails up Merced Canyon and down the Grand Canyon of the Tuolumne. But the final suggestion on their list was the most surprising. They asked for a trail up Tenaya Canyon, justified because it would allow visitors to reach the eastern part of the park more directly and earlier in the season. This would be a major engineering feat, and would do considerable violence to the landscape since "a great deal of blasting will be required." In sum, these improvements would sacrifice the wildest canyons of Yosemite as wildernesses, so that the less adventurous visitors could see them more conveniently. Thus it was that the Club and Muir became committed to recreational development as a first priority, at the expense of wild areas in the parks and other wild areas outside parks to which they paid no heed. Such attention to parks as islands was and is dangerous.[9]

When Mather, as director of the National Park Service, purchased and improved the Tioga Road, which now bisects the Yo-

semite Park, he was implementing Muir and Colby's 1908 suggestion, so we can perhaps trace the genesis of the new Tioga Highway
and others like it to the policy of "rendering accessible" to which
Muir and the Club committed themselves early in the nineties. Because access is so closely associated with development, I don't think
it is reaching too far to suggest that Mission '66 (which after mid-
century would bring not only improved roads, but also many new
and redesigned visitor service centers to the parks) was a further
extension of the strategy which required graduated experiences for
a divided clientele in the national parks.

Holway Jones has presented a sort of apology for the Club, and
it goes like this: the Sierra Club was really a small organization;
it had very little power and only a couple of hundred members; and
so it had to focus its attention on gaining power, and had to limit
its influence mostly to the running of Yosemite National Park. (All
right. So the Club never said a word about the desertification of
the Owens Valley, which was precisely contemporaneous with and
analogous to the Hetch Hetchy controversy.) And as a result of its
own limitations the Club instigated a policy directed largely at protecting and developing national parks as islands. These were the practical decisions we might expect. But it turned out that *the strength
of the Club was not in its political power, but in the attractiveness
of the ideas it promoted.* So it was of the highest importance that
the Club promote carefully a coherent and far-seeing plan for parks
and wildernesses. It failed to do this, and when one of its own converts, Stephen Mather, gained power and took charge of the parks
as director of the newly formed National Park Service, the Club's
ideas of access and development were put to the test. Mather believed in good roads, good meals, and comfortable accommodations
in the parks. He was an effective bureaucrat, but hardly a great intellect. His ecological education was embarrassingly poor, even by
nineteenth-century standards. Taking congressmen into the wilderness, he applied the methods of Sierra Club Outings to his own political machinations, and the gospel he preached was a vulgar form
of what he had learned from the Sierra Club. So it should be no
surprise that we have a system of national parks designed by a vulgar intellect for what he assumed was an ignorant and physically
handicapped American public.[10]

THE SIERRA CLUB OUTING

The idea that a National Park would be designed as a facility to encourage the experiences of novices in the wilderness evolved as part of the Sierra Club's Outings Program. Mather's most famous mountain trip took place in 1915, when he wined and dined influential politicians in the Sequoia, Kings River, and Mount Whitney country. Perhaps this trip can be seen as a parody of a Sierra Club Outing, but it was based on a Club outing in style and in strategy. Mather was taking people into the wilderness who could simply not get there by themselves, who could never go it alone.[11]

The Sierra Club Outings were a far more essential part of the Club's activities than one might at first suspect. And Muir was far more likely to take an active part in a Sierra Club summer outing than he was to be present at a Club meeting in San Francisco. William Colby gave Muir credit for enthusiastic support of the program. Certainly the outings represented an extension of the strategy Muir used on Robert Underwood Johnson. It is still being used; the first Sierra Club Outing in 1901 was planned and carried out in a style that remained unchanged at the Club's base camps of the 1960s. Further, the Club's outing style had a major influence on the style of recreation and ecological education which Mather brought to the national parks, and which has continued to predominate this day.[12]

When William Colby announced the first summer outing in 1901, to Tuolumne Meadows, he pointed out that it would be a tool for the Sierra Club: "An excursion of this sort, if properly conducted will do an infinite amount of good toward awakening the proper kind of interest in the forests and other natural features of our mountains, and will also tend to create a spirit of good fellowship among our members." Thus Colby recognized the importance of the outing, "properly conducted," for providing not only an environmental education, but also for forming a communal relationship among participants. With these two goals in mind, he also realized that the outing would have to be a compromise which would allow the greatest range of members to participate: "The first trip should combine comparative ease and comfort with the opportunity to see some of the grandest scenery of the Sierra, not too commonly visited as to lack distinction." The comfort was significant, requiring that the Club pack the participants' gear into the base camp at Tuolumne, and that it provide a "commissary department" to prepare food for the campers. Colby pointed out that a group outing would also offer considerable monetary savings to participants. But the real virtue of the communal outing was its possibility as an educational tool. The ninety-six people who came to Tuolumne Meadows that summer listened to William Dudley's talks on forestry, C. Hart Merriam's lectures on birds and animals, and Theodore Hittle's history of Yosemite; Muir himself spoke on a wide range of subjects. Colby prepared the members for this kind of education by recommending that they read beforehand Le Conte's *Rambles* and Muir's *Mountains of California.*[13]

When I first arrived in Tuolumne Meadows more than fifty years later, the recreational atmosphere was similar. During my two-week stay in a Park Service campground, I listened to campfire talks by Naturalists Carl Sharsmith and Allan Shields. I followed Park Naturalists on hikes up Mount Dana and Mount Conness, and had I been a little older I could have followed Carl Sharsmith to the summit of Mount Lyell. Like the Sierra Club's Outings, the Yosemite Naturalists' Program led large numbers of campers on hikes, and like the participants of the Club outings the people in the Tuolumne Meadows campground in the 1950s felt a sense of community. We were all being educated in the "proper kind of interest" in the parks.

The Sierra Club Outings were, then, highly influential in creating the kind of recreation which would become a standard in the parks. And the National Park Service, in trying to create converts who would return home to the cities prepared to defend the parks, further applied Club strategy. It was a good strategy, but by the 1960s the strategy was creating problems in the Club, and those same problems were becoming evident in parks like Yosemite.

In 1966 the Sierra Club base camp was of the most civilized sort; the campers' personal gear was packed into the backcountry, and a hired crew prepared sumptuous meals such as roast leg of lamb and omelettes made from fresh eggs. The educational aspect of the trips continued, though it was not as spectacular as it had once been. Still, Norman Clyde was there as a naturalist, and David Brower might walk in for a visit and talk to the campers. Even after the base camp had been scaled down from more than a hundred to only sixty campers, it was still clear to the crews that the Club had been too long in reviewing its policy of providing unnecessarily extravagant comforts for its members on the outings. The Club was slow to see that elaborate accommodations were a severe hindrance to the spiritual growth of the participants. So too, on a nationwide scale, the elaborate accommodations of the national park system were becoming a serious problem for park maintenance. Too many people were expecting overly comfortable accommodations. It is unreasonable to expect that Muir could have anticipated a problem of this kind in the future. But it is true that the Club was very slow in changing its access policy and its outings program; policies have a way of becoming entrenched paths, and are difficult to revise or overthrow. From the very beginning, rendering the wilderness accessible was a philosophical contradiction which, hand in hand with encouraging tourism, could only lead to long-term problems; but these might have been foreseen if only the Club, or Muir, had appreciated the pressures of increased population and the overwhelming power of technology.

Yet it seemed to them, perhaps unavoidably, that access and tourism were their best tools. For the same reason, I can see no better strategy in places like Utah and Alaska than trying to counterbalance industrial development with increased tourism. It is better to have crowded parks and forests than no parks and forests. Getting people into the woods, even too many people into the woods, was perhaps the only step that could be taken.

People needed trees, and the trees needed people. The Club was providing a kind of philanthropy by bringing the uninitiated into the wilderness. I myself was fortunate enough to learn to appreciate the Sierra while on Park Service hikes and Sierra Club Outings, and I do not now desire to bite the hands which fed me so well. But the Club Outings seemed to be based on an anthropocentric philosophy, which even Muir finally accepted when it came from the mouth of E. H. Harriman: "What I enjoy most is the power of creation, getting into partnership with Nature in doing good, helping to feed man and beast, and making everybody and everything a little better and happier." When Muir went on Harriman's Alaska Expedition in 1899 he saw Harriman doing exactly that sort of thing for the scientists on board his cruise ship. And when I worked for the Sierra Club Outings Program, that is what we did for the predominantly professional people who came to the base camps. We took care of an interesting group of Americans, and we tried to make these urban folk as comfortable as possible in the wilderness. We hoped we were making friends for the trees.[14]

Ah, but were we? Yes and no. The problem then was similar to the problem facing the national parks today: the clientele would come back from year to year, and would not graduate to more rugged and self-reliant outings. When we pointed this out to the Outings Committee of the Sierra Club, the committe pointed out in turn that the base camps, which were the most luxurious kind of Club outing, were also the most financially profitable, and that they had become a financial necessity since they supported the other smaller, less profitable and more rugged outings. Likewise, the typical visitor to Yosemite, the archetypal National Park, has learned to repeat certain kinds of activities. He wants a short, easy, heavily-signed "nature trail," and he expects to get it. He wants elaborate exhibits at the Visitor Centers, and he has learned to expect them. He has grown accustomed to smooth, high-speed roads, and is surprised when he finds anything different. Yet he represents support for parks. He is encouraged to return, because numbers mean support. He is not encouraged very much to graduate to more austere kinds of recreation, so when he goes to the next park down the line he will engage in his usual activities. The hierarchy of roads, trails, and services has helped to entrench and perhaps create a static caste system in the parks — from the residents of the Ahwahnee Hotel to the Winnebago owners, to the pickup truck and van campers, to the backpackers, and finally to the mountaineers and river-runners. Each group seems fixed in its own sphere of activity, and none benefit from the insights available through commerce with the others. Further, the parks now need a great number of visitors in order to justify the services they offer.

In the same way, Sierra Club Outings have become a hierarchy of different excursions, rated by difficulty, each of which appeals to a different group of members. There is no longer a sense of community among participants of the same outing, let alone a sense of community among the participants of different kinds of outings.

Accidental and yet lasting relationships of the sort that Muir made on his excursion in 1895, when he led a diverse group of people in the mountains — those seem a thing of the past.

POLITICS AND COMMUNITY

The Sierra Club, as a communal organization, had possibilities which reached far beyond those of a pleasure group, and Muir must have seen in it the potential for a new kind of cross-political, cross-cultural alliance. On outings, when this new community was born in the wilderness, a new set of allegiances suggested themselves — allegiances to Earth instead of State, allegiances which reached deeper into the soul of Man than business, money, or even family. Members like Colby, Parsons, and Badè, who were closest to Muir, realized immediately that this was a different kind of club, an organization which transcended, or might transcend, other hopeful organizations in California. The Club suggested "a passage to more than India," a vision of a California that was more than just a Mediterranean of the American West, and most of all, a new western ethic. This ethic had always been the heart of Muir's message: men's allegiances ought to reach higher than the State or the city of their birth; men's works ought to reflect their reverence for the land.[15]

But even as the Club's communal dream was born, it entered the political realm along with Muir and Johnson and Colby. As the Club became involved in the mundane day-to-day battles over the disposition of Yosemite National Park and the recession of the Valley to the federal government, as the Club became muddled in what Muir had once called the "political quagg," it lost its longer-range, more powerful vision. It gradually ceased to explore its visionary horizon, and paid closer attention to the more pressing, immediate political and practical matters.

Yet the Club would have to face the larger problems which tested its possible utopian aspirations. The Club was a diverse group of professional people, and embodied the tensions evident in Californian society as a whole. A divided loyalty in its own membership was dangerous, even as the group buried itself in the transitory, crisis-oriented battles raging around Yosemite. For while the Sierra Club focused on these details, the larger political and economic forces which would come to be called "conservation" were at work. What Muir wanted the Sierra Club to represent was very different from what the "conservationists" stood for, and at stake was more than an internecine struggle between warring factions of American progressives.

The conservationists, with their "resource conservation and development" approach, were essentially at odds with someone like Muir. As Samuel Hays's definitive history of conservation points out, the larger and more powerful movement suggested a whole new way to visualize the future of America: "specialization," "nationalism," "growth," "use values," "efficiency" — the very language of conservation implied a technological future and acceptance of an urban, centralized society. Muir's Club, with its new communality and its worship of the wilderness, suggested a decentralized homeostasis between humans and their planet. Even if most Sierra Clubbers didn't realize it — and still don't realize it — the conflict between values born of the wilderness and those of the conservationists was destined to grow.

This conflict was not a matter of personalities, and it's time that historians stop pretending that the particular political figures involved in the battle were the real participants. The real participants were two separate world-views. Unfortunately, those two separate world-views had been uncomfortably merged in the organization of the Club itself. No wonder the Club divided over the management of Yosemite Valley, and again over the proposed damming of Hetch Hetchy. In the same way the Club has been hampered in modern-day battles, in which patriotism seems to be an opponent of ecological consciousness, particularly when the MX missile system is debated. This kind of internal split impeded the Club's ability to articulate a clear and permanent policy. It caused the Club to focus on certain issues, and to not even mention others which were essentially related to them. It created the problems that exploded in the controversy over Hetch Hetchy, and resulted in the symbolic and powerful absence of Muir at Roosevelt's Governor's Convention in 1908. His exclusion from mainstream conservation by Pinchot simply dramatized a larger truth: he never was a conservationist.

As Muir himself became buried deeply in the temporal affairs of Yosemite during his last years, he came to be identified not with the world-view he had tried so hard to foster, but instead with the specific issues which were symptomatic of the larger growing pains of America. Thus he has taken a less than rightful place in the history of this period, and is still generally viewed as a spokesman for a particular special-interest group. Though Muir shared in many of the inner conflicts of the Sierra Club, he was able to remember what was essential, remaining far more radical in his outlook than the Club was able to be. So it is necessary to deal with the political alliances Muir actually made during the period 1890–1905, to see the style and intention of his own politics, before one can assess the importance of the battles over Yosemite and Hetch Hetchy which represented the applied aspect of his views.

POLITICS IN THE MOUNTAINS

The lure of Washington, and of the East, was great in post–Civil War America. After the war San Francisco was emptied of the brightest members of its literary renaissance. Even in the seventies Muir's close friend John Swett advised Henry George to go to New York if he wanted to get a hearing for *Progress and Poverty*. Washington was becoming the central power which, for the first time, would support serious scientific explorers. Men like John Wesley Powell linked their careers irrevocably to the government. Yet Muir resisted the lures of eastern academia and government service. In 1895 he reviewed for Robert Underwood Johnson the history of the academic East's seductive arguments, and remembered that in the seventies he "never for a moment thought of leaving God's big show for a mere prof-ship, call who may." For the same reason he did not become a member of the National Forestry Commission. Perhaps one could say that he was temperamentally a loner, but his reasons were more deliberate. Like Thoreau, to whom he compared himself frequently in the early years of the twentieth century, Muir thought of himself as a "majority of one." If he were to influence the government, he would do so as an upright and independent citizen, not as a civil servant.[16]

He had neither the desire nor the ability to become a bureaucrat, or even to become a lobbyist. Indeed, he preferred to leave the running of the Sierra Club to younger, more organizationally inclined allies like Colby. If he were to wield any power, he wished to do so with his pen and his ideas. Thus it was with great caution that he entered the political realm during the battle for the recession of Yosemite Valley from state to federal control. His first foray in this battle was a disappointment. He wrote to T. H. Lukens early in 1897 that he had gone to Sacramento to talk to legislators about recession. Warren Olney and Eliot McAlister, the Sierra Club's secretary and legal counsel, had refused to go with him. He went alone, despite his feeling that he was "far from the right man for such work." But when he arrived, he discovered that the legislature had already voted against recession. He was out of his realm.[17]

He was not like the men who would run the National Park Service. Unlike Mather and his successor Albright, who were mediators, Muir's strength grew from his uncompromising integrity; he did not like to work out compromises. He was not a joiner. But neither was he a "man without politics," as Mather tried to be. Muir's interests were not so much apolitical as trans-political, and the kinds of allies he made suggested his ability to appeal to a wide range of people, his ability to make himself a catalyst, not a leader. Bill Devall suggests that Muir's politics could be glossed with a passage from the Tao Te Ching:

> If the sage would guide the people, he must serve with
>   humility.
> If he would lead them, he must follow behind.
> In this way when the sage rules, the people will not
>   feel oppressed;
> When he stands before them, they will not be harmed.
> The whole world will support him and will not tire of him.
>
> Because he does not compete,
> He does not meet the competition.[18]

Like a sage, Muir appealed to his allies in the last two decades of his life not as a leader, but as a fellow traveler of the Way. Even as he spoke to men like Taft and Roosevelt as equals, so he was spoken to by his correspondents—Johnson, Colby, and others—as a fellow. He did not wish to be held in awe, and resisted for years the appeals by Harriman, Johnson, and Page that he write an autobiography. For a man whose fellow citizens in Martinez considered him strange and dislikable, Muir made a remarkable number of friends of all sorts; and these were not just chance acquaintances, but loyal allies. Politicians, businessmen, poets, artists, scientists, and even ministers found him an irresistible talker and a valued friend. Muir, on the other hand, was remarkably tolerant of their frailties.

This is not to say that he was a conciliatory sort of person. Muir's relationship with the artist William Keith was notoriously stormy, and even though the two men had great affection and regard for each other, they also frequently disagreed in voluble terms. Likewise, Muir's friendship with the writer John Burroughs was punctuated by disputes and grumblings. Charles Sprague Sargent, the botanist, was perhaps the crankiest of men, yet Muir knew that the love of trees which he shared with Sargent was more important than irrelevant day-to-day temperamental differences. Muir could never resist the lure of a quibble, and he often said things which punctured the egos of his acquaintances in ways that they thought cruel.

Muir did like to do all the talking. Burroughs complained that, on the Harriman Alaska Expedition, Muir "would not allow the rest of the party to have an opinion on the subject" of glaciers. And when ranger Charlie Leidig tried to listen in on a conversation between Muir and Roosevelt as they camped near Glacier Point in 1903, he noticed that "some difficulty was encountered because both men wanted to do all the talking." Yet there was also something disarming about Muir's innocent enthusiasm. Just as Joseph Hooker and Asa Gray had enjoyed teasing Muir in the late seventies because he was "so eternally enthusiastic," so William Howard Taft could tease Muir as the two men walked down from Glacier Point in 1909. Muir was capable of absorbing as well as giving ridicule. He could bend, and did. In fact, I believe that Muir's careless and innocent demeanor was part of a calculated charm. William Kimes recounts an incident that took place during Roosevelt's visit to Yosemite. Muir had received a letter from Charles Sprague Sargent which commanded Muir to get some letters from the president that might be of use to Muir and Sargent on their anticipated world tour. Muir simply handed Sargent's letter to Roosevelt, apparently forgetting that Sargent had commented in the letter that Roosevelt "takes a sloppy unintelligent interest in forests, although he is altogether too much under the influence of that creature Pinchot." What could Roosevelt do but laugh at Muir's disarming naïveté?[19]

At times like these Muir must have seemed totally unselfconscious and unegotistical. But it is probably fair to say that this was a conscious style. He recognized and admired in E. H. Harriman the "wonderful manager of men." He suspected that there was a greatness in Harriman's ability to touch so many lives. And Muir's series of letters to William Colby, written while both men worked for so many years to save Hetch Hetchy, are a testament to Muir's ability to support and encourage an ally through the ups and downs of a long political battle. In a similar manner, Muir constantly gave Robert Underwood Johnson credit for many of the activities that the two men had conceived in common. It is naive to think of this as selflessness on Muir's part; rather, it was good political sense.

Muir's politics, to the extent that he was capable of manipulating the circumstances, were carried on in the mountains. Men like Roosevelt and Taft, Burroughs and Harriman, came to his world in Alaska and Yosemite. Muir did not go to Washington, or even to Sacramento, unless he had to. This *was* important. Mountain thinking was different, and so consequently was mountain society. If only the conversion in the wilderness could be made strong enough, it would be carried back down to the lowlands and change the cities. All of this suggested that the Sierra Club Outing carried the possibility for a re-creation of human society.

When I worked on Sierra Club Outings, there was still hope that the outings would enlist the "support and cooperation" of the participants. The air was alive with it. How could people fail to gain something after camping for two weeks in the company of Norman Clyde? There was a place on a Sierra Club Outing for a young man like George Dyson, a place where he could get away from his father's obsessional vision of nuclear-powered escape from a polluted and overpopulated world. He could find a congenial group, a cult of revolutionaries who believed that our own world was our only world, and one worth saving. Even doctors and lawyers became something different when they went into the wilderness; they learned

a new set of manners, and a new set of values. That was the promise of the Sierra Club, and of Muir's kind of Sierra Club Outing
politics. Americans could sense, for a while, what it meant to be at
home in Nature, and then they would write to their congressmen.[20]

The dream of the Sierra Club Outings had always been essential to Sierra Club politics, but the reality of the outings suggests
something else. People haven't always gotten along with each other,
and there have been frequent moral conflicts between the younger
crews and the older campers over precisely the question of what
constitutes the "right manners of the wilderness." On one trip we
invited along two boys, nine and eleven years old, from the Oakland
ghetto. Duke and John. They were miserable. They missed the television set and even the noise of traffic. They could not understand
why sane adults would want to spend any time out in that wilderness. We were shocked to discover firsthand that the taste for wilderness was culturally determined, a privilege enjoyed only by the
sons and daughters of a certain comfortable class of Americans. One
could cultivate a sense of utopian community on the outings only
by beginning with a group of people who already agreed closely
about certain basic values. Mountain thinking and mountain politics were not likely to become a ground swell in the evolution of
American culture and politics. The Sierra Club Outing had always
been designed to appeal only to middle- and upper-class people. And
it worked effectively only within those groups. The most popular
crew members, not surprisingly, were the young men who had gone
to elite prep schools like Phillips Exeter and Cate. The doctors, college professors, and lawyers loved them.

These were the kinds of people that Muir had been able to convert when he took them to the mountains. These were people who
would walk the John Muir Trail. The openness with which he greeted
influential people — politicians like Mather, Pinchot, Roosevelt, Taft,
Noble, and Kent; businessmen like Harriman, Carnegie, Lukens —
allowed these men who were so different from Muir to become his
allies, or at least to be willing to listen to him. Yet Muir also gained
and kept the respect of scientists and scholars like C. Hart Merriam, Henry Fairfield Osborn, Charles Sargent, Joseph Hooker, Asa
Gray, and Joseph Le Conte. He was equally capable of appealing
to humanists, poets, and artists like Francis Fisher Browne, Robert

Underwood Johnson, William Keith, Charles Robinson, Thomas Hill, and Harriet Monroe. His own friendship and political alliance with such people indicated that he wanted to foster a coalition of Americans which would cut across the increasingly rigid cultural boundaries.

He encouraged his own daughters to pursue their interests despite the social costs, and he took joy in seeing more and more women in the mountains — indications that he hoped for a more equal alliance between men and women. Perhaps Pinchot appealed to genteel women's groups like the Daughters of the American Revolution because he wanted to cement an alliance between his own "directed social organization" and the middle and upper classes of America. So Pinchot might appeal to the conservation of "traditional American Virtues." But Muir's appeal to women was directed toward them as human beings, and he hoped that they might join men as equals, seeking their spiritual recreation as partners. As early as 1873 Muir had gone to Hetch Hetchy and the Grand Canyon of the Tuolumne with Jeanne Carr, defying Victorian standards of behavior. He never changed his attitude about women's place in the wilderness, and perhaps Jeanne Carr was responsible for this. Certainly Muir's participation in the outings program showed his continued interest in women's equal role in the mountains. Still, even in the early 1960s women working on the crews of Sierra Club Outings were more likely to be assigned duties in the commissary than duties as guides.[21]

Muir's belief in not just the Sierra Club, but in "the more clubs, the better," argued that he wished to see a decentralized and universal movement which would bring together communal groups all over America, united by their evolving consciousness and their commitment to the preservation of Nature. As Muir conceived it this would be a grass-roots movement, nonbureaucratic, nonspecialist, and certainly antithetical to the burgeoning growth of American culture at the turn of the century.[22]

Thus the Sierra Club, and ecological resistance, could be seen as an alternative way of life, a contrary vision which hoped to stop the bulldozer of progress. Perhaps I am trying too hard to suggest the radical possibilities of the Sierra Club and of Muir's own style of politics. And for the moment I am ignoring the practical impossibility of such a vision. Yet this alternate way of life was part of the dream born with the Sierra Club. Perhaps the dream was never heard, or perhaps it died between 1895 and 1905. It was certainly not possible to hold together alliances made up of monopolists and progressives, conservationists and artists, rural folk and urban.

1905

A political victory . . . or some other favorable event raises your spirits, and you think good days are preparing for you. Do not believe it. Nothing can bring you peace but yourself. Nothing can bring you peace but the triumph of principles.
Emerson, "Self-Reliance"

From the very beginning of his campaign with Johnson to preserve the region surrounding Yosemite, Muir saw that it would be necessary to return Yosemite Valley to federal control. But he also knew that the issue was likely to be sensitive: "These Californians now sleeping in apathy, caring only for what 'pays,' would then blaze up as did the Devil when touched by Ithuriel's spear. A man may not appreciate his wife, but let her daddie try to take her back!" The question of recession smoldered through the middle nineties, while Muir and other radicals like C. E. Robinson became anxious about the state's poor management. Robinson, in his fiery style, accused the Sierra Club of the same apathy that Muir attributed to all Californians. "The Sierra Club . . . has a mere existence for its own pleasure — that is all," he said. But perhaps the reason for the Club's inaction was less basic; at the time it seemed more appropriate to make the strategic choice to work in a spirit of cooperation with the state's Yosemite Commission. Yet Muir too was ashamed of the Club's stand on parks and reservations. Its attitude, Muir knew, was really quite naive. In 1895 he wrote to Johnson complaining of the Club's gullibility in Yosemite matters. Already the Sierra Club had been diverted from its duty to Yosemite by the Yosemite Commission's willingness to make some cosmetic changes in the Valley; the commission promised to hire a landscape gardener. Muir wrote, "I never believed that the Yosemite Commissioners really meant to turn over a new leaf in the management. California does not truly care for Yosemite for itself, and here lies the difficulty." There was no marriage between California and the Valley, Muir knew, and no love either.[23]

Muir hoped that the Sierra Club would press for the preservation of Yosemite's flora, but he was disappointed with the Club's lack of interest in the matter. "Our Sierra Club altogether refuses to make a fight at present," he had written to Johnson in 1893; four years later he was still complaining to Johnson, "I am trying to get the Sierra Club to take plain open ground on the Yosemite question."[24]

The problem was precisely as Muir saw it. The Club itself was an organization made up of Californians, so the membership was divided in its loyalties and had not decided whether its allegiance went to the state or went to the Valley. This confusion was serious, and brought into question the very integrity of the Club. Of course the members who favored state control would have argued that the question was state versus federal control, but that, Muir knew, was a red herring. The state had demonstrated its inability to care for the park, and at the same time the federal government had shown that it could care for the watershed surrounding the park. When the Club finally did take open ground in 1905, its reasons for advocating the recession of the Valley to the federal government were couched in purely practical terms; rather than addressing the real issue of concern for the Yosemite itself, the Club argued that federal jurisdiction would bring improved accommodations and services, and would provide growing revenues for the state. It may be that the Club's argument was directed toward the expected opposition of the state's citizens, but nevertheless its public statements were not based on the deep reasons for changing the administration of the Valley.[25]

In the meantime, Muir and Colby had enlisted the aid of Harriman and his paid-off men in Sacramento. And it is likely that the nine visits Muir and Colby made to the legislature during the debate were less significant than one call made by William Herrin, who was Harriman's chief counsel in California. Thus the real force which lobbied effectively for Yosemite in 1905 was not the Club, but the Southern Pacific Railroad. This was a bad omen. When it came to the question of Hetch Hetchy, Muir and Colby would not be able to use Harriman, because to do so would involve confronting the more powerful anti-monopoly progressives who stood behind Roosevelt. So the lesson of the recession might not have been very cheering to Muir, despite his enthusiastic and forward-looking comment to Johnson: "Now, ho! for righteous management." In fact, the battle had taken a serious personal toll, as he wrote to Johnson in the same letter: "I am now an experienced lobbyist; my political education is complete. Have attended legislature, made speeches, explained, exhorted, persuaded every mother's son of legislators, newspapers reporters, and everybody else who would listen to me. And now that the fight is finished and my education as a politician and lobbyist is finished, I am almost finished myself."[26]

In its proper perspective, the fight for the recession of Yosemite Valley pales into a small skirmish in a much larger war. By 1905 San Francisco had made its first moves to gain the Hetch Hetchy as a reservoir, and Los Angeles was well on its way to gaining the watershed of the Owens Valley for its own use. Wild and rural California were already hearing the death knell; California was pursuing a policy of sacrificing all for the growth of its large urban centers.

On a national level, the picture was even bleaker. As Samuel Hays documents this history, by 1903, the very year of Roosevelt's visit to Yosemite with Muir, the Roosevelt administration was realizing its objective of "efficient maximum development" of resources. And in 1905, the same year in which the California legislature approved the recession of the Valley, the forest reserves were transferred to the Department of Agriculture, representing a "victory for the development point of view in the Roosevelt administration. The change of name from 'forest reserves' to 'national forests' symbolized its significance." The whole conservation program of the Roosevelt administration was planned along the lines of "divide and conquer," as the public domain was classified into economic categories. As Secretary of Agriculture, Pinchot continued to press for more control of public lands by his department, which he thought should be responsible for National Parks, the Geological Survey, the General Land Office, and even the Office of Indian Affairs.[27]

More than a year elapsed between California's decision to give up Yosemite Valley and the federal government's decision to accept it. During that year Muir received the news of Pinchot's doings in Washington with more equanimity than the future would warrant. He wrote to Johnson about the forests being put under the control of the Department of Agriculture, "What a glorious chance this gives Pinchot to distinguish himself and bless the world; but politicians I fear will try as hard as ever to get in their deadly work in spite of all we can do." In the same letter he commented that there were rumors of a renewed interest in a reservoir at Hetch Hetchy. He had heard that Pinchot had approved of such a plan, but could not believe that was possible if Pinchot really knew the valley. One can only sigh at a distance. Muir's impact on Roosevelt had not been as great as he had hoped it would be. Even if, in 1903, Muir had "stuffed him" regarding timber thieves and the destructive work of lumbermen and other forest despoilers, the newest threat to wild lands, in the form of reservoirs and pipelines, was to be a worse menace. Pinchot didn't care to see Hetch Hetchy; his decision was not based on the value of the valley *for itself.* He was more interested in the welfare of San Franciso.[28]

And the question of water would again raise the problem of conflicting loyalties in the Sierra Club. Even though it might have been possible to compromise, the issue was perceived on both the east and west sides of the Sierra—by Washington, Pinchot, Roosevelt, Los Angeles, and San Francisco—as a simple choice between humans and Nature, between the cities and the landscape. Conservationists and engineers had already planned their arguments, and the fight would be fought by their rules, and under their standard utilitarian test for public policy: "the greatest good for the greatest number." In 1905, the battle was won in Washington by the "resource developers" before Muir even entered the fray.

HETCH HETCHY

Finally let us remember that the conservation of natural resources . . . is yet but a part of another and greater problem . . . the problem of national efficiency, the patriotic duty of insuring the safety and continuance of the nation.

T. Roosevelt, Conference of Governors, May, 1908

John Muir did not hear Roosevelt say these words, because he was conspicuously absent from Pinchot's carefully orchestrated Conference of Governors in Washington.[29] Yet he undoubtedly read the published proceedings. Muir had appealed to Roosevelt on the matter of damming Hetch Hetchy in 1907, and Roosevelt had replied that he, the President, found it difficult to "interfere with the development of the State for the sake of keeping a valley which apparently hardly anyone wanted to have kept, under national control." Muir wrote again to Roosevelt in April of 1908, repeating his plea, this time arguing that the integrity of Yosemite National Park was threatened by able, but perhaps ignorant, "capitalists, engineers, lawyers, or even philanthropists." Though Roosevelt had been pleased to set aside Petrified Forest National Monument on Muir's advice in 1906, and had accepted William Kent's gift of Muir Woods as a National Monument early in 1908, this matter of Hetch Hetchy was entirely different. Muir wished to believe, all the while, that the Big Stick politician was "not the real Roosevelt," and suspected that the president had only been too heavily influenced by Pinchot. So it seems that Muir was quite thoroughly deceived, either by his own hopes or by his own political naïveté. Roosevelt was the nationalistic and conservationist enemy, despite the concessions he was willing to make to preservationists on matters which did not threaten the efficient development of resources in America.[30]

Samuel Hays views the Roosevelt program with sympathy, praising "the role it played in the transformation of a decentralized nontechnical, loosely organized society, where waste and inefficiency ran rampant, into a highly organized, technical, and centrally planned and directed social organization which could meet a complex world with efficiency and purpose." The Roosevelt administration's emphasis on applied science, and Roosevelt's insistence that "the National Government shall proceed as a private businessman would," led to decisions about national resources imposed from the top. Even though Roosevelt and Pinchot tried to make their programs appeal to middle- and upper-income urban dwellers, they wanted their program to be run by Hamiltonian means. What this meant, quite simply, was that the decision on Hetch Hetchy would be a political one, based on a kind of thinking Muir abhorred. Muir once said that playing at politics sapped the "foundations of righteousness." Yet politics was the arena in which the fate of Hetch Hetchy had already been decided. Conservationists would not listen to a popular outcry; they would only try to hush the cry or outshout the objectors.[31]

So the story of Hetch Hetchy, as a political struggle, was determined by forces which had already been mustered, alliances of "reformers" more powerful than Muir or the Sierra Club. The time was not right for raising the issue that Hetch Hetchy suggested. San Francisco was attempting to recover from its earthquake and was struggling to get out from under the corrupt politics of its past. The Lincoln–Roosevelt Republican League was trying to end the influence of the Southern Pacific Railroad. The Californian progressive was beginning to be heard. More than ever before, San Francisco was turning its attention to itself, and was pursuing aspirations to partake of the world power that Roosevelt had promised. And newspapers like the *San Francisco Bulletin*, which had been friendly to Muir in the past, were heavily committed to this new direction in Californian aspirations. On top of that, a fierce competition was growing between San Francisco and Los Angeles. In this time of growth, nobody in the West seemed interested in national parks or wildernesses.[32]

Between 1905 and 1913, the Sierra Club might have learned important lessons in politics, and the nation might have come alive to the importance of wilderness in its future. But it is probably overly optimistic to argue, as William Everson does about Hetch Hetchy, that

this was one of the main turning points in the spiritual life of the nation, perhaps the chief turning point, as far as the future was concerned. It marked the real closing of the concept of unlimited expansion, and insisted on the point that man was going to have to think of depriving himself, rather than abusing his environment. But more than that, it marked the moment when the implicit religious attitudes of the people gained explicit status, and through a kind of reflex America violated its conscience, dammed the Hetch Hetchy, opted for the norms of the past rather than those of the future.

No, America was not changing its mind about wilderness, but was moving with tremendous momentum away from its Jeffersonian conscience and from any care about its past values. America was embracing a highly organized, technical, centrally planned, and seemingly efficient businesslike or bureaucratic organization. As one engineer put it, the nation would "relegate all such archaic questions to the past, and concern [itself] with that which confers the greatest good upon the greatest number." But Everson's hope, so well expressed, might represent a watershed for late twentieth-century thinkers. We might review the failure of Muir and the Sierra Club in the battle over Hetch Hetchy and try to discover what kept this "implicit religious attitude" from gaining an "explicit status." What did keep Muir and his colleagues from making the strongest possible plea, in spiritual terms, for a new view of life in America? What kept them from turning defeat into a spiritual victory? These, I think, are the most fertile grounds for an investigation of the battle over Hetch Hetchy, and the first thing one notices is that Muir might have made more powerful arguments had he recognized, at the onset, that the battle would be lost. His hope that he could fight this battle on his opponents' ground blunted and diminished the effectiveness of his own arguments. Yet he made far fewer concessions to utilitarian rhetoric than his allies did. His integrity during the battle was a landmark in the geography of environmental politics.[33]

THE SYMBOLIC VALLEYS

Joseph Sax observes that national parks have come to take on a symbolic significance in the minds of preservationists. Lately, the Owens Valley and Mono Lake have taken on similar significance. Nevertheless, it is wise to remember that Hetch Hetchy, and the Owens Valley as well, are very real parts of the larger ecological systems which interpenetrate in the land we call California. Though the oak groves of Hetch Hetchy are dead and the Owens Valley has become a dust bowl, the places are still living ecological communities. Such places don't go away when they are "utilized." They take on a new form, and, though no longer "specimen sections of our natural flora," they become newly created environments. Thus a significant question to be asked about these places is, why should we have changed or not changed them? What did they mean to us in 1905, and what do they mean to us now? How do Man's changes give direction to his own evolving life?[34]

Muir would not reduce Hetch Hetchy to an abstraction. He knew that it was both real and significant. Of course, it had a private and personal meaning for him, but it also had a meaning for itself that reached far beyond his own experience there, and as far as he was able he wanted to describe it in terms equal to the task at hand. Though the valley held some of the roots of his own enlightenment, it also had its own flow and life. And even though he compared it to Yosemite, he knew that it was incomparable.

Hetch Hetchy was a part of the flow of Nature. It was filled with waterfalls, and was the path of the Tuolumne River. It was the path of ancient glaciers, and a path new life had taken as it entered the mountains. And damming it was an act by men which bespoke their arrogance. Men who built dams believed that they could control and harness the flow of Nature. Hetch Hetchy was also a consummation, as all the inseparable sections of the flow were. It was not an "exceptional creation," since none of God's gardens were. It was part of a larger whole, and edenic as it was, it was not the only edenic valley. Yet when men chose to stop its flowing life, and did so not for the farmers of the Central Valley but for the businessmen of the City of San Francisco, Muir saw in this action civilization's willingness to kill Nature for its own convenience. In theory—for the young Muir certainly—all dams in all valleys were arrogant gestures by men. When he insisted that damming Hetch Hetchy was damning Hetch Hetchy, he was seriously pointing to the arrogance of men who pretended that they were gods. It was a wild place, and civilized men preferred to have it tame and dead.

But Hetch Hetchy had gained a certain human significance over the years. The names of its geographical features bespoke its importance to Indians. Above it, in Pate Valley, pictographs on the granite suggested its sacred significance. Although white men had seen it in agricultural terms, it had finally been preserved as the wild Yosemite, a part of the wild half of Yosemite National Park. It was, as Muir would argue, a part of the natural pathway to Tuolumne Meadows, and thus it offered a path toward the fountain peaks. The purpose of a park, Muir thought, was to allow humans to follow such ways toward enlightenment. In this sense the canyon was an important cultural resource: "Dam Hetch Hetchy! As well dam for water-tanks the people's cathedrals and churches, for no holier temple has ever been consecrated by the heart of man." When men had decided to create national parks, thought Muir, they had consecrated these places as inviolate temples. Thus men were damning themselves when they dammed Hetch Hetchy. They were denying their own spiritual selves.[35]

The entire idea behind Yosemite Park, an idea so long in taking shape, was to hold inviolate the whole watersheds of the Merced and Tuolumne rivers. To violate that precedent was to damage the concept of a national park as more than a collection of scenic features. So it was that the principle of a national park as an ecological whole was also at stake. Worse, Yosemite had already been "improved." Hetch Hetchy should not suffer the same fate. Perhaps the most important contribution Muir had made to public policy was the idea that national parks contain both wild and pastoral ecological systems.

But on the deepest level, the issue was between the growth of the city and the preservation of wilderness. Muir saw this, quite simply, as the question of Evil versus Good. And if, as Muir argued, the only reason that San Francisco preferred to dam Hetch Hetchy was monetary, if the city could get its water elsewhere by paying a little more, then he questioned the conservationists' chief value: efficiency. If they called efficiency progress, then he would question that too, but not in public. It was by this, the deepest issue, that Muir and the Sierra Club would be most troubled, and it was in relation to this issue that the Owens Valley formed an analogue to Hetch Hetchy.

At the same time that San Francisco was trying to lay its hands on the watershed of the Tuolumne River, Los Angeles was attempting to buy up the watershed of the Owens Valley. If San Francisco wanted to drown Hetch Hetchy, Los Angeles wanted to drain the Owens Valley dry. If James Phelan, the proposer of Hetch Hetchy dam, represented a capitalistic evil to Muir, "to the farmers of the Owens Valley" William Mulholland "represented greed, arrogance, and overwhelming financial power." Just as Pinchot had supported San Francisco, so he helped Mulholland and Los Angeles in 1906. Clearly, the same conservationist ethic was at work on the east and west sides of the Sierra simultaneously. And the same argument in favor of the cities — efficiency and centralized urban power, under the rubric of "the greatest good for the greatest number" — was also at work. There were two significant differences between the sacrifices of the Owens and the Hetch Hetchy valleys. First of all, the Owens Valley was not a national park, and second, the desertification of the Owens Valley was a decision in favor of urban California at the expense of rural — not wild — California. But entering that battle would have been too taxing for Muir.[36]

For the same reason that "Wild Wool" had not been included in *The Mountains of California*, so too the speaker of "Wild Wool" could not come forth in the twentieth century. Muir could not, at this late date, remind America of the false dogma which "regards the world as made especially for the uses of man." He could not try to teach again the "relations which culture sustains to wildness." Nor could he even insist that civilization was on a wrong track if it could consider only quantity, and never quality. On a more personal level, he had accepted in the early nineties the robes of the genial prophet, and he had grown into them. A photograph taken in 1896 at Thomas Lukens's home in Pasadena shows an impeccably dressed, well-combed Muir — he even sports a gold watch fob — surrounded by fine furniture and elegantly framed landscape paintings. This was no iconoclast. How could a man in his seventies return to the vigor of his thirties? It was too late to break idols, particularly when that would mean breaking friendships and political alliances. If there was a wolf in this sheep's clothing, he was well hidden. Muir was confined in his arguments between two uses of Hetch Hetchy Valley — both uses for men: the choice was between the valley as park or as water tank.

Muir loved the glare of the Owens Valley, and had subscribed to a basically agrarian hope for California; he should also have been in sympathy with the citizens on the east side of the Sierra. He must have recognized that their cause, too, dramatized the conflict between two views of America's future. But unlike Mary Austin, a writer with roots in the Owens Valley, he chose to remain silent about the battle there. One need only look at the Sierra Club and Muir's eastern allies to understand why he argued only about Hetch Hetchy.

CITIES AND WILDERNESS

For many reasons, the Sierra Club was not prepared for the battle over Hetch Hetchy. The most significant problem was in the allegiances of the members themselves. Did they, for instance, think of themselves as conservationists? Then what would they think about Muir's direct attack on conservationists in *The Yosemite*? The Club itself had not only been supporting parks, but had been heartily in favor of forestry; the Sierra Club *Bulletin* had included William Dudley's "Forestry Notes" for several years. Like many modern Americans, Club members might have thought of themselves as conservationists without knowing what the term stood for. Conservation seemed to represent the appropriate right-thinking, progressive attitude at the time.

Indeed, what might be called the "California progressive" represented the perfect portrait of the typical Sierra Club member. Like sixty percent of California's population in 1910, he was urban. He was a professional man, a member of the middle class and proud of it. He might be a member of the Lincoln–Roosevelt Republican League. And for good reason. Before Phelan and the other progressives cleaned up the politics of San Francisco, the citizens had their choice between a Republican Party dominated by railroads and a Democratic Party run by a combination of power companies and underworld figures. No wonder the citizen felt threatened by monopolies on one side and organized labor on the other. He had been raised a Protestant, and might be attracted to the secularized version of pantheism that the Sierra Club represented. Yet men like William Kent or Chester Rowell were also likely to belong to Chambers of Commerce, and wanted to "preserve the fundamental pattern of twentieth-century industrial society." Like Roosevelt himself, the progressive believed that none should be for a class and that all should be for the State. In this way we can understand that conservation was only a part of Roosevelt's larger Progressive movement. A member of the Sierra Club was very likely to sympathize with this movement, if he was not actively engaged in fighting for its aims.[37]

Did these men think they could have their growing cities and the wilderness too? Apparently they did. They were not prepared to take a stand on an issue which would seem to entail not just the preservation of the forests and natural features of the Sierra Nevada, but the involvement of the Club in the political arena. For many of them the decision to dam Hetch Hetchy was a decision to insure the growth of their beloved cities, and was perhaps even crucial to the long-range security of their nation. Particularly after the great earthquake of 1906, San Franciscans hoped their city would "Rise From the Ashes a Greater and More Beautiful City than Ever." Perhaps even Muir was sympathetic to their causes. And when people like University of California President Benjamin Wheeler and Congressman William Kent turned against him over Hetch Hetchy, he must have understood that it was too much to expect them to be any different from what they were at root, men who wanted the country to grow.[38]

Muir could not rely on Harriman's help precisely because any part Harriman might take would only add fuel to the arguments of the San Franciscans that the people who opposed the Hetch Hetchy Dam were the monopolists who wished to control San Francisco's water and power supplies. But Muir's relationship with Harriman had always been ambivalent. He liked the man well enough, but he didn't know whether he liked what Harriman stood for. This must have troubled him, and you can see it in his language. He wished to attribute the Hetch Hetchy scheme to "monopolizing San Francisco Capitalists." And he insisted that "these temple destroyers, devotees of ravenging commercialism, seem to have a perfect contempt for Nature, and instead of lifting their eyes to the mountains, lift them to dams and town skyscrapers." He was vehement in his condemnation of the park despoilers, as he saw the proposers of the Hetch Hetchy plan to be. The parks were being attacked "mostly by despoiling gain-seekers—mischief-makers and robbers of every degree from Satan to senators, supervisors, lumbermen, cattlemen, farmers, etc., eagerly trying to make everything dollerable, often thinly disguised in smiling philanthropy, calling pocket-filling plunder 'Utilization of beneficent natural resources, that man and beast may be fed and the dear Nation grow great.'" Buried in this harangue was the anti-anthropocentric speaker of "Wild Wool," but buried he was. And perhaps Muir did not want to examine his opposition to the smiling face of philanthropy too closely. For Harriman had presented himself to Muir with precisely that face.[39]

In 1911 Muir wrote a small book as a memorial to Harriman, in spite of the protests of many friends—friends, one can guess, like Edward Taylor, a poet whom Muir had known for years and who followed Phelan as mayor of San Francisco in 1902. Muir's friends —perhaps Taylor—worried that he had "gone capitalistic." In this book Muir documented his gradual but complete conversion to Harriman's point of view. "No enterprise calculated to advance humanity failed to interest him," Muir asserted. And for Harriman, Muir tried to explain, money was not an end but only "a tool like a locomotive or ship." But most interesting is the philosophy of philanthropy which Muir claimed Harriman had expressed during the Alaska Expedition in 1899: "helping to feed man and beast, and making everybody and everything a little better and happier." This echoed the very philosophy expressed by the gain-seekers whom Muir attacked in his 1909 pamphlet on Hetch Hetchy. How was one to know that Harriman's work, "damming the Colorado flood, filling a way across the Great Salt Lake, tunnelling the Sierra above Truckee, and helping San Francisco after the great earthquake and fire," was different from Phelan's plan to dam the Tuolumne? It was a fine distinction at best, and it must have worried Muir deeply. His most powerful ally and his worst enemies seemed to subscribe to the same philosophy, and they were all humanists and philanthropists.[40]

Since the philosophies of his allies and his enemies seemed indistinguishable, Muir had to argue in practical terms. He couldn't expect the public to make subtle distinctions which troubled even himself. It was no wonder, then, that he saw the need to temper his arguments and repeat the more moderate view of the New York *Outlook* in a pamphlet: "While the Yosemite National Park might very properly be sacrificed to save the lives and health of citizens of San Francisco, it ought not to be sacrificed to save their dollars." Colby, Edward Parsons, Badè, Johnson, and Muir decided that the argument for Hetch Hetchy would be most effectively made in terms of the "utility of recreation." They were willing to quote Horace McFarland when he spoke of the money value of tourism. They were willing to concede improvements which would damage the valley's ecology, if such concessions would in turn save it from the dam makers. For instance, when opponents suggested that the lower end of Hetch Hetchy was a mosquito bog, the defenders were willing to allow that the meadows at the bottom of the valley could be drained, as had been done in Yosemite Valley. Muir knew that this would accelerate forest succession and diminish the meadows, but almost anything seemed a lesser evil than the dam itself. Muir and his allies were willing to answer "park invaders" in utilitarian terms, so their arguments could be easily countered by Pinchot, who simply asserted that "at this stage of the game" the aesthetic side of conservation could not "go ahead of the economic and moral aspects of the case." When the issues were reduced to the realm of utilitarian and materialist ideology, there was not much doubt that water for San Francisco would be seen as a greater good for a greater number.[41]

Muir might point out in the pages of *American Forestry* the disastrous precedent that Hetch Hetchy represented, arguing in a very subdued and businesslike way that the Hetch Hetchy controversy was "a national question" that pitted the citizens of the United States against "certain individuals in San Francisco." He might insist that "the commercial invasion of the Yosemite Park means that sooner or later under various specious beguiling pleas, all the public parks and playgrounds throughout our country may be invaded and spoiled. The Hetch-Hetchy is a glaringly representative case . . ." Yet the arguments that he and his allies created had stooped to a consideration of the practical merits of the Hetch Hetchy case, even to the extent of examining and criticizing the engineer's report. They had admitted in so doing that the parks would always be subject to this kind of invasion, and would always have to be defended, not on principle, but on the merits of the invader's case.[42]

Consequently, during World War I and World War II, when the question of invading the parks arose, the same kind of issues would recur. And now, when war seems to be a constant state of mind in the United States, when agribusiness, coal, missile sites, or nuclear waste dumps threaten not just our American landscape but also our national parks, there is in the public mind a constant need to invade untouched natural resources. Muir and his colleagues tried to say that San Francisco could get its water elsewhere. And so too, at Olympic National Park during World War II, the Sitka spruce was defended by a study which showed that the wood could be gotten elsewhere. But there will come a time the park invaders will perceive a need, and the National Park Service, the Sierra Club, and all others who want to preserve the parks will discover that there is no other place to get the coal, spruce, or whatever. Then what?[43]

Indeed, the proponents of the Hetch Hetchy scheme delivered to all United States congressmen a copy of an editorial printed in the *San*

Francisco Examiner on December 2, 1913. In this editorial the *Examiner* argued that Los Angeles had been allowed to take its water from the Owens Valley, so how could San Francisco be refused? How indeed? The *Examiner* spoke of "A certain class of citizens . . . who may be called chronic opponents. They never originate ANYTHING and they always oppose EVERYTHING." So the battle was lost and a precedent was set. The rights of the cities were more important than the rights of the wilderness or of the rural areas. If the Owens Valley could be drained, then Hetch Hetchy could be dammed.[44]

PARKS AND SERVICES

Much has been said about the compensatory good which would follow the defeat suffered when San Francisco gained the rights to Hetch Hetchy. Muir wrote to Henry Fairfield Osborn, "Fortunately wrong cannot last; soon or late it must fall back home to Hades, while some compensating good must surely follow." One might wish that this were true. But nothing is ever so simple, and the divine plan in which Muir believed continues to elude us.[45]

Certainly many of the very men who tried to discredit Muir over the Hetch Hetchy debate became active supporters of the Park Service bill, which finally gave us a National Park Service in 1916. John Raker and William Kent in particular were instrumental in seeing the National Park Service formed, and were glad to accept help from the western railroads. Did they do so because, as Muir believed in 1914, "the conscience of the whole country has been aroused from sleep"? Did they do so because they felt guilty? Whatever their reasons, they were not speaking out for wilderness; they were creating a government bureaucracy, and that is a significant distinction. They had already made their stand for conservation, and by putting the parks under the National Park Service they were subscribing to a utilitarian version of recreation which was far from the Pathless Way that Muir had perceived.[46]

What would a conversationist's national park look like? It would be a highly organized, centrally planned and directed machine for the purpose of providing recreation. It would have at its core the purpose of marketing efficiently an experience for its visitors, and so it would welcome technological improvements which furthered that aim by providing the greatest number of vacations possible, in the smallest compass of time, and with the most comfort, given the economic resources of the visitor. This is what the National Park Service set out to do under Mather.

12

The End
and the Beginning

     Muir buried much of his energy in the interminable politics of conservation during the last twenty years of his life; perhaps he almost lost himself in the battles over Yosemite. No wonder these years carry a pervading tone of tragedy. The man who always preferred a pure quick death in the mountains was being ground down and worn out by the ghostly machine of civilization. He wondered how that was possible, and remembered when such a fate seemed unimaginable. He could only be glad that he had spent so many years in commerce with the realities of the mountains.

     Wasn't that where his life had gathered its meaning? What *had* his life meant? Was there something exceptional, something about his spiritual path which should be told so that others might be redeemed? What had saved him from becoming the typical American immigrant of his generation?

     In 1893, the year before Muir published *The Mountains of California*, Frederick Jackson Turner had wondered about the end of the Frontier. In his persuasive essay, Turner argued that American development exhibited a "return to primitive conditions on a continually advancing frontier line." He claimed that "wilderness masters the colonist" and "strips off the garments of civilization." The sodbuster, trapper, gold hunter: all were simply the products of this peculiarly American phenomenon. At root, Turner knew, at issue was the evolution of men. How did it occur? Muir's idea on this

339

subject went to a deeper level. Muir's idea — like that which Clarence King put forth, and like a similar theory suggested by a Nunamiut hunter in *Of Wolves and Men* — was that all species, be they wolves, Eskimos, mountaineers, or mountain sheep, go through a process which might be spoken of an convergent evolution. All animals, men included, were products of their environment, and were most governed when they were wildest. "Who, at the end, knows more about the land — an old man or an old wolf?" an anthropologist asked. "The same. They know the same," answered the old Nunamiut hunter. But civilized men, unlike the other beasts, could deceive themselves. They could not only choose their environment, thus creating themselves, but they could also choose to ignore their environment, like the sodbusters whom Muir remembered from his youth, who cut their straight furrows through the prairie, inattentive to anything except the size and shape of their farms.[1]

Unlike the frontiersman Turner spoke of, Muir embraced the new identity he received when he went to the wilderness. He abandoned deliberately most of the ideology which the immigrant had used as a defense against the wild new land. Family, religion, civilization: Muir tried to rid himself of all artificial encumbrances. And so in his youth he had hoped to become sensitive to a new self which might in time germinate into a new society, based not on the old European or New England relations of men to each other, but on a new relationship of all men toward the wonderful possibilities inherent in the North American continent. This was the utopian significance of California, and this ideology was at bottom the set of values which had been developed by natives like Ishi, long before white men had seen the coast. Though Muir never became fully aware of the kinship he shared with Indians, he did know that his consciousness was new and old, revolutionary and eternal.[2]

Even a poor Scottish immigrant like him could attune himself to the song of Nature in the New World. But he must have had certain advantages in his past. What were they, and how had he made the most of them? He began to reconsider his boyhood and youth in the light of what he had become. And his increased tendency toward introspection was linked to an acceptance of what he had become. He was a writer. Men called him a poet of Nature, and perhaps he was, but he was also a scientist. The two were inseparable, and he wondered if some influences in his early youth had allowed the poet and the scientist to merge in him, producing a new consciousness, a new sensibility.

His musings on his life were, he thought, personal and private. While he visited many of the scenes of his youth during the nineties, those journeys into his past did not at the time seem so important as the pressing issues of the present. He always knew that the world which had allowed him to evolve was far more important than any one man. But by the turn of the century his two editors, Walter Hines Page of *Atlantic* and Robert Underwood Johnson of *Century*, had both encouraged him to begin an autobiography. Johnson suggested in 1899 that he might use a "thread of biography" and "string upon it your observations of life, the awakening of a scientific spirit, and the contrast between boyhood and manhood." In 1900, Muir told Page that he planned to write at least six volumes: first, a Yosemite Guidebook for Johnson, second, a "California tree and shrub book," third, a mountaineering book "all about walking, climbing, and camping, with a lot of illustrative excursions," fourth, a book on Alaska, and fifth, "a book of Studies . . . my main real book in which I'll ask my readers to cerebrate"; only last on this ambitious list did he mention the autobiography so many people were asking for. It hardly seemed worthwhile "in the midst of so much that is infinitely more important," though "such a book would offer fair opportunities here and there to say a word for God."[3]

Though he completed *The Yosemite* and *Travels in Alaska* before he died, autobiography proved to be his most important writing task in the twentieth century, and most of that was done after his wife's death in 1905. He left no written remembrance of her, yet her death marked a major transition in his life. For several years he immersed himself in a study of the petrified forests of Arizona as a kind of consolation, and wrote about nothing. When he returned to his writing he knew he was beginning a new phase, turning a new page. Still, he was ambivalent. *Century* had published an early version of *Stickeen* as "Adventures with a Dog and Glacier," but now he didn't want simply to tell tales of adventure. When Johnson suggested that his further contributions be "nature and life in about equal proportions," Muir balked again, answering that they would "be all nature — animated nature."[4]

But he had come to think seriously about the life he had lived, and in *Story of My Boyhood and Youth, Stickeen,* and *My First Summer in the Sierra,* he began to investigate the values he had developed in the years before he settled down. Somehow Scotland, Wisconsin, the Sierra, and Alaska, were braided together by the green thread of his life. And those worlds of his youth were rapidly being lost, despite his best efforts for parks and wilderness. His autobiography might be a means of making a plea for the Nature to which he was devoted. Perhaps he might influence a new generation of young Americans, and then his values might find ascendancy after the conservationists had passed away.

That, of course, is what has happened. The Muir who has so influenced my generation is the Muir the old man remembered, the innocent fellow who could scarcely wait to get out of camp at sunrise, who took off his shoes and climbed barefoot across the polished granite, who followed the rhythm of his feet, fell in love with the song of the lark and the voice of flowers, who knew that "the clearest way into the Universe is through a forest wilderness."[5]

BOYHOOD AND YOUTH

It is a truism about American literature that many of our great classics are boys' books. If Muir wrote children's literature in his later years, he did so as a conscious choice. As early as 1883, John Swett, Chas. H. Allen, and Josiah Royce had included selections from Muir's essays in textbooks they edited for fourth and fifth grade California students. Muir was pleased that his stories appealed to children. He always thought of *Story of My Boyhood and Youth* as a young folks' animal book, a chance to say some good words for "our poor earth bound companions and fellow mortals." Long before he wrote it down, *Stickeen* too had been a favorite story of his daughters and other little children, like Gifford Pinchot. These kinds of tales allowed him to present a gentle argument against the ingrained anthropocentric views of society, and he was also interested in furthering the long-neglected ethical education of children.[6]

In 1907, for instance, he wrote a letter to Daniel Beard, published in the *Woman's Home Companion* as "A New Top Notch for the Sons of Daniel Boone." In it he attempted to establish a kind of wilderness ethic for this precursor of the Boy Scouts. He wished to encourage "walking in wild places, so that our boys may gradually grow out of natural hunting, blood-loving savagery into natural sympathy with all our fellow mortals — plants and animals, as well as men." He recommended the kinds of excursions in which the walker "sees most, learns most, loves most, and leaves the cleanest track." He was taking a stand for a better sort of education, trying to counteract the primitivist's version of wilderness experience, with its hunting and fishing, or the Roosevelt version of exposure to wild Nature which developed "hardihood, resolution, and scorn of discomfort and danger."[7]

The ethical issues which arose from men's inhumane treatment of animals became the basis for most of *Story of My Boyhood and Youth*. The book began with Muir's remembrance of discovering "a mother field mouse with half a dozen naked young hanging to her teats." Was this a "real" incident, or the memory of a poem by Burns? The allusion to Burns was more obvious when Muir compared the little dog Stickeen to the field mouse of Burns, the "wee, hairy, sleekit beastie." In *Story of My Boyhood and Youth*, this was only the first of many anecdotes about the essential humanity of wild and domestic animals. Oxen, pigs, horses, and dogs served Muir's purposes as much as did the wild animals he encountered in his youth. They all shared the emotions of humans, and so Muir argued that "almost any wild animal may be made a pet, simply by sympathizing with it and entering as much as possible into its life." Not that he thought boys should make pets of wild animals or birds. In an anecdote about caged skylarks in Scotland, he remembered how pitiful it was to look at the "imprisoned soarer of the heavens." Any boy's conscience would require that the bird be set free. He seemed to disregard flagrantly the very distinction he had once made between wild sheep and tame. And perhaps one must remember that Muir was writing a children's book. The stories which seemed to be aimed at reminding young boys to be good to animals and to allow them as much freedom as possible were also aimed at the freedom of the boys, who needed to run in the woods instead of being caged in schools, churches, and front parlors. Muir attempted to trace his own progress as he was first caged like a bird, then served as a beast of burden in Wisconsin, and finally freed himself from the leash and ran free. He learned the meaning of freedom by observing the conditions of the wild and domestic animals that surrounded him in Scotland and Wisconsin. But the stories came out sounding simplistic, and after a while, repetitive.[8]

The structure of the book grew out of its peculiar method of composition. E. H. Harriman insisted that Muir planned and brooded too much, and enforced upon him an unnatural strategy. He made Muir dictate his memoirs to a personal secretary when Muir was a guest at the Pelican Bay Lodge at Klamath Lake, Oregon. The so-called "Pelican Bay Manuscript" was long, rambling, and disjointed, though Muir thought it might serve as "a sort of foundation for more than one volume." It was five years before he sorted out the chaotic and casual collection of remembrances, and he seems to have decided that the best method of presentation was to juxtapose incidents. He also attempted to comprehend, in one short volume, the lessons of his first twenty-five years. By the juxtaposition of incidents, the structure of this book suggested that Muir's life consisted of an alternation between wilderness and civilization. As it originally appeared, serialized in *Atlantic* at Muir's request, it was divided into four sections called "My Boyhood," "Plunge into the Wilderness," "Lessons of the Wilderness," and "Out of the Wilderness"; the last section ended with Muir leaving "the Wisconsin University for the University of the Wilderness." Clearly he meant to dramatize the dilemma of a youth caught between two worlds.[9]

In an almost painstaking way, he argued that his personal odyssey consisted in transcending a Scylla and Charybdis where the natural Indianlike savagery of youth beckoned on one side while the rote education of school and home on the other side threatened, by rigid discipline, to crush any development of sensibility. He believed he was saved, not by the Bible he had to memorize or by his aggressive and savage youthful energy, but by the poetry of Burns and by the inexhaustible wonders of Nature. So too, after he had arrived in America, and even after he had lost the savagery of boyhood, he would need to resist the dulling labor and cares of farm life, and an interest in mere mechanical inventions. He would need to attend the University of Wisconsin, but recognize the limits of a merely academic view of Nature. In the end, when he returned to the wild world of his boyhood, he was changed, and able to appreciate it as an older and wiser being.

The idea is interesting, but the book is dull. Strange to say, the method of composition, which Harriman hoped would result in spontaneity, had the opposite effect. The spark of inspiration never caught. More important, Muir failed to catch the true significance of his past in shaping *him*, if that was indeed his aim. Though the book sometimes succeeded in harking back to a vision of childhood, when everything seemed to be brother, when the young boy was green and carefree and ran his heedless ways, the later chapters were superficial. Muir wrote to one friend that it did not contain much that was likely to interest anybody but children. One doesn't find much serious self-analysis in this book.[10]

What about the question of men's relationship with animals? Muir mourned the extinction of the passenger pigeons. He expressed a fear of the dominion of men who thought they were civilized. Whether they killed wild animals whom they perceived as enemies or tame dogs who relished the taste of chickens, nineteenth-century farmers lived by the justice of Manifest Destiny. So too they robbed the Indians of their lands, and justified themselves by claiming more efficient farming methods. Muir called this the "rule of might."

A modern writer has tried to deal with this dilemma, and has gone a step further than Muir did, by realizing that the eradication of Indians and wolves amounted to the same thing:

> In a historical sense, we are all to blame for the loss of wolves. In the nineteenth century when the Indians on the plains were telling us that the wolf was a brother, we were preaching another gospel. Manifest Destiny. What rankles us now, I think, is that an alternative gospel still remains largely unarticulated. You want to say there never should have been a killing, but you don't know what to put in its place.

The alternative gospel was at the heart of Muir's narrative, but never quite crystallized in *Story of My Boyhood and Youth*. Muir knew that he had lived out his life forever caught between the values of civilization and those of wildness. Once a man had passed the point in history where he could never become an Indian, he could never return. So his story was at bottom a narrative of loss.[11]

Whitman asked the question in 1855: "The friendly and flowing savage, who is he? / Is he waiting for civilization, or past it and
mastering it?" Muir could only answer that question ambiguously.
After all, he remembered how he had as a boy abused his pet pony,
Jack. And once an Indian had stolen a horse named Nob from his
father's ranch and treated it with "terrible cruelty." Worse, he remembered the irony of Nob's death, caused by his father's abusing
her in order to arrive at a church meeting on time. "Civilized" or
"primitive," all men had failed in a sacred duty to respect their brother
mortals. Maybe, with better education, the future might be brighter.

STICKEEN

If a man would reveal his true character in his behavior toward animals, it was also true that animals often revealed the true kinship
of all beings when they became the companions of men. In *Stickeen,*
Muir used this analogy in order to look at himself from an external
perspective. Even if this dog story was a tale for children, in it he
began to question the value of his early adventures for himself and
for the others he led into the wilderness. He claimed that the story
caused him as much pain as any he ever wrote, and perhaps this
was the reason. As a leader of men, he had come to know the heavy
responsibility for those who followed, but perhaps he had forgotten what it meant to be young and afraid.

If the Muir of the narrative was an experienced, taciturn mountaineer, so was the dog who accompanied him. This, he thought,
was surprising in so small an animal, but perhaps we all have more
courage than we suspect. Stickeen was "cold as a glacier," a "true
child of the wilderness, holding the even tenor of his hidden life
with the silence and serenity of Nature." Like Muir, Stickeen seemed
to bury his true self, but a sensitive observer could see it flashing
in his eyes. This dog who persisted in following wherever Muir went,
and for reasons which were not altogether clear, since he was offered no food and none of the usual encouragements — why would
even a dog want to follow Muir? This was virtually the same as asking why Muir would want to follow his own impulse to wander into
a wilderness of ice. Stickeen became a second self.[12]

Certainly one would expect a glacier to be at the heart of Muir's Alaskan adventures — a glacier obscured by a storm, a grand wild landscape, impossible to comprehend from a distance. "I tried to draw the marvelous scene in my note-book, but the rain blurred the page in spite of all my pains to shelter it, and the sketch was almost worthless," he remembered. Grinding large trees to pulp along its margin, the glacier was involved in its own massive creation and dwarfed Muir's dealings with paper. Because he could not see it from a distant prospect, and because art would not capture it, Muir chose to enter into its life. And so he set off, in July of 1880, upon this "seemingly boundless prairie of ice," the Taylor Glacier.

Stickeen's motives for following were perhaps more obscure. He "showed neither caution nor curiosity, wonder nor fear, but bravely trotted on as if glaciers were playgrounds." Just as Muir's companions back at camp might have wondered about a man who wandered about in glaciers, so Muir suspected Stickeen's good sense. Like Muir's, his courage "seemed to be due to dullness of perception, as if he were only blindly bold." Yet Muir portrayed Stickeen's wild soul, and the dog in turn spoke sentiments that Muir would have been embarrassed to speak in his own person. He later used the same narrative technique in *Travels in Alaska*, allowing Indians to speak for him at times. And Stickeen had an Indian soul as well as an Indian name. This was not surprising, since, "before the whites came, the Thinkits held, with Agassiz, that animals have souls." When these two mountaineers were hard beset by dangers, Muir said they "doggedly persevered." Their roles were complementary; Muir's will was leading not only his own, but also another's soul into the unknown. There they would be faced with crossing a sunken ice bridge, a "tremendous necessity."[13]

They became marooned on a giant island of ice in the midst of the glacier because, going into a bewildering maze of crevasses, Muir had broken the "rule of mountaineers who live long" by following a route he could not retrace. He portrayed himself as highly rational and calmly deliberate, but his reasoning was specious. "At length because of the dangers behind me, I determined to venture against those that might be ahead," he explained. So they finally arrived at the great unknown, a seventy-foot sliver of ice, a thin knife-edge which bridged a huge and bottomless crevasse.

It was indeed a symbolic bridge. Could it bear the weight of a man? Would a dog be able to descend and ascend the vertical walls which embraced it? This was the unexpected trial that always waits for the unwary. Yet it was also an opportunity, a promise, and a test of faith. It could lead the man and the dog who followed out of the vast glacier which was "an emblem of the valley of the shadow of death."

Muir could be highly rational when investigating the nature of an ice bridge. Such bridges were formed when a crevasse opened; they melted and sank below the edges of the crevasse when they grew old and frail. This one had sunk down considerably and was consequently very old. He could also describe his crossing of it in technical terms, which he had probably gleaned from the narratives of Tyndall. Yet he claimed that while actually engaged in his perilous crossing he was unselfconscious and beyond rationality: "At such times one's whole body is eye, and common skill and fortitude are replaced by power beyond our call or knowledge." So he could not tell the reader how he got over the ice bridge, how he was delivered, or how he felt about the risk. If you are all eye, you have neither memory nor voice.[14]

His attempted analysis of his encounter with death was overrational, abstract, and like a sermon. Though he claimed he "oftentimes felt that to meet one's fate on a noble mountain, or in the heart of a glacier, would be blessed," such a "quick and crystal pure" demise was hard to face. But he could see that Stickeen was not such a stoic.

The scene became nicely emblematic. The willful, rational Muir and his second, emotional self stood divided by the abyss, isolated in the snowy gloom of late afternoon. The dog muttered and whined, and his fears seemed as human to Muir as those of a frightened boy. He would preach to the dog even as he might preach to himself: "'No right way is easy in this rough world. We must risk our lives to save them. At the worst we can only slip, and then how grand a grave we will have, and by and by our nice bones will do good in the terminal moraine.'" But such a sermon was hardly reassuring, the small dog, who "was able to weigh and appreciate it so justly," was not fooled by empty words. He tested Muir's assumptions, reacted emotionally, but finally followed. "His voice and gestures, hopes and fears, were so perfectly human that none could mistake them; while he seemed to understand every word." Thus Muir discovered in the dog what he had willed to ignore in himself. As Stickeen finally made his crossing from death to life, from despair to joy, as he called up the courage in himself, Muir learned what it was to be human. He became what he saw so clearly in his companion; he embraced his own redemption: "The joy of deliverance burned in us like fire, and we ran without fatigue, every muscle with immense rebound glorying in its strength."

Stickeen is a sentimental but thoughtful dog story, and Muir did not mean to transcend the conventions of his chosen genre when he wrote it. Its message is straightforward. "Through him," said Muir, "as through a window I have ever since been looking with deeper sympathy into all my fellow mortals." But the story was also about Muir himself, about the rebirth of the boy in him who was frightened by danger, and joyous when he had passed over. As Muir turned the focus of the narrative onto the dog, and through the dog back onto himself, he was beginning to look back on his own experiences with a more critical eye and ask whether such adventures really had been valuable. Why was it better to live life and risk death in the mountains? Because he could only appreciate life after facing death? Perhaps; but also because he needed to be reminded that he was, at bottom, only a child.

A second theme also emerged in *Stickeen*. How could he ask other mortals to take the risks he had taken? Of that he was not so certain. No amount of sermonizing about Noble Deaths could justify his insistence that others, or even he, should set foot on such uncertain ground. In the summer of 1880, he had been a husband for four months. "Surely you are not going into the awful place," said Stickeen when he saw his master crawling down onto the ice bridge. God may have led Muir into the wilderness, but He did not necessarily invest him with the authority to lead other unsuspecting mortals into the same dangerous paths.

It was hard to know where responsibility began in these things. A year before Stickeen followed Muir onto the Taylor Glacier, Hall Young had foolishly followed him on an ascent of Glenora Peak. In both cases Muir warned his companions, but they decided to continue against his advice. Hall Young was seriously injured: he dislocated both shoulders on his excursion. Was Muir responsible? Certainly not in the most literal sense. But then he always taught by example, and he knew that many followed his ways into the wilderness alone, perhaps to their deaths. Just as animals sometimes followed blindly, so did men. So he felt responsible, and in the nineties and later was increasingly reticent to recommend dangerous excursions. More than that, he feared that those who read his essays and books would misunderstand him and would follow the path of adventure for its own sake, not for its spiritual goal.

FIRST SUMMER

In *Story of My Boyhood and Youth* he wondered about the path which led him to wildness. In *Stickeen* he reconsidered the cost of the lessons of the wilderness. In *My First Summer in the Sierra* he reappraised that critical time in his life when he gave himself fully to Nature, no matter what the cost.

My First Summer in the Sierra is a deceptively straightforward narrative. When it tells the story of Muir's baptism in the mountains, of his finding a true home, most readers assume that Muir had simply transcribed forty-year-old journals, turning them into a naturally coherent whole. That is hardly likely, and it is contradicted by the few remaining early drafts of the book. For one thing, the narrative is organized thematically. Crucial passages are heavily revised and worked over in one manuscript that remains. Significant structuring episodes are added or elaborated. The journals also contradict certain incidents in the book: Muir's progress toward understanding the glacial history of the Sierra was certainly not as far advanced in 1869 as the book suggests, and he was not yet committed to a long stay in the Sierra; at the end of that summer he seriously considered moving on to South America. All of this simply suggests that the book is carefully crafted. Like *Walden*, it telescopes the actual experiences of several summers. Late in his life Muir accepted his kinship with Thoreau, calling himself "a self appointed inspector of gorges, gulches, and glaciers."[15]

"Though *First Summer* is an honest and truthful book, it is also narrated with all the skill that a novelist might muster. We may well believe that Muir's colleague, the shepherd Billy, expressed his ignorant and selfish views of an employee's responsibility to his employer on the Fourth of July, even if it is a little harder to take literally the fact that ripe summer appeared that year on July first. Like the artist of the city of Kouroo in *Walden*, Muir knew "the material was pure, and his art was pure; how could the result be other than wonderful." He was right; he was minting the gold of his youth. So it is possible to learn a great deal about what the old Muir thought of his former self from the structure of the book alone.

After choosing to make *First Summer* dramatize his own baptism into the Sierran wilderness, he developed a context for the drama. By juxtaposing revised versions of several journals written in his youth with certain, perhaps fictional, incidents, he could remind the reader of the social pressures which had surrounded this pilgrimage. After all, the old Muir was not only selecting and editing the journals, but also deciding upon their sequence. The structure of *First Summer* allowed both a young naturalist and an older creator of parks to speak. The young narrator could travel his own innocent and sometimes heedless ways, while the older and wiser man constructed the bleak social context of the young man's travels. If young Muir was primarily interested in his personal spiritual quest, the old Muir dramatized his repeated encounters with civilization, and also documented the destruction of that world which the youth sought. The young Muir was not yet committed to preservation, or even to a life in the wilderness, but an older, sterner Muir knew that he would be, and knew further that while the young man would never achieve the complete freedom for which he hoped, his vision of freedom was nonetheless essential to accomplishing anything. Sometimes he even put words into the young man's mouth which were obviously those of a more mature man.

The result is a carefully orchestrated structure which shows young Muir torn between his desire to wander free in the wilderness until he found a home and the necessities that required him to earn his bread and to encounter other men — shepherds, tourists, Indians, educators from his past, and his employer, Patrick Delaney.

Throughout the book the hero moved back and forth between society and the wilderness, while the author constantly tested his idealistic aspirations. Both men had their say.

PORTRAIT OF THE ARTIST IN A SHEEP CAMP

The young hero of *First Summer* had no illusions about the pleasures of pastoral life. He joined Patrick Delaney and his shepherd Billy as they followed the flocks out of the Central Valley and into the Sierra because that was the surest way for him to enter the mountains. Though Delaney assured him that he would be left perfectly free to pursue his studies, and though Muir "was in a mood to accept work of any kind," he was saddled with responsibility for his employer's sheep. Delaney wanted Muir to be the "man about the camp whom he could trust to see that the shepherd did his duty." Caught by duty from the beginning, he might be able to rationalize that "we never know where we must go, or what guides we are to get,— men, storms, guardian angels, or sheep," but he was still responsible to an enterprise which he knew was degrading.[16]

To see this one need only look at the way young Muir characterized Delaney, whom he called Don Quixote, and Billy, who was Sancho Panza. The Don, "bony and tall, with sharply hacked features," had been educated as a priest, but then participated in the Gold Rush. And what the narrator thought of the Gold Rush is significantly different in an early draft of *First Summer* from what he thought in the final version. Originally Muir had written that it was a brutal period of history: "On no virgin landscape were such savage blows rained & such marked damage done by so small a band of men in so short a time." Since he was not writing a book about the Gold Rush, he deleted his outburst. But its shadow remained; when the small band of the sheep camp climbed out of the deadly heat of the plains and passed the abandoned gold country, its men escaped from dead worlds and sought eternal summer as they invaded the mountains. The parallel was obvious, though Muir would not attack Delaney so directly. The young man only commented that the Don had been "overflowed and denuded and remodeled by the excitements of the gold fields"; which made him a typical Californian of his generation. Though Muir noted that "the California sheep-owner is in haste to get rich" and that the sheep business "blinds and degrades," he seemed to like Delaney. The Don was no Ahab. But the sheep business was a natural extension of the get-rich ethics of the Gold Rush, and Delaney was an example of the men who continued the rape of the mountains. He appeared with no staff, but rather carried "a heavy rifle over his shoulder intended for bears and wolves." It was about as useful as Don Quixote's lance, and when it did not work Delaney had a ready supply of strychnine. Thus he conducted his war against bears, coyotes, mountain lions — in fact, against all Nature — not as a monomaniac, but in a banal and businesslike sort of way. It was not comforting for young Muir to think that he was Delaney's trusted lieutenant.[17]

The book evades the issue somewhat by making Billy, the "proud shepherd," play Sancho Panza, whose aphorisms spice the narrative. Like Sancho, Billy hoped one day to govern his own realm. But the shepherd was doomed to servitude: "For, though stimulated at times by hopes of one day owning a flock and getting rich like his boss, he at the same time is likely to be degraded by the life he leads, and seldom reaches the dignity or advantage — or disadvantage — of ownership." Muir developed Billy's portrait from the picture of lumbermen he had drawn in "Puget Sound" and "American Forests." In this book, he allowed the hired hand to wax philosophical.[18]

Billy was totally insensitive to Nature. Of the sacred fern forests he said, "Oh, they're only d — d big brakes." When Muir tried to entice him to go see the Valley, he responded, "What is Yosemite but a cañon — a lot of rocks — a hole in the ground — a place dangerous about falling into — a d — d good place to keep away from." Even when Muir worked on him, "like a missionary offering the gospel," he only replied, "You can't humbug me. I've been in this country too long for that." In other words, he was humorously but hopelessly degraded.[19]

His lack of interest in anything he couldn't eat failed to guarantee that he would be a good shepherd. On the Fourth of July, while Muir and Billy waited anxiously for the Don to bring food for the camp, they were forced to eat their own mutton, which neither of them could stomach. A nice irony there. Billy became "somewhat demoralized," and showed his true mettle: "He says that since the boss has failed to feed him he is not rightly bound to feed the sheep, and swears no decent white man can climb these steep mountains on mutton alone. 'It's not fittin' grub for a white man really white. For dogs and coyotes and Indians it's different. Good grub, good sheep. That's what I say.' Such was Billy's Fourth of July oration." Billy was physically distasteful. Covered with the remains of his food, his trousers were so dirty that Muir suspected they had "geological significance." Such a "queer character" was "hard to place in this wilderness."[20]

Young Muir's worst fear was that he might have to take up Billy's duties, as he almost did when the shepherd quarreled with the Don and left for the lowlands in August. The fears were all there in the narrative. What if you are what you eat? Worse, what if Muir's participation in this "white" business of sheep herding degraded him into a Billy? Well, he had inner resources of wildness to save him. Muir would play neither the Don's role nor Billy's, even if he was trapped in a sheep camp.

This mutton eating seemed like a crucial issue. After an idyllic and botanical June, Muir and Billy ran out of bread early in July, and they reached their low ebb just as ripe summer arrived. In an early draft Muir described in great detail the gastric distress occasioned by an all-mutton diet. But the real significance of the incident was spiritual. Mutton was "the least desirable of food," and young Muir preferred to eat lupine and saxifrage like the Indians. All men, he knew, must eat, but it irked him that one could not go for "a few days' saunter in the Godful woods without maintaining a base on a wheat-field and grist-mill." Later in the summer he wished to live on pine buds "for the sake of this grand independence." He could not, just as he could never live like a juniper overlooking Tenaya Lake. It was in this context that he argued, "Man seems to be the only animal whose food soils him." A problem as old as Genesis. Unlike the clean wild animals, fallen Man soiled himself whenever he labored for food. All labor for bread was degrading in the eyes of young Muir.[21]

It is no coincidence that he began to notice immediately after this incident that the sheep were destroying Nature's lily meadows; "man alone, and the animals he tames, destroy these gardens," he lamented. As he pursued his studies in the mountains, the sheep business seemed more and more distasteful. There was simply no way out of young Muir's dilemma. Though he could not eat the mutton he guarded, he also knew that the bread he ate was earned in the sheep business. Billy might be depicted as more soiled than young Muir, but it was only a matter of degree. And while the Indians whom Billy hated were able to get their living from wild plants and animals, Muir suspected that the dirty Indians he saw on occasion were no more natural than the fashionable "glaring tailored tourists." Thinking about the wild foods that Indians ate, he said, "Our education has been sadly neglected for many generations," yet he contradicted himself later by saying that Indians were "not a whit more natural in their lives than we civilized whites." The author of *First Summer* insisted that young Muir accept his membership in white civilization, and argued that all men sell their souls for food to some extent. He never allowed young Muir to escape from this dilemma.[22]

HUMAN ALTERNATIVES

If Muir never wished to be a shepherd or a sheep owner, but found that he could not become an Indian, there was one other human alternative — that of the tourist, the visitor to Nature who came from the city. Muir never wanted to see himself as a tourist. When he saw one party of travelers early in the summer, he was surprised at their inattentive attitude toward Nature, but hoped that in the Valley they would "forget themselves and become devout." If these visitors seemed out of place and a disturbance in the woods, "What," Muir wondered, "may we say of ourselves and our flock?"[23]

When Dr. James Davie Butler, a representative from Muir's past life at the University of Wisconsin, arrived in the Valley, the young man mysteriously sensed his presence and came down into the world of hotels and tourists. Called to the Valley by a strange telepathy, Muir puzzled over this singular event in a section of his autobiographical notes, and decided that such "mysterious things" could probably be explained if men only understood the natural forces which created them. In any case, he was attracted to Butler as if the man was a magnet, and their meeting became a significant part of the plot of *First Summer*.[24]

When he met the professor and his traveling companion, a General Alvord, he pitied the men, "bound by clocks, almanacs, orders, duties, etc., and compelled to dwell with lowland care and dust and din, where Nature is covered and her voice smothered, while the poor, insignificant wanderer enjoys the freedom and glory of God's wilderness." He was both glad that he was not great enough to be missed in the busy world, and disappointed to see that Butler and other tourists in the Valley were "little influenced by its novel grandeur, as if their eyes were bandaged and their ears stopped." Just as he had Delaney, he criticized Butler by implication. When the professor gave Muir a book, Muir gave him a sketch for his son. He remembered Butler's six-year-old son, before the Civil War, making patriotic speeches from a tall stool, and his memory suggests his implicit understanding of his own role. Though he wouldn't be as selfish as Billy, neither would he commit himself to a blind obedience to civilization. He could no more be a son to Butler than he could to Delaney. Yet the student of Muir's life must remember that Butler taught Muir how to read literature, and encouraged him to keep a journal. The young Muir of *First Summer* didn't know he would be a writer, but the older Muir recognized his debt to men like Butler who gave him books and also made demands — in this case, that the young Muir write at least one letter a year.[25]

After this visit, young Muir recognized that his commerce was with Nature, not with men. He dismissed the telepathic incident as a distraction from his past, and stepped into his future. He finally understood that "the natural and common is more truly marvelous and mysterious than the so-called supernatural." And so he returned to the mountains. Though he continued to wonder whether it was natural for him to prefer the company of rocks, flowers, trees, and animals to that of his own species, he also began to see that "the whole wilderness seems to be alive and familiar, full of humanity." He chose to ignore the values of civilization, to the best of his ability. He would return to the wilderness, knowing that "wherever we go in the mountains, or indeed in any of God's wild fields, we find more than we seek." Thus far had the pilgrim progressed toward eternal truth.[26]

I have said that *First Summer* is an honest book, and I believe that the unresolved conflicts faced by young Muir in his musings are signs of this honesty. When the older Muir placed his younger self in a more complex world than he might have wanted, when he kept reminding the reader that civilization is constantly piercing and breaking into the wilderness, when he continued to reveal the large social forces which were so capable of crushing not just the tender flowers of the glacial meadow, but also the soul of his younger self, then he was trying to dramatize the continuing conflict between civilization and Nature. The young self he presented in his book was only partly capable of dealing with these problems. Like Huck Finn, he had an intuitive perception that something was wrong with the world he shunned, but he was incapable of analyzing what was wrong.

Just as Muir later had to earn his bread by running a sawmill for Hutchings or by guiding tourists, so too in *First Summer* young Muir was forced to participate in the invasion of the mountains which he would later try to quell. The book, then, could not depict an escape to the self-consistent world of Nature, but was filled with the sorts of interruptions that constantly hindered Muir's studies. When he was able to leave the sheep camp for short excursions, his orbit of freedom was small. Like the real Muir, he was constantly drawn back to civilization, incompletely fulfilled. One could never simply "light out for the Territory ahead of the rest."[27]

Old Muir did not see his former self as a tragic victim, but neither did he see himself as triumphant. Young Muir was not to be fully conscious of his victimization, but old Muir recognized the limitations that the world imposed upon him, and built them into the architecture of his narrative. The years which intervened between the summers of his journals and the writing of the book had taught him that even the creator of parks would be able to save only specimen sections of wilderness; there men could go for temporary respite from the grinding machine of civilization. Young Muir did not want his first summer to be a temporary experiment, but old Muir knew something about the laws of life. He only hoped to save a specimen section of his young and innocent wildness.

When Muir's later books juxtaposed wilderness and civilization, they indicated his staunch belief that the two could not be reconciled. When these books refused to create a pastoral middle ground between the wild and the civilized, when the hero of these books refused to settle down, it was because Muir always refused to believe that such compromises were possible. It was not "progress," but only a sad historical necessity which destroyed the dreams of his youth. So it was with his life: once he had been civilized, he could never return to the wild and innocent state of the narrator of *First Summer.* His only victory might be in the image he could write of the struggle for freedom.

Yet I believe that the young Muir presented in *First Summer* is subtly different from the one I introduced in early chapters of this book. As Muir looked back on his early years in Yosemite, he tended to see himself as less rebellious and less dependent on human society than he really had been. The young Muir of *First Summer* does not attack the values of civilization, nor does he question explicitly the values of books and bookmaking. He does not act the rough wild man who was disliked by residents of Yosemite Valley. He does not see himself in conflict with the tourists or the shepherds. Nor does he show the real need he had for intellectual contact with the Butlers and Carrs and Keiths, who spoke intelligently to him and also sent him many invaluable books. Rather, he attempts to accept the social and economic realities which surrounded him, and simply transcends them. He is more innocent than the thirty-year-old man who came to California in 1868.

CREATION'S DAWN

Each time young Muir escaped from the sheep camp on an excursion into the wilds he was furthering his education in the University of the Wilderness. During his botanical June he began to sense the true freedom, the "good practical sort of immortality" implicit in "vast calm, measureless mountain days." On his excursion to the top of Yosemite Fall, he looked down into the "heart of the snowy, chanting throng of comet like streamers," and it was like looking into the depths of the Universe. Over the days that followed this intense, even apocalyptic vision of his own death, pounding in the "death song of Yosemite Creek," he began to hear more clearly the "eternal song of creation." He was immersed in the flow. A rock like South Dome, which had appeared earlier as sculpture, suddenly seemed "full of thought, clothed with living light . . . steadfast in serene strength like a god." On Mount Hoffman he wakened to the dizzying radiance, "every crystal, every flower a window opening into heaven, a mirror reflecting the Creator." He became what he beheld. As he sauntered through bogs and gardens, crossed mirrored glacial pavements and soft carpets of bryanthus, he began to feel through his feet the rhythm of the great heart of Nature. He climbed the mountains and trees. As he looked into the mirror of Lake Tenaya, he seemed to be entering heaven.[28]

So on August ninth he is fully alive when he races ahead of the flock and enters Tuolumne Meadows alone. He thinks, "Every feature already seems familiar as if I have lived here always." He is finally home. In the meadows he sees "how ineffably spiritually fine is the morning-glow on the mountaintops and the alpenglow of evening." He knows that he is in the midst of the Range of Light, where everything is interesting, where one is "constantly reminded of the infinite lavishness and fertility of Nature."[29]

In the midst of the world of Tuolumne stands Cathedral Peak, sometimes shadowed with clouds. Early in his summer Muir had wondered at clouds, watching them grow "as if new worlds were being created"; they were "another version of the snowy Sierra," and when they merge with the rocks of the mountains, matter and spirit become one. Muir has lived in the world of Tuolumne for nearly a month when the mountain, shadowed with clouds, reveals its true nature, "drawing earth and sky together as one." It is Sinai. Even seeing it from a distance, Muir feels "part of wild nature, kin to everything." When he goes to the mountain as he must, on his last excursion of the summer, and finally sits on its summit at noon, he has arrived at the center of the world. As fine as the views from the summit appear, "no feature, however, of all the noble landscape as seen from here seems more wonderful than the Cathedral itself, a temple displaying Nature's best masonry and sermons in stone."[30]

It is true. Of all the peaks surrounding Tuolumne, Cathedral Peak is prime. One sits on the summit and feels not so much above the landscape as truly in it. I have been there perhaps twenty times, once on the centennial of Muir's ascent, when the clouds sailed through the mountains, riding the west wind. Each day on Cathedral Peak that I remember seems sacred. The world seems to flow about that granite altar in all its wholeness.

Yet Muir was not sure that sitting on the summit consummated his experience in the Sierra. Writing to his brother Daniel several weeks after his ascent, he said that when he sat on Cathedral Peak, he was hungry when he looked up, and ate his bread; but when he looked down he felt full. He wondered what that meant — perhaps that he was satisfied with the spiritual bread of the Sierra, and yet longed for something more. (When you get to the top of the mountain, keep on climbing!) Cathedral Peak had become young Muir's church: "In our best times everything turns into religion, all the world seems a church and the mountains altars." On this mountain altar he is offered a promise, not a fulfillment.[31]

Part of the promise is fulfilled when he discovers while descending that cassiope grows upon his sacred mountain. Cassiope, or white heather, "the highest name of all the small mountain heath people": in some ways, his meeting with this plant is more important than the climb to the summit. Why?

Winter and summer, you may hear her voice, the low, sweet melody of her purple bells. No evangel among all the mountain plants speaks Nature's love more plainly than cassiope. Where she dwells, the redemption of the coldest solitude is complete. The very rocks and glaciers seem to feel her presence, and become imbued with her own fountain sweetness.

Here is an angelic and emblematic flower speaking the message Muir had wanted to hear: the world is not a desert, but is saturated with light. Hearing cassiope brings the final enlightenment of his first summer, and allows him to say with certainty, "How delightful it is to be alone here! How wild everything is,— wild as the sky and as pure!"[32]

At seventy-four years of age, Muir knew this had drawn him to the mountains, a promise of purity and wholeness. He learned that he could immerse himself over and over again in the realm of Nature and not want for more. Though he would never learn all the answers to his life's problems, he had learned that he did not have to reason his way through the world. "The charms of these mountains are beyond all common reason, unexplainable and mysterious as life itself." He could never exhaust, and never explain, the mysteries of the mountains. After all, he was not a prophet, he was only a man.[33]

The twentieth century would bring historians and ecologists who would attempt to write the critique of modern technological culture. But Muir, more than any of them, attempted to live that critique. His life and career are perhaps not models, but they offer an affirmation of what is good in the world, and a rejection of what is only dross. One looks for that last great lyrical passage which encapsulates his philosophy and his life, but one does not find it. Like the spirit of the wilderness, it is a part of the fabric of his life in the mountains, and cannot be abstracted from the world he loved.

Epilogue

As I was sitting in the morning sun in front of the McCauley cabin, I wondered when I would ever finish this book, or whether it was even worth writing. I was not alone with my thoughts. Jesse, my infant son, was learning how to stand, and was vocalizing his problems. His song harmonized with the voices coming from a flicker's nest high in a lodgepole pine. Valerie, his mother the ranger, had been working for a couple of hours already. She had left when the frost was still glittering on the meadows. Now it was mid morning, and the day gathered its warmth about it.

In Tuolumne Meadows one is never alone with one's thoughts, and that is what makes it home. Every day seems to share itself with its participants. One never gets lost, since the landmarks seem to cluster themselves around in unmistakable cordiality. Fairview Dome, Cathedral Peak, the great shoulder of the Kuna Crest, the red masses of Dana and Gibbs. Across the meadow, Lembert Dome rises like a glimmering wave. These are the landmarks of my world, and I suppose of my thought. The meadows themselves undergo that strange and subtle modulation of colors: white under snow in early June, brown, green, and then the islands of gold appear. The summer flows by and one becomes part of it.

It has not always been that way. I can remember summers when I arrived at the meadows and everything seemed flat and unreal, like a movie set. The air was so clear, the days so bright, I thought this landscape could not be real. I had become ghostly and disoriented after a year away from the mountains. It is an unfortunate

362

human failing that one has to be continually reminding oneself about reality, about what is important and what is not. There may be a "phenomenological ecology" which leads us to enlightenment in the mountains, but the cities reverse that process and allow us to fall away from our best moments.

I have spent many summers in Tuolumne Meadows, and all of them have been important. For several seasons I lived in the old Sierra Club campground which had been here at Soda Springs. For several summers I lived in what we used to call the Mountaineer's Center, an old Civilian Conservation Corps mess hall which has recently been transformed into a Visitor's Center. Later I lived above the confluence of the Dana and Lyell forks of the Tuolumne River, in the tent cabins where most of the rangers reside. And now for the past three summers, out here at Soda Springs in the McCauley cabin, near John Muir's favorite camping spot. They are all good places, but this might be the best.

Each camping spot has been associated with a different community of humans. The campground, when I stayed there, was filled with young rockclimbers and wanderers of the mountains, like myself. There was an unspoken agreement among us. We knew why we were here and didn't need to communicate it. Later, at the Mountaineer's Center, many of the same people became a legitimate part of the machinery within the park which entertained the public. We were rockclimbing instructors and guides, or at least that is how we earned our bread. In our free hours, we preferred to climb and ramble in the mountains as we had before we began to work for a living. The communal living arrangements brought us closer together than we had been. We were unlike the other employees of the concessionaire because we had our own kitchen, worked on commission rather than on salary, grew beards, and did not come under as close a scrutiny as the others. We were proud. We thought we were an elite and superior group.

Since Valerie has been working for the National Park Service, my status has changed. Now I no longer need to work during the summers, and I am only loosely connected to the community of Park Service employees. I am certainly not isolated, and have frequent conversations with a variety of people who come out to Soda Springs. Michael, for instance, runs an interpretive program for the Natural

History Association. He walks by most mornings, and we often discuss park affairs over a cup of tea. I notice, in general, that almost every valued friend from the past fifteen years sooner or later shows up at the meadows and comes for a visit.

In other words, Tuolumne Meadows has never been a wilderness for me. Living here has always had its sense of community. I believe it is a good place for my young son to spend his first summer, and perhaps every summer thereafter, because it has been such a good place for Valerie and me. But I wonder about the changes that have come about since Muir was here, and perhaps more important, since I have been coming. A scholar once asked me why I could not simply write a natural history of John Muir, why I had to talk about myself, and this is the answer to his question:

It was early summer and the river was high as I crossed the bridge and walked across the meadow. The old Mountaineer's Center was being dedicated as the new Tuolumne Meadows Visitor's Center. It was a short walk, and Jesse made appreciative noises as he watched the glittering mountain bluebirds we flushed out of a small lodgepole, which had taken root in the old road cut that bisected the meadow. As usual, he had great expectations. When he was put in his pack, that meant adventure. He could hardly wait. I had smaller expectations. I wanted to see the Visitor's Center, particularly because it was being created on a "John Muir theme," but I knew enough about National Park Visitor's Centers to suspect that this one would be like all the rest. Somehow, it was true: they were all the same, whether they were on the rim of the Grand Canyon or in Yosemite Valley. Yet I hoped that wouldn't be true here.

After all, the building itself had a rich history. For the past few winters my friends Anne and Chas had wintered in it, achieving the life John Muir had longed for during his First Summer. Many of my friends had lived there at one time or another. And the meadows themselves had a rich human history. Here was the scene of John Muir's baptism into the Sierra. Here too was the site of the first Sierra Club Outing. Here was the place where I had been introduced more than twenty years ago to the wonders of the Sierra. Carl Sharsmith, the most important teacher I had in those summer days, was still working as a Naturalist; he would be present at the

Visitor's Center. I also knew several of the people who had planned the new exhibits. I respected them. They were young seasonal Naturalists who had also learned from Carl.

But the Visitor's Center was a disappointment. Certainly the building itself had been cleaned and painted. The new exhibit cases were professionally done, and the large canvas banners with quotations from Muir's writings provided some food for thought. But they had been selected only for their superficial references to Tuolumne, not because they had something special to teach. I thought little of the many color photographs, which were so unnecessary since the scenes they depicted were available in Nature, right outside the door. By far the most upsetting part of the exhibit was the trays containing "natural objects" like pine cones, rocks, deer horns, staghorn lichen, and even a small patch of bear skin for the visitor to touch. What was the point, I wondered, when outside the windows all of these were available in the forest in their natural and appropriate setting?

Jesse was having a great time. He loved to be in a crowd of milling people, and he smiled, chortled, waved to everyone. That was how he was. He had already discovered his favorite trail in Yosemite, the asphalt path from Happy Isles to Vernal Fall, where there were so many people to see. I mentioned this to Carl Sharsmith, and he smiled, observing that humans were an important part of natural history. Inside the Visitor's Center one could learn quite a bit about the natural history of tourism, I supposed. Jesse simply liked people because they created such a friendly environment. And people were happy there, I realized, with other humans safely surrounding them. Perhaps they even preferred to see the forest through the windows.

But I felt uncomfortable in the midst of the people who surrounded me, and I thought as I looked around that the Naturalists too seemed ill at ease. This was borne out by subsequent visits. I tried to guess what was the matter. Maybe I was made uncomfortable not only by seeing Nature enclosed in showcases, but also by seeing Naturalists imprisoned in the Visitor's Center. Carl looked particularly out of place. He wore his dress uniform, Class A's, as they are called. This was not the man I remembered from my past, in his clean but threadbare and patched clothes, his old mountain boots worn down at the outside of the heels. It was simply not possible for his spirit to come through in this context.

I realized that Muir's spirit had been lost too. Just as it couldn't be imported to the cities, it couldn't be displayed indoors. Late in his life, Muir had told an interviewer, "You say that what I write may bring this beauty to the hearts of those who do not go out to see it. They have no right to it." But there were other problems as well. The people who created the exhibits had not decided what they had to say about Muir or Tuolumne Meadows. I talked to Michael about the design of the Center. We agreed that a Visitor's Center ought to teach people how to see, and ought further to explain what Muir had called "the right manners of the wilderness." It ought to explain what the needleminers were doing, what all of Nature was doing out there, he thought. I agreed, and added that the focus could have been on a guide to vision, perhaps to Muir's vision, but in any case a means to turn the tourist into a visitor and a visitor into someone capable of dwelling in the meadows. A Visitor's Center, in the words of one of my friends, ought to allow humans who had been alienated from Nature to re-inhabit the earth. Wasn't that the purpose of national parks? Wasn't that what Muir had thought?

I wondered if that was what I had to say about Muir. Wasn't that, finally, his most important contribution? Hadn't he articulated for America just how important it was for men to live in and through a loving relationship to Nature?

July 1980

Notes
Index

Notes

ABBREVIATIONS

Alaska   John Muir, *Travels in Alaska* (1915; repr., Boston: Hough-
                      ton Mifflin, 1917).

Badè   William Frederick Badè, *The Life and Letters of John Muir*,
                      2 vols. (Boston: Houghton Mifflin, 1923–24).

Boyhood & Youth   John Muir, *The Story of My Boyhood and Youth* (1913; repr.,
                      Madison: University of Wisconsin Press, 1965).

Corwin   John Muir, *Cruise of the Corwin*, ed. William F. Badè (1917;
                      repr., Boston: Houghton Mifflin, 1918).

First Summer   John Muir, *My First Summer in the Sierra* (Boston: Hough-
                      ton Mifflin, 1911).

H   Huntington Library, San Marino, California.

Hadley   Edith Jane Hadley, *John Muir's Views of Nature and Their
                      Consequences*, (Ph.D. diss. University of Wisconsin, Madi-
                      son 1956).

Harriman   John Muir, *Edward Henry Harriman* (New York: Doubleday,
                      1912).

Hays   Samuel P. Hays, *Conservation and the Gospel of Efficiency:
                      The Progressive Conservation Movement, 1890–1920* (Cam-
                      bridge, Mass.: Harvard University Press, 1959).

John of Mountains   *John of the Mountains: The Unpublished Journals of John
                      Muir*, ed. Linnie Marsh Wolfe (1938; repr., Madison: Univer-
                      sity of Wisconsin Press, 1979).

Jones   Holway Jones, *John Muir and the Sierra Club: The Battle
                      for Yosemite* (San Francisco: Sierra Club, 1965).

JP   Robert Underwood Johnson Papers, Bancroft Library, Uni-
                      versity of California at Berkeley.

Kimes

William F. Kimes and Maymie B. Kimes, *John Muir: A Reading Bibliography* (Palo Alto: William P. Wrendon, 1978).

Letters

John Muir, *Letters to a Friend: Written to Mrs. Ezra Carr, 1866–1879* (1915; repr., Dunwoody, Georgia: Norman Berg, 1973).

Mountains

John Muir, *The Mountains of California* (1894; repr., Berkeley: Ten Speed Press, 1979).

MP

The John Muir Papers, Stuart Library, University of the Pacific, Stockton, California.

Nash

Roderick Nash, *Wilderness and the American Mind* (New Haven: Yale University Press, 1967).

Parks

John Muir, *Our National Parks* (1901; repr., Boston: Houghton Mifflin, 1917).

Picturesque California

Picturesque California and the Region West of the Rocky Mountains, from Alaska to Mexico, ed. John Muir, 2 vols. (San Francisco: J. Dewing, 1888).

Remembered Yesterdays

Robert Underwood Johnson, *Remembered Yesterdays* (Boston: Little, Brown, 1923).

Richardson

Elmo Richardson, *The Politics of Conservation: Crusades and Controversies, 1897–1913* (Berkeley: University of California Press, 1962).

SCB

Sierra Club *Bulletin*

Starr

Kevin Starr, *Americans and the California Dream* (New York: Oxford University Press, 1973).

Steep Trails

John Muir, *Steep Trails*, ed. William F. Badè (Boston: Houghton Mifflin, 1918).

Stickeen

John Muir, *Stickeen* (1909; repr., Garden City, N.Y.: Doubleday, 1974).

Studies

John Muir, *Studies in the Sierra*, ed. William E. Colby (San Francisco: Sierra Club, 1950).

To Yosemite and Beyond

John Muir, *To Yosemite and Beyond, Writings from the Years 1863 to 1875*, ed. Robert Engberg and Donald Wesling (Madison: University of Wisconsin Press, 1980).

Walk

John Muir, *A Thousand Mile Walk to the Gulf*, ed. William F. Badè (1916; repr., Boston: Houghton Mifflin, 1917).

West

West of the Rocky Mountains, ed. John Muir (1888; repr., Philadelphia: Running Press, 1976). This is an abridged reprint of *Picturesque California*.

Wolfe   Linnie Marsh Wolfe, *Son of the Wilderness: The Life of John
                  Muir* (1945; repr., Madison: University of Wisconsin Press,
                  1978).

Worster   Donald Worster, *Nature's Economy: The Roots of Ecology*
                  (San Francisco: Sierra Club Books, 1977).

YNP   Yosemite National Park Archives.

Yosemite   John Muir, *The Yosemite* (1912; repr., Garden City, N.Y.: Dou-
                  bleday, Natural History Library, 1962).

METHODS OF CITATION USED IN THE NOTES

Catchphrases   Catchphrases from the text are used in the notes to identify
materials being cited. A catchphrase may be either the opening words of a quoted
passage, or a key word or words indicating a subject of discussion.

Where a single catchphrase from a quoted passage references a paragraph
containing several quotations, the citation for the catchphrase documents the other
materials in the same paragraph as well.

Many notes contain several catchphrases. In notes to paragraphs containing
referenced materials from several sources, the material relevant to each source is
flagged by a catchphrase. A sequence of quoted phrases or lines from the same
source is sometimes indicated by catchphrases from the first and last quotations
in the sequence, to distinguish them from materials from other sources.

Where materials in an entire section of a chapter, or in a series of consecutive
paragraphs within a section, follow the same source (such as an essay by Muir),
one note is used, where possible, to document the relevant materials for the section or paragraphs. References for materials from other sources, within such sections and paragraphs, are cited in separate notes. Certain landmark passages from
Muir's writings are also cited separately.

Kimes Citations   Because John Muir's articles frequently went through many
revisions, from articles in newspapers to chapters in books, I cite all articles, essays, and pamphlets by title and key them to William F. Kimes and Maymie B.
Kimes, *John Muir: A Reading Bibliography.* The Kimes have carefully traced the
complex publishing history of Muir's works. Some of Muir's articles were published under excessively long titles; I have used short titles for convenience, where
appropriate.

Manuscripts, Papers, Letters   Manuscripts are referenced by file, box, or cata-
logue number, according to the system used by the library source. The Muir Papers became increasingly better organized during the time I used them, and certain
materials I used in the Yosemite National Park Archives will now be found in the
Muir collection at the University of the Pacific. Hadley's dissertation contains many
of the letters that are in the Johnson Papers.

Chapter 1. THE MACHINE AND THE FLOWER

1 "I wish I knew where I was going . . .": *Letters*, p. 32, Aug. 30, 1867.
2 "The folks think it funny . . .": MP, Box 1, Nov. 18, 1860. "In case anything . . .": H, FAC 625 (11), Sept. 7, 1867.
3 Manuscript notebook of A Thousand Mile Walk to the Gulf: YNP, File 9161.
4 "conventional or traditional man . . .": R. W. B. Lewis, *The American Adam: Innocence, Tragedy, and Tradition in the Nineteenth Century* (Chicago: University of Chicago Press, 1955), p. 23. Thoreau after *Walden*: Worster, pp. 89–97.
5 Muir's inventions: *Boyhood & Youth*, pp. 192–222; Wolfe, pp. 65–66.
6 "done for the real good . . .": *Letters*, p. 4, Jan. 21, 1866. "To what end . . .": H, FAC 625 (11), Dec. 20, 1863.
7 The meaning of machines: see Lewis Mumford, *The Myth of the Machine: the Pentagon of Power* (New York: Harcourt Brace, 1970), pp. 164–96. "All flesh is grass . . .": *Boyhood & Youth*, p. 205.
8 *Boyhood & Youth*, p. 196.
9 David Ehrenfeld, *The Arrogance of Humanism* (New York: Oxford University Press, 1978), pp. 16–17.
10 "I have about made up my mind . . .": H, FAC 625 (11), May 7, 1866. The industrial accident: H, FAC 625 (11), Aug. 12, 1866. "I should like to invent . . .": *Letters*, p. 9, Sept. 13, 1866.
11 "How intensely I desire . . .": *Letters*, p. 9. "my mind seems to so bury itself . . .": *Letters*, p. 9.
12 "great book of Nature": *Letters*, p. 13. Emulating Humboldt: *Boyhood & Youth*, p. 207.
13 Ezra S. Carr, *The Patrons of Husbandry on the Pacific Coast* (San Francisco: A.L. Bancroft, 1875). Mrs. Carr as guiding power: Verne A. Stadtman, *The University of California, 1868–1968* (New York: McGraw Hill, 1970), pp. 69, 76, 80.
14 Carr's alliance with Henry George: Stadtman, *University of California*, p. 74. "Social man . . .": H, CA 12, Ezra Carr, "Forestry: Its Relation to Civilization" [ca. 1873], p. 26. This document refers to George Perkins Marsh, *Man and Nature*, ed. David Lowenthal (1864; repr., Cambridge, Mass.: Harvard University Press, 1965).
15 "Love thy neighbor . . .": H, CA 22, Jeanne Carr, "Christmas" [speech delivered to a Granger group, Dec., ca. 1875], p. 26.
16 "He says that woman speaks . . .": Susan Griffin, *Woman and Nature: the Roaring Inside Her* (New York: Harper and Row, 1978), p. 1. "You do not know . . .": MP, Box 1, Oct. 12, 1867.
17 "eye within the eye . . .": MP, Box 1, March 15, 1867. "Patron Saint . . .": H, CA 40. "the greatest extent . . .": *Walk*, p. 247.
18 Saint Francis as Patron Saint of Ecology: see Lynn White, Jr., "The Historical Roots of Our Ecologic Crisis," in White, *Machina ex Deo: Essays in the Dynamism of Western Culture* (Cambridge, Mass.: Harvard University Press, 1968).

"We carried no tent . . .": H, CA 40, "Mrs. Carr's Lecture on the Big Tuolumne Cañon, before the Oakland Farming Club" [1873], pp. 3, 2.

19 Muir's notebook: MP, File 39.29. "We know ourselves . . .": Griffin, *Woman and Nature*, p. 226. "He gave you . . .": MP, Box 1, March 15, 1867.

20 "But to me the most captivating piece . . .": Jeanne C. Carr, "John Muir," *Californian Illustrated Magazine*, vol. 2 (June, 1892), p. 90.

21 "Some plants . . .": YNP, File 9161, pp. 62–63. "Is not your experience . . .": *Letters*, p. 32.

22 "We are taught . . .": YNP, File 9161, p. 50.

23 "Nature's grandeur . . ." through "one of the useful, practical men . . .": *Walk*, pp. 254–55.

24 "I believe in Providence . . .": *Walk*, pp. 276–77.

25 "musty orthodox arguments": YNP, File 9161, p. 19.

26 "Hammer in hand . . .": *Walk*, p. 265.

27 "A serious matter . . .": *Walk*, p. 321.

28 "I gazed awe-stricken . . .": *Walk*, p. 301.

29 "*Alone*": YNP, File 9161, p. 45. Loitering negroes: YNP, File 9161, p. 56. "civilized swarm . . ." and "one of the Lord's . . .": YNP, File 9161, pp. 45–56.

30 "obliterating all memory . . ." through "the most notable . . .": YNP, File 9161, p. 52.

31 "the forest trees . . .": H, FAC, 625 (11), Sept. 22, 1869.

32 ". . . not a mark . . .": *Walk*, p. 316. "starving unfriended condition": YNP, File 9161, p. 82. "handsome as a minister . . .": *Walk*, pp. 316–17.

33 "no man knows himself . . .": YNP, File 9161, p. 84. "the proprieties of civilization": YNP, File 9161, p. 98; *Walk*,, p. 324. Drawing of alligators: YNP, File 9161, p. 99.

34 "Take that!": *Boyhood & Youth*, p. 104.

35 "Why . . . should man . . .": *Walk*, p. 356.

36 Lewis Mumford, *The Brown Decades: A Study of the Arts in America, 1865–1895* (New York: Harcourt, Brace, 1931), p. 78.

37 "mutations": Marsh, *Man and Nature*, p. 19.

38 "there was nothing sacred . . .": David Lowenthal, Introduction to Marsh, *Man and Nature*, p. xxv. "The fact . . ." and "for usufruct alone . . .": Marsh, *Man and Nature*, p. 36.

39 "a perpetual struggle . . ." and "in proportion to the magnitude . . .": George Perkins Marsh, "The Study of Nature," *Christian Examiner* (Jan. 1860, p. 34.

40 "when he sinks . . .": Marsh, "Study of Nature," p. 34.

41 "closet researches of the clergy": *Walk*, pp. 356–59; corrected with YNP, File 9161, p. 157.

42 "Well, I have precious little sympathy . . .": YNP, File 9161, p. 130.

43 "I used to imagine . . .": *John of Mountains*, p. 8, Jan. 1, 1869. Coyote as hunter: MP, File 38.12, "Coyote." "The sheep of my flock . . .": YNP, File 9165, "At Smokey Jack's Sheep Camp," p. 35.

44 "Fearing he might attack . . .": MP, File 19.2; *First Summer*, pp. 178–85.

45 "Bears are made . . .": *John of Mountains*, pp. 82–83.

46 "I never tried . . .": Wolfe, p. 95.
47 "a clearly defined correspondence . . .": *John of Mountains*, p. 8, Jan. 1, 1869. "who believes in the literature . . ." and "purely a manufactured article": *Walk*, p. 355. "in the free unplanted fields . . ." and "invisible, measureless currents": *John of Mountains*, p. 8.
48 Crisis in scientific world-view: Thomas S. Kuhn, *The Structure of Scientific Revolutions* (Chicago: University of Chicago Press, 1962), pp. 5-11, 82-83.

Chapter 2. THE GLACIAL EYE

1 "a large sheetful . . .": *Letters*, p. 49, Feb. 24, 1869.
2 "I have no fixed practical aim . . .": *To Yosemite and Beyond*, p. 65, June 4, 1871. "exemplary, stable . . .": Wolfe, p. 144.
3 "You must live within . . .": Henry David Thoreau, *Walden and Civil Disobedience*, ed. Owen Thomas (New York: Norton, 1966), p. 235.
4 Gary Snyder, *Myths and Texts* (1960; repr., New York: New Directions, 1978). T. S. Eliot, "These fragments . . .": "The Waste Land," line 431; "We shall not cease . . .": "Little Gidding," lines 241-44 *Collected Poems, 1909-1935* (New York: Harcourt, Brace, 1936). "stay together . . .": Gary Snyder, *Earth House Hold: Technical Notes and Queries to Fellow Dharma Revolutionaries* (New York: New Directions, 1969), p. 86.
5 Snapshots: see Susan Sontag, *On Photography* (New York: Farrar, Strauss, and Giroux, 1977). Urban commentator: see Theodore Roszak, *Where the Wasteland Ends: Politics and Transcendence in Postindustrial Society* (New York: Doubleday, 1972), p. 27.
6 "to go into solitude . . .": "Nature," *Selections from Ralph Waldo Emerson: An Organic Anthology*, ed. Stephen E. Whicher (Boston: Houghton Mifflin, 1957), p. 23.
7 "memories made up . . .": "Rambles of a Botanist among the Plants and Climates of California," pp. 767-70; Kimes #12.
8 His observations would cohere: MP, File 37.14. "blotted and storm-beaten . . .": "Yosemite Glaciers"; Kimes #2; reprinted in *To Yosemite and Beyond*, pp. 77-87. "books never yet opened": "Exploration of the Great Tuolumne Cañon," p. 147; Kimes #22.
9 "Yet why should one bewail . . .": *To Yosemite and Beyond*, p. 54. "rather stand . . .": *John of Mountains*, p. 103.
10 "Equal interest . . .": Francis P. Farquhar, *History of the Sierra Nevada* (Berkeley: University of California Press, 1969), pp. 156-58.
11 "the ambitious amateur . . .": quoted in Farquhar, *History of the Sierra Nevada*, p. 163.
12 "I had remained . . .": "Exploration of the Great Tuolumne Cañon," p. 141; Kimes #22. "self-styled . . .": "The Creation of Yosemite National Park, Letters of John Muir to Robert Underwood Johnson," Sept. 13, 1889; Kimes #393.
13 "I only went out . . .": *John of Mountains*, p. 439.

14 "I spring to my feet . . .": *John of Mountains*, p. 84. The effect of environment on mind: see Raymond F. Dasmann, *A Different Kind of Country* (London: Collier Books, 1968), p. 99. "mountains and deserts . . .": George B. Schaller, *Stones of Silence: Journeys in the Himalaya* (New York: Viking, 1980), p. 6.

15 "dainty little fall . . .": Badè, 1:185. "Oh, no . . .": MP, File 70.12; reprinted in *To Yosemite and Beyond*, p. 43.

16 Muir's reading: see Hadley.

17 "When he can read God . . .": "The American Scholar," *Selections from Ralph Waldo Emerson*, ed. Whicher, p. 68.

18 "a great longing for Gray . . .": *Letters*, pp. 125–26. "He is a most cordial lover . . .": *Letters*, p. 128, July 27, 1872. "I think . . .": *Letters*, p. 140, Oct. 14, 1872.

19 John Ruskin on "Mountain Gloom" and "Mountain Glory": chapters 19 and 20, *Of Mountain Beauty*, vol. 4 of *Modern Painters: The Works of John Ruskin*, ed. E. T. Cook and Alexander Wetterburn, 39 vols. (New York and London: G. Allen and Longman, Green, 1904). "were he . . . to dwell . . .": *Letters*, p. 123.

20 "The deep stillness . . .": Joseph Le Conte, *A Journal of Ramblings Through the High Sierra of California by the University Excursion Party*, ed. Francis P. Farquhar (1874; repr., San Francisco: Sierra Club Books, 1960), pp. 73–74.

21 King on Ruskin and Tyndall: Clarence King, *Mountaineering in the Sierra Nevada*, ed. Francis P. Farquhar (1871; repr., New York: Norton, 1935), pp. 305–6. "There are no harsh, hard dividing lines . . .": *John of Mountains*, p. 89, Aug. 21, 1872. "When you get to the top . . .": These words are ascribed to Japhy Ryder [Gary Snyder] in Jack Kerouac, *Dharma Bums* (New York: Signet, New American Library, 1958).

22 "This was my 'method of study'": . . .": "Exploration of the Great Tuolumne Cañon," p. 141; Kimes #22.

23 "methodless rovings": *John of Mountains*, p. 108.

24 "We must trust . . .": "Nature," *Selections from Ralph Waldo Emerson*, ed. Whicher, p. 22.

25 *Études:* Louis Agassiz, *Studies on Glaciers*, trans. Albert V. Carozzi (New York: Hafner, 1967). "In particular the great Valley . . .": Badè, 1:294, Sept. 8, 1871.

26 "No scientific book . . .": *Letters*, p. 157. "tough grey clothes . . .": *Letters*, pp. 157–58.

27 "I then began to creep . . .": "Exploration of the Great Tuolumne Cañon," p. 144; Kimes #22.

28 "Philosophers have yet to learn . . .": Louis Agassiz, *Essay on Classification*, ed. Edward Lurie (Cambridge, Mass.: Harvard University Press, 1962), p. 20.

29 "no healthy man . . .": "Exploration of the Great Tuolumne Cañon," p. 146; Kimes #22. Muir's revised version of this essay: MP, File 27.15.

30 "realms that eye hath not seen . . .": "Exploration of the Great Tuolumne Cañon, p. 146; Kimes #22.

31 Skiing powder: Delores LaChappelle, *Earth Wisdom* (Los Angeles: Guild of Tutors Press, 1978), p. 53.

32 "imagination . . . must be strictly checked . . .": John Tyndall, *Hours of Exercise in the Alps* (New York: Longmans, Green, 1871), p. 230. "sweet music . . ." through "the whole world . . .": *John of Mountains*, p. 226.

33 "You'll find me rough . . .": Badè, 1:325.

34 "A Geologist's Winter Walk," Kimes #20; reprinted in *Steep Trails*, pp. 19–28. Quoted passages in the following eight paragraphs are from this source.

35 "Not one of all the assembled rocks . . .": *Steep Trails*, p. 28.

36 "Much as I enjoy . . .": Tyndall, *Hours of Exercise in the Alps*, p. 11. Tyndall's gift of a barometer: James Mitchell Clarke, *The Life and Adventures of John Muir* (San Diego: The Word Shop, 1979), p. 108. "[We] live with our heels . . .": MP, File 37.14; *To Yosemite and Beyond*, p. 57.

37 "In the woods . . .": "Nature," *Selections from Ralph Waldo Emerson*, ed. Whicher, p. 24. Emerson's abstract version of Nature, and William Ellery Channing's analysis of it: see F. O. Matthiessen, *American Renaissance: Art and Expression in the Age of Emerson and Whitman* (New York: Oxford University Press, 1941), pp. 160–61.

38 "sponge steeped in immortality": "Rambles of a Botanist Among the Plants and Climates of California," p. 768; Kimes #12. "Emerson observes . . .": Introduction to *The Wilderness World of John Muir*, ed. Edwin Way Teale (Boston: Houghton Mifflin, 1954), p. xi.

39 "Winter blows the fog . . .": *John of Mountains*, p. 190. "Now we observe . . .": *John of Mountains*, p. 138.

40 "Darwin's mean ungodly word . . .": Badè, 1:380.

41 "the two major advances . . .": quoted in Nash, pp. 193–94.

42 "there is some impropriety . . .": Jonathan Edwards, "Dissertation Concerning the End for which God Created the World," in *Major Writers of America*, ed. Perry Miller, vol. 1 (New York: Harcourt Brace, 1962), p. 171.

43 "more intensive scientific reconnaisances . . .": William H. Goetzmann, *Exploration and Empire: The Explorer and the Scientist in the Winning of the American West* (New York: Random House, 1966), p. xiii–xiv.

44 Galen Clark: see Shirley Sargent, *Galen Clark: Yosemite Guardian* (San Francisco: Sierra Club Books, 1964), pp. 52, 81–85. "Go east . . . ," "earth hath no sorrows . . .": *John of Mountains*, p. 99.

45 "Scenes Among the Glaciers' Beds," in "Yosemite Glaciers"; Kimes #2.

46 "the foot-prints . . .": "The Living Glaciers of California"; Kimes #14. See also *Letters*, pp. 135–37, Oct. 8, 1872.

47 The *Harper's* version: "Living Glaciers of California"; Kimes #52.

48 "the Sierra Nevada of California . . ." through "main lateral moraines . . .": "Living Glaciers of California," pp. 770–72; Kimes #52. "A series of rugged zigzags . . .": "Living Glaciers of California," p. 772; Kimes #52.

49 "a sample of rashness . . .": Kimes #52, p. 776.

50 "the tops of mountains . . .": Henry David Thoreau, *The Maine Woods* (1848; repr., New York: Bramhall House, 1950), pp. 271–72.

51 "There is no life in thee . . .": "The Masthead," in Herman Melville, *Moby Dick or, The Whale*, ed. Charles Feidelson, Jr. (1851; repr., New York: Bobbs-Merrill, 1964), pp. 214–15.

52 "Why should man value . . .": *Walk*, p. 356.

53 The early draft of "Ancient Glaciers of the Sierra," Kimes #109, is in MP, File 29.11.

54 "only daring and insolent men . . .": Thoreau, *The Maine Woods*, p. 272. Sacred initiation: Mircea Eliade, *The Sacred and the Profane: The Nature of Religion*, trans. Willard R. Trask (New York: Harcourt Brace, 1959), pp. 53–54, 196–97.

55 "the ruins of a bygone geological empire": King, *Mountaineering in the Sierra Nevada*, p. 306.

56 "When after the melting . . .": *Studies*, p. 88. "mountain flowers . . .": *John of Mountains*, p. 94.

57 "The clearest way . . .": *The Wilderness World of John Muir*, ed. Teale, p. 312.

58 "I left the woods . . .": Thoreau, *Walden*, ed. Thomas, p. 213. "I am hopelessly and forever . . .": Badè, 2:28–29. "to give himself . . .": *To Yosemite and Beyond*, p. 158.

Chapter 3. THE PATHLESS WAY AND THE RANGE OF LIGHT

1 Awakening: The discussion in this chapter is indebted to Doug Robinson, "The Climber as Visionary," *Ascent*, vol. 6, no. 3 (May, 1969), pp. 6–9; and Tom Lyon, "A Mountain Mind," *The Mountain Spirit*, ed. Michael Tobias (Woodstock, N.Y.: Overlook Press, 1979), pp. 22–27. "made one, unseparate . . .": *John of Mountains*, p. 82. "Mountains holy as Sinai": *John of Mountains*, p. 92. Natural Man and the sacred spiritual state: Lewis, *American Adam*, pp. 23–25. "got religion": Badè, 1:218, April 10, 1870.

2 "put off thy shoes . . .": Exodus 3.5. "navel of the earth": see Eliade, *The Sacred and the Profane*, p. 20.

3 Baptism in Yosemite Fall: *John of Mountains*, pp. 61–62, April 3, 1871; his best published account of the baptism, "Treasures of Yosemite," *The Century Magazine*, vol. 40, no. 4 (Aug., 1890); Kimes #181. "In the Heart of the California Alps," Kimes #100; this narrative, retitled "A Near View of the High Sierra" as it appears in *Mountains*, pp. 48–73, is most accurate, and I follow it, with exceptions noted. All quoted passages in the following two sections of the chapter are from the retitled narrative, except those documented otherwise in the notes; long extracts from *Mountains* are also separately cited, as are shorter passages where clarity so requires.

4 The nature of Enlightenment: D. T. Suzuki, *Essays in Zen Buddhism*, 1st ser. (New York: Grove Press, 1961), p. 156.

5 "After gaining a point . . .": *Mountains*, pp. 64–65.

6 "the style . . .": *Studies*, p. 15. "finding the ordinary . . .": Wolfe, p. 163. The devouring fire: Exodus 24.17. "cut off . . .": Wolfe, p. 163.

7 "the unfolding . . .": Suzuki, *Essays in Zen Buddhism*, p. 230. "satori is the most

intimate . . .": Suzuki, p. 263. Athletic event: This is completely misunderstood by Clarke, *Life and Adventures of John Muir*, p. 114.

8 Forgetting himself in the woods: *Letters*, p. 7. "limbs moving . . .": *Mountains*, p. 60. The "watercourse way": see Allan Watts, *TAO: The Watercourse Way*, with the collaboration of Al Chungliang (New York: Pantheon Books, 1975), pp. 39, 41, 76. "Down through the midst . . .": *Mountains*, p. 50.

9 The tension: see Eugen Herrigel, *Zen in the Art of Archery*, trans. R. F. C. Hull (New York: Random House, 1953), pp. 54, 65. "Big Two-Hearted River," *The Short Stories of Ernest Hemingway* (1938; repr., New York: Scribner's, 1958).

10 Ecological thinking: Gregory Bateson, *Steps to an Ecology of Mind* (New York: Ballantine Books, 1972), pp. 314, 499. "*uncommitted potentiality* . . .": Bateson, pp. 462–63; Herrigel, *Zen in the Art of Archery*, p. 54. "we should trust . . .": Bateson, p. 463.

11 "one feels far from home . . .": *West*, p. 458.

12 "In climbing . . .": *John of Mountains*, p. 296.

13 "far less striking . . .": "Summering in the Sierra. The Summit of South Dome . . ."; Kimes #60.

14 "the former is a colossal cone . . .": "Mount Whitney . . ."; Kimes #48. "the glaciers of Ritter . . .": *John of Mountains*, p. 157.

15 yin-yang: Peter Matthiessen, *The Snow Leopard* (New York: Bantam Books, 1979), p. 171.

16 Ritter: in "Mountain Building," chapter 7, *Studies*, pp. 94–95.

17 "most influential agent . . .": *Studies*, p. 92.

18 *Axis mundi*: Eliade, *The Sacred and the Profane*, pp. 33–35, 94. "Standing here . . .": *Mountains*, pp. 69–70.

19 The Golden Age in the Sierra: see Farquhar, *History of the Sierra Nevada*, p. 145. "I rang my hammer . . .": King, *Mountaineering in the Sierra Nevada*, p. 94.

20 "accepting the equal alternatives . . .": quoted by H. E. G. Tyndall, ed., in his introduction to Edward Whymper, *Scrambles Amongst the Alps* (1871; repr. London: John Murray, 1936), p. vii.

21 John Ruskin's view of mountaineering and mountains: see *Sesames and Lillies* in *Works*, vol. 18, pp. 22, 25, 89, 90; see also *Works*, vol. 4, p. 457; and Roger B. Stein, *John Ruskin and Aesthetic Thought in America, 1840–1900* (Cambridge, Mass.: Harvard University Press, 1967).

22 Muir's answer to Ruskin: Badè, 1:377–78. "without a particle . . .": Tyndall, *Hours of Exercise in the Alps*, p. 33. Henry James's view: see Stein, *John Ruskin and Aesthetic Thought*, p. 83.

23 "No tongue can tell . . .": King, *Mountaineering in the Sierra Nevada*, p. 142. "The varying hues . . .": King, p. 305. "no sentiment of beauty . . .": King, p. 97. "a fearful sense . . .": King, p. 303.

24 "'no aspect of destruction'" and "descending masses . . .": Whymper, *Scrambles Amongst the Alps*, p. 110. "a strong smell of sulphur . . .": Whymper, p. 93. "to prove . . .": Leslie Stephen *The Playgrounds of Europe* (1871; repr. London: Longman's, Green, 1899), p. 69.

25 "Now the first merit . . .": Stephen, *Playgrounds of Europe*, p. 316.

26 "do not usually yield . . .": Whymper, *Scrambles Amongst the Alps*, pp. 119–20.

27 Muir's discussion of artists and aesthetics: "In the Heart of the California Alps," pp. 345–49; Kimes #100. I follow this early version in my discussion; quoted passages in this section of the chapter are from that source, unless otherwise indicated. Long extracts are documented separately..

28 "When looking . . .": "In the Heart of the California Alps," p. 351.

29 "No one can decipher . . .": Stephen, *Playgrounds of Europe*, p. 319.

30 "I am glad to know . . .": Badè, 1:320. "development of manliness . . .": Whymper, *Scrambles Amongst the Alps*, p. 332. "In Clarence King . . .": Starr, p. 187.

31 Mallory and mountaineering: see Gregory Bateson, *Mind and Nature: A Necessary Unity* (New York: Bantam, 1980), pp. 154–55. "Have we vanquished an enemy? . . .": George Leigh Mallory, "Mont Blanc from the Col du Géant by the Eastern Buttress of Mont Maudit," *Alpine Journal*, vol. 32 (Sept., 1918), p. 162.

32 "The sense of peace . . .": Suzuki, *Essays in Zen Buddhism*, p. 153.

33 "Muir despised . . .": Starr, p. 187.

34 Muir's elegy to Clark: "Galen Clark"; Kimes #291. An accurate picture of the relationship between Muir and Hutchings is clouded by local gossip even today.

35 Susan Brownmiller, *Against Our Will: Men, Women, and Rape* (New York: Bantam, 1976), pp. 211–12.

36 Muir on "Mr. Short": "Summering in the Sierra. The Summit of South Dome." Kimes #60. Climbing as a game: Lito Tejada-Flores, "Games Climbers Play," *The Games Climbers Play*, ed. Ken Wilson (San Franciso: Sierra Club Books, 1978), pp. 19–27.

37 Sir John Hunt's *The Conquest of Everest* (New York: E. P. Dutton, 1954), describes the first ascent of the mountain.

38 "A wilderness . . .": Section 2 (C), The Wilderness Act of September 3, 1964 (Public Law 88–577, 78 Stat. 890, 16 USC 1131).

39 Rare I and II: Roadless Area Review Evaluation I and II; BLM: Bureau of Land Management; FLPMA: Federal Land Planning and Management Act of 1976. On environmental legislation, see Samuel P. Hays, "From Conservation to Environment: Environmental Politics in the United States Since World War Two," *Environmental Review*, vol. 6, no. 2 (Fall 1982), pp. 14–41.

40 "while the word . . .": Nash, p. 1.

41 "the Sierra, instead of being a huge wrinkle . . .": *Studies*, pp. 4–5.

42 "all may sing excelsior . . .": "The Summit of South Dome"; Kimes #60.

43 The Muir Wall: Yvon Chouinard, "Muir Wall–El Capitan," *American Alpine Club Journal*, vol. 15, no. 40, pp. 46–51.

Chapter 4. THE WAY OF GEOLOGY

1 "Suppose I should give . . .": Badè, 1:296, Sept. 8, 1871. "Well, here it is . . .": Badè, 1:296–97.

2 François E. Matthes, *The Incomparable Valley: A Geologic Interpretation of the Yosemite*, ed. Fritiof Fryxell (Berkeley: University of California Press, 1950).

3 "curtail his poetic exuberance . . .": Wolfe, pp. 171–72.

4 "Everything is so inseparably united . . .": Wolfe, p. 171. The critic and philosopher: Phillip Wheelwright, *Heraclitus* (New York: Atheneum, 1964), p. 13. "most of the words . . .": Badè, 2:7. The vitalist point of view: Worster, p. 378.

5 "one vast undulated wave . . .": *Studies*, p. 3. "disinter forms . . ." and "only developed . . .": *Studies*, p. 16.

6 "in Sierra architecture . . .": *Studies*, p. 15. "'He hath *builded* . . .'": *Studies*, p. 5. "Nature is not so poor . . .": *Studies*, p. 21.

7 "seeds so to speak . . ." and "domes appear . . .": MP, File 27.16. "No Accidents or Caprice . . .": Alphonso Wood, *Classbook of Botany* (New York: Barnes and Burr, 1861), p. 8. "the ripening . . .": *Studies*, p. 15.

8 "While the snow-flowers . . .": *John of Mountains*, p. 90. "The beautiful conoid . . .": I quote the original version, MP, File 27.16; revised in *Studies*, pp. 8–9. "In all this sublime fulfillment . . .": *Studies*, p. 100. "Opposition brings concord . . .": Wheelwright, *Heraclitus*, pp. 98, 116.

9 "It is hard not to invest . . .": King, *Mountaineering in the Sierra Nevada*, p. 304. "Glaciers move in tides . . .": *John of Mountains*, p. 89. Muir's perceptions from the Owens Valley: *John of Mountains*, p. 188.

10 ". . . to me a mountain is a Buddha . . .": Kerouac, *Dharma Bums*, p. 54. "When we thoroughly study . . .": Dōgen, "Treasury of the True Dharma Eye: Book XXIX, The Mountains and Rivers Sutra," *The Mountain Spirit*, ed. Michael Tobias, trans. Carl Bielefeldt (Woodstock, N.Y.: Overlook Press, 1979), p. 59. "To be 'in the mountains' . . .": Dōgen, *The Mountain Spirit*, p. 41.

11 "no temple made with hands . . .": "The Treasures of Yosemite," pp. 484–85; Kimes #181.

12 "Desert," in Richard Shelton, *Chosen Place* (Crete, Neb.: The Best Cellar Press, 1975).

13 "I looked up . . .": Kerouac, *Dharma Bums*, p. 68. "If for a moment . . .": *Yosemite*, p. 65.

14 "lingering beneath cool shadows . . .": *Studies*, p. 4.

15 Uniformity vs. Catastrophe: The best general discussion of these issues is by Stephen Jay Gould, "Uniformity and Catastrophe," in Gould, *Ever Since Darwin: Reflections in Natural History* (New York: Norton, 1977), pp. 147–52. I follow his analysis of the controversy.

16 "Natural Laws . . .": Gould, *Ever Since Darwin*, p. 150. "Linnaeus says . . .": *John of Mountains*, pp. 153–54, Aug., 1873.

17 "calculated to foster indolence . . .": Charles Lyell, *Principles of Geology* (London: J. Murray, 1831), vol. 3, p. 1.

18 "obliging him to allow . . .": *The Education of Henry Adams* (1918; repr., New York: The Modern Library, 1931), p. 227.

19 "processes now operating . . .": Gould, *Ever Since Darwin*, p. 150. "The

erosive energy of ice . . .": *Studies*, p. 45. "Here is the first man . . .": Wolfe, p. 160.

20 "Geologic change is slow . . .": Gould, *Ever Since Darwin*, p. 151. "seeming to account . . .": *Studies*, p. 18.

21 "the earth has been fundamentally . . .": Gould, *Ever Since Darwin*, p. 151. "Since I saw the glaciers . . .": quoted in Edward Lurie, *Louis Agassiz: A Life in Science* (Chicago: University of Chicago Press, 1960), p. 99.

22 "huge ocean of ice . . .": Agassiz, *Studies on Glaciers*, p. 169. "The surface of the earth . . .": Agassiz, *Studies on Glaciers*, p. 175.

23 "separate the knowable . . .": *John of Mountains*, p. 108.

24 "setting out . . .": *Studies*, p. 34.

25 Muir's revised copy of "Exploration in the Great Tuolumne Cañon": MP, File 27.15.

26 "unconscious interpreters . . .": Agassiz, *Essay on Classification*, p. 37.

27 Gray's comparison of Agassiz and Darwin: Asa Gray, *Darwiniana: Essays and Reviews Pertaining to Darwinism*, ed. A. Hunter Dupree (Cambridge, Mass.: Harvard University Press, 1963), p. 16.

28 "[Man] is often obliged . . .": Asa Gray, *Lessons in Botany and Vegetable Physiology* (New York: Ivison, Blakeman, and Taylor, 1876), p. 495.

29 "When a page is written over . . .": *Walk*, p. 376.

30 "Two years ago . . .": "Yosemite Glaciers," Kimes #2; reprinted in *To Yosemite and Beyond*, p. 77.

31 "ice-chiselled and storm-tinted . . .": King, *Mountaineering in the Sierra Nevada*, p. 306.

32 "The ice-sheet of the glacial period . . .": *Studies*, p. 52.

33 "strange brightness . . .": *Studies*, p. 50.

34 "When Nature lifted . . .": *Studies*, p. 72.

35 "more intense delight . . .": *Letters*, p. 1.

36 "monumental fictional contexts . . .": Murray Krieger, *Theory of Criticism: A Tradition and its System* (Baltimore: The Johns Hopkins University Press, 1976), pp. 146–47.

37 "must create forms . . .": Krieger, *Theory of Criticism*, p. 224.

38 "instead of disappearing . . .": *Studies*, p. 77.

39 "smooth rough glacial soils . . .": *Studies*, p. 87.

40 The great green wall: see Elna S. Bakker, *An Island Called California* (Berkeley: University of California Press, 1971), pp. 173–93.

41 "Nature Loves the Number Five": *Letters*, p. 149. "five expressions of the same idea": Louis Agassiz, *Methods of Study in Natural History* (Boston: Tichnor and Fields, 1868), p. 268.

42 "yosemite" as a term: *Studies*, p. 17. Nash's term "wilderness": Nash, pp. 1–7.

43 "Nature manifests her love . . .": *Studies*, p. 40.

44 "The affinities of all the beings . . .": *Darwin: A Norton Critical Edition*, ed. Phillip Appleman, 2d. ed. (New York: Norton, 1979), p. 87.

45 Worster, pp. 159–69.

46 "yet so little understood . . .": *Studies*, p. 18. "In Yosemite there is an evergreen oak . . .": *Studies*, p. 24. "things frail and fleeting . . .": *Yosemite*, p. 5.

47 Coleridge's theory: Samuel Taylor Coleridge, "Shakespeare's Judgment Equal to His Genius," in *Critical Theory Since Plato*, ed. Hazard Adams (New York: Harcourt Brace, 1971), p. 460.

48 "the greatest obstacle . . .": *Studies*, p. 21. "the abundance . . .": *Studies*, p. 31.

49 "When we walk the pathways . . .": *Studies*, p. 47.

50 "Glacial denudation . . .": *Studies*, p. 82.

51 "The winds that sweep . . .": *Studies*, p. 72.

52 "mystics understand the roots . . .": Fritjof Capra, *The Tao of Physics: An Exploration of the Parallels between Modern Physics and Eastern Mysticism* (Boulder, Colo.: Shambhala, 1975), p. 307. "*Contraria Sunt Complementa*": Capra, p. 145.

Chapter 5. STORMY SERMONS

1 "Squirrelville . . .": Badè, 1:270–73. The manuscript is in YNP, File 9189. The letter is written in ink prepared from Sequoia cones. Quoted passages in the first four paragraphs of this section are from the letter.

2 "Destruction is creation": *Studies*, p. 100. "The One is united . . .": "The Hidden Harmony," chapter 7 of Wheelwright, *Heraclitus*.

3 "I *wished* I had not . . .": Badè, 1:20. "save Jesus Christ . . .": *Boyhood & Youth*, p. 203. "It is no use . . .": Badè, 1:21.

4 "deeply interrelated . . .": Phillip Wheelwright, *The Burning Fountain: A Study in Language and Symbolism* (Bloomington: Indiana University Press, 1954), pp. 73–74.

5 "blank fleshly apathy . . .": Badè, 1:220. "overadvertise how satisfying . . .": David Brower, "Publisher's Foreword," Steve Roper, *A Climber's Guide to Yosemite Valley* (San Francisco: Sierra Club Books, 1964), p. 12.

6 "The Valley is full of people . . .": Badè, 1:226. "I can proclaim . . .": Badè, 2:7.

7 "Winter blows the fog . . .": *John of Mountains*, p. 190.

8 "You are a true lover . . .": MP, Box 1, Dec. 16, 1866. "Try your pen . . .": MP, Box 1, March 3, 1872. "Book-making frightens me . . ." and "You tell me . . .": Badè, 2:6–7.

9 "only to entice . . .": Badè, 2:28. "I have seen Montgomery Street . . .": "Shasta in Winter"; Kimes #36.

10 Emerson's friends: see James Bradley Thayer, *A Western Journey with Mr. Emerson* (Boston: Little, Brown, 1884), p. 98. "I felt lonely . . .": *Parks*, pp. 148–49.

11 "better people": Badè, 1:259–60.

12 "telling us most solemnly . . .": Badè, 1:319.

13 "Glorious are these rocks . . .": *Yosemite*, p. 40.

14 "probation and sequestration . . .": Badè, 1:254.

15 "as the John Baptist angel . . .": This letter, held at the Harvard University Library, is printed in Hadley, pp. 436–38. I follow the letter, and quote from it,

in this and the three subsequent paragraphs; quotations from other sources are documented separately.

16 "not in doubt . . ." and another variant of the Yosemite earthquake: "Yosemite in Spring"; Kimes #9; quoted by Wolfe, p. 157.

17 San Francisco earthquake: letter to Margaret Lunam, May 13, 1906; MP, Box 17.

18 "When you transform Nature . . ." and "if philosophers . . .": George Santayana, "The Genteel Tradition in American Philosophy," *Winds of Doctrine: Studies in Contemporary Opinion* (New York: C. Scribner, 1913), pp. 213–14.

19 "Yosemite Valley in Flood"; Kimes #10. Quotations in the two subsequent paragraphs are from this source, pp. 347–50.

20 "a perfect hell . . .": *John of Mountains*, p. 43.

21 "Visions like these . . .": "Yosemite Valley in Flood," p. 350.

22 "it will doubtlessly be remembered . . .": "Flood-Storm in the Sierra," p. 490; Kimes #43.

23 Early drafts of "Flood-Storm in the Sierra" are in MP, Files 28.13 and 30.4.

24 "Don't pity me . . .": Wolfe, p. 179. "True, some goods were destroyed . . .": "Flood-Storm in the Sierra," pp. 494–95.

25 "How terribly downright . . .": "Flood-Storm in the Sierra," p. 494.

26 "I wish to speak a word for Nature . . .": Henry David Thoreau, "Walking," *The Portable Thoreau*, ed. Carl Bode (New York: Viking, 1964), p. 592.

27 "Civilization needs pure wildness . . .": MP, File 30.4. "The West of which I speak . . .": *The Portable Thoreau*, ed. Bode, pp. 609–10.

28 "The rain brought out . . ." through "The world needs the woods . . .": "Flood-Storm in the Sierra," pp. 495–96.

29 "After one has seen pines . . .": "A Wind Storm in the Forests of the Yuba"; Kimes #81. Quotations throughout this section are from that source, pp. 55–59, unless otherwise documented.

30 "Peace I leave with you . . .": John 14.27. "I am the true vine . . .": John 15. 1–5.

31 "We hug the earth . . ." through "above men's heads . . .": *The Portable Thoreau*, ed. Bode, p. 627.

32 "Found in a Storm": with apologies to William Stafford. The essays on Shasta storms: "Shasta in Winter"; Kimes #36. "Snow Storm on Mounta Shasta," in *Harper's*; Kimes #70. "Mount Shasta," in *Picturesque California*, reprinted in *Steep Trails*, pp. 57–81. Quoted passages in this section are from "Snow Storm on Mount Shasta," pp. 521–30, except where otherwise documented.

33 "Vide Rain Storm on Mount Yuba": MP, File 29.2

34 "lying like a squirrel . . .": "Shasta in Winter"; Kimes #36. "But the next spring . . .": *Steep Trails*, p. 67.

35 Muir's writing as too subtle: Wolfe, p. 174.

36 Sleeping out-of-doors: *Walk*, p. 305; YNP, File 9161, p. 57. "Not like my taking the veil . . .": *John of Mountains*, p. 439. "strange dread . . .": *Parks*, p. 147.

37 "felt God's presence . . ." and "fix myself in order to view . . .": Jonathan Edwards, "Personal Narrative" in *The Norton Anthology of American Literature*, ed. Ronald Gottesman et al. (New York: Norton, 1979), vol. 1, p. 210.

Chapter 6. SACRED ANIMALS: ECOLOGICAL CONSCIOUSNESS

1 Standard college ecology text: Eugene P. Odum, *Fundamentals of Ecology*, 3d ed. (Philadelphia: W. B. Saunders, 1971), pp. 3–6, 150. Subversive science: Paul Shepard and Daniel McKinley, eds., *The Subversive Science: Essays Toward an Ecology of Man* (Boston: Houghton Mifflin, 1969), p. 9. New prophet of science: Worster, pp. 343–44. "a radical form of consciousness . . .": Bill Devall, "Ecological Consciousness and Ecological Resisting: Theory and Practicing" (Humboldt State University, 1980). Clothes: "I say beware of all enterprises that require new clothes and not rather a new wearer of clothes," Thoreau, *Walden*, ed. Thomas, p. 15.

2 Merriam: see Worster, pp. 195–98. Communities of life: *John of Mountains*, p. 147. Microclimates: *John of Mountains*, p. 120.

3 Taxonomical notes: *Corwin*, pp. 281–96. Ecological vision in "Flood-Storm in the Sierra": see John Leighly, "John Muir's Image of the West," *Annals of the Association of American Geographers*, vol. 48 (1958), pp. 313–14. Muir's diagram: "Snow Storm on Mount Shasta," p. 522; Kimes #70.

4 "not a shell . . .": Shepard, in Shepard and McKinley, eds., *The Subversive Science*, p. 122.

5 "the dark chilly reasoning . . .": Wolfe, p. 103.

6 "mystery of harmony": *John of Mountains*, pp. 107, 168.

7 "unify and thereby sanctify . . .": Bateson, *Mind and Nature*, p. 19. Pantheism: see William Everson, *Archetype West: The Pacific Coast as a Literary Region* (Berkeley: Oyez Press, 1976); La Chappelle, *Earth Wisdom*; Roderick Nash, "Can We Afford Wilderness," in *Environment, Man, Survival: Grand Canyon Symposium*, ed. L. H. Wallstein et al. (Salt Lake City: University of Utah Press, 1970), pp. 97–111. "a sense sublime . . ." and "rolls through . . .": William Wordsworth, "Lines Composed a Few Miles above Tintern Abbey . . . ," lines 95–103. "The first time . . ." and "circular power . . .": Emerson, "Nature," Selections from Ralph Waldo Emerson, ed. Whicher, pt. 1.

8 "But I *do* love the world": Loren Eiseley, *The Star Thrower* (New York: Times Books, 1978), p. 182.

9 "How little we know . . .": *Walk*, p. 262. "It is my faith . . .": *John of Mountains*, pp. 436–37.

10 "Let us not doubt . . .": Ernest Hemingway, *The Sun Also Rises* (New York: Scribner's, 1926), p. 122. Muir's call for preservation: "God's First Temples. How Shall We Preserve Our Forests?"; Kimes #55.

11 "the expression of love . . .": Eiseley, *The Star Thrower*, p. 182.

12 Melville's *Encantadas:* see Worster, pp. 115–29.

13 "Honorable representatives . . .": *Walk*, pp. 324–25. "Men and other bipeds . . .": *Walk*, p. 356.

14 "Man and other civilized animals . . ." through "in sad measure . . .": *Walk*, p. 313.

15 Thomas Huxley: Worster, p. 178.

16 Muir's library and "Man is fallen . . .": see Hadley, p. 255. "When charmed . . ."

and "don't you think . . .": Herman Melville, *The Confidence Man*, ed. H. Bruce Franklin (1857; repr., New York: Bobbs-Merrill, 1967), p. 267.

17 "Killed a rattlesnake . . .": *John of Mountains*, p. 28. Muir on rattlesnakes: "In the San Gabriel," Kimes #72; "Amongst the Animals of the Yosemite," Kimes #222; "The Snakes of Fresno," Kimes #A6.

18 "When we came across a tarantula . . .": Gifford Pinchot, *Breaking New Ground* (New York: Harcourt Brace, 1947), p. 103. Albert Fall, snake killer: Robert Shankland, *Steve Mather of the National Parks* (New York: Knopf, 1951), p. 219.

19 Emerson's view of Nature: F. O. Matthiessen, *American Renaissance*, pp. 160–61.

20 "[He] informed me . . .": Nathaniel Hawthorne, *The English Notebooks*, ed. Randall Stewart (New York: M.L.A., 1941), p. 433, Nov. 20, 1856. "conceived Nature . . .": Stephen Crane, *The Red Badge of Courage*, ed. Sculley Bradley et al. (1895; repr., New York: Norton, 1976), p. 41.

21 LeConte on God: *Evolution and its Relation to Religious Thought* (New York: D. Appleton, 1888), pp. 279, 285, 313.

22 Muir on evolution: "Three Days with John Muir," *World's Work* (March, 1909), pp. 11355–56.

23 "Man also is surrounded . . .": LeConte, *Evolution and its Relation to Religious Thought*, p. 329.

24 "Resource Conservation and Development": see John R. Rodman, "Theory and Practice in the Environmental Movement: Notes Toward an Ecology of Experience," in *The Search for Absolute Values in a Changing World, Proceedings of the Sixth International Conference on the Unity of the Sciences* (San Francisco, 1977), p. 456; see also George Sessions, "Shallow and Deep Ecology: A Review of the Philosophical Literature," in *Proceedings Earthday X: The Humanities and Ecological Consciousness, April 21–24, 1980* (Denver: University of Denver, 1980). "made of the same dust . . .": *John of Mountains*, p. 82. "Our tidal civilizations . . .": manuscript variant of *John of Mountains*, p. 82, quoted by Gretchen Robertson in "John Muir" (Southern Utah State College, manuscript, n.d.).

25 "struggle for existence": Worster, pp. 35, 143. "survival of the fittest": Richard Hofstadter, *Social Darwinism in American Thought*, rev. ed. (New York: George Braziller, 1959), p. 29.

26 "balanced order . . .": Worster, p. 150. "although tame men . . .": "Wild Sheep of California," p. 359; Kimes #23.

27 "Life seems neither long . . .": *First Summer*, pp. 52–62.

28 "I can't understand . . ." and "A quick electric flame . . .": *First Summer*, pp. 58–59.

29 "tickly acid body . . ." through "how many mouths . . .": *First Summer*, p. 62.

30 "biology as a whole . . ." through "Moments of great catastrophe . . .": Clarence King, "Catastrophe and Evolution," *American Naturalist*, vol. 11, no. 8 (Aug., 1877), pp. 449–70.

31 "diverging from their parents . . .": Worster, pp. 160–61.

32 "the whole subject is too profound . . .": quoted in Bert James Loewenberg, "The Mosaic of Darwinian Thought," in Appleman, ed., *Darwin*, pp. 217–18.

33 Badè, 1:383–84.
34 "an echo . . .": *John of Mountains*, p. 165. "complete compliance . . ." through "our ouzel . . .": "The Humming-Bird of the California Water-Falls," pp. 545–54; Kimes #74. Quotations in the following paragraph are also from Kimes #74.
35 "this bright chip of nature . . .": "The Douglass Squirrel of California", Kimes #83. Quotations in this and the following paragraph are from Kimes #83.
36 "How blessed it would be . . .": *John of Mountains*, p. 166.
37 "constituted the best support . . .": Goetzmann, *Exploration and Empire*, p. 42; see also Hofstadter, *Social Darwinism in American Thought*, p. 19.
38 "Wild Sheep of California"; Kimes #23.
39 "the domestic sheep is expressionless . . .": "Wild Sheep of California," p. 359.
40 "more guileless . . ." through "flowing undulations . . .": "Wild Sheep of California," p. 361. "a lithe figure . . .": Thérèse Yelverton, *Zanita: A Tale of Yosemite* (1872; reprinted in *To Yosemite and Beyond*, pp. 102–5).
41 "modern deification of survival . . .": quoted in Hofstadter, *Social Darwinism in American Thought*, p. 201.
42 "strong self-reliance . . .": "Wild Sheep of California," p. 363. The quotation in the following paragraph is also from this source.
43 "No dogma taught . . .": "Wild Wool"; Kimes #41; reprinted in *Steep Trails*, pp. 3–18.
44 "The entire universe . . ." and "Most of the world . . .": MP, File 28.13.
45 "what English breeders . . .": Charles Darwin, *The Origin of Species* (London: John Murray, 1873), p. 23. "wild species remain . . .": Agassiz, *Methods of Study*, p. 147.
46 "Wildness . . .": "Wild Wool," in *Steep Trails*, p. 18. Swett and George: see Wolfe, p. 181; and John Swett, *Public Education in California* (Chicago: American Book Co., 1911), p. 234. "our greatest product . . .": Henry George, *Our Land and Land Policy: Speeches, Lectures, and Miscellaneous Writings* (New York: Doubleday and Page, 1872).
47 "Moral improvers have calls . . .": *Steep Trails*, p. 3. "divine call . . ." and "old man devotes . . .": MP, File 28.13. "Not content . . ." through "Culture is an orchard apple . . .": *Steep Trails*, pp. 3–4.
48 "in the manufactures of Nature . . ." through "Wild wool is finer . . .": *Steep Trails*, pp. 4–5. Quotations in the rest of this section are from "Wild Wool," in *Steep Trails*, pp. 3–18.
49 "Were it not for the exercise . . .": *Steep Trails*, pp. 12–13.
50 Coyote: MP, File 38.12. "poor persecuted, twice damned Coyote": *Letters*, p. 113.

Chapter 7. SACRED GROVES: MAN IN THE WOODS

1 "Man seems to be . . .": *First Summer*, p. 104. "meat of any kind . . .": *John of Mountains*, p. 97. "Is it not a reproach . . .": Thoreau, *Walden*, ed. Thomas, p. 143.

2 Indians and acorns: "The YoSemite Valley: Another Claim Raised Against It," *Mariposa Gazette* (Aug. 20, 1869); Concentrated food: *Letters*, p. 104.

3 "never killed . . ." and "We little know . . .": *John of Mountains*, p. 199.

4 Hunting: Paul Shepard, *Man in the Landscape: A Historic View of the Aesthetics of Nature* (New York: Knopf, 1967), pp. 211–13; Paul Shepard, *Thinking Animals* (New York: Viking, 1978), p. 13; Gary Snyder, *Earth House Hold*, p. 120; José Ortega y Gassett, *Meditations on Hunting*, trans. Howard B. Wescott (New York: Scribner's, 1972), p. 150. Split in consciousness: Nash, chapters 8 and 9.

5 Muir as Victorian: Everson, *Archetype West*, p. 50. "tower beyond tragedy": George Sessions, "Spinoza and Jeffers," *Inquiry*, vol. 20 (1977), pp. 481–528. "the wild Indian power . . .": *First Summer*, p. 72.

6 Gary Snyder, *The Old Ways* (San Francisco: City Lights, 1977); Carl O. Sauer, *Agricultural Origins and Dispersals* (New York: American Geographical Society, 1952), p. 104.

7 "Perhaps if I knew them better . . .": *First Summer*, p. 304.

8 "miserable degraded savages" through "perfect equality . . .": Charles Darwin, *The Voyage of the Beagle* (New York: P. F. Collier, 1909), pp. 210–34.

9 Jordan: see Starr, p. 312.

10 "the wild wailing came . . ." through "wondered that so much . . .": Badè, 2:22. "panthers": "Modoc Memories"; Kimes #38.

11 "I don't agree with you . . .": MP, Box 2, Jan. 10, 1873.

12 "more experienced and wiser . . .": Thoreau, *Walden*, ed. Thomas, p. 27. Marsh's position: Marsh, "The Study of Nature," pp. 34–35.

13 "to become a gentle shepherd . . .": "By-Ways of Yosemite Travel. Bloody Cañon," pp. 271–72; Kimes #30.

14 "gray, ashy wilderness": "By-Ways . . ." was rewritten for *Picturesque California*, and the passage from the 1888 version to which I refer is in *West of the Rocky Mountains*, pp. 45–46.

15 John G. Mitchell considers, but does not resolve, this problem when he discusses "subsistence hunting" by Alaskan natives in "Yunguaquaquq," in Mitchell, *The Hunt* (New York: Knopf, 1980), pp. 149–204.

16 Aldo Leopold, "The Conservation Ethic," *Journal of Forestry* (Oct., 1933); reprinted in *The Ecological Conscience: Values for Survival*, ed. Robert Disch (Englewood Cliffs, N. J.: Prentice Hall, 1970), p. 46.

17 Leopold and European forestry: Susan Flader, *Thinking Like a Mountain: Aldo Leopold and the Evolution of an Ecological Attitude toward Deer, Wolves, and Forests* (Lincoln, Neb.: University of Nebraska Press, 1978), pp. 139–44. "who are slow to suspect . . .": "Wild Sheep of California," p. 359; Kimes #23.

18 Ecological theory: Worster, pp. 195–212. Ecological conscience: this theory is reviewed by Bill Devall in "Ecological Consciousness and Ecological Resisting"; see also Theodore Roszak, *Person/Planet* (Garden City, N. Y.: Doubleday, 1978), p. 98; and Arne Naess, "Notes on the Methodology of Normative Systems," *Methodology Science*, vol. 10 (1977), pp. 64–79.

19 "all of mine . . .": *John of Mountains*, p. 86.

20 "unlooked for treasure . . .": "The Mountain Lakes of California"; Kimes #85; reprinted in *Mountains*, p. 416.

21 "awakened to the monstrous evils . . .": Wolfe, p. 183.

22 "visit the valley at once . . .": "Summering in the Sierra. A New Yosemite . . ."; Kimes #47.

23 "too good to live long": Asa Gray, *Sequoia and Its History, An Address* (Salem, Mass.: The Salem Press, 1872), pp. 7–8.

24 Competition: see Hofstadter, *Social Darwinism in American Thought*, p. 110.

25 "Will he cut down . . .": *John of Mountains*, p. 215. "The sunset, autumn . . .": Northrop Frye, "Archetypes of Literature," in Frye, *Fables of Identity: Studies in Poetic Mythology* (New York: Harcourt, Brace, and World, 1963), p. 16. Muir's journal, on Sequoia groves: *John of Mountains*, pp. 209–35; quotations in the rest of this section are from these journal pages, unless otherwise noted.

26 "Our crude civilization . . .": *John of Mountains*, p. 234.

27 "God's First Temples. How Shall We Preserve Our Forests?"; Kimes #55.

28 "On the Post-Glacial History of Sequoia Gigantea"; Kimes #63. "Species develop and die . . .": "Summering in the Sierra. A Bit of Forest Study . . ."; Kimes #50.

29 "New Sequoia Forests of California"; Kimes #80. Material and quotations in the following two paragraphs are from this article.

30 Muir was wrong in many details of his analysis of the Sequoia forests' ecology. See Richard Harlesvelt et al., *The Giant Sequoia of the Sierra Nevada* (Washington, D.C.: U.S. Dept. of Interior, National Park Service, 1975). Like Matthes's book on Sierran geology, this study is structured by the themes Muir discussed.

31 Lester Ward's view of Nature: see Hofstadter, *Social Darwinism in American Thought*, p. 74. "The fact is not however a gloomy one . . .": MP, File 28.18.

32 "I have often tried to understand . . .": "New Sequoia Forests of California," p. 824; Kimes #80. Warmer: Worster, p. 199.

33 "unfortunately *man* is in the woods . . .": "On the Post-Glacial History of Sequoia Gigantea," p. 252; Kimes #63.

34 "unless protective measures . . .": "On the Post-Glacial History of Sequoia Gigantea," p. 253; Kimes #63. "Whether our loose-jointed Government . . .": "God's First Temples. How Shall We Preserve Our Forests?"; Kimes #55.

35 "Naturalistic Calvinism": Hofstadter, *Social Darwinism in American Thought*, pp. 10, 51. "chains of duty . . .": *John of Mountains*, p. 235.

36 "what has destroyed all previous civilizations . . .": Henry George, quoted in Hofstadter, *Social Darwinism in American Thought*, p. 112. "the property of men . . .": Hofstadter, p. 62.

Chapter 8. TOURISM AND THE PASTORAL LIFE

1 Sheep flocks: Raymond F. Dasmann, *The Destruction of California* (New York: Macmillan, 1965), p. 68. "The heavy masonry . . .": Badè, 1:319.

2 "Oh, do not ask . . .": T. S. Eliot, "The Love Song of J. Alfred Prufrock," lines 11–12.

3 "Twenty Hill Hollow": Kimes #13. "By-Ways of Yosemite Travel. Bloody Cañon": Kimes #30.

4 "descriptions of California scenery . . .": "Twenty Hill Hollow," p. 81; Kimes #13. Quoted phrases and passages throughout this section are from "Twenty Hill Hollow," pp. 80–86, unless otherwise indicated.

5 "lawful article fit for *outsiders*": *Letters*, p. 112.

6 "Plant gold is fading . . .": *Letters*, p. 112.

7 "Florida is indeed . . .": MP, Box 14, July 19, 1868.

8 "sheep, wild as antelopes . . .": MP, Box 14, July 14, 1868. "the rich mellow light . . .": MP, Box 14, Feb. 27, 1869.

9 "At first I could not guess . . ." through "wipe off all marks . . .": *John of Mountains*, pp. 9–10.

10 The revised encounter with the eagle: "Twenty Hill Hollow," p. 83; Kimes #13. "It may be asked . . .": "Twenty Hill Hollow," p. 86.

11 "The migrating buffalo . . .": Thoreau, *Walden*, ed. Thomas, p. 214.

12 "industrialized version of the pastoral ideal": Leo Marx, *The Machine in the Garden: Technology and the Pastoral Ideal in America* (New York: Oxford University Press, 1964), pp. 220–22.

13 Man's impact on Yosemite's flora: Robert P. Gibbens and Harold F. Heady, *The Influence of Modern Man on the Vegetation of Yosemite Valley* (n.p.: University of California Division of Agricultural Sciences Publication, 1964). "climax": Sauer, *Agricultural Origins and Dispersals*, p. 15.

14 "lovers of clean mountain wildness . . .": "By-Ways of Yosemite Travel: Bloody Cañon," p. 273; Kimes #30. Quotations throughout this section are from "By-Ways . . . ," unless otherwise documented.

15 "The influences of pure nature . . .": "The Glacier Meadows of the Sierra," p. 480; Kimes #87. "the artist must employ . . .": Ralph Waldo Emerson, "Art," in *Essays, First Series*, vol. 2 (Boston and New York: Houghton Mifflin, 1883), p. 328.

16 "To depict America . . .": Marx, *The Machine in the Garden*, p. 43.

17 "characteristic processes . . .": "Salmon Breeding. . . ."; Kimes #31. "All are more or less sick . . .": *John of Mountains*, p. 191. "those strangely complicated filths . . .": "Salmon Breeding"; Kimes #31.

18 "I think he would pine . . .": quoted in Wolfe, p. 135.

19 "Of all the overworked and defrauded toilers . . .": "Shasta Bees . . ."; Kimes #40.

20 The Olmsted report, originally written in 1865: F. L. Olmsted, "The Yosemite Valley and the Mariposa Big Tree Grove," with an introduction by Laura Wood Roper, *Landscape Architecture*, vol. 43 (Oct., 1952), pp. 12–25. Garland on farmers: see Henry Nash Smith, *Virgin Land* (Cambridge, Mass.: Harvard University Press, 1950), p. 194.

21 "life is so profoundly in transaction . . .": Shepard, *Man in the Landscape*, p. 53.

22 "We must not dwell . . .": Badè, 1:376–77.

23 "slaves, duty bound . . ." and "Ho weary town worker . . .": "Summering in

the Sierra. John Muir Shakes the Dust of the Town from his Feet . . ."; Kimes #56. The shake maker: *Parks*, pp. 321–22.

24 "No matter into what depths . . .": *John of Mountains*, p. 353.

25 "Come to Yosemite . . .": "Summering in the Sierra. John Muir discourses of Sierra Forests . . ."; Kimes #46.

26 "Many a poor, defrauded town dweller . . .": "Summering in the Sierra. A New Yosemite—the King's River Valley . . ."; Kimes #47.

27 "as translucent as Tahoe . . .": "Summering in the Sierra. John Muir's Description of a Wonderful Region . . ."; Kimes #49. "King of them all": "Tahoe in Winter . . ."; Kimes #75. "most singular and beautiful . . .": "Pyramid Lake"; Kimes #77. "as accessible as any watering place . . .": "Notes from Utah"; Kimes #67.

28 "Laplands and Labradors . . .": "Summering in the Sierra. John Muir's Description of a Wonderful Region . . ."; Kimes #49. "Not quite 33 per cent . . ." through "There is too much Niagara . . .": "Yosemite in June"; this article is not listed in Kimes, but is in MP, File 29.13, June, 1880.

29 "The regular tourist . . .": "Summering in the Sierra. 'The Season' at the Yosemite Valley . . ."; Kimes #59.

30 "I would advise . . .": "Summering in the Sierra. John Muir, the Naturalist, Tells us Something . . ."; Kimes #44. "wild life . . ." through "speedily becoming . . .": "Notes from Shasta"; Kimes #73. "dabble away . . .": "In the San Gabriel"; Kimes #72.

31 "As far as the falls are concerned . . .": "Summering in the Sierra. John Muir, the Naturalist, Tells us something . . ."; Kimes #44. "The waters of the new valley . . .": "Summering in the Sierra. A New Yosemite—the King's River Valley . . ."; Kimes #47. "no special geological significance": "Mount Whitney"; Kimes #48.

32 "Mass-saying . . .": "Summering in the Sierra. John Muir Visits One of the Famous Mountain Caves . . ."; Kimes #58.

33 "as well say a man is conquered . . .": "South Dome . . ."; Kimes #54.

34 "like a child . . ." through "I'm the first . . .": "Mount Whitney": Kimes #48. Muir's journal, when he guided John Swett: *John of Mountains*, p. 203.

35 "When one comes out of the woods . . .": "Summering in the Sierra. Tulare Levels . . ."; Kimes #53.

36 "[There] is a block of land . . ." through "grander miracles . . .": "Semi-Tropical California"; Kimes #71. "in the search the seekers . . .": "Nevada's Dead Towns"; Kimes #86.

37 "How sad the tones . . .": "Summering in the Sierra. A Bit of Forest Study . . ."; Kimes #50. "monuments of fraud . . .": "Nevada's Dead Towns": Kimes #86. "In spite of all . . ." through "wildcat farming . . .": Kimes #50; "reached old deathbeds . . .": Kimes #86.

38 "perhaps greater than the entire wheat crop . . .": "Nevada Forests . . ."; Kimes #79. The Homestead Act: see Smith, *Virgin Land*, p. 191.

39 "If tillers of the soil . . .": "Nevada Farms . . ."; Kimes #78. "strange, dark

man . . ." through "All this prospective affluence . . .": "In the San Gabriel";
    Kimes #72.
40 "I suppose nothing less . . .": *Letters,* p. 193, April 9, 1879.
41 "California Agriculture": MP, File 37.3.
42 ". . . fortunately farming on so collossal a scale . . .": "California Agriculture,"
    p. 9; MP, File 37.3.
43 "The agrarian utopia . . .": Smith, *Virgin Land,* p. 191.
44 "Bee-Pastures of California: In Two Parts: I"; Kimes #145. "Bee-Pastures of Cali-
    fornia: In Two Parts: II"; Kimes #146. Quotations throughout this section are
    from this two-part essay, unless otherwise documented.
45 "exerts a more degrading influence . . .": "City of the Saints"; Kimes #65.
46 "last efforts were on the preservation . . .": *Letters,* p. 192. Elna S. Bakker, "Red
    Winged Blackbird," in *An Island Called California,* pp. 134–46; "Frank C.
    Craighead, Jr., *Track of the Grizzly* (San Francisco: Sierra Club Books, 1979).
47 "exactly delicious . . .": "Shasta Bees. A Honeyful Region . . ."; Kimes #40.
48 The perennial glory of the Central Valley: Dasmann, "The Prairies that Van-
    ished," *The Destruction of California,* pp. 58–76.
49 "In short, notwithstanding . . .": *Mountains,* p. 381.
50 "was praised as a piece of sentiment": MP, Box 2, Feb. 19, 1879.
51 "hardy and virtuous yeomen . . .": Smith, *Virgin Land,* pp. 169–73.
52 Legislative efforts in 1881: Wolfe, pp. 227–28. "The love of Nature among Cali-
    fornians . . .": Badè, 2:237.

Chapter 9. THE GENTEEL WILDERNESS

 1 Samuel Taylor Coleridge, "On the Principles of Genial Criticism Concerning
    the Fine Arts," in *Criticism: The Major Texts,* ed. Walter Jackson Bate (New
    York: Harcourt Brace, 1952).
 2 "with the conceit and lofty importance . . .": Badè, 1:377. "The wonder is . . .":
    Wolfe, p. 150.
 3 The new humanism: see Norman Foerster, *American Criticism* (1928; repr.,
    New York: Russell & Russell, 1962), pp. 236–41.
 4 *Picturesque America, or the Land we Live in,* ed. William Cullen Bryant, 2
    vols. (New York: D. Appleton, 1872).
 5 *Gentle Wilderness, the Sierra Nevada: Text from John Muir: Photographs
    by Richard Kauffman,* ed. David Brower (San Francisco: Sierra Club Books,
    1964).
 6 "Photography implies . . .": Susan Sontag, *On Photography,* p. 21.
 7 "wilderness as opportunity and idea": Wallace Stegner, "Coda: Wilderness Let-
    ter," in Stegner, *The Sound of Mountain Water* (New York: E. P. Dutton, 1980),
    pp. 145–53. "Snow Banners of the California Alps," published in *Harper's*; Kimes
    #68.
 8 "in the strictest sense of the word": "Snow Banners of the California Alps,"

p. 163; Kimes #68. Materials and quotations in this and the following three paragraphs are from "Snow Banners . . ." pp. 162–64; Kimes #68.

9 "a deep chasm drawn between . . .": "In the Heart of the California Alps," p. 349; Kimes #100. "The lessons and enjoyments . . .": "In the Heart of the California Alps," p. 345.

10 The oak tree: *Studies*, p. 24. The elm tree: "The Mountain Lakes of California," p. 412; Kimes #85. "when, like a young eye . . .": "The Mountain Lakes of California," p. 413.

11 "everything about you . . .": "The Glacier Meadows of the Sierra," p. 483; Kimes #87.

12 "And I know something . . .": Badè, 1:378.

13 Sierran conifers: "Coniferous Forests of the Sierra Nevada. I"; Kimes #124; "Coniferous Forests of the Sierra Nevada. II"; Kimes #127; I follow and quote from the slightly expanded and combined version of the two essays in chapter 8, "The Forests," in *Mountains*. "gone far enough . . .": *Mountains*, p. 140.

14 "How a tree book can be exhaustive . . .": *Letters*, p. 191, Apr. 9, 1879.

15 "the noblest pine yet discovered" through "No two are alike . . ." *Mountains*, pp. 152–62. The juniper through "Its fine color and odd picturesqueness . . .": *Mountains*, pp. 204–07.

16 "It is the most staid . . .": *West*, p. 93. "proper and exact . . .": "The Treasures of Yosemite," p. 495; Kimes #181.

17 "It is not nearly so grand . . .": *West*, pp. 91–92.

18 "What a bright appreciative traveller . . .": MP, Box 16, Oct. 22, 1887.

19 "To sketch picturesque bits . . .": *Picturesque California*, p. 193.

20 "for the elements . . ." through "the various aspects . . .": *Picturesque America*, pp. iii–iv.

21 Tourism in *Picturesque California*: pp. 77, 204, 488.

22 "During the last few centuries . . .": *West*, p. 490–91.

23 "hairy harvests": *West*, p. 432. "hacking, burning . . ." and "grawing like beavers . . .": *West*, p. 446. "love of the freeholder . . .": *West*, p. 192.

24 "a striking . . ." through "There is nothing in California . . .": *West*, pp. 415–18.

25 "classical and heroic . . .": quoted in Starr, pp. 121–22.

26 "declare to man . . ." and "The railroads have enough . . .": *Picturesque California*, p. 432.

27 "The National Park as a Camping Place": "The Yellowstone Park"; Kimes # 165. Published in the *San Francisco Bulletin* as one of a series of letters from Muir.

28 "We almost thought he was Jesus Christ . . .": Wolfe, p. 154.

29 "as well whitewash . . .": *West*, p. 93. M.C.A., the Park concessionaire, painted cliffs in the 1970s while filming a television series on Yosemite rangers.

30 "He was not a 'dreamer' . . .": *Remembered Yesterdays*, p. 316.

31 "To foster concern . . .": untitled Yosemite Institute brochure (Yosemite National Park, Calif.: Yosemite Institute, n.d.), p. 4.

32 "power of understatement": "The Creation of Yosemite National Park. Letters of John Muir to Robert Underwood Johnson," SCB, vol. 29, no. 5 (Oct., 1944), p. 50.

33 "I can't make my way . . .": *Remembered Yesterdays*, pp. 279–80.

34 "getting into a sort of second youth . . .": Badè, 2:235–36, June 3, 1889.

35 "the wildest region . . ." through "The detritus of the wall . . .": *Remembered Yesterdays*, pp. 283–84.

36 "'No,' said Muir, 'we do not . . .'": *Remembered Yesterdays*, p. 287.

37 The three essays: "The Treasures of Yosemite": Kimes # 181; "Features of the Proposed Yosemite Park": Kimes #182; and "A Rival of Yosemite. The Cañon of the South Fork of King's River, California": Kimes #185.

38 "Any one accustomed to walk . . .": "Features of the Proposed Yosemite Park," p. 662; Kimes #182.

39 "Heaven knows . . .": *John of Mountains*, p. 86. "Then it seemed to me . . .": "The Treasures of Yosemite," p. 483; Kimes # 181.

40 "peacefully gliding . . .": "The Treasures of Yosemite," p. 485; Kimes #181. Materials and quotations in this section are from "The Treasures of Yosemite," pp. 483–500, unless otherwise indicated.

41 The definitive history on Yosemite politics is Jones, *John Muir and the Sierra Club*.

42 Muir as "publicizer": see Nash, pp. 122–40.

43 "Most people who visit Yosemite . . .": "Features of the Proposed Yosemite Park," pp. 663–64; Kimes #182.

44 "The Tuolumne Cañon is so closely related . . .": Badè, 2:244.

45 "The members had never heard . . .": *Remembered Yesterdays*, p. 228.

46 "I think you might call . . .": MP, Box 3, May 1, 1891.

47 Johnson pressures Muir: MP, Box 3, July 22, 1891. "my stock of cliff and cascade adjectives . . .": JP, July 14, 1891; quoted in Hadley, p. 547. "I fear you will find . . .": JP, Aug. 15, 1891, quoted in Hadley, p. 549.

48 "this new yosemite is longer and deeper . . .": "A Rival of Yosemite," p. 77; Kimes #185. Quotations through the rest of this section are from "A Rival of Yosemite," pp. 77–97, unless otherwise indicated; several landmark passages are also documented separately.

49 "the highest, most elaborately sculptured . . ." through "It is upward of a mile in height . . .": "A Rival of Yosemite," p. 82; Kimes #185.

50 "At first sight it would seem . . .": "A Rival of Yosemite," p. 88; Kimes #185. "favorable consideration . . .": Badè, 2:254.

51 "notwithstanding its tremendous rockiness . . .": "A Rival of Yosemite," p. 95; Kimes #185.

52 "But if instead of crossing . . .": "A Rival of Yosemite," p. 79; Kimes #185.

Chapter 10. FOREST RESERVES

1 "it was natural that each of these men . . .": John Ise, *Our National Park Policy: A Critical History* (Baltimore: The Johns Hopkins Press, 1961), p. 323. Biographies: Shankland, *Steve Mather of the National Parks*; Donald Swain, *Wilderness Defender: Horace M. Albright and Conservation* (Chicago: Univer-

sity of Chicago Press, 1970); Shirley Sargent, *Theodore Parker Lukens: Father of Forestry* (Los Angeles: Dawson's Book Shop, 1969).

2 Books not previously noted about conservation in the 1890s and early 1900s: Hans Huth, *Nature and the American: Three Centuries of Changing Attitudes* (Berkeley: University of California Press, 1957); Elmo Richardson, *The Politics of Conservation; Crusades and Controversies, 1897–1913* (Berkeley: University of California Press, 1962); Joseph L. Sax, *Mountains Without Handrails: Reflections on the National Parks* (Ann Arbor: University of Michigan Press, 1980); Joseph M. Petulla, *American Environmental History: The Exploitation and Conservation of Natural Resources* (San Francisco: Boyd and Fraser, 1977). These books provide more complete bibliographies.

3 Muir giving Johnson credit for the idea of Yosemite National Park: JP, Dec. 24, 1901; Hadley, p. 642.

4 "defense association": Jones, pp. 7–11.

5 "progressives": see George E. Mowry, "What Manner of Men: The Progressive Mind," chapter 4 of Mowry, *The California Progressives* (Berkeley: University of California Press, 1951).

6 "To explore, enjoy, and render accessible . . .": Jones, p. 173. "secular religion": Sax, *Mountains Withou Handrails*, p. 2.

7 "preservationists": Sax, *Mountains Without Handrails*, p. 54; Donald Worster, "The Protestant Roots of American Environmentalism" (University of Hawaii, Manoa, manuscript, n.d.). "we gave up our belief . . .": Roderick Nash, "Can We Afford Wilderness," in *Environment, Man, Survival: Grand Canyon Symposium*, ed. L. H. Wallstein et al. p. 102. "It follows that to obtain . . .": Nash, p. 104.

8 "The primary function of the national forests . . .": Horace McFarland, "Are National Parks Worthwhile?" SCB, vol. 8, no. 3 (Jan., 1912), p. 237.

9 In *Mountains Without Handrails*, p. 48, Sax gives the profile of a typical wilderness user.

10 The early outline called "The California Alps": MP, File 38.4. "write a hard geological book": JP, Nov. 7, 1894; Hadley, p. 580. "take what you want . . .": JP, Oct. 24, 1891; Hadley, p. 550. "charming collection": MP, Box 4, July 18, 1894. "You will say . . .": MP, Box 16.

11 "In it I have ventured . . .": JP, April 3, 1894; Hadley, p. 573. Muir's diction in *Mountains*: Wolfe, p. 267.

12 "the three great gorges . . .": MP, Box 4, June 30, 1894.

13 "Johnson's view of the Forestry Commission: *Remembered Yesterdays*, pp. 296–300.

14 The Forest Reserve Act of 1891: see Ise, *Our National Park Policy*, p. 48.

15 "Muir's journey in 1895: Sargent, *Theodore Parker Lukens*, pp. 23–45; *John of Mountains*, pp. 342–48. Despair about the Valley: Badè, 2:294. "The preservation of specimen sections . . .": "The National Parks and Forest Reservations," speech by John Muir in *Proceedings of the Sierra Club*, SCB, vol. 1, no. 7 (Jan., 1896), p. 276; Kimes #203 (hereafter cited as *Proceedings*). "As I have urged over and over . . .": Badè, 2:244, May 8, 1890.

16 Wolfe, pp. 272–73.

17 "found botany a chaos . . .": "Linnaeus"; Kimes #201.

18 "Had the bright lines . . .": "Sargent's Silva," p. 20; Kimes #248.

19 "The battle we have fought . . .": *Proceedings*, p. 276. "The very first forest reserve . . .": JP, Dec. 6, 1894; Hadley, p. 583.

20 "And it always is refreshing . . .": *Proceedings*, p. 275. See also JP, Oct. 29, 1894; Hadley, p. 577.

21 "Republicans and Democrats . . .": Letter to Johnson, March 4, 1890, in "The Creation of Yosemite National Park, Letters . . ."; Kimes #393.

22 Railroads: see Petulla, *American Environmental History*, p. 102, 182.

23 "But it is impossible . . .": Muir letter published as part of "A Plan to Save the Forests," *Century*, Feb., 1895; Kimes #198.

24 "Leopold in Germany: Flader, *Thinking Like a Mountain*, pp. 30–31. "The Land Ethic": Aldo Leopold, *A Sand County Almanac and Sketches Here and There* (New York: Oxford University Press, 1949), pp. 224–25.

25 Muir, the Commission, and grazing: Laurence Rakestraw, "Sheep Grazing in the Cascade Range: John Minto *vs.* John Muir," *Pacific Historical Review*, vol. 27, no. 4 (Nov., 1958), pp. 375–76; Pinchot, *Breaking New Ground*, p. 179; Hays, p. 48.

26 "good forest fellows . . .": JP, July 5, 1896; Hadley, p. 599.

27 "a most fascinating talker": Pinchot, *Breaking New Ground*, pp. 100, 101, 171.

28 "I'm sorry to see . . .": JP, Sept. 3, 1910; Hadley, p. 706. Living accommodations: *John of Mountains*, pp. 356–64.

29 The McCrae–Pettigrew Bill: *Conservation in the United States: A Documentary History*, 2 vols., ed. Frank E. Smith (New York: Chelsea House, 1971), pp. 763–66; Pinchot's response: *Breaking New Ground*, p. 116.

30 The three articles: "The National Parks and Forest Reservations," *Harper's*, Kimes #208; "The American Forests," *Atlantic*, Kimes #209; and "Wild Parks and Forest Reservations of the West," *Atlantic*, Kimes #217. The *Atlantic* articles became the first and last chapters of *Our National Parks*, cited as *Parks*.

31 Merriam's appointment by Roosevelt: Hays, p. 189.

32 William Kent and John Muir: see Nash, p. 173.

33 "should be reserved . . .": "The National Parks and Forest Reservations," p. 567; Kimes #208.

34 "Gold stings . . ." through "All of our precious mountains . . .": "The National Parks and Forest Reservations," pp. 566–67; Kimes #208.

35 "Muir, Johnson, and their colleagues . . .": Nash, p. 181.

36 "Those Western Corporations . . .": JP, June 18, 1897; Hadley, p. 610.

37 "an invading horde of destroyers": *Parks*, p. 363. Quoted passages in the rest of this section are from "The American Forests," in *Parks*, pp. 357–93, unless otherwise indicated.

38 Timber and Stone Act: *Conservation in the United States*: ed. Smith, pp. 602–09.

Chapter 11. NATIONAL PARKS

1 Muir's trip in 1895: Sargent, *Theodore Parker Lukens*, pp. 27–30; *John of Mountains*, pp. 342–48.

2 "He said fishing wasted . . .": Pinchot, *Breaking New Ground*, pp. 100–101. "boyishness of killing things": *Remembered Yesterdays*, p. 388.

3 "Few are altogether deaf . . .": *Proceedings*, p. 282. "inciting people to come . . ." through "Even the scenery habit . . .": *Parks*, pp. 3–4.

4 "Nothing can be done well . . .": *Parks*, p. 63. Quotations through the rest of this section are from *Parks*, pp. 63, 38, 190.

5 Toll roads: Sargent, *Theodore Parker Lukens*, p. 28.

6 "up the South Fork . . .": "A Rival of the Yosemite," p. 97; Kimes #185. "lead many a lover of wildness . . .": *Parks*, p. 15. "in the presence of such stupendous scenery . . .": "The Grand Cañon of the Colorado"; Kimes #245; reprinted in *Steep Trails*, pp. 347–48.

7 Muir and autos: Holway Jones, "John Muir, the Sierra Club, and the Formulation of the Wilderness Concept," *The Pacific Historian*, vol. 25, no. 2 (Summer 1981), pp. 73–75. Badè, 2:378–80.

8 Mission '66: Conrad Wirth, "Working with the Conservationists: Reflections of a National Park Service Director," *Journal of Forest History*, vol. 24, (July, 1980), p. 155. "a rather wide range . . .": Sax, *Mountains Without Handrails*, p. 100. "people want illusions . . .": Sax, p. 99.

9 "a great deal of blasting . . .": SCB, vol. 6, no. 4 (Jan., 1908), p. 262.

10 Jones's apology: Jones, pp. 150–169. National Parks as islands: F. Fraser Darling, "The Park Idea and Ecological Reality," *National Parks Magazine* (May, 1969), pp. 21–24.

11 Mather's mountain trip: see Shankland, *Steve Mather of the National Parks*, pp. 68–74; and Swain, *Wilderness Defender*, pp. 46–52.

12 Muir and the outings program: Farquhar, *History of the Sierra Nevada*, p. 226.

13 "An excursion of this sort . . .": SCB, vol. 3, no. 3 (Feb., 1901), p. 250. "The first trip should combine . . .": SCB, vol. 3, no. 3 (Feb., 1901), p. 251. The 1901 outing: E. T. Parsons, "The Sierra Club Outing to Tuolumne Meadows," SCB, vol. 4, no. 1 (Jan., 1902), p. 19.

14 "What I enjoy most . . .": *Harriman*, p. 36.

15 The Sierra Club as communal organization: see Starr, pp. 418, 249. I disagree with Starr's analysis.

16 Swett and George: Wolfe, p. 183. Powell in Washington: Wallace Stegner, *Beyond the Hundredth Meridian: John Wesley Powell and the Second Opening of the West* (Boston: Houghton Mifflin, 1953), pp. 116–18. "never for a moment thought . . .": Badè, 2:292.

17 "far from the right man . . .": Theodore Lukens Papers, L 14-6, Feb. 14, 1897, Huntington Library.

18 Bill Devall, "John Muir as Deep Ecologist" (Paper presented at "The World of John Muir," a conference at the University of the Pacific, Stockton, Calif.,

Nov. 15, 1980). "If the sage would guide the people . . .": Lao Tsu, *Tao Te Ching*, trans. Gia-Fu Feng (New York: Random House-Vintage, 1972), #66.

19 "would not allow the rest . . .": John Burroughs, *Harriman Alaska Expedition* (New York: Doubleday, Page, 1901), vol. 1, p. 18. "some difficulty was encountered . . .": "Charlie Leidig's Report of President Roosevelt's Visit in May, 1903," YNP, Box 921, mu. 2. Muir and Taft: Wolfe, pp. 194, 323. The Sargent letter: William F. Kimes, "With Theodore Roosevelt and John Muir in Yosemite," YNP, File #979.447Y-40.

20 George Dyson: see Kenneth Brower, *The Starship and the Canoe* (New York: Holt, Rinehart and Winston, 1978), p. 30.

21 "directed social organization" and "traditional American Virtues": see Hays, p. 142.

22 "the more clubs the better": Jones, p. 63.

23 "These Californians now sleeping . . .": Badè, 2:238. "The Sierra Club . . .": quoted in Jones, p. 57. "I never believed . . .": JP, June 18, 1895; Hadley, p. 590.

24 "Our Sierra Club altogether refuses . . .": JP, Feb. 19, 1893; quoted in Jones, p. 58. "I am trying . . .": JP, Jan. 7, 1897; Hadley, pp. 601–02.

25 Recession of the Valley: Jones, pp. 64–65.

26 Herrin's influence: Jones, pp. 71–72. "Now, ho! . . ." and "I am now an experienced lobbyist . . .": Badè, 2:356.

27 "efficient maximum development": Hays, p. 69. "victory for the development point of view . . .": Hays, p. 191.

28 "What a glorious chance . . .": JP, March 23, 1905; Hadley, p. 660.

29 "Finally let us remember . . .": quoted in Richardson, p. 125.

30 "interfere with the development . . .": Roosevelt to Muir, Sept. 6, 1907, quoted in Richardson, p. 44. "capitalists, engineers . . .": Badè, 2:417. "not the real Roosevelt": Wolfe, p. 329.

31 "the role it played . . .": Hays, p. 265. "the national Government . . .": Roosevelt, quoted in Hays, p. 130. Hamiltonian means: Hays, pp. 130, 270.

32 Hetch Hetchy as a political struggle: Elmo Richardson, "The Struggle for the Valley: California's Hetch Hetchy Controversy, 1905–1913," *California Historical Society Quarterly*, vol. 38, no. 3 (Sept., 1959), pp. 249–58.

33 "this was one of the main turning points . . .": Everson, *Archetype West*, p. 53. "relegate all such archaic questions . . .": Charles McDonald to the American Society of Civil Engineers, 1908, quoted in Hays, p. 127.

34 Sax, *Mountains Without Handrails*, p. 12.

35 "Dam Hetch Hetchy! . . .": *Yosemite*, p. 282.

36 "to the farmers of Owens Valley . . .": Richard Coke Wood, *The Owens Valley and the Los Angeles Water Controversy: Owens Valley as I Knew It*, Pacific Center for Western Studies, Monograph no. 1 (Stockton, Calif.: University of the Pacific, 1973), p. 3; see also Page Stegner, "Los Angeles Water Wars: Bleeding the Owens Valley Dry," *Harper's*, vol. 262, no. 1570 (March, 1981). Stegner points out that Muir's ally, E. H. Harriman, was among those who profited from the Owens Valley water scheme.

37 "preserve the fundamental pattern . . .": Mowry, *The California Progressives,* p. 102.
38 "Rise From the Ashes . . .": *San Francisco Chronicle,* quoted in Starr, p. 293.
39 "monopolizing San Francisco Capitalists . . .": "Let Everyone Help to Save the Famous Hetch-Hetchy Valley and Stop the Commercial Destruction Which Threatens Our National Park. To the American Public," p. 17; Kimes #287. "mostly by despoiling gain-seekers . . .": "Hetch-Hetchy—The Tuolumne Yosemite," p. 6; Kimes #275.
40 "gone capitalistic": Wolfe, p. 322. "No enterprise . . ." through "damming the Colorado . . .": *Harriman,* pp. 32–36.
41 "while the Yosemite National Park . . .": quoted from the *Outlook* (Jan. 30, 1909) in "Let Everyone Help to Save the Famous Hetch-Hetchy Valley . . .," p. 1; Kimes #287. "at this stage of the game . . .": Pinchot, at the Governor's Conference in 1908, quoted in Hay, pp. 194–95.
42 "the commercial invasion . . .": "The Hetch-Hetchy Valley: A National Question," p. 269; Kimes #289.
43 Invasion of parks during the World Wars: Swain, *Wilderness Defender,* pp. 74–75; Sax, *Mountains Without Handrails,* pp. 64–66.
44 "A certain class of citizens . . .": this editorial is reproduced by Roy W. Taylor, *Hetch Hetchy: The Story of San Francisco's Struggle to Provide a Water Supply for her Future Needs* (San Francisco: Ricardo J. Orozco, 1926), p. 36. The *Examiner's* attitude is echoed by James Watt, President Reagan's Secretary of the Interior; see Ron Wolf, "New Voice in the Wilderness: James Watt," *Rocky Mountain Magazine,* vol. 3, no. 2 (March/April, 1981), pp. 29–34.
45 "Fortunately wrong cannot last . . .": Badè, 2:386, Jan. 4, 1914.
46 Raker and Kent: Swain, *Wilderness Defender.,* pp. 56–60. "the conscience of the whole country . . .": JP, Jan. 1, 1914; Hadley, p. 744.

Chapter 12. THE END AND THE BEGINNING

1 "return to primitive conditions . . .": Frederick Jackson Turner, "The Significance of the Frontier in American History," in *Frontier and Section: Selected Essays of Frederick Jackson Turner,* ed. Ray Billington (1894; repr., Englewood Cliffs, N.J.: Prentice Hall, 1961), p. 39. "Who, at the end, knows more . . .": Barry Lopez, *Of Wolves and Men* (New York: Charles Scribner's Sons, 1978), p. 86.
2 Ishi: Theodora Kroeber, *Ishi in Two Worlds: A Biography of the Last Wild Indian in North America* (Berkeley: University of California Press, 1961).
3 "thread of biography . . .": MP, Box 6, March 9, 1899. "California tree and shrub . . ." through "such a book . . .": Badè, 2:341–42.
4 *Stickeen* and "Adventures with a Dog and a Glacier": see JP, Dec. 6, 1897; Hadley, p. 622. "be all nature—animated nature": JP, Nov. 16, 1899; Hadley, p. 635.
5 "the clearest way . . .": *Wilderness World of John Muir,* ed. Teale, p. 312.

6 Muir's essays in textbooks: Kimes #152, #153, #154, #155. "our poor earth bound companions . . .": MP, Box 17, letter to Mrs. Hooker, June 9, 1909; letter to Mrs. Hanna, May 20, 1910.

7 "walking in wild places . . ." and "sees most . . .": "A New Top Notch for the Sons of Daniel Boone"; Kimes #257, in MP, Box 16. "hardihood, resolution . . .": Nash, p. 151.

8 "a mother field mouse . . .": *Boyhood & Youth*, p. 4. "wee, hairy, sleekit beastie": *Stickeen*, p. 59. "almost any wild animal . . .": *Boyhood & Youth*, p. 149. "imprisoned soarer . . .": *Boyhood & Youth*, p. 40.

9 "Pelican Bay Manuscript": MP, Box 31. "a sort of foundation . . .": *Harriman*, pp. 22–24. Juxtaposed incidents: see Herbert Smith, *John Muir*, Twayne's United States Authors series (New Haven, Conn.: College and University Press, 1965), p. 24. The four sections of *Boyhood & Youth*, in *Atlantic*: Kimes #311, #312, #313, #314.

10 Muir's view of *Boyhood & Youth*, as a children's book: MP, Box 18, letter to Florence Merriam Bailey, March 27, 1913.

11 "In a historical sense . . .": Lopez, *Of Wolves and Men*, p. 138.

12 "cold as a glacier . . .": *Stickeen*, p. 15. Quotations throughout this section are from *Stickeen*, pp. 13–78, unless otherwise indicated.

13 "before the whites came . . .": *Alaska*, p. 285.

14 Tyndall and *Stickeen*: the flyleaves of Muir's copy of *Hours of Exercise in the Alps* contain notes on step-cutting and notes which refer to the little dog; in MP (no file or box no.).

15 "a self appointed inspector . . .": MP, File 42.71.

16 "was in a mood to accept work . . .": *First Summer*, p. 4. Quotations throughout this section are from *First Summer*, pp. 4–51, unless otherwise indicated. Certain landmark passages from within these pages are also separately documented. "we never know . . .": *First Summer*, p. 331.

17 "On no virgin landscape . . .": MP, File 19.1, pp. 89–90; this is a recopied and perhaps revised version of Muir's 1869 journal.

18 "For, though stimulated at times . . .": *First Summer*, p. 30.

19 "Oh, they're only d——d big brakes": *First Summer*, p. 55. "what is Yosemite . . ." through "You can't humbug me . . .": *First Summer*, pp. 197–98.

20 "He says that since the boss has failed . . .": *First Summer*, p. 100.

21 Gastric distress: MP, File 19.1, p. 123. "a few days' saunter . . .": *First Summer*, p. 103.

22 "man alone . . .": *First Summer*, p. 126. "Our education has been sadly neglected . . .": *First Summer*, p. 106. "not a whit more natural . . .": *First Summer*, p. 304.

23 "forget themselves and become devout": *First Summer*, p. 138. Quotations throughout this section are from *First Summer*, pp. 238–57, unless otherwise indicated. Landmark passages from *First Summer* are also indicated by separate documentation.

24 "mysterious things": in autobiographical notes, MP, Box 31.

25 "bound by clocks . . .": *First Summer*, p. 250. "little influenced by its novel grandeur . . .": *First Summer*, p. 255. Butler's influence on Muir: see Hadley, pp. 109–13.

26 "the natural and common . . ." and "the whole wilderness . . .": *First Summer*, p. 256. "wherever we go in the mountains . . .": *First Summer*, p. 251.

27 "light out . . .": Samuel Clemens, *Adventures of Huckleberry Finn*, ed. Scully Bradley (1885; repr., New York: W. W. Norton, 1961), p. 226.

28 "good practical sort of immortality": *First Summer*, p. 52. "vast, calm . . .": *First Summer*, p. 82. "heart of the snowy . . ." through "every crystal, every flower . . .": *First Summer*, pp. 170–205. Quotations throughout this section are from *First Summer*, unless otherwise indicated. Significant phrases and passages from *First Summer* are also indicated by separate documentation.

29 Entering Tuolumne Meadows alone: *First Summer*, pp. 265–324.

30 "another version of the snowy Sierra": *First Summer*, pp. 177. "drawing earth and sky together": *First Summer*, p. 326. The ascent of Cathedral Peak: *First Summer*, pp. 326–341. "no feature . . .": *First Summer*, p. 336.

31 Muir's letter to Daniel Muir: H, FAC 625 (11), Sept. 22, 1869. "In our best times . . .": *First Summer*, p. 336.

32 "Winter and summer . . .": *Mountains*, p. 59. "How delightful it is . . .": *First Summer*, p. 338.

33 "The charms of these mountains . . .": *First Summer*, p. 347.

Index

dience, 229; in "Bee-Pastures," 231; moderation, 235, 240–43; for Yosemite, 256, 257–58, 260, 264–73; tourism, 259–60, 294, 301; political, 278; for Hetch Hetchy, 332, 335; in *First Summer,* 357
— writings: "The American Forests," 299; "Ancient Glaciers of the Sierra," 61; "Bee-Pastures," 249, 254, 285; "By-Ways of Yosemite Travel. Bloody Cañon," 207, 214–17; "California Agriculture," 229; *Cruise of the Corwin,* 189; "Douglas Squirrel," 171–72; *Edward Henry Harriman,* 334–35; "Exploration of the Great Tuolumne Cañon," 42, 44, 103–4; "Features of the Proposed Yosemite Park," 265–67; "Flood-Storm in the Sierra," 138, 140, 142; "A Geologist's Winter Walk," 47, 50, 64; "The Glacier Meadows of the Sierra," 216, 234–35; "God's First Temples. How Shall We Preserve Our Forests?," 196; "The Humming-Bird of the California Water-Falls," 171; "In the Heart of the California Alps," 67, 242; "Jubilee of Waters," 137, 263; King Sequoia Letter, 122–23, 130, 282; "Living Glaciers of California," 56, 73; "The Mountain Lakes of California," 243; *The Mountains of California,* 67, 189, 234, 258, 284; *My First Summer in the Sierra,* 166, 186, 238, 350–61; "National Parks and Forest Reservations," 297; "A Near View of the High Sierra," 67; "New Sequoia Forests of California," 197–204; "A New Top Notch for the Sons of Daniel Boone," 242–43; "On the Post-Glacial History of Sequoia Gigantea," 196, 198–204; *Our National Parks,* xiv, 283, 302–5; *Picturesque California,* 144, 238, 240, 245, 246–53, 260, 280; "A Rival of Yosemite," 267–73; "Snow Banners of the California Alps," 240; "Snow Storm on Mount Shasta," 145–47; *Stickeen,* 264, 341, 346–50; *Story of My Boyhood and Youth,* 19, 342–46; *Studies in the Sierra,* 73, 89–121, 168; *Thousand Mile Walk,* 3–27, 32, 38, 60, 148, 158;

original journal of *Thousand Mile Walk,* 3, 18–19, 106, 156–57; *Travels in Alaska,* 341, 347; "Treasures of Yosemite," 246, 247, 260–65; "Twenty Hill Hollow," 207–14; "Wild Sheep of California," 173–75; "Wild Wool," 175–79, 180, 187, 193, 203, 210, 231, 285, 332; "Wind Storm in the Forests of the Yuba," 142, 149; *The Yosemite,* 264, 341; "Yosemite Valley in Flood," 137
Muir, Wanda, 302
Muir Glacier, 248, 267
Mulholland, William, 331
Muybridge, Edward, 207
MX Missile System, 316
Mysticism, 128. *See also* Awakening

Nash, Roderick, 87, 184, 276, 282, 298
National parks, 251, 257, 258, 265, 280; spiritual significance of, 213, 252, 329; as campgrounds, 252, 266; as watershed, 252, 260–67, 288, 330–31; educational significance, 252, 254; not wilderness, 252–53, 294, 296, 301, 311; roads and developments, 265, 271–72, 282, 306–8, 313, 335–36; as recreation, 265, 283, 295, 335; administration, 287, 290, 297. *See also* National Park Service; Tourism
National Park Service, 47, 309–10, 314, 337–38; administration of, 275–76, 283, 318; visitor's centers, 304, 312, 314, 364–66
Nature as flow, 18, 50, 70, 92, 104, 112, 118, 239, 261, 330
Nelder, John, 55, 226
Nevada, 227–28
Nevada Fall, 246, 307; "mended," 251, 254
New York Tribune, 34
Noble, John, secretary of the interior, 258, 268
North Dome, 24

Oakland, California, 89, 131
Olmsted, Frederick: on national parks, 213, 252, 287, 306; on tourism, 218; on recreation, 219, 220
Olney, Warren, 283, 318

DESIGNED BY QUENTIN FIORE
COMPOSED BY METRICOMP, GRUNDY CENTER, IOWA
MANUFACTURED BY CUSHING-MALLOY, INC., ANN ARBOR, MICHIGAN
TEXT AND DISPLAY LINES ARE SET IN PALATINO

Library of Congress Cataloging in Publication Data
Cohen, Michael P., 1944–
The pathless way.

Includes bibliographical references and index.
1. Muir, John, 1838–1914. 2. Nature conservation –
United States – History. 3. Naturalists – United States –
Biography. 4. Conservationists – United States –
Biography. I. Title.
QH31.M9C64 1984   333.7'2'0924 [B]   83-40260
ISBN 0-299-09720-X